Egypt and the rise of fluid authoritarianism

Manchester University Press

Egypt and the rise of fluid authoritarianism

Political ecology, power and the crisis of legitimacy

Maria Gloria Polimeno

MANCHESTER UNIVERSITY PRESS

Copyright © Maria Gloria Polimeno 2024

The right of Maria Gloria Polimeno to be identified as the author of this work has been asserted in accordance with the Copyright, Designs and Patents Act 1988.

This book will be made open access within three years of publication thanks to Path to Open, a program developed in partnership between JSTOR, the American Council of Learned Societies (ACLS), University of Michigan Press, and The University of North Carolina Press to bring about equitable access and impact for the entire scholarly community, including authors, researchers, libraries, and university presses around the world. Learn more at https://about.jstor.org/path-to-open/

Published by Manchester University Press
Oxford Road, Manchester, M13 9PL

www.manchesteruniversitypress.co.uk

British Library Cataloguing-in-Publication Data
A catalogue record for this book is available from the British Library

ISBN   978 1 5261 7660 8   hardback

First published 2024

The publisher has no responsibility for the persistence or accuracy of URLs for any external or third-party internet websites referred to in this book, and does not guarantee that any content on such websites is, or will remain, accurate or appropriate.

Typeset
by New Best-set Typesetters Ltd

Raise your words, not voice. It is rain that grows flowers, not thunder.
Jalal al-Din Rumi

Contents

List of figures	*page* viii
List of tables	ix
Glossary	xi
Preface	xii
Acknowledgments	xvi
List of abbreviations	xviii
Introduction	1
1. Political legitimacy in fluid authoritarianism: a liquid interregnum	24
2. Not an Arab phoenix	52
3. Reinventing a different political machine	68
4. A hero in search of a political role: playing myths and symbols	106
5. God, the political seductor	134
6. The political economy of resurrection: power and nature as a critical ecosystem	167
Conclusion	213
Appendix	227
References	231
Index	271

Figures

1.1	Sub-levels that participate in the modified conception of political legitimacy in autocracies after shockwaves which impacted with sub-transformations of the state structure	*page* 38
3.1	Graffiti of Tahrir Square. A SCAF tank symbolically presented as suppressing social and political freedom	78
3.2	Trends in authority, 1943–2013; 2011–2013 transition to a closed anocracy	86
3.3	Quantitative analysis for sub-node 6.1	96
3.4	Quantitative analysis for sub-node 6.2	96
4.1	Extended quantitative analysis of the celebration of the army between 2016 and 2019 in a no-longer purely military regime	110
4.2	Military expenditure of % GDP in the broader Mediterranean region and the EU	123
6.1	Egypt consumer price index 2014–2022	168
6.2	Combine-coded data on Egypt's national strategy in the sector of sustainable development and milestones	198

Tables

1.1	Phases for the legitimating process	page 39
1.2	Frames and interpretative levels	42
1.3	Categorisation of meta-frames and definitions	43
1.4	Vertical approach to the leadership's process of legitimation	48
2.1	Table of leadership's polarised paradigm	58
3.1	Nvivo codebook for the EAF's 1 July 2013 statement	71
3.2	Codebook for 3 July coup-staging speech	74
3.3	Frames and qualifiers of resonance	81
3.4	Codebook of al-Sisi's motivations for March 2014 speech	84
3.5	Codebook of 2015 BBC interview with al-Sisi	88
3.6	Extrapolated list of nodes for Law No. 107 of 2013 and Law No. 94 of 2015	93
3.7	Combined codebook for Anti-Terrorism Law No. 94 of 2015, Law No. 107 of 2013 and Law No. 70 of 2017	95
3.8	Transformation of authoritarianism in Egypt in the immediate post-2013 period	101
4.1	Combined codebook for al-Sisi's speeches at the military graduation ceremony of July 2016 (1), commemoration of the 23 July Revolution at the Military Academy in 2019 (2), and commemoration of the October War in 2019 (3)	108
5.1	Transformation of Islamists after the 2013 coup and the leadership's corresponding transformative process	135
5.2	Codebook of al-Sisi's December 2015 speech at the al-Azhar	151
5.3	Combined codebook of al-Sisi's speeches at the Laylat al-Qadr celebrations, 2018 (A)–2019 (B)	153
5.4	Codebook of al-Sisi speech at Laylat al-Qadr, March 2019 (B)	156
5.5	Strategic and tactical frames attached by al-Sisi to religion and revolutionising Islam as attached to the reconstruction of the state	160

5.6 Codebook for the December 2015 (A) speech at the al-Azhar and September 2016 (B) speech at the UN General Assembly	161
6.1 Two levels of post-2013 economic reforms as attached to stateness	172
6.2 Codebook of the Youth Conference speech, October 2016	175
6.3 Codebook of al-Sisi's speech at the World Economic Forum in Davos, 2015	179
6.4 Codebook for al-Sisi's speech at the 71st UN General Assembly, 2016	180
6.5 Political implications behind subsidies	182

Glossary

Diffused support	A form of support towards the political establishment which can take different forms. While it can remain hierarchical, though not necessarily confined to the oligarchy, it takes the form of a diffused network which additionally expands to non-elite segments. Diffused support is considered a proactive, coopted mechanism of bargain of constituencies
Liquid State	Changing institutional structures in contrast to the idea of weakness
Macro-structural	Macro-scale dynamics which could be intraregional, transregional and influenced by global trends or shocks
Micro-systemic	The inner and specific mechanisms of states' functioning. It is a narrowed approach that complements the macro-structural approach in the production of political knowledge
Omnibalancing	The process of internal repositioning of social and political actors along the state infrastructures. The repositioning is then followed by intra-realignments amongst different categories of actors which is interests driven. The two-level process impacts the overall political materiality of institutions and recalibrates rulers' struggle for internal legitimation and interferes with the overall dynamics of consensus building
Specific support	Classical forms of support found in autocracies, foundations of which are rooted in a regime party. The support is confined to the oligarchy, who in turn are intertwined with the regime party. This form of support is pyramidally conceived and excludes the cooptation of constituencies. It destabilises the 'social contract of informality'

Preface

At the time of writing, illiberal powers are on the rise on a global scale – one that transcends regionalisms such as North–South or Western–Eastern divides. Illiberal regimes are proving themselves to be attractive in poisoning the fundamental political, social and moral values of liberal democracies. Likewise, populist narratives are being revived, and while they aim at dividing nations, preventing democratic reforms, in other contexts populist narratives, by relying on ethnosymbolism, aim at recreating the idea and identity of nations, after shockwaves. Myths, memories and symbols have not returned to playing out against neoliberal projects but to tactically reclaiming a welfarist-ethical role and legitimation for business elites' mandate in new projects of development. In the complexity of these processes, populist narratives and neonationalisms have emerged within a distorted 1950s–1960s socialist-welfarist claim, which is presented as the host-ideology, but anachronistically in a neoliberal capitalist regional system that remains fondly linked to the International Monetary Fund's loans, and thus condemned to enduring financial indebtedness. The erosion in the qualities of democracies and untransitioned systems, as well as the gap in internal legitimation, that persist in autocracies have been accompanied by a reinterpreted institutionalisation of identities, at which core the idea of the greatness of nations started to be employed as a legitimation device. While much is known about the role of regime type and democratisation in international cooperation and the spread of liberal norms (Mansfield et al., 2000; Pevehouse, 2005; Tallberg et al., 2020), we know relatively little about the regional and international consequences of reverse processes, alias the structural consolidation of autocracies and the role of nature in this process. This book will contribute to the study of internal political legitimacy from a structural, socio-political, and economic perspective in systems that have undergone transformations after shockwaves, like Egypt after the 2013 coup.

From a theoretical perspective, the book engages with the broader debate on autocratic restorations, though it approaches the phenomenon through the prism of non-continuity. What it establishes is intertwined with the theory of rupture and change in times of transition. To this end, the Introduction presents a combined reinterpretation of the Gramscian interregnum through a Baumanian flavour, which sees further development in the theory of fluid authoritarianism, against the immobilism of the scholarship, and which goes beyond empirical and regionalised focuses. In the early phases of this work, the term shockwaves has been limited to Egypt, as the first country that experienced a coup one year after democratic elections in 2012. As the conclusions of the book are approached, other shockwaves have occurred in the region, and Tunisia deserves a mention, next to Lebanon where the persistence of the elite in the country has been at the core of internal protests but also impacted on transforming the system. In a global context of referred 'authoritarian restorations', lying in democracy has become normalised in international politics, and this act of lying ended up revealing a struggle to create new bases of internal consensus beyond old practices of coercion, repression and torture. Shockwaves organically can upgrade political machines, thus determining a transition at the level of the organisation of state structure, even from within, and from which the conception of fluid authoritarianism stems. Despite this, violence and coercion have tactically entered a new era of routinisation in the everyday life of the Middle East region, turning into new modes of governmentality that transcend former exceptionalisms. After 2011 elites have returned, playing and consolidating a strategic central function in the economic and development sector, surfing new industrial waves, which have ended up institutionalising and moralising the environment and nature. In Tunisia, after the collapse of Ben Ali's regime in 2011, prosperous companies were sold to factions of the elite, which started consolidating their business. This finds application in Egypt, though under different premises and in a sub-transformed political structure in which the architecture of power emerged as polarised for the first time since 1953. Green reforms promoted under the Social Development Goals, including the greening of desert lands, the commercial development of the Suez Canal Area, and the Siwa Oasis project, among others, projected towards green energy transition, saw a constructive presentation through the lenses of a political programme of economic development, were environmentally ethical and committed to making natural resources accessible by all and sustainable. The political seduction of this discourse aimed at a consolidation of the deep internal legitimation void. Despite this, Egypt remains profoundly based on a precarious political and economic stability, which is internationally and diplomatically negotiated with the parable of economic opportunities and growth under the umbrella of Agenda 2030, but which in fact implies major structural and socio-economic risks, which in turn can become boomerang determinants due to the internal realignment of domestic religious, social and military actors along the infrastructural and international spectrum. This lens of analysis with application in the context of Egypt can be exported to other contemporary autocracies in the way illiberal green policies lying about sustainability are being internationally turned into dispositives for political and economic legitimation on the one hand, and for the functioning of a new frontier of moral green capitalism on the other.

Since 2013 Egypt has radically changed many of the historical state's structural assets, and presents some features reminiscent of a form of 'personalist' authoritarianism, though non-exclusivist, embedded into an organically transformed societal materiality which impacted with the linearity of internal alignments. This book distances itself from existing debates, arguing for a simplistic restoration of a militarised structure in the country, and for a continuum between al-Sisi and Mubarak's model of regime. Illiberal regimes have many sub-faces, they are not static or single level-built entities along the spectrum of their taxonomies. The process of internal legitimation is here designed beyond classical approaches confined to Max Weber. Rather, the book has designed a framework for reinterpreting internal political legitimacy in sub-transformed systems in which micro-structural shifts in the nature of relations are projected towards new categories of material resources. The framework will go beyond Egypt and the Middle East.

A central argument of this book concerns the idea of authoritarian continuity in post-shockwaves settings and the rise of what the book defines as 'fluid authoritarianism' as a sub-structural and organic result of shockwaves that collapsed historical and structural certainties and impacted with the transition period. On a transregional scale, this idea of illiberal fluidity is embedded into a regional context that considers the interconnections of domestic political survival with readjustments in transnational alignments in times of transition. The reconstruction of the Egyptian machine of governance through the prism of internal political legitimacy has permitted this book to expand on the broader political design derived at the regional and international level as directly stemming from intra-countries' structural change. These interconnections can directly influence new forms of political and economic ambitions and rehabilitation along the international system and market that are straightforwardly modulated by the inner-transformations and relationship that take place within the political system itself. In addition, the intradisciplinary multil-level built framework designed in the book has permitted a twofold theorisation where the rise of fluid authoritarianism as a brand-new taxonomy of autocracy that emerged after shockwaves is interlinked with the fluidity of Arab states. The book unpacks these aspects before turning, in the final chapter, to offer a critical radical discussion on political ecology and power as constituting a critical ecosystem for political legitimacy. While the focus is on Egypt, in fact the critique here finds application to what the book calls the fluid Middle East, alias a region in which political, intra-societal and economic relations have become more fluid than in the past as a result of changes at the level of the political structures. The Middle East region remains profoundly brittle, but this is an aspect that is still neglected by Western actors, who continue to view new governments that have emerged and 'consolidated' since 2011 or so as politically stable entities and trustworthy economic partners in the Mediterranean area. As the book highlights, these premises risk renegotiating the boundaries and structure of power where nature will become a new locus of political power, exclusion and contestation, in Egypt and beyond.

Acknowledgments

The early origins of this book can be found way back in Cairo but also in the infinite days and late nights spent in SOAS library in London and at the University of Exeter. Egypt has been the last stop on a long nomadism in the Middle East, which started in North Africa and ended up by the Syrian–Turkish border on the eve of the Syrian uprisings. Some cities, places, libraries and communities I had the privilege to visit and appreciate no longer exist today. The months spent in Egypt, conducting empirical observations, breathing the uncertainties and protests that protracted during the 2012 presidential campaign and elections have represented a moment of departure in the core conceptual foundations and empirical analysis of this book. I also felt privileged for living within the chaotic political events and a transitioning society with all its enduring challenges and hopes for dignity, but also for having learnt a lot from ordinary Egyptians.

In the middle of the campaign for the presidential elections, it was a warm, apparently quiet, and beautiful Cairo night when the house of the Islamist Hazem Salah Abu Ismail, not so distant from the coffee house where I was with a group of close friends and colleagues, was torched. On the same night new protests once again animated Tahrir Square, making sense not only of a society that was transforming after January 2011 but of the fact that Egypt officially entered its chaotic presidential electoral stage, which culminated with the, at that time, much acclaimed victory of Mohammed Morsi. However, I also had the privilege of witnessing the complexities, tragedies, societal and individual economic and political challenges and doubts of the middle and lower-middle class living in relative poverty, their political mistrust yet hope for a brighter future. I lived the curfew, clashes, smoke of tear gas, political protests, Islamist manifestations and the balthageya (thugs) and experienced the persistence of the policy of daily electrical blackouts and energy cuts, April's and May's sandy sky above Cairo, fuel shortage and its related crisis, and the unsustainable traffic jam, next to the wonderful Fatimid Cairo, which happened to be detracted from by small hills of rubbish and an illegal and illicit market. All of these are issues that have returned to play a crucial role in the re-making of politics and fluid authoritarianism in the country and, more broadly, the region, and which entered this book in the form of political ecology, power and the crisis of legitimacy.

At the time of writing, I feel grateful to so many people for having contributed to the long journey, and who it would be simply impossible to thank one by one. I am particularly thankful to Zeynep, Miryana and the inspirational Friedrich, for our chats on the state of Egypt and Egyptian politics and culture, for our cultural dinners, but also for having accessed remote villages and inaccessible archaeological sites together and with the rest of the crew.

Once returned from Egypt I moved to the UK and joined the School of Oriental and African Studies and former London Middle East Institute, where I also returned in my entity of visiting fellow a few years later. However, it is at the University of Exeter, my Alma Mater, that my project found an intellectual home, and which also funded the fieldwork for this book. My sincerest thanks go out to my now colleague and friend Jonathan Ghitens-Mazer and Eleanor Gao for their support.

I was able to present and discuss some of this book's early extracts at many conferences and world congresses, amongst which the World Congress of Middle Eastern Studies, but principally in Seville, Wroclaw and London. My gratitude goes also to the interviewees based in the UK, Middle East, the US and across Europe who offered me their precious time and provided information impossible to find elsewhere. Their names remain anonymous in this book to protect their identity.

I want to thank Robert Byron and Humairaa Dudhwala for being two incredible editors and for their support from the early acceptance of the book. I am honoured that this book met the interest and support from the prestigious Manchester University Press.

The road to this book has met some intense moments. My sincere appreciation goes out to my closest friends, amongst whom Giusy who lent me an ear whenever I needed it. Thank you all for the dinners, laughs and chats that lightened my mind, for having amplified my passion for mountains, and for the hazardous trips across different latitudes.

My love to my family for their unconditional support and grounded faith from the beginning of this work. This book is dedicated to them.

While I hope that I haven't forgotten to thank anyone, in the end, any errors are my own.

Abbreviations

AB	Arab Barometer
ACA	Administrative Control Authority
AOI	Arab Organisation for Industrialisation
ASU	Arab Socialist Union
ATP	Arab Transformations Project
BTI	Bertelsmann Transformation Index
CAPMAS	Central Agency for Public Mobilisation and Statistics
CBE	Central Bank of Egypt
CPI	Corruption Perception Index
COP	Conference of the Parties to the United Nations Framework Convention on Climate Change
EAF	Egyptian Armed Forces
EC	European Commission
ENI	hydrocarbons national body
ENPI	European Neighbourhood Programme Instrument
EU	European Union
FAO	Food and Agricultural Organisation
FDI	foreign direct investment
FJP	Freedom and Justice Party
FSI	Fragile States Index
GCDCAF	Geneva Centre for the Democratic Control of Armed Forces
ILO	International Labour Organization
IMF	International Monetary Fund
MENA	Middle East and North Africa
NDP	National Democratic Party
NFB	Nation's Future Block
NGO	non-governmental organisation
NSPO	National Services Project Organisation
SAP	Structural Adjustment Programme
SCAF	Supreme Council of Armed Forces
UAE	United Arab Emirates
WEF	World Economic Forum

Introduction

Purpose and scope of the book

This book takes a transformative approach to the study of authoritarianism, its variations in sub-taxonomies and its transformations within a regional and global scenario in which processes of autocratisation are globally on the rise at the expense of democracy, and in which quality and processes of erosion can be measured. This has led to the rise of new forms of neonationalistic projects infused by anachronistic social-welfarist ideas of populist tendencies and narratives deeply embdedded into an economic-industrial model of production and development that has a financialised and institutionalised nature. This volume focuses on Egypt after the 2013 military coup and redefines its transformed authoritarian identity by entering the theorised concept of fluid authoritarianism. Fluid authoritarianism here defines regimes in which relations between internal actors are less defined and are subjected to unpredictable change. Fluid authoritarianism is here captured against a Baumanian-Gramscian reinterpretation of the classical Gramscian interregnum (Gramsci, 1971). Borrowing from Bauman's conceptual elaboration of Gramsci's theory of the 'interregnum', time represents a rupture in the otherwise (seemingly) monotonous continuity of government, law and social order (Bauman, 2012).[1] The crisis that emerges at this time, at least according to Gramsci, is rooted in an alienation of the masses from their political representation, giving rise to a mismatch between 'represented and representatives' (Gramsci, 1971). Thus, the 'mummified and anachronistic' actors of the past, in Bauman's words, are unable to solve the crisis within the framework of the dying order (Bauman, 2012). This in turn leads to a 'crisis of authority', which leaves an ideological void and thus the possibility for different crisis solutions. What it is debated here, through different lenses, is the concept of power and its architecture in upgraded autocracies during phases of political crises and in connection to its sub-transformation, which would be captured as a 'solution' to a political crisis and scepticism.

Focusing on the specific case of Egypt, against this Baumanian-Gramscian-inspired background, the book problematises the Gramscian idea of transitional immobilism in the context of the political authorities' struggle for political legitimation and the nature of the transformative process. Here power is not captured as a variable that remains static, nor as a regime of truth (Foucault, 1988). It is, rather, approached for its transformative and fluid aspects and as an adaptive and living variable to internal and external shocks, which keeps evolving along phases that correspond to its rise, consolidation, stagnation and eventually dissolution (Khaldun, 1958). Along the cycle, power and authority may rely on qualifiers that serve the purpose of obtaining authority and thus creating the idea of the state but also expressing grievances (Khaldun, 1958; Weber, 1968). While this premise is reminiscent of Khaldunian cyclical theory, here *asabiyya* (social cohesion) at the core of Khaldun's thought is alienated from the contemporary socio-political and economic-diplomatic context of the Middle East in which the book is located. Rather, the Khaldunian theory of power as a cyclical force here attains to specific qualifiers that, at least on conceptual premises, replace *asabiyya* with some forms of modernity that find in Weber more affinity in how the rule of law, charisma, alias characteristic qualifiers, and religion interplay for the purpose of creating political consensus and legitimacy around a ruler and the political system.[2]

Yet in systems that underwent a transformation during times of transition, from where the Baumanian-Gramscian inspired redefinition of the 'interregnum' stems in this book, the three qualifiers that connote Weber become obsolete in the way they neglect the intra-transformations that took place at the level of the (Arab) social materiality after shockwaves (i.e. coups, protests, revolutions). Classical approaches to the study of political legitimacy in the context of illiberal systems are criticised for being static and less based on a momentum that intrinsically remains highly cyclical (Khaldun, 1958). Here, fluid authoritarianism wants to conceptualise a form of viscosity in the political, diplomatic and social relations, which interferes with sub-changes.

The book takes a top-down approach to the process of internal legitimation contextualised in a system that has undergone a structural sub-transformation at the inner level of the infrastructure of power and as a result of shockwaves that, in Egypt, started taking place in 2011 and 2013 and protracted during the time of transition up to 2022. The departure point is the July 2013 military coup-initiated mechanisms of a gradual regime upgrade, which have sub-transformed Egypt's infrastructures of power, impacting on the level of political leadership and consequently on the forging of a legitimation claim. This has determined for the first time since the 1950s, when the waves of nationalist populisms were on the rise, a rupture. Yet the post-2013 setting in Egypt remains a blurred moment in which the struggle for filling the legitimacy and political void ended up restructuring the nature and organisation of the regime identity. In this, the book shares Runciman's critique of Barker and conceptualises the overall struggle for legitimacy as a theatrical and cinematic representation of politics (Runciman, 2003: 115; see also Barker, 2001).

The approach taken with this book is highly transformative, and relies on critical analytical lenses to the study of the process of internal transformations in what the book defines as a sub-transformed autocracy, which distances itself from a strictly military past – at least in historical purist terms. The focus on the process of internal legitimation allows reflection on the internal variation of regimes' authoritarian traits, bringing up to date the broader debate on regimes' functioning and legitimation, and adding to knowledge on Egyptian authoritarianism since 1953 and the sub-functioning of contemporary illiberal systems, even beyond the Middle East (Frantz and Geddes, 2016). Stepping away from the recent scholarship on Egyptian politics, the definition of restored militarism is further problematised by the civilian face of the regime, and its combination with the rehabilitated army's role; this study argues that the post-2013 regime has undergone a sub-variation to a pre-existing militarism, which enables its characterisation as a non-exclusivist personalism. This neocoined sub-category of personalist autocracy recognises the determinant of identity through the recalling of myths and symbols.

The transition period located during 2013–2022 has straightforwardly impacted a transformation at the inner level, which has made the state structure more liquid and the regime more fluid. The book considers and questions the phases of political transition and regime redefinition that took place between 2013 and 2022, though major intensifications took place between 2014 and 2018. This span of time is portrayed as highly transformative and 'liquid', in which intra-systemic and ruler-societies' relations are shown as deeply precarious from within but stable from the outside – to the point of identifying these systems as a point of reference for the political and energy stabilisation of the Mediterranean area by international actors.

The debate that unfolds in this book therefore takes a twofold approach: internally, it re-engages with the open-ended debate on the transformation of non-liberal governments, the routinisation of state violence as a political dispositive, and the rise of a new approach to recreate a new cycle of political power and eventually its mechanisms of corruption. Broadening the lenses, Arab states in the Middle East and North Africa (MENA) have become liquid political entities since the 2011 protests due to the volatility of those connections that govern intra-state relations and states versus international Western and non-Western actors' relations. This conception applies to Egypt under al-Sisi, though the definition of liquid states – used in opposition to

Ayubi's definition of Arab states as weak entities (Ayubi, 1995) – meaning fragile and changing institutional structures, can find theoretical application also beyond the case of Egypt in a Mediterranean region in which the overall political architecture of power has undergone forms of adaptations to survive internal shocks.

In this framework, Egypt constitutes a stepping-stone for future avenues of research inquiring the intersections between political and infrastructural sub-change that take place at the level of political relations and new trends in economic interests, that is, green transition as internationally promoted under Agenda 2030. This connection questions not only the *quo vadis* of democratisation in the region – a theme which has been extensively dominating a divided scholarship since the 1970s (Albrecht and Schlumberger, 2004; Bicchi and Voltolini, 2013; Hollis, 2012; Rahbek, 2005; Schlumberger, 2000; Springborg, 2007) – but mainly the values and moral repositioning of international actors along the region. The reference is primarily set on the European and Western elites who have recently relocated their interests from the security level (see Hollis, 2012), to the incentivisation of regional interests more projected towards energy politics and the broader environmental sector. This risks the turning into utilitarian elements of the legitimation process by newly emerged and transformed illiberal systems in the region. What this process de facto complicates is the locus of political power where nature risks becoming a new ecology for political negotiation and exploitation for elite resilience.

Hence, the core argument is that the 2013 military coup in Egypt, which led to the consolidation of al-Sisi to power in the 2014 elections, initiated a change in the sub-infrastructures of the regime, which also posed, and still does, questions about the process of institutional political and social legitimation of non-liberal authorities in post-shockwave contexts that organically transformed the materiality of societies and the regime's premises of durability. In the specific case of Egypt, this book theorises that after the 2011 and 2013 shockwaves the materiality of Egyptian society underwent a cultural, ideological and political organic transformation. This is an aspect that remains neglected, but which finds an explanation and application in this book.

In taking a modified and interdisciplinary conception to political legitimacy and the overall struggle for legitimation, as not exclusively based on classicist-Western assumptions like the rule of law, charisma and tradition as qualifiers or preconditions for gaining consensus in contemporary autocracies (Weber, 1968), the goal of this book is to de-Westernise and de-colonise the approach to the study of autocrats' legitimation processes after shockwaves by additionally looking at the micro-materiality of societies and transformations of local political-social actors and their potential reconfiguration along the international system, both diplomatically and economically.

Thus, the intradisciplinarity of the framework theorised for Egypt and the transition period, de facto embeds elements and a broad interdisciplinary multil-level theoretical architecture that will go beyond the empirical contextualisation to autocracies in the Mediterranean area to meet a transregional application to illiberal contexts in the Global South and in systems that, while they did not transition toward de facto democracies, thus remaining defective, still underwent a combination of societal-political and infrastructural sub-adaptations. This in the framework is intertwined with the impact in the reorganisation of the foundation of states and the idea of nations.

With regard to Egypt, the book asserts that al-Sisi's regime (*nizam*) still faces a legitimacy crisis, despite what in July 2013 looked like a popularly supported counter-revolution against the Muslim Brotherhood and the Freedom and Justice Party (FJP), accused of having betrayed the popular demands of the 2011 revolution by attempting to create a religious authoritarian system based on dogmas, though views on this regard remain fragmented (Totten et al., 2012; see also Lacroix, 2013).

As the attempt to frame the 2013 counter-revolution as legitimate has failed, despite al-Sisi's attempt to emphasise his authority in charismatic key (in fact, rather uncharismatic), a vacuum is left in internal legitimation, which, in one way or another, needs to be filled. The attempts of self-framing as a determinant pillar for the country's stability contributed to an authoritarian escalation which has necessitated redesigning the Egyptian state's foundations. This has increased the authoritarian character of the system, even when compared to Egypt's historical military authoritarian traits under the regimes of Gamal Abdel-Nasser, Anwar al-Sadat and even Hosni Mubarak.

From an internal perspective, the work aims to offer a ground-breaking analysis through which deconstructing, defining and explaining a political, structural, social and economic condition within the Egyptian politics that has not yet been fully explored – the struggle for constructing internal political legitimacy after shockwaves beyond the classical idea of domination – as well as the impact of this internal struggle at the level of the state's inner processes of reinvention of the political machine and its broad architecture of power. From a more international perspective, the book aims to connect the process of the internal legitimation of transformed non-liberal systems along their internationalisation of the business network to the changing nature of Western priorities and interests in the broader Mediterranean area, which remain fragmented between military cooperations that in turn empower elites and moral values.

From a critical perspective, the issue of political legitimacy in Egypt has become even more relevant given that the Arab world, long after the uprisings of 2011, still struggles to develop a clear agenda on domestic political and economic stabilisation, and democratisation has become a utopian and obsolete externally preconceived project that exposes the fragility of values it sustains (Perthes, 2008; Ridge, 2022; see also Geddes, 1999a). Despite al-Sisi's constitutional amendments, apparently projected towards forms of welfarisation of the Egyptian economy and model of social justice, and speeches on the country's stability, the trajectories of domestic politics after 2013 suggest an ever-deepening process of top-down political legitimation, structural internal imbalance, and interconnection with regional realignments in the Arab Gulf, particularly repositioning Egypt's economy towards Saudi Arabia and the United Arab Emirates (UAE), and contributing to the isolation of Qatar. Similarly, Egypt's international realignments remain oriented towards two colluding directions that mainly attain to the way in which opposing economic relations between the Western bloc (primarily the EU) and Russia and China are managed in the sectors of renewable energies and sustainable development. Egypt's plans are set on creating an economic model of sustainable system which entails a market economy but with no chance of negotiating forms of socio-political pluralism and in which logics of redistributive politics are off the table.

Despite some externally perceived improvements in macroeconomic indicators (i.e. external debt, bonds, GDP and foreign direct investment (FDI)), these developments have merely served to persuade international stakeholders and state actors of Egypt's stability, providing to the outside a positive image of the political system and its in-the-making economic foundations (Polimeno, 2022). These authoritarian internal changes ultimately did, and still does, resonate at the international level. This is an aspect that remains neglected mainly by Western state actors, such as the EU and some of its member states who persist in looking at emerged systems in the MENA region, and in particular Egypt under al-Sisi, as reliable economic and military partners and stable political entities, despite their internal, brittle, fragile and precarious internal relations.[3] From an internal perspective, margins of expression and political inclusion have narrowed after the second presidential elections held in 2018, which al-Sisi, it is believed, won with 97 per cent of the vote with a 41 per cent turnout in the absence of any real opposition, due to the disappearance of the leftist and youth parties that emerged in 2012 and before that date as movements that put pressure on Ahmed Shafiq in November 2011 for transferring power from Mubarak to a civilian leadership (see Durac 2018). As well as the youth parties and movements, then the Nasserites and the Tagammu, belonging to the 'Arab Socialist' sphere similarly disappeared from the political scenario (Abdalla, 2016; see also Durac, 2018).[4] Thus, what exactly these social, political, economic and cultural changes in Egypt will lead to, how they might resonate on the international level, and how they might bolster the regime's claim of legitimacy finds a critical discussion in this book. The political-diplomatic repositioning of Egypt along the international spectrum poses questions that are both intellectual and empirical and relate also to the broader connection between liberal and non-liberal systems, and environmental politics. In 2020 the regime pushed forward the idea of additionally investing in alternative systems boosting the industrial production and aimed at greening desert lands and areas.[5]

Yet the coup that took place in 2013 represented a critical juncture that set in motion infrastructural sub-change, including the discarding of the structural premises of Mubarak's resilience such as the importance of a regime party since 1978 (i.e. the National Democratic Party (NDP)) and the apparent civilian nature of the government; the 'state legitimation' of the politics of disappearance of opposition forces and parties which had emerged before 2013 when the country experienced a transitory political opening to new 50 parties; the instauration of a permanent state of exception under the emergency law renewed for at least 17 times from 2013 until 2021; and the overall bureaucratisation of politics which depoliticised the parliamentary assembly functions, reduced to a bureaucratic element of the state. With the goal of understanding the struggle for legitimation in the face of the crisis left by the 2013 coup, the underlining argument in this book is that the coup – as the Supreme Council of Armed Forces (SCAF) framed it, a counter-revolution – appears to have structurally interfered with the process of political legitimation, diversifying strategies implemented by post-2013 authorities from those previously enforced under the NDP. A change in the political authority's strategies and paths for legitimation directly influences a change in the state structures, alliances and definition, and this in turn can affect and interfere with the stability of the entire political system.

As a general norm, in autocracies a change at sub-systemic level, theorised in connection to a contested process of political legitimacy, can provoke interferences with the reconfiguration of the new autocracy in the international system and the country's readaptation of its foreign policy in accordance with an internal rebalance of power, interests and alliances. The focus on the contested struggle for political legitimacy in Egypt and in the context of the crisis determined by the post-2013 coup – and in turn the efforts to deconstruct the political essence of post-2013 authorities and the mechanisms that led to the gradual reinvention of the political machine, under different premises, goals and ambitions – permits reconsideration of two key aspects, which if and when combined can generate two contributions: (i) a new and comprehensive understanding of the reconfiguration of Egypt's aspirations as well as on the redefinition of its diplomatic and economic international relations with Western (i.e. EU) and non-Western state actors (i.e. Russia, China, UAE and India); (ii) a new understanding of the non-linearity of legitimation struggles in the Mediterranean area, which until now keeps being approached through a classical Weberian lens. Rather, the critique and empirical analysis that set the foundations of this book unfold how the Weberian trilogy is obsolete as it neglects the materiality of non-Western societies.

In connection to the focus on crisis, data for Egypt indicate that in early 2014, a year after the coup, the people's level of satisfaction with government performance in economic development was 58.9 per cent while concern towards authoritarianism stood at only 2 per cent (ATP, 2014). Regardless of the form of government, citizens' main concern was for economic recovery. Despite some limited trust in the economic reforms and urban planning that the government promised, there was a perception of corruption and a related concern about government inaction. Indeed, 53.6 per cent of Egyptians in the survey saw the government as still corrupt to a large extent, with an additional 23.3 per cent believing in corruption to a medium extent. Only 4 per cent believed there was no corruption at all.[6] The analysis of data on consensus building gathered from the ATP and here combined with that obtained from the Transformations Index (2018), show that consensus in Egypt in 2018 was rated at 3.2 on a 0–10 scale, demonstrating that the political model that was emerging was already poorly functioning. Gaps persisted in people's hope for economic growth and their trust in the institutional design that was underway, regardless of the nature of the government, indicating a lack of institutional trust and dissatisfaction in the government's performance across sectors.

The rationale: the fluid faces of autocracies

Contemporary states are a form of power structure that requires legitimation, not so much to function, or even to survive over a timespan, but to achieve those purposes that depend on the support of its population, and to maintain its political system intact in the face of serious policy and economic failures or challenges (Mattheson, 1987: 118). Thus, this book's theme is located in the renewed and recent debate on autocratisation processes, at the expenses of democratic erosion and untransitioned systems towards more inclusive structures, and their dynamics of adaptation. These reflections will also go beyond the Middle East. On theoretical premises, this volume captures political legitimacy as a highly transformative activity inserted in the context of systems that have undergone a social, cultural and systemic transformation after major structural and societal shockwaves (i.e. social protests, coup and turmoil). While legitimacy can be captured as a fluid and transformative concept, it is assumed in this book that the dynamics of power and the mechanisms through which it is assured in non-democratic regime types can vary in relation to the country's cultural, ideological, political and social contexts. These themselves can shift through turmoil and protests that contribute to the breakdown of former structural and political conditions, which interferes with changes in diktats and legitimating discourses that are the necessary conditions for long-term stability.

Legitimacy affects state strength and political authorities' survival; when legitimacy breaks down, so too do stability and order (McLoughlin, 2015). Crises of legitimacy are often cited as catalysts for regimes' 'transformations, delegitimation and civilian revolutions' (Arendt, 1965: 20; see also Huntington, 1991; Johnson, 1964). A different view is provided by Cavatorta who, borrowing from Przeworski, upholds that a system can survive even without significant legitimacy (Cavatorta and Kraetzschmar, 2010; Przeworski, 1986). While Przeworski notes that crisis or decline in legitimacy may coincide with the end of a regime, Lipset argues that the lack of political legitimacy could instead cause regimes to rely more heavily on coercive practices and suppression (Lipset, 1994). Achcar (2013) nonetheless notes that brutal force alone cannot provide regimes with durability. This latter argument is reminiscent of the Weberian definition of states as a human community that claims a monopoly on the legitimate use of physical force within a given territory (Weber, 1978). From a more modern perspective, and considering the international human rights law introduced by the UN in 1948, however, the Weberian understanding of state and the legitimate use of force raise concerns in judicial terms.

Building on these premises, the book approaches the case of Egypt and the process of political legitimacy as a top-down oriented transformative and adaptive activity after the 2013 military coup and inserted in a context of regional structural liquidity. The ascent of the Muslim Brotherhood to power in 2012 with the FJP's election victory corresponded with the people's demands for political change and a more redistributive approach to resources. However, popular satisfaction with the political performance and thus the legitimacy of the Muslim Brotherhood deteriorated during 2012 and 2013. This was not so much linked to the perception of the creation of a theocratic political ideology, but rather the accusation of the Muslim Brotherhood pursuing a Mubarak-inspired authoritarian system, albeit in different garb (Monier and Ranko, 2013: 61–63). This offered the military an opportunity to start creating a pro-Egyptian Armed Forces (EAF) narrative of legitimation, under the, at that time, commander-in-chief al-Sisi. Taking a fluid and transformative approach to the practices of authoritarian restoration against transformed societal fabrics and a newly emerged regional order in the broader Mediterranean area, this book considers and questions the phases of political transition and regime redefinition that took place between 2013 and 2020 in Egypt. The analysis shows that this timespan was highly transformative and 'liquid', in which intra-systemic and ruler-societies relations are shown as deeply precarious and subjected to a high level of fluidity and fragility. Conversely, relations are externally presented as based on solid grounds to fulfil precise diplomatic goals obeying a clear principle of conditionality on both an internal and international level.

State liquidity

Beyond the definition of states as weak political subjects, this book defines contemporary illiberal states that emerged after upheavals as 'liquid' rather than 'weak' power structures. The liquidity of states is intertwined with the concept of fluidity in the way both underpin uncharacterised, at times catatonic, trajectories undertaken by political authorities, which do not seem to move along a unique trajectory determined by the state's belief system or attain to a specific and convincing political programme as a flagship. Rather, they fluctuate and take new turns depending on the internal adament of political and economic relations between internal actors. As such, this is translated into (i) non-strictly categorised definitions of states, like in the 1950s–1970s as influenced by ideologies, and (ii) a more interchangeable and less perennialist use of the myth-symbols and memories complex that participates in the making of nations and states.[7] On an international level, this translates into double game strategies. With this argument of states as liquid entities, the book distances itself from Ayubi's early definition of Arab states as weak political entities (Ayubi, 1995). States' liquidity in turn entails a form of more ductile legitimation claim and readaptation to achieve economic and structural purposes that strictly depend on the support of the population, and to keep their political existence intact in the face of serious policy failures or external and internal challenges and shocks that rulers are called to confront. This enables a micro-systemic consideration of the mentalities and ideologies of subaltern classes (i.e. peasants, workers), their active and/or passive affiliations to dominant or competing political, civic and religious associations.[8] In turn, this captures their involvement in, or disengagement from, the formation of internal political alliances that might help in a set of purposes, such as (i) conserving bottom-up dissent, (ii) maintaining control or contesting the authority-making process at an intra-hierarchical level, (iii) contributing to the external narrative and frame of the possibly of forging an internal authoritarian legitimation and constructed form of acceptance in the multilateral international system. Indeed, legitimation strategies cannot be considered as 'cheap talks' (Burnell, 2006). They bring and have fundamental political consequences in impacting the relations between state and citizens. Given the purposes, the relations between the authorities and internal social-religious forces remains a core determinant that has not found extensive discussion in studies on authoritarian resistance and dynamics of existence. Looking into the dynamics and strategies of political legitimacy, their transformation along the infrastructural organisation of the political machine, the new idea of nation and political powers also equals exploring as to whether a state can be considered structurally, politically stable beyond narratives and mechanisms of neoliberal political propaganda (Easton, 1965; Weber, 1978).

In countries that have experienced a political variation in authoritarianism, or internal 'upgrade' (see also Heydemann and Leenders, 2014) in response to social protests, the mechanisms and formulas involved in the justification and legitimation of the political authority become subjected to a recombination and readaptations of characteristics and sources. Thus, under political-structural circumstances, the process of leadership legitimation could also undergo an internal variation, taking into account the internal axis over the external.

In the context of Egypt, the post-2013 system that has gradually emerged is built on extremely fragile political and economic relations with internal actors, principally the armed forces and their rehabilitation and repositioning in the state infrastructure, in which relations are still being tested. This is one of the aspects that remains neglected in the academic debate, which seems more projected towards a form of historical static approach in the definition of Egypt under al-Sisi as a continuation of a Mubarakian mode state combined with some elements that are reminiscent of a Nasserian authority (Adly, 2016; DCAF, 2016; Roll and Miehe, 2019; Springborg, 2017).

The intra-systemic variation and change in internal alliances eventually led the country to seek new relocations along the economic and diplomatic international order. Despite the theory of a change in the organisation of power and regime sub-transformation put forward in this book, there are scholarly divisions on the ground which still consider Egypt as a de facto militarised state, with the military rehabilitated in the institutionalised state apparatus and granted more influence than under the NDP since its establishment back in 1978 by Anwar Sadat and in the context of the Infitah (Albrecht, 2005; Bellin, 2004; Weinbaum, 1985; Blaydes, 2008, 2010; Buehler and Ibraheem, 2018; Diamond, 2002; Fukuyama, 2013; Galal, 2011; Geddes, 1999b; Geddes et al., 2014; Haber, 2006; Hinnebusch, 2006; Kelly, 2016; Levitsky and Way, 2002; Gandhi and Lust-Okar, 2009; Lust-Okar, 2005; Magaloni, 2008; Mandour, 2024; Rutherford, 2013; Schlumberger, 2010; Schlumberger and Matzke, 2012). This is considered a simplistic reading of the inner implications that events were micro-structurally determined in Egypt. In the system that emerged after 2013 the Egyptian army remains the strongest army in the region, historically perceived as the pillar of the republican establishment, but also the only source of authority over civilians

(Moughira, 2015). In the immediate aftermath of the uprising in 2011, the armed forces re-emerged as the dominant actor on the political scene, and the 2013 coup provided the SCAF with a carte blanche to strengthen its hold over the state in exchange for security, stability and an improving economy: this is what has been extensively reported, though in a simplistic manner (see Mandour, 2017). Since 2015 it has been reported as a 'Nasserisation' of al-Sisi's discourse and personalisation of charisma. This indicates some largely diffused confusion over the political system(s) which emerged after 2011 and 2013. The armed forces' control of the mass media, and the resulting press freedom, facilitated the recall of Nasser's domestic politics, as the past leader had controlled the press with the aim of preventing the rise of intra-Arab Socialist Union (ASU) and intra-army challengers (Crabbs, 1975; Diong, 2015; el Issawi, 2014). Now, these conventions are treated as tautological assumptions.

The legal framework introduced soon after the 2013 coup may have implications that can more accurately be said to have impacted the internal repositioning of actors within the legal and institutionalised infrastructures of power to the point that defining Egypt as a continuation of the Mubarak regime would be historically, and structurally, wrong. These interfered with the process of leadership legitimation and the new role played by the armed forces within the country's state structures, which de facto remain militarised. Moving beyond tautological meanings is a key departure moment as it also captures, from an international perspective, the new position of Egypt and its balance of power along the international spectrum diplomatically, financially and economically. This will be a further departure moment for questioning, in terms of evidence-based analysis, the effective stability of Egypt or exposing the risks beyond the communality of propagandistic interests.

The 2013 military coup initiated mechanisms of regime upgrade that have transformed Egypt's infrastructures, impacting on the level of political leadership and consequently on the claim of legitimacy. The testing of the army–al-Sisi relationship is intimately connected with the process of legitimation and the theory of a possible post-2013 regime upgrade. The 2013 coup-initiated mechanisms of regime upgrade that have transformed Egypt's infrastructures of power, impacting on the new role played by the military in the institutional structures and the testing of the army–al-Sisi relationship over power in the book is therefore viewed as intimately intertwined with the process of a transformative legitimation and the theory of a possible post-2013 regime upgrade. The book builds on Albrecht and Schlumberger as well as Heydemann's argument of 'changes at sub-systemic level' and 'changes within a regime' (Albrecht and Schlumberger, 2004: 385; see also Heydemann, 2007). However, the 2013 coup escalated a process of de facto structural change that may have turned the regime from being strictly militarised and semi-competitive, as it was from the late 1980s until the late 2000s under the ruling NDP, into being more personalist in nature and inserted into a state that remains culturally militarised, and thus strictly in antithesis to the core model of reformism and democratisation it claims. While the country embarked into a programme of economic modernisation, the projects it launched did not in fact reform the economic apparatus of the state, which remains deeply anchored to a form of neoliberal capitalism framed in a social key, as discussed in Chapter 6. From a political perspective, the apparatus of cronyism has ended up capitalising on aid assistance by creating 'crony capitalism' (Arab Barometer, 2018; Benjamin et al., 2014). This has ultimately affected voter politics and given military elites an entry into politics to assure the advantages of the militarised production under the National Services Project Organisation (NSPO), dating back to 1979.[9]

Yet personalism is not considered as an exclusive trait of al-Sisi's regime, as the 2013 coup appears to have structurally interfered with the process of political legitimation, diversifying strategies implemented by post-2013 authorities from those previously enforced under the NDP since the 1990s after the Washington Consensus. A change in the political authority's strategies for legitimation may influence a change in the state structure and definition, which in turn can affect the stability of the system. Thus, under these political-structural circumstances, it is here posited that in the shift in the institutional infrastructures of power, the process of political and institutional legitimation could undergo an internal variation, taking into account the internal axis over the external as a result of inherited internal political and economic challenges.

The lack of understanding of the post-2013 authoritarian transformative process of internal legitimation taking a micro-structural approach represents a notable gap in the existing scholarship on the sub-transformation of state and institutions in the long effects of post-2011 Middle East. In comparison to Egypt under Hosni Mubarak – when the regime's durability was mainly granted through recurring multi-party elections, cooptation of the wright-wing opposition and clientelist relations between the military and international state actors – in Egypt under al-Sisi the social and political panorama became smaller (Albrecht, 2005; Blaydes, 2006; Lust-Okar, 2009; Meital, 2006; Sharp, 2011). The subsequent suppression of all forms of civilian and political opposition – especially the lack of a regime party, after the collapse of the NDP and the freezing of all its assets, next to its replacement with a technocratic Parliament mainly represented by a pro-ruler block – significantly complicates the understanding of political legitimacy and dynamics of regime durability and stability in the country.

In the context of 'upgraded authoritarianisms', as a process resulting from protests or coups, the determinants of legitimation cannot be considered as an autonomous set of variables. Rather, they should be considered as closely tied to, and in constant interaction with, the circumstances, settings, socio-political contexts and structures, and international superstructures in which governments operate and implement policies and economic agendas (Lucca-Silveira, 2016). It follows that the legitimating process organically goes further when the intersection of certain political, structural and economic variables is considered.

Despite the argument of a possible regime sub-transformation towards a 'non-exclusivist personalism' which took place in Egypt as a direct and internal consequence to the 2013 coup, the debate remains highly fragmented in this regard, and still there is a consideration of Egypt as a restored and de facto militarised state (Aziz, 2017; Mandour, 2024; Noll, 2017; Sayigh, 2019; see also Bush and Greco, 2020), with the military rehabilitated in the institutionalised state apparatus and granted more influence and power than under the NDP. This state of affairs has been described as 'Mubarakism without Mubarak' (Goldberg, 2011). Instead, it is worth remembering that the legal framework introduced soon after the 2013 coup may have implications that can more accurately be said to have impacted the internal repositioning of actors within the legal and institutionalised infrastructures and interfered with the process of leadership legitimation and the new role played by the armed forces within the state structures. Al-Sisi has established a military electoral authoritarian state with a non-dominant party electoral system. In this regard the book will enter a critical analysis in Chapters 3 and 5 where the internal realignment of the SCAF along sub-transformed state structures is discussed.

This book proposes that, rather than a return of the function of the EAF to the Mubarak era, or its adoption of the Algerian military model, the military's involvement in the economy through the EAF, the Arab Organisation for Industrialisation (AOI) and NSPO, in combination with a supposedly civilian political leadership represented by Abdel Fattah al-Sisi and his coalition 'For the Love of Egypt', displays more similarities to the Sudanese model since the ouster of Omar al-Bashir in 2019, in which a civilian component has existed within the idea of a state and nations rooted into a persistent military culture (for reasons considered in Chapter 6). The 2013 military coup in Egypt set in motion infrastructural changes, including the collapse of the structural premises of Mubarak's resilience such as the important role of a regime party (i.e. the NDP) in 2011 and the confiscation of all assets, the disappearance of opposition forces and leftist parties which had emerged before 2013, the apparent civilian nature of the government led by al-Sisi, and the extreme bureaucratisation of politics with specific reference to the function of the Parliament, which deserve mention in the analysis of the regime and the background to political legitimacy. In the context of the Middle East after the 2011 wave of protests, the concept of legitimacy has today become particularly relevant because it is inextricable from understanding institutional trust. This work focuses specifically on the internal dynamics of a state's legitimacy, or the set of conditions by virtue of which the Egyptian government in fact is working to enjoy the right to rule over those living within its territorial jurisdiction. By definition, and in the context of more liberal political orders, a right to rule is correlated with an obligation to obey on the part of those subject to authority (Raz, 1985: 3). The concept 'obligation to obey' but also the 'voluntarily act to obey' as strictly Weber-inspired, takes a different conceptualisation in this work (Weber, 1978). The act of obeying is not here necessarily understood as a moral or civic obligation in autocracies, rather it can undergo structural and, eventually, online forms of contestations. In more simplistic terms it is concerned with the redefinition of the boundaries between rulers and ruled, between accepting certain conditions, imposed with violence or repression, from above and the right to contest them from below, and this regardless of the form of power exercised by the state.

Empirical and critical caveats

Economic liberalisation policies over more than three decades have already influenced, though not organically, the emergence of cronyism, intensifying the spread of fraud and patronage (*wasta* in Arabic), both in terms of access to economic resources and political advantages (Adly, 2009, 2014; Blaydes, 2010; Chekir and Diwan, 2012; Gormus, 2017; Hanieh, 2013; Hinnebusch, 1993; King, 2009; Stein, 2012; see also Barnett et al., 2013).[10] Economic liberalisation was proposed in the MENA region as an enlightening project which could apparently contribute to the process of democratisation (in fact, democratic capitalism) through market liberalisation and the mobility of global capital. Deregulation and privatisation, it was promised, would increase firms' economic activity. This in turn would increase the level of productivity, stimulating domestic and foreign investments, which as a result would contribute to economic expansion, including a decrease in the unemployment rate (Joya, 2020). However, from a Marxist perspective on economic-social relations in illiberal systems, market liberalisation in the Middle East, and broadly speaking the Global South, ultimately represented a political project under which capital found its realisation (Joya, 2020: 18–20). The emergence of cronyism since the 1990s after the International Monetary Fund (IMF)'s Structural Adjustment Programmes (SAP), and the brutal embrace of the International Financial Institutions under the Washington Consensus, rather than achieving what was labelled as a 'democratic capitalist economy', has ended up antagonising and polarising the state–society relationship, with high rates of unemployment, a widening poverty gap, and poor market performance compared to countries which did not embrace the Washington Consensus.[11] Indeed, economic adjustments to be effective structurally require opposition parties and their management. In the context of developing countries, as also found in Waterbury (1989), the coalition commonly entails the military and parties with exports-oriented interests and privatisation of industries. Thus, rather than bolstering the participation of civil society, economic liberalisation led to clashes with the elitist social and political structures governing Egypt. The economic failure determined by the contextualisation of neoliberal policies was converted into direct confrontation in the socio-political fabric between the state and Islamists, primarily represented by the Muslim Brotherhood, in light of the latter's long-lasting internal and consolidated capacity to attract communities living in marginalised areas in its anti-Mubarak campaigns, but also its structural capacity to interfere with the country's economic sector through the Faisal Islamic Bank of Egypt and intra-organisation donors (Denis, 1994).[12] The diffusion of anti-regime sentiments in the 1990s and 2000s was also fostered by the state absence as a social and welfare actor from Cairo's areas of informal housing, as government spending in healthcare and education under Mubarak is estimated as falling below the regional line (World Health Organization, 2000–2010) and UNESCO Institute for Statistics (2000–2008). Data go against more internal and non-objective readings of social expenditure under Mubarak like those provided by Galal in 2003 and later more objectively revised by Tadros (2007).

During the 2000s, the government's institutional absence from society meant it was structurally replaced mainly by the Muslim Brotherhood, which acted as the main social service provider, while the NDP continued with its economic liberalisation manoeuvres (Dorman, 2007; El-Sherif, 2014). While Salafi groups are found, in existing studies, to have additionally acted as social services providers, attempting to turn this social function into votes (Al-Anani, 2014; European Parliament, 2013), Salafis' involvement in the social sector was arguably somewhat similar to the NDP's tactic of attempting to limit the political implications of the Muslim Brotherhood's social presence. Informal neighbourhoods, therefore, were represented in the regime's discourse as places requiring the force of direct state intervention to prevent the spread of political ideologies that would put the durability of the regime at risk, but which also reflected the Egyptian state's inability to manage the growth of its capital (Dorman, 2009; Dorman and Stein, 2013). This corresponded to the state's securitisation of society and reliance on the intelligence services in arresting dissenters and patrolling certain areas, amongst which Bulaq al-Dakrur became representative of many other neighbourhoods in undergoing a process of political stereotyping from the late 1990s until the late 2000s (Ismail, 1998). In 2015, the area of Matariyya suffered a similar fate after a collusion between police officers and unidentified gunmen on motorbikes (Howeidy, 2015). The mechanisms of direct securitisation of informal areas through police personnel, and stereotyping, marginalisation and exclusion of communities as linked to terrorist threats, became ineffective after 2013 (see Bayat, 2000; Bayat and Denis, 2000; Ismail, 2006).[13]

In this book there is a bypassing of the understanding of power as a pure domination in political contexts shaken by mobilisations and major protests that eventually produced a major shockwave at the level of the political establishment and the social materiality of urban fabrics, like in Egypt between 2011 and the post-2013 events and created a void in leadership and power. Leadership and political power are two closely related concepts. Power has played an important role in leadership practices, while leadership is considered attached to the idea of power (Barker, 2001). The existing belief is that leadership cannot be conceived of separately from power, and while an individual can exercise power without being a leader, they may not be a leader without power (Lunenburg, 2012; see Parson 1963).

There is, in addition, a caveat requiring further reflection and this relates to the understanding of legitimacy as a temporal determinant. Legitimacy requires a continuous struggle, negotiation, and faith to be achieved, maintained and safeguarded. The perpetuation of negotiations by political authorities, both in democratic and autocratic systems around the world, is both a reminder of the fragility of the set of conditions that permit authorities to act as legitimate mandate of power, and a historical alert over time. When citizens are not willing to concede legitimacy, the crisis of legitimacy enters the debate.

As a concept, political legitimacy remains trapped in right-wing conservative assumptions that do not transcend the subversive nature it can embed, and rather confine it to the reductivism of a normative obedience, while in fact it cannot be reduced to a set of norms and restrictions. Despite constitutional reforms implemented after 2014 and the state's narrative on security, and even its social policies and growth, Egypt is still classified as a de facto highly fragile and highly authoritarian state (Freedom House, 2017–2022; see also Shenker, 2016). The Bertelsmann Transformation Index (BTI) in 2018 identified Egypt as a hard-line autocracy, a model which is functioning poorly (BTI, 2018). According to the US-based government-funded non-governmental organisation (NGO) Freedom House, Arab Barometer (AB), and the project on political government organisations Polity IV, Egypt in 2017 was listed 74th of 100 countries regarding political freedom, hence located amongst the less free countries (Freedom House, 2018; Arab Barometer, 2018; Polity Project V, 2017). This trend was confirmed in subsequent years due to the routinisation and abusive politics of repression on civilian and political fronts which continued up to 2023.

Regarding economic and political stability, based on the Global Economic Index between 2005 and 2006 the country's overall stability decreased to –0.84 but the economic performance was framed as "impressive" (–2.5 weak/+2.5 strong) (Global Economy Index, 2016; see also Bertelsmann Transformation Index, 2006–2007, International Monetary Forum, 2007). However, based on World Economic Forum' (WEF) indeces, there was an impossiblity of doing business in the country mainly due to crime and theft, (World Economic Forum, 2007). A different approach to stability is found in the Heritage Foundation, according to which institutional integrity in 2006–2007 was overall very poor, though not poorer than the level of integrity scored in 2014, 2018–2019 and 2022 (the Heritage Foundation, 2006–2022). There was a slight improvement between 2007 and 2009 when the country shifted from –0.55 to –0.51 (Global Economy Index, 2016). The score was not surprising, as at the time the NDP was attempting to regain consensus through programmes of urban upgrading and improvement (Khalifa, 2015). Nevertheless, stability dropped again in 2011 to –1.44. A year after the 2013 coup, consensus towards political authorities dropped even further, to –1.64, equalling Egypt's lowest historic level. The situation slightly improved in 2016 with a score of –1.42, reflecting the new government's launch of its economic agenda (Global Economy Index, 2016). In 2022 the most recent value for political stability was scored at –1.03 (World Bank Index, 2022): –2.5 weak/above 2.5 strong. These indicators are indicative of a severe lack of institutional trust in the Egyptian government led by al-Sisi. Yet they are also indicative of fluctuating and unstable government performance. According to data provided by the Arab Transformations Project (ATP) (2014, 2017), the failure to capture consensus was linked to perceptions of high levels of corruption after 2013. Perception of corruption in politics and public sector started fluctuating after 2013 with a new peak between 2017 and 2018, to fall down in 2019 and again in 2022 to rise again in 2023. (Transparency International, 2023). Indeed, after an initial denial in which al-Sisi himself accused the media of slandering the armed forces, the regime in 2017 replaced most of the heads of the military, presenting these changes as aimed at transparency and tackling political corruption. However, such reshuffles of high-ranking military figures have been common since al-Sisi assumed power but have done little to halt the spread of corruption (Gamal, 2019a). The government's failure to gain public confidence and trust in state institutions could be read as a symptom of the government's inability to reach stabilisation. Based on statistics, despite the launch of the economic agenda, in 2014 there was still no broad social consensus over the regime's actions in the economic and financial sectors.

The symbolic importance of the 2011 protests demonstrates that the legitimation of political rulers has shifted towards reliance upon internal dynamics and cannot be considered as linked to rhetoric construction alone but is dependent on the effective capacity to bring change. The cooptation of political opposition and civil society organisations have been practices through which autocrats have attempted to achieve a form of durability as enduring ordinary practices in autocratic systems, even beyond the Arab world. However, in the specific case of Egypt for at least three decades, repressive power controlled the political and social destiny of the country. Even though the 2011 protests failed in establishing a new regional order as based on a redefinition of the social contract and in the making of a more inclusivist social dimension centralising citizens' needs at the core of economic redistributive agendas, protests succeeded in redefining the boundaries between ruled and rulers. Despite a gradual process of autocratic restoration and rehabilitation of elite in the new state foundations, political power as a premise can no longer be approached as coercive (Achcar, 2013). Coercions and persecutions from an economic perspective remain costly, unsustainable and expose power to the risk of collapse. As such, with a particular emphasis after major shockwaves coercion and repression can no longer be a recipe for governing in the way they contribute to the accumulation of dissent in the context of organically, culturally and socially transformed societal fabrics. Class struggles, labour strikes and bread riots in the region are historically representative for structured mass dissent against the effects determined by the alliance between capitalist neoliberalism and illiberally designed institutions but, echoing Gerschewski, repressing opposition in the long-term is a costly endeavour as the latter creates counterproductive incentives (Gerschewski, 2018: 655). Thus, persuasion and seduction are two qualifiers of transmission in the legitimation process.

Structure of the book

The overall structure of the book reflects the transformative approach and the four-phases model in the way it initially critically reinterprets traditional Western-based approaches to the study of political legitimacy through Weber's rational-legal, charismatic and traditional determinants. The goal is that of entering the theorised structural architectural transformation in the reorganisation of power structures. Here the elements of seduction, persuasion and the retelling of myths, symbols and memories are recalled through a critical transformative approach. This serves the purpose of redirecting into the modified conception of legitimacy, which in turn is aimed at unpacking and acknowledging the transformations in the social materiality of society in Egypt, beyond Eurocentrist-neocolonial approaches. This is done by considering internal realignments and the existing relations, despite social repression and amendments to the penal code, which prevent forms of civic and political engagement between armed forces and social-religious actors as well as the projections of new business interests and aspirations along the international political and economic spectrum like new trends in development as represented by the international programmes supporting and urging green transitions under Agenda 2030.[14] In the four phases the book shifts and considers the economic side of political legitimation in a political system in which the legal foundations of the state, as shown in the first three phases, gradually generated a shift in the architecture of political power, which entered disequilibria. This is done by considering the global policy regulations pushing for green transitions and how the latter risks being institutionally weaponised as a new tool for renegotiating the foundations of legitimacy (and effects on the social contracts) on the one hand, and on the other greenwashing the resilience of corrupted autocracies in the region. The overall approach taken will reflect the main repositioning of the work in the debate on authoritarianism and its cut-off disengagement with the debate on illiberal continuity.

Chapter 1 introduces the theoretical framework, explaining the reason for an interdisciplinary and modified conception of internal political legitimacy, and considers the scope of the design beyond Egypt and the Middle East. The interdisciplinarity of the framework pushes for a structural and infrastructural micro-understanding of the inner socio-political materiality of non-Western societies. The chapter reflects on a dominance of Westernised and Eurocentrist premises to the legitimation of non-democratic systems in developing countries and broadly in non-Western countries. It calls for post-Orientalist and de-Westernised critical lenses of analysis, which in this book will find contextualisation through Wallerstein, Marks and Abdelhalim and Abu-Lughod, to better appreciate the cruciality transformations in the urban materiality of non-Western dominated societal fabrics after shockwaves (Abu-Lughod, 1971; 1989; Marks and Abdelhalim, 2018; Wallerstein, 1997). This is captured as a precondition for understanding the non-linearity of legitimation struggles in illiberal systems that happened to be closer to a form of less immobilistic (and thus fluid) authoritarianism.

Chapter 2 looks at the main transformation that took place in the aftermath of the 2013 coup in Egypt, amongst which the disappearance of a regime party and the transformation in Islamism with an emphasis on the rise of political Salafism. The chapter argues how the capitulation of the Mubarak and Morsi regimes did not lead to a form of restoration of the status quo ex-ante but rather, in line with the Khaldunian theory of cyclical change and the Baumanian reinterpretation of the Gramscian interregnum, it is likely there will be a transformation along the authoritarian spectrum. To this end the chapter engages with a redefinition of personalist regimes. The rupture here is with the scholarship that remains set on the idea of a purist military restoration, an argument from which the book distances itself.

Chapter 3 focuses on how a legitimation claim as forged from above and addressed to civil society started to be forged immediately after the 2013 coup. It explores the implications of al-Sisi's strategy of playing with the rule of law which directly impacted with polarising the architecture of power in the country for the first time. This set the bases for and the reinvention of the liquid state and the reinvention of the regime's legal foundations.

Chapter 4 traces the evolution of the political authorities' legitimation strategies between 2014 and 2016, focusing on the function played by charisma and how the interplay of myths and symbols with collective memories from the past, acting as host-symbolism, were manipulated by political authorities and promoted as neo-socialist and neo-welfarist with the goal of recreating not so much a Nasserian national greatness from the past – a theory from which the book ruptures – but to justify the new role played by armed forces in projects of green transitions through their joint ventures. However, the more authoritarian and personalist the regime became, the more it needed the army, rather than civil society and this is at odds with its promoted idea of a neo-Nasserian socialism and a return to neo-Nasserism, as conventionally and broadly agreed. Likewise, this is at odds with the dynamics of populism in the way charisma aimed at a form of intra-hierarchical consensus on the one hand, while on the other populism ended up manipulating myths, symbols and memories not with the goal of dividing the nation for preventing democratic reforms but rather with the scope of marginalising the political-societal sub-stratum linked to the Muslim Brotherhood. This links to the next chapter, in which the book enters the ethnosymbolism of religion.

Chapter 5 expands on the use made of religion by the authorities between 2015 and 2020. The chapter considers how al-Sisi's appropriation of religion attempted to influence the process of internal legitimation and provide access to power structures. It also investigates the securitisation of the Muslim Brotherhood, and al-Sisi's discourse on terrorism as a prelude to a politics of political fear and obsession. It expands on state violence and its routinisation in everyday life while understanding how sub-transformations additionally impacted power imbalances. It offers a critical analysis into the internal fragmentations that exist within the al-Azhar, with the Muslim Brotherhood trend being more predominant over others and still present within the armed forces. The chapter analyses the communality of interests that brings the Muslim Brotherhood and the armed forces closer, when compared to the interests that bring together al-Sisi and the armed forces. This very deep legacy and the risks it entails remains unacknowledged.

Chapter 6 discusses economic performance and the regime's new business trajectories as more oriented towards meeting the IMF's demand. It additionally presents a critical overview on political ecology as intertwined with the overall struggle for political legitimacy. It outlines the main socio-economic developmental challenges facing Egypt from the issue of resources distribution to the health sector and education, to projects of green transitions as part of the agenda of sustainable development. While centralising nature as a new political ecology of power struggle, the chapter looks at the creation of the youth pro-ruler bloc connected to the ruler's struggle for legitimation and the meaning for the regime's political structure.

The book closes re-engaging with the discussion on internal political legitimacy and the theory of fluid autocracies following shockwaves in authoritarian states that became more liquid.

The final chapter also expands to Western actors and the European Foreign Policy in the Mediterranean area in connection with the legitimation, and renewal, of sub-transformed fluid autocracies framed as a necessary condition for the functioning of the international agenda on development, but which system remains discussed through 'neocolonialist' lenses, despite the unsustainability of financial indebtedness. This in turn poses ethical issues around the institutionalisation and financialisation of nature as a 'critical ecosystem' of power and legitimacy.

Notes

1 Interregnum, borrowing from Baumna, was originally used to denote a time-lag separating the death of one royal sovereign from the enthronement of the successor (Bauman, 2012).
2 Charisma is conceptualised in this work 'as a certain quality of an individual personality by virtue of which he is considered extraordinary and treated as endowed with supernatural, superhuman, or exceptional powers or qualities' (Schweitzer, 1974: 151). According to Spencer, Weber uses the concept of charisma in at least three senses: '(i) the supernatural "gift" of the leader, (ii) charisma as a sacred or revered essence deposited in objects or persons, [and] (iii) charisma as the attractiveness of a personality' (Spencer, 1973; see also Weber, 1947: 352). There is wide agreement in the scholarship on Nasser's case of what Weber defined as 'charismatic legitimacy' as deriving from the attractiveness of his personality, despite being an autocrat. Expanding the classical Weberian interpretation, there is not necessarily any contradiction between despotic rules and legitimacy, as long as the latter is classified as either traditional or charismatic (Dusza, 1989).
3 Since 2019 Italy has boosted joint economy and military production cooperation with Egypt. Sectors include defence and civil industries and comprise a total of

nine agreements. The arms deal amounts to 10–12 billion US dollars: all this, despite human rights records. In 2020 al-Sisi was the recipient of the Gran Cross of the Legion d'Honneur (France 24).
4   In the 2014 elections al-Sisi won with 96.1 per cent of the vote, instead (EODS, 2014).
5   An early project of greening desert lands was launched in 1997. The headquarter is al-Wahat al-Baharia desert on Giza's governorate. It remains unclear who the funders of the project are, as state institutions are not displayed in the Sekem Wahat project. As well as this, the ministries of environment and housing are backing the construction of the Green River in the New Administrative Capital which started in 2019.
6   On corruption and legitimacy see Seligson (2002).
7   On early definition of perennialism and the role of myth and symbols see Smith, 1991.
8   That is, the Muslim Brotherhood movement, the Egyptian Trade Union Federation syndicate, the independent syndicates, the Salafis movements.
9   NSPO (National Service Projects Organization). Available at: http://www.nspo.com.eg/nspo/about.html.
10 It should be noted that the practices mentioned above were strictly associated with the NDP's hegemonic power, consolidated between the late 1990s and the early 2000s.
11 On International Financial Institutions see also Abu-Odeh, 2009: 352. The Washington Consensus, dating to the 1980s, proposed itself as a new paradigm of development, pushing for fiscal discipline, privatisation, liberalisation of FDI and trade, and tax reform, amongst other goals (see on this Joya, 2020).
12 This was especially evident in Cairo neighbourhoods such as Bulaq el-Dakrur and Imbaba, from which dissent against Mubarak spread in the 1990s. The Muslim Brotherhood's success in attracting communities in informal areas was organically linked to the genesis of the organisation in the late 1920s under its spiritual guide Hassan al-Banna.
13 On consequent state interventions in areas under Mubarak see Dorman, 2007. On associated internal programmes retrieved in 2016 European Union External Action Service 2016.
14 *Desertec Project* and the *Mediterranean Solar Panels Programme*, supported and financed both by the private sector and the European Bank of Investment, deserve a mention here.

1

Political legitimacy in fluid authoritarianism: a liquid interregnum

The problem of political legitimacy in modern autocracies

A Weber inspired reading (1968, quoted in Bensman, 1979: 360) defines legitimacy as 'the belief in a political or social order', though another frequently acknowledged theory, recalling Lipset (1959), explains legitimacy as the capacity of a political system to engender a belief that certain political institutions, regardless of their form and normative foundations, are 'beneficial' for society.[1] Legitimacy here is captured as evaluative, while performance is instrumental (Lispset, 1984: 88). The Gramscian interregnum (1971), as introduced in this book, and as based on processuality, organicity and morbidity, finds a critical application to Egypt in the way the political event of 2013 has been captured as a process that internally and organically set up a crisis which had existed latently at the inner level since the early 2000s but which become more evident, though not predominant, after 2006–2008. Hence, the 2013 set-up of a series of internal processes that substantively attempted to change the structural identity of the state, thus interfering with the making of a new order in which authoritarianism attempted to renegotiate the foundations of consent and political legitimacy from above. In unpacking every single process that started taking place in the aftermath of 2013 up to 2020, this book goes beyond Gramsci's 1930s immobilism of the dying order as a transition period that due to the persistence of certain global structures (i.e. capitalism) prevented the rise of a newborn order. While from a global perspective the book does not contest Gramsci's criticism of capitalism, in the specific contextualisation of post-2013 Egypt under al-Sisi, it demonstrates how the process of crisis, that is, the 2013 coup and, before that, the 2011 protests, undermined the historical conception of power and authority as mainly based on diplomatic political cooperation until 2010 and instead pushed for a redefinition of the entire state assets and the internal legitimation process of the authority.

The transition period identified in this book from 2013 up to 2020 has been here captured as liquid, where by liquidity is meant the volatility of the internal phases that started emerging soon after 2013 and which interested not only the state structures from above and the overall impact liquidity exercised over the nationalistic identity of the state that emerged in the post-2013 setting under the mythisation of al-Sisi, but mainly the relations that started becoming more uncertain and fluid, at the meso-level due to organic intra-societal transformations.[2] The liquidity of the relations and new state identity is, in this book, used in antithesis to Ayubi's theory of Arab states' weakness (Ayubi, 1995) defined as a result of Arab states' inability to impose a neoliberal restructuring (Ayubi, 1995; see also Achcar, 2021: 58). The renegotiation of internal premises of legitimation in a top-down fashion through differing categories through which al-Sisi framed political, economic and social actions and decisions are an account of the liquid and changing dynamic of authoritarianism in Egypt in response to a new order that started to emerge from the inner level (sub-structural system) and which attempted to negotiate the sphere of obedience with the sphere of a form of consensus.

In acknowledging the limitations that a purist Weber-based approach faces in bypassing Westernised and Eurocentrist explanations of political legitimacy in non-Eurocentrist political systems, there are different levels of analysis. Addressing the limitations posed by Weber follows an intellectual engagement with Wallerstein (1997) and the critique of Eurocentrist approaches in the broader study and understanding of social science theories and political systems. To this end, the theoretical foundations further incorporate Marks and Abdelhalim (2018) and the general critique of Eurocentrism and Western-oriented approaches of the study of non-Western political contexts. In addition, the work then combines this critique with Abu-Lughod's problematisation of the dominant colonialist-Orientalist culture in deciphering the Middle East and its anthropological substratum (1989). Hence, the modified Weberian conception will bypass the limitations posed by classical and Western definitions of legitimacy, which neglect internal and societal change in non-Western illiberal systems. The chapter will specifically propose a modified Weberian conception of political legitimacy in combination with three more selected theories: David's (1991) theory of omnibalancing, Easton's (1975) theory of specific support as embedded into the systems theory, and Gerschewski's (2013) theory of internal support.[3]

This multi-level framework sets the foundations through which to study political legitimation in the context of sub-transformed systems and infrastructures that reacted to political and social episodes of transformations – the 2011 uprising initially, and more specifically the 2013 military coup, are representative. While the modified conception here provided has found an empirical application to the specific case study of Egypt, from a broader intellectual perspective the foundations here go beyond the paradigm of 'survival' on a transnational level in the Middle East and in countries that bear similarities to Egypt after 2013.

The designed model recognises the many intellectual approaches in discussing political legitimacy and will critically comment on definitions and critiques put forward by Barker (2012), Beetham (1991), Booth and Seligson (2009), Dogan (1992), Gilley (2012), Hechter (2009), Hurd (1999), Levi and Sacks (2009), Linz (1988), Marx and Engels (1959), Raz (1985), Stinchcombe (1968), and mainly Weber (1963, 1978). The modified framework has been created to better fit with the repositioning of social actors along the spectrum of domestic politics. While the theoretical framework of this study expands on Weber's theory of legitimacy and specifically traditional legitimacy, it also modifies and combines it with aspects extrapolated from Scharpf's theory of legitimacy as based on inputs and outputs (Scharpf, 1970). For the purpose of this book and its double contribution to international comparative politics and Middle Eastern politics, the work will additionally refer to three main determinants, as also found in Van Soest and Graugovel (2017). In the second part of the framework, the multi-level designed model aims to understand how these have been modified under the post-2013 executive, and the extent that they may have had a role in the process of legitimation. Expanding on Weber's (1963) concept of the authoritarian state, he defined the German political system as *Obrigkeitsstaat* (authoritarian), in which the maintenance of a social order ultimately depended upon the continuity of its members' perceptions of the order as legitimate.[4]

Combining Weber's theory of legitimacy with more empirical works on Middle East politics and dynamics of military authoritarianism in pre-2013 Egypt (Geddes, 1999b; Gilley, 2006; Lipset, 1960, 1994; Mitchell, 2002; Schmitter, 2010), the isolated variables that participate in the process of legitimation fall within the normative, moral and social legitimacy realm. Linking the multi-level theoretical framework at the foundation of this book with the focus on the architecture of legitimacy, and recalling the isolated variables patronage and corruption, cooptation of the Islamist opposition and elections, and the manipulation of the judiciary, all used to create the foundations for durability, this chapter outlines the mechanisms through which, according to existing theories on authoritarianism, military and personalist regimes attempt to consolidate power and legitimise their political authority (Blaydes, 2010; Geddes, 2008; Geddes et al., 2017; Gerschewski, 2013; Gandhi and Lust, 2009; Hamzawy, 2005; Janowitz, 1977; Lust-Okar, 2009; Magaloni, 2008; Merkel and Gerschewski, 2011). The focus on these two categories of authoritarianism, as opposed to other taxonomies, is connected with the theory of a regime sub-variation towards a certain personalism, referenced in this work, as intertwined with the post-2013 political authorities' construction of a new form of political legitimacy.

It follows that in some political contexts experiencing profound social and eventually ideological transformations, like Egypt after the 2013 coup, despite the historical legacy of authoritarianism, legitimacy still plays a fundamental role in the regime's durability and resilience, and its construction may follow different formulas from those historically implemented by past regimes (Hudson, 2014; see also Patriotta and Schultz, 2011). This book contends that the need for reconsidering the approach to sustainability, durability and legitimation may also be determined by strictly structural changes that influence the recreation of power structures. Al-Sisi's legitimation strategy does not necessarily follow those adopted by his predecessors, from Nasser to Mubarak. This line of argumentation paves the road to a total reconsideration of authoritarianism in Egypt since its inception in 1953. Hence, the empirical contribution added by the new model of theories outlined above is one of challenging existing works that have drawn, in one way or another, a form of post-modern continuity between the 1950s and post-2013 setting.

As indicated above, there is an urgency to rethink the approach to legitimacy in the broader Mediterranean area beyond a purist Weber-rooted conception, derived from the need to recognise the context which is the object of inquiry (Marks and Abdelhalim, 2018: 305), as a quickly changing environment that can shift from a social and political condition of stability to structural regional insecurity, which would end up constituting satellite worries for the, geographically close, EU and its member states. Equally, there is an urgency in reconsidering the dominance of Orientalist, ontological and epistemological stylised approaches in defining, describing and explaining non-Western social or political contexts through the dominance of neocolonialist Western eyes.

It was in 1997 that Wallerstein argued that social science is a product of the modern world system, and Eurocentrism is a constitutive element of what he called 'the geoculture of the modern world' (1997: 21). The work goes a step further and expands this critique, with Wallerstein establishing a connection between the persistency of Eurocentrism in social science and colonialism, he argued how specific European historical achievements, the idea of civilisation, the theory of progress and its Orientalism constituted certain categories that expressed the deep-rooted and dominant Eurocentric approach in social science. From an intellectual perspective, this book gets closer to Wallerstein's critique, which suggests the need to reanalyse, through different analytical eyes, not only European historical 'achievements' but also the definition and interpretation of the non-Western world (1997: 35). In arguing thus, there is further needed to embed Abu-Lughod's (1989) more specific contestation of Western-rooted Orientalist explanations of the Middle East. Orientalists are mostly Westerners that, implicitly or explicitly, attempt to uphold European domination of the Middle East in their works (Abu-Lughod, 1989). This results in structural inequalities between the world of Western scholars and their 'Third World' subjects, as disciplines have been influenced by Western-oriented constructivist views of the societal and political functioning of the Arab world and its ethno and non-ethno societies.

Thus, a purist Western-induced conception of legitimacy, applied to a structurally, socially and politically changing country like Egypt in response to the 2011 protests and 2013 coup and their subsequent and protracted processes until 2022 would fail in capturing the internal determinants that interact in forging a legitimation claim (Abu-Lughod, 1989). Expanding Abu-Lughod's critique and recalling Bourdieu's conceptualisation of *habitus* (2005), neglecting the action and role of internal actors risks neglecting the structures that shape the social and political world from which authority emerges and how domination occurs. Therefore, this work suggests a modified conception of legitimacy, which considers the action and role of internal political and religious actors in a transformed society, where state and religion bypass limitations posed by purist and classical Weberian analysis as mainly applied to the sphere of inputs.

The idea of political authority can be established at all hierarchical levels, and can be exercised upward, downward, or horizontally. This chapter argues that the construction of a political authority in post-2013 Egypt shifted from being strictly verticalised (top-down) and prevalently based on *wasta* politics, into more horizontal and diffused dimensions. The shift of political power from a pyramidal hierarchy, as that which produced political power and regime resilience under Mubarak's NDP, to a network as theorised in this work, implies in turn a shift in the organisation and conceptualisation of legitimation by political authorities. This result, it is argued, may possibly lead to two effects: a change in the definition and nature of leadership, a break from the continuum of the past in regard to the authoritarian state structures (i.e. the existence of a regime party since the 1950s, first the ASU and then the NDP from 1978 to 2011) after the 2013 coup, and a depoliticisation of the parliamentary assembly.

In introducing the multi-level based modified framework of analysis combining Weber with David (1991) plus Gerschewski (2013) and Easton (1975), this chapter will theorise that regimes following a moment of political breakdown, with the emergence of new political actors (such as the Salafis) next to the existence of former political threats (such as the Muslim Brotherhood and FJP after their experience of governmental politics), may opt to realign themselves with forces previously considered 'enemies' (i.e. Salafis) to counter the threat from those framed as the greater enemies (i.e. the Muslim Brotherhood). This argument borrows from David's (1991) omnibalancing theory of intra-alignments, which in turn capitalised on international relations' redefinition of Walt's (1985) balance of power theory. However, it also links to Easton's theory of internal and specific support, discussed in the final part of this chapter. Easton (1975) suggests that the specific realignment between political authorities and state-identified actors (e.g. religious actors) does not necessarily have to be strictly political, but can, nevertheless, influence the process of political legitimation adding cohesion (Easton, 1975; von Soest and Graugovel, 2017). However, borrowing from Dogan's (2009: 195) critique of Weber and the argument that his trilogy of legitimacy is outdated, this study agrees that, specifically in non-democratic regime types, legitimacy is never unanimously achieved due to forms of resistance and rebel cultures, but it is worth considering the societal substratum in which legitimacy is forged, beyond Western-Colonialist and Eurocentric definitions and stylised understanding of non-Western societies and political systems (Marks and Abdelhalim, 2018; Abu-Lughod, 1989).

Legitimacy and the right to rule

In *The Evolution of Prestige*, Henrich and Gil-White aimed to define the motivation behind power (Henrich and Gil-White, 2001). They differentiate between dominance and prestige motivations for power (Henrich and Gil-White, 2001). While 'Dominance reflects an approach in which individuals attain and use power via force and the selfish manipulation of group resources', prestige reflects an approach whereby people attain influence because they garner respect and employ valuable skills or knowledge to help the group achieve its goal (Mead and Maner, 2010). Henrich and Gil-White are not the only theorists who differentiate between self-interested and group-interested motives; a distinction has also been made between personalised power (using power for personal gain) and socialised power (using power to benefit other people) (French and Raven, 1959; McClelland, 1970, 1975; Winter, 1973). Knowing the motivation behind power can explain why someone chooses to employ a certain basis over another.

A person motivated by dominance/personalised power will utilise the reward and coercive bases, while one motivated by prestige/socialised power will utilise the referent and expert bases. Taking one step further, a person whose aim is simply to maintain a power position is motivated by dominance/personalised power; whereas a person whose aim is to be an effective leader is motivated by prestige/socialised power. Henrich's and Gil-White's views connect to a deeper level of analysis linked to the right and power to rule, which regulates understandings of why and on what premises non-democratic systems possess legitimacy. Regarding the right to rule, the theory of rights is highly prescient, combining claims with interests. The intersection between claim, right and interest determines the level of legitimacy, but when interests and positions prevail over claims, a justified non-democratic rule could arise even without a right to rule, for example, legitimacy. Thus, the absence of the right to rule forces justification or legitimation to be sought by other means.

Legitimacy is still considered a crucial element in the creation and survival of organisational forms and alliances (Aldrich and Fiol, 1994; Dacin et al., 2007; Freeman and Hannan, 1983; Hannan, 1989). It is believed that being the determinant to provide a solution to political problems mainly relates to the justification of political institutions. The problem of justifying a non-democratic political structure, its architecture and form of power mainly attains to non-democratic systems and in post-conflict systems that did not transition towards expected outcomes, that is, democracies. In the context of non-democratic political systems, legitimacy can be understood as an acceptance of authority by both elite and non-elite groups, although this definition undergoes problematisation as not all citizens share equally in their capacity to confer legitimacy (McCullogh, 2015: 7).

In the context of non-democratic political systems, legitimacy can be understood as an acceptance of authority by both elite and non-elite groups, although not all citizens are equal in their capacity to confer legitimacy. Thus, the modified conceptual framework through which political legitimacy is reapproached is initially and utilitarianly based on Weber's (1963, 1978) theories of legitimacy, and additionally combines McLoughlin (2014) with Easton (1975) and Gerschewski (2013). Political legitimacy remains one of the most used, but also misused, concepts. It ranks with power in terms of its importance (Schmitter, 2010) and the popular acceptance of the state's right to rule (Mcloughlin, 2015). It can also refer to the stability and transformations of political orders, or factors that provide legitimacy to political rulers (von Haldenwang, 2016: 1). Broadly, the concept of right is understood as correlated with an obligation to obey on the part of those subject to the authority (Raz, 1985). Nevertheless, political legitimacy becomes a subject of debate and analysis particularly when it is missing or deficient (Schmitter, 2010: 1), and it is when a state, government or regime is challenged by citizens that the lack of legitimacy is usually invoked as a driver for the crisis (Schmitter, 2010). However, crises in turn inevitably lead to organic transformations.

The Weberian idea of charisma is one of the most historically debated sources of political legitimacy with fragmented views on it. It is conceptualised in this book 'as a certain quality of an individual personality by virtue of which he is considered extraordinary and treated as endowed with

Political legitimacy in fluid authoritarianism 31

supernatural, superhuman, or exceptional powers or qualities' (Schweitzer, 1974: 151, see also Scheitzer, 1984).[5] While Weber considered charismatic legitimacy as emerging relatively spontaneously, legal legitimacy was defined as subject to people's confidence in the system. Indeed, to borrow from Weber, charisma is understood as subject to people's recognition, but it is also considered transitory, and is often transformed into legal-rational legitimacy (Weber, 1978). Hence, as opposed to norms, charisma can be understood as a transitory form of domination. Distanced from Weber, Szelenyi argues that it is hard, almost impossible, to pass charisma on from one leader to the next, and the concept is utopian in the way it promises 'miracles' or 'salvations' through revolutions (Szelenyi, 2016). On general premises, processes of charismatic legitimation are more likely to be overthrown by revolutionary waves, which in Weber's view are considered illegitimate in form (Weber, 1978). Revolutions stemming out of charismatic failures are replaced by new forms of legal-rational legitimacy, which in turn obey the same logic of being overthrown by popular protests and replaced by new sources of legitimacy, thus repeating a vicious circle. Weber's theory of legitimacy is not entirely consistent due to the circularity of the concept, the claim that legitimacy is the belief of citizens in the legitimacy of the system (Grafstein, 1981).

Problematising classical Weberian interpretations, the most moral source remains legal-traditional as profoundly anchored to the Latin origin of the verb 'legitimare' which stands for 'making lawful', rather than 'according to the law', as misread by the German interpretation instead.[6] The transnational debate on political legitimacy has attempted to recentralise the old debate which asked whether autocratic regimes can make their rule more stable and based on consensus by seeking the support of the citizens (Dukalskis and Gerschewski, 2017; Kailitz and Stockemer, 2017; see also Gerschewski, 2013). While for decades the debate on legitimation process of non-democratic systems attempted to examine the role of multi-party and semi-competitive elections as catalysts for democratisation-legitimation of non-democratic structures. In fact, as this book deepens in Chapter three, in the Middle East semi-competitive elections just served the purpose of vehiculating external funding towards parties' cadres and through the manipulations of constitutions and legal amendments.[7]

There is a recurring heavy Weberian approach to the normative definition of political legitimacy in how the state is defined. One of the many limitations here stems from Weber's static view of states, which is in antithesis to the theory of (Arab) states' liquidity theorised in this book in post-shockwaves contexts. David Beetham's conception of legitimacy as here combined with Weber is influential in the way bypasses the narrowed idea of legitimacy and power as attained to the spheres of coercion and domination, alone. Beyond Weber, in Beetham legitimacy does not depend on people's belief, but on the justification of rule on the basis of people's beliefs (Beetham, 1991). Beetham begins by criticising Weber, stressing that Weber's (1978) typology of legitimacy is misleading, and that the German scholar's belief in legitimacy (*Legitimitätsglauben*) is too simplistic to grasp the state's legitimacy appropriately. The 'typology of Weber' is a misleading tool for the analysis of the modern state; especially for the comparative analysis of transformational political systems' (Beetham, 1991: 34). The "normative structures of legitimacy' suggest a need for a multi-dimensional analysis' (Beetham, 1991: 64–99). Beetham's conceptualisation of legitimacy is threefold on different premises: on the first level, legitimacy lies in conformity to established rules; on the second level, rules can be justified by reference to beliefs shared by both dominant and subordinate groups; and on the third level, legitimacy stems from evidence of the consent of the subordinate to the particular power relation (Beetham, 1991). Unlike Weber's, in Beetham's theory, legitimacy is thought to be accessed through the combination of perceptions and actions.

The complexity of the concepts of legitimacy and authority has generated an extensive body of literature that deals with the legitimation of non-democratic rule (Abulof, 2016; Andersen, 2012; Gerschewski, 2013; Holbig and Gilley, 2010; Kailitz, 2015, 2013; Lust-Okar, 2006; Magaloni, 2006, 2008). Dogan (1992) argues that regimes usually secure power through force. A different view is expressed by Huntington (1991) who, instead, posits that regimes' possession of legitimacy also includes factors such as economic performance, which ultimately in authoritarian systems represents the output or the instrumentalist tool towards a trustworthy government in which performance is captured as a utilitaristic justification for staying in power.[8] The concept of performance has so far been discussed as a self-referential strategy put in place by rulers to claim political legitimacy (Saliba, 2014; see also Gerschewski et al., 2013). It refers to regime legitimacy that stems from success in satisfying citizens' needs (see Listhaug, 1998). However, while some studies acknowledge the consistent importance of performance for legitimising political rule, others like Saward uphold the limits that a definition of legitimacy based on efficiency and accountability may pose (Saward, 1992: 33). The focus on performance in this study reflects the extent to which a regime either deliberately cites its achievements in fulfilling societal demands such as material welfare and security, or, alternately, employs claims of achievements in the absence of real improvements. Hence, different components can comprise the notion of 'performance', among them the claim that the state organises equal redistribution and access to public goods including healthcare and education (Van Soest and Grauvogel,

2017), as well as the presentation of a regime as a guarantor of stability and territorial integrity (Radnitz, 2012). Rather than using proxies such as economic growth, inflation and unemployment to measure a regime's performance-based support, as is common practice, this work asks to what extent a regime explicitly invokes such performance-related claims. Thus, while performance is indicative of the rulers' self-narrative to legitimise and justify themselves, it does not determine whether political authorities benefit from genuine popular trust. This argument clashes with Geddes (1999b), de Mesquita et al. (2003) and de Mesquita and Smith (2011), in the views of whom economic performance is at the core of regimes' success, as good economic outcomes and stable GDP contribute to regimes' durability.

On the contrary, performance in non-democratic systems has been considered as lying at the core of legitimacy decline over time, due to unrealised promised. Poor performance in the economy, human rights and law tends to disaffect the masses by generating mistrust and the formation of opposing groups (Bellin, 2004). Equity in income distribution and per capita income under the broader umbrella of 'performance' have been regarded as generators of legitimacy crisis (Bellin, 2004; Epstein et al., 2003). However, whilst von Soest and Graugovel (2017) sees in performance a possible driver for and determinant of legitimation, Mcloughlin (2014) differs in not considering the delivery of services as the basis of state legitimacy. Service delivery can instead positively impact on perceptions.[9] Mechanisms of elections, cooptation and clientelism have for decades been considered as drivers behind the longevity and legitimacy of particularly military and semi-competitive military regimes. This has been the subject of extensive discussion in the context of Mubarak's Egypt, as a result of the country's institutionalised multi-party system. Very few studies have instead attempted to understand how performance in Egyptian politics may be employed as driver of legitimation by outputs. While specific or performance-based support can be measured using indicators such as economic growth, inflation and unemployment, the goal of adopting performance as output legitimation is to understand the extent to which a regime deliberately uses its achievements in fulfilling societal demands such as material welfare or security or, alternately, employs claims of achievements in the absence of real improvements in order to back up its claims to legitimacy (Dimitrov, 2009). While in democratic systems performance is included in the state input, as a result of shared ideas about what the political system represents, in the context of non-democratic states it is explored as an output process (Mazepus et al., 2016: 353; see also Przeworski and Limongi, 1993).

The points of departure set out above are never so important as in a country like Egypt under al-Sisi. The concept of right is understood as correlated with an obligation to obey on the part of those subject to the authority (Raz, 1985). Nevertheless, political legitimacy becomes a subject of debate and analysis, particularly when it is missing or deficient, and it is when a state or government is challenged by citizens that the lack of legitimacy is usually invoked as a driver for the crisis (Schmitter, 2010). The centres of power through which legitimacy is achieved should not be conceived as monolithic, rather they can be identified around institutions and social groups. The relationship between the regime and its centres of power(s) is important to the maintenance of the regime itself (Stinchcombe, 1968). The centrality of the debate evolves around the modus operandi, as unpopular and non-democratic government can retain authority by calling on centres of power, in particular the armed forces (i.e. the military, police and secret services), which can also be considered an institutionalised centre of power (Stinchombe, 1968). Broadening the debate, the role of the armed forces in sustaining regimes is established in comparative politics, and there are numerous examples of militaries backing a regime in trouble for which a crystal-clear example is 1989 China when Deng Xiaoping and the Chinese Communist Party ordered the army to use force to suppress protests in Tiananmen Square. However, it is worth adding how the framing of the military as an institutional centre of power finds validation to the extent authoritarian leaders do not implement policies aimed at interfering and undermining the organisational structure and cohesion of the armed forces (see Albrecht and Ohl, 2016). As long as the armed forces' integrity is preserved the army remains acquiescent (Makara, 2013). Empirically and historically, this is exactly what happened in Egypt between 2004 and 2009 when the EAF's royalties were exposed to risks derived from the intra-NDP fragmentations.

The second source constituting a centre of power remains society itself, or particular groups within it. The societal-based centres of power also encompass the traditional Eastonian view of legitimacy dominant in political science, which conceptualises legitimacy as popular (public) support. However, Stinchcombe's definition extends the centres of power even to particular and narrowed groups and sections of the social structure, rather than limiting it to support from a majority of the public (Stinchcombe, 1968). There is here a form of continuity in sharing the idea of legitimation as influenced by specific domestic sets which in turn find a linkage with Easton's (1975) specific support. Taking a cue from Lipset and Rokkan (1967), potential centres of power can be conceptualised as arising from 'critical lines of cleavages': (i) workers versus owners or employers; (ii) church versus state; (iii) centre versus periphery; and (iv) urban versus rural. Any of these cleavages could indeed be the basis for group mobilisation that ultimately becomes a centre of power in the legitimation process (Lipset and Rokkan, 1967).

A second way to understand society-based centres of power is to consider the important ethnic, religious and linguistic groups into which society may be divided. In other words, the underlying social structure and the way it transforms may give rise to certain societal groups that can form a new centre of power. This will become particularly evident and questionable in the rise of an Egyptian 'pro-regime Salafism', as discussed later in the book.

An interdisciplinary framework for political legitimacy in post-shockwaves contexts

In introducing the modified Weberian framework of analysis combining Weber with David (1991) plus Gerschewski (2013) and Easton (1975), the underlining critical position is that following a moment of political breakdown – with the emergence of new political actors (such as the Salafis that, despite existing since 1922, did not represent, at least until 2012, a new face of politics) next to the existence of former political threats (such as the Muslim Brotherhood and FJP after their experience of governmental politics) – actors may opt to realign themselves with forces previously considered 'enemies' (i.e. Salafis) to counter the threat from those framed as the greater enemies (i.e. the Muslim Brotherhood Terrorist Designation Act of 2015).[10] This argument borrows from David's (1991) omnibalancing theory of intra-alignments, which in turn capitalised on international relations' redefinition of Walt's (1985) balance of power theory. It also links to Easton's theory of internal and specific support. Specific realignment between political authorities and state-identified actors (e.g. religious actors) does not necessarily have to be strictly political, but can, nevertheless, influence the process of political legitimation adding cohesion (Easton, 1975; see also von Soest, 2017). However, borrowing from Dogan's (2009: 195) critique of Weber and the argument that his trilogy of legitimacy is outdated if not obsolete, the book agrees that, specifically in non-democratic regime types, legitimacy is never unanimously achieved due to forms of resistance and rebel cultures, but it is worth considering the societal substratum in which legitimacy is forged, beyond Western-Colonialist definitions (Marks and Abdelhalim, 2018; Abu-Lughod, 1989).

Out of the debate on political legitimacy and its critical remarks introduced above, this book rejects the idea that legitimacy in authoritarian contexts should follow a culture of moral and civic obedience (Weber, 1978). Rather, it captures it as contestable regardless of structures, and this problematises the perspective of the political authority and their resistance in office. This work argues in favour of an integration of Max Weber's conception of political legitimacy with two theories extrapolated from international relations theories, these are: omnibalancing and the theory of specific/internal support in opposition to the idea of a diffused clientelist network of support that emerged in non-liberal system when they shifted to the neoliberal economic model (Weber, 1968; Easton, 1975; see also Gerschewski, 2013).[11] The theory of omnibalancing deals with the specific case of internal realignments, which in this book corresponds to the repositioning of specific domestic actors along the political and structural spectrum of the state structures (i.e. the Salafis and some sub-segments from the armed forces). It also opts for a taxonomy of threats and focuses not on the internationalisation but on their internalisation. However, the book builds an idea of threats as classified into main and secondary, depending on the level of perceived danger they pose. This brings into focus the actors' agency without neglecting the structural and institutional background on their respective desires.

Internal realignments and their dynamics are an alternative model for understanding the world beyond obsolete bipolar views. In explaining third world leaders' alignments, the benefits relate to the focus on threats to rulers' leaderships rather than to states as units. Thus, leaders in non-democratic systems may follow a certain logic of internal alignment with a secondary domestic enemy. This interaction helps rulers deal more successfully with internal threats to the durability of their tenure. This is a strong point of departure for three main reasons: (i) exploration of the rationality behind alignments with secondary threats; (ii) the understanding that leaders tend to adopt the divide-and-rule principle against forces or groups that threaten them; and (iii) rulers may act for their own security, but at the expense of the state unit (David, 1991: 235). Thus, the benefit for analysing the internal dimension of the legitimating narrative in Egypt after 2013 is that it can be revealed more about leaders' mechanisms and strategies for legitimacy. Omnibalancing establishes a different framework in which political actors do not simply align or re-align themselves against 'threats' to power; rulers appease secondary enemies (or adversaries) so that they can use their resources to counter primary enemies, represented as threats to the regime's stability (David, 1991: 235). Third World countries' understanding of external realignment is usually reductive; threats are externally as well as internally understood in ways reflective of the changeable domestic social and political contexts to which regimes are exposed and to which they are called to adapt. Thus, rulers of third world countries may split any alignment against them by focusing their energies on domestic opponents perceived as non-competitive, but still influential for the purpose of buying societal acceptance amongst opponents' followers, by aligning with them (David, 1991: 235). In addition, the construction of legitimation, understood as a process, may involve and be strictly dependent on two distinct levels: the internal, seeking consensus from internal actors to legitimise power; and the external, seeking consensus from international actors to legitimise power (Kneuer, 2013).

While in the case of military regimes (including electoral and multi-party systems) the seeking of internal legitimation is straightforwardly linked to the elites (or military elites) and the juntas (as discussed previously), in personalist regimes the legitimising process is less straightforward, as it is not dependent on elites or the winning coalition. Existing theories discussing military and personalist regimes have usually overlooked the variable of support as directly connected to the legitimation of non-democratic powers.

The hybridisation of the internal-specific support nexus

Specific support is used here in support of the theory of internal realignments (i.e. omnibalancing) which constitutes an addition with the goal of reinforcing the shift to the internal and micro-side of political legitimation in a system theorised as sub-transformed towards a form of 'non-exclusivist personalism' or which have broadly upgraded from the within their state structures and in which power underwent a polarisation and internal relations fragmentations. Adding Easton's (1975) distinction between specific and diffuse support the modified framework investigates how different aspects of political trust impact political legitimacy. In doing this, the interpretation distances itself from Easton's early definition as more attached to vote shifting between parties and vote shifting into non-substantial voting choices as connected to trust mechanisms. Rather, specific support theory is used as an addition to omnibalancing (David, 1991) and to Easton's classical argument. The theorised framework reconnects support to specific types of trust (or legitimacy) directed by selected (or specific) actors not to particular officeholders, but the ruler, based upon their performance. To some extent this finds a form of conceptual connection with de Mesquita's selectorate theory (de Mesquita et al., 2003). Specific support is argued as having stronger effect than levels of the more 'diffuse' types of trust. Gerschewski here complements Easton in that the theory of specific support is reinforced by internal support theory in autocracies and the role that social or political actors may have in determining the resilience of an autocracies, in opposition to the role of external-international supporters legitimating the durability of a regime (Gerschewski, 2013). This finds a more specific application based on the premises of sub-change at the regime level as theorised in Egypt after 2013 in which the focus shifted from the external side of the legitimation process to the internal one due to a reconfiguration of social and non-strictly political actors along the domestic spectrum (i.e. Salafis and the armed forces as non-belonging to a party cadre due to the collapse of a regime party).

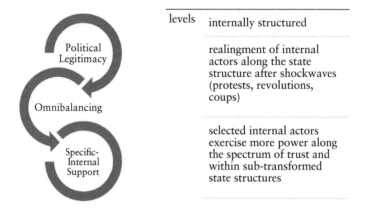

1.1 Sub-levels that participate in the modified conception of political legitimacy in autocracies after shockwaves which impacted with sub-transformations of the state structure

Easton's specific support corresponds to the 'quid pro quo' for the fulfilment of demands, including performance orientation. Diffused support corresponds to what the regime aims to represent and is based more on 'a reservoir of favourable attitudes or good will that helps members to accept or tolerate outputs to which they are opposed' (Easton, 1965: 273; see also Gerschewski, 2018). This second category of support, instead, is considered oriented towards the longer-term, as it can stem from 'political ideologies', but also nationalist claims invoking the unity of the country and the use of the 'we identity' by charismatic leaders. Thus, in line with the modified Weberian conception in combination with the trilogy made up of David, Gerschewski and Easton, the specific support theory, as opposed to diffused support, was theorised in Egypt under Hosni Mubarak and even Sadat as distributed amongst the regime party's cadre, and is centralised in the way it deals with the problematisation of interests over identity (Easton, 1965). Specific-internal support suggests a realignment of internal social and, eventually, military actors along the spectrum of evolving material interests, which could be of two types: accessing economic resources and recreate mechanisms of corruption; accessing political power to shape the political future of a given country.[12]

A four-phases transformative model

In connection with the theory of state's liquidity introduced above, theorised as an outcome of the process of legitimation in the 2013–2020 transition

Table 1.1 Phases for the legitimating process

Inputs	(i)	Reference to the rule of law and the polarisation of power
	(ii)	Reference to charisma and the critique of a welfarist (populist) post-modern nationalism[a]
	(iii)	Religion as a departure from Weberian tradition and captured as an element of political stability and shift in internal alliances and in which intra-alignments are subjected to logic of economic developmentalist opportunities.
Outputs/ Transmission	(iv)	Economic performance and regime functioning (internal-international level)/sustainable environmentalism through the SDG17.

[a]Modern nationalism in Egypt embeds both perennialist and industrial-functionalist elements.

timespan, the approach is deeply transformative and so is the four-phases model that will inform the rest of the volume. These four phases of analysis have been split into readjusted inputs and outputs and their combinations. Inputs correspond to: (i) the rule of law, (ii) charisma and the recalling of myths and memories in the creation of the political hero, (iii) reference to religion as a source of populist divine-given legitimation and driver for seducing society and clerics. Religion in this book is not understood in connection to transcendental legitimacy, at least in Weberian terms, but rather to the seduction of clerics for negotiating the moral conducts with institutional interests. The concept of seduction in this book thus gets closer to Auriol and Platteau's (2016) idea of clerical seduction, which this book, however, replaces with the idea of God seduction in the way in certain illiberal contexts, like al-Sisi in Egypt – but also Erdogan in Turkey or beyond the region – taking a more comparative lens, attempting to bypass the religious establishment or to manipulate it. There is ample evidence to the effect that, in its relationship to the sovereign, the religious officialdom (the coopted clerics) tends to sacrifice values to the altar of personal interests. As per outputs, the fifth phase in the book includes a close analysis of economic-business performance and transformations, where performance is captured as the transmission (see Gerschewski, 2018).

One of the core assumptions in this book is the fact that regimes usually secure access to power through force and domination (Dogan, 1992), but the transformed materiality of societal fabrics remains neglected and treated as immutable. The concept of right is normally understood as correlated with an obligation to obey on the part of those subjected to the authority (Raz, 1985). However, this book contests the Weberian conception of transmission and the fact that rights are correlated with an obligation to obey, 'Gehorsamspflicht' (Weber, 1978: 129). The understanding of political power here goes both beyond the idea of hegemony and domination, and the fact that in non-democratic systems power can be exclusively used as a form of dispositive for exercising punishment (Foucault, 1988). The modified Weberian conception of political legitimacy adopted in the book bypasses these conceptual stereotypes and instead focuses on power and legitimacy more as a product of negotiation from a top-down perspective. Recalling Beetham, the existence of a belief system as a core aspect that in autocracies may impact the process of authoritarian legitimation and resistance to exported democratisation is centralised (Beetham, 1991). To some extent, this view in the book connects with von Haldenwang's definition of legitimacy as also influenced by a sense of identifications rooted in cultural, more than ethnic, or religious premises at least in non-strictly ethnic setting (von Haldenwang, 2011).

On method and data

The modified framework here presented bypasses limitations confined to the sphere of abstractness and rather makes the process of legitimation an observable activity that also depends on outputs, and not just on a certain set of inputs on the functioning of an institution and the public assessment of the relevance and quality of the institution's performance (von Haldenwang, 2016; Listhaug, 1998; Weatherford, 1992). Therefore the work is based on a multi-method-based methodology, with extensive qualitative analysis combined with combined quantitative data and supported by integrative fieldwork conducted with different profiles based in the UK, Middle East, US and the wider European Continent. It should be highlighted that, although an alternative approach to the study could have been based on ethnography, the deterioration of the security situation in Egypt and the impossibility of conducting ethnographic research has made a top-down approach to this work and its scope more suitable. The top-down approach introduced earlier in this book focuses on how power is reproduced, and thus how the political regime and the ruler adapted to a society organically transformed by the 2011 and 2013 political episodes, in which the process of political legitimation still continues to undergo certain struggles determined by the permanent collapse of pre-existing state structures: the regime party and the absolutism of power in the hands of the authority left space to forms of polarisation in how the architecture of power was formed. The qualitative analysis of sources builds on thematic and framing analysis applied to selected political texts and speeches that were given by al-Sisi between 2013 and 2019 (Benford and Snow, 2000; Entman, 1993; Minsky, 1977; Snow and Benford, 1988 and Snow et al., 2014). Framing has been defined as both an objective part of practices aimed at generating meanings, and a systematic methodology that allows the operationalisation of mixed methods research (Pan and Kosicki, 1993). It has been described as a more focused and narrowed approach than broader discourse analysis, of which it is considered an extension (Della Porta, 2016). The focus on the language and how language constructs frames is intended to provide an understanding of how the former affects policies and impacts social political transformations and transitional political processes.

Meanwhile, thematic content analysis allows the deciphering of what is being communicated, and why it is being communicated (Babbie, 2004). In terms of functionality, the usefulness of content analysis relates to the relevance and importance of the message. It builds on different elements and levels that interact to deliver the content of the message (cohesion), namely coherence, intentionality, acceptability, informativity and situationality. Framing analysis is employed in this work in combination with thematic analysis. To return to framing analysis, framing denotes the way in which issues are presented. To make use of Entman's words 'frames select and call attention to particular aspects of the reality described' (Entman, 1993: 54).

In other words, the scope of the methodology of this book lies in capturing and contextualising from a political and state-structural perspective the frames of the rule of law, charisma, religious-internal alliances and economic governance-performance, identified as the four phases of legitimation in the 2013–2020 timespan from the perspective of the political authorities and the top-down contested legitimation struggle that this book debates. The benefit of framing is a more focused and narrowed approach to discourse analysis. Thus, the use of framing captures the fluidity of political processes and how they evolved with the goal of forging a legitimation claim and in making the state more 'liquid', rather than weak, as overstated by Ayubi (1995) and accepted as such. Instead, the combination with thematic content analysis allowed to decipher what was being communicated, and why it was being communicated (Babbie, 2004).

The book is based on examining keywords and metaphors in speeches given by al-Sisi and official texts (e.g. ratified decrees and laws), identifying what was included in the selected frames as well as what they left out. This work's approach does not concentrate only on words and their repetition in written texts, since it is acknowledged that words repeated most often in the text may not be the most important from a political and strategic perspective. Instead, insisting on the value of frames and the political meaning

Table 1.2 Frames and interpretative levels

Categorisation	Definition
Diagnostic	Identification of a problem and its causes
Prognostic	Providing solutions to the problems (i.e. strategies to undertake)
Motivational	Action needed to change a specific status quo or situation

they embed, this study wanted to take first a more general approach to frames, considering the three levels on which frames develop: cognition, discourse and discourse product (Entman, 1993; Scheufele, 1999; Tuchman, 1978; see Entman, Matthews and Pellicano, 2009). Secondly, the specific focus on the level of the discourse unpacked the political meaning from the perspective of the ruler, alias al-Sisi, and his intentions. Differently from Western democracies where political legitimacy is the result of free and fair elections, in authoritarian contexts, regimes activate framing elements which package socio-political events and issues in a manner that is consistent with the regime's overarching legitimation (Dukalskis and Gerschewki, 2017; see also Matthes, 2012).

Three different categories of frames deconstruct the top-down struggle for legitimation against structural transformations: diagnostic, prognostic and motivational. 'Diagnostic framing' mainly refers to the identification of a problem and its causes, and the attribution of blame in a specific direction; 'prognostic framing' consists of providing solutions to the problems identified and the strategies needed to achieve them; and 'motivational framing' refers to the action needed to change the situation. Diagnostic and prognostic frames help to create a direct connection between a leader's reproduction of power and the consequent actions derived from the implementation of power.

Diagnostic and prognostic frames as a distinct category must meet three criteria: (i) frame consistency, meaning there are no contradictions between frame and the frame-maker's behaviour; (ii) empirical credibility, meaning there is congruence between the proposed frame and world realities; and (iii) credibility of frame articulator, based on the status and knowledge of the frame-maker. As per motivational frame, instead, they represent a solution to the problem.

Focusing on distinguishing the different categories of frames in the book also considers the parameter of resonance as determined by three main determinants: (i) *consistency* – completeness of the beliefs, claims and actions promoted in the frames; (ii) *cultural compatibility* – compatibility of the frames with the society's cultural identification, heritage, and symbols; and (iii) *relevance* – frames that fit between cultural myths, the narrative and

Table 1.3 Categorisation of meta-frames and definitions

Meta-frame	Definitions
Tactical	Organisation of structures which hide the strategic intention of the actor
Strategic	Effort towards constructing a formula in which actors are central
Game	In which main politically related issues are referred in strategic ways that fulfil the political purpose

events in the world. However, regarding this study's focus on power and legitimacy crisis in post-2013 Egypt, Benford and Snow's theory of cultural compatibility draws closer to both Weber's (1968) claim of legitimation as stemming from tradition (habits, heritage or religion), and von Haldenwang's (2012) theory of 'performed legitimacy', also defined as a practice of identification. Thus, the scope has been the one of understanding how these three master frames and their resonance fit in the post-2013 political authorities' narrative and strategies of internal legitimation and their interconnection with the infrastructural reorganisation of the regime, towards an alternative model type.

The above tripartition of framing is followed by a focus on the construction and function of more complex frames categories such as meta-frames, which include 'tactical', 'strategic' and 'game' frame (Aalberg et al., 2012: 168; Aalberg and Brekker, 2007; Lawrence, 2000; Scheufele, 1999: 402; Strömbäck and Dimitrova, 2006). Meta-frames are made up of tactics for winning and/or staying in power, strategies addressed to emphasise actors' personality, but also games in which politically related issues are referred in strategic ways that fulfil the political purpose.

The above combination of more categories of frames, however, is not driven by an exclusionary approach. At different stages of the process of legitimation, different frames play different functions or overlap, depending on the conditions that determine their use (Strömbäck and Luengo, 2008).

From the general perspective of framing, if a political leader breaches their own frame, this jeopardises their status as a credible and consistent framer and, in the literature, this is highlighted as an important political attribute. The consequence is that the ruler risks being positioned outside the normative context in which their frames were originally deployed. Consequently, over time political leaders can become increasingly constrained by the frames to which they have expressed political and personal commitment. But the process of framing politics additionally implies distinction between image schemata and frames (Wood, 2018: 245–249). While the former is viewed as a form of personal culture, the latter is conceived as a form of public culture that activates the former. Frames also require distinction when linked to frame modelling, theoretically defined as a set of declarative instructions used to create a certain frame. As a result, framing does not impose meanings, but rather attempts to evoke them through reassembling the materiality of political, social and historical situations that activate networks of schemata (or filters), which in turn are expected to evoke associated desires and responses.

The book works on the analysis of frames to specifically focus on the meaning and function attached to three selected determinants from the perspective of al-Sisi: the armed forces, Islam (religion) and economic performance as connected to domestic, regional resistance and diplomatic existence along the international system. The analysis looks at how these three axes eventually connected to or interfered with the construction of a form of internal political legitimacy in a social context of political dissent, such as for the purpose of this book in Egypt after the 2013 military coup.

So far, works that have employed frame analysis as a methodology have drawn from various theoretical and methodological approaches, leading to working definitions that are often tentative and specific to the purposes of the respective study (Benford and Snow, 2000; Strömbäck and Shehata, 2007). This has resulted in relatively little consensus regarding how frames can be operationalised and detected. The approach taken in this book is inductive and top-down as aimed at providing an understanding of the verticalisation of the state's input and output sides of the narrative behind the legitimating process, in a society that has culturally, politically and socially changed after the FJP's experience in power. The first task in the empirical investigation of frames is the detection of keywords. The automatic generation of these keywords has even been suggested, simply by mapping the most frequently repeated words or strings within the data (Koella, 2003: 7; Miller, 1997: 70).

However, the operationalisation has taken a different approach from the standard ones: rather than looking for the recurrence of keywords in qualitative sources used, it has elaborated and interpreted the meaning attached to them, while also considering possible associations in the system of cultural and political values that started gradually in the transition period in post-2013 Egypt. The approach gets closer to Hertog and Mcleod's view that certain themes and words are still considered central to the meaning of the text even though they may not occur the most frequently (Hertog and Mcleod, 2001: 152). Coding took place through existing nodes. Although nodes did not readily reveal frames, they directed the analyst to important concepts in a text which may help 'diagnose' or 'nominate' central ideas around which frames are constructed (such as the frames of the armed forces, the rule of law, the leader and the attached moral duty, religion in politics and economic sacrifices). By identifying themes with unusually higher frequency in comparison with other norms, the themes' function has made it possible to elicit words that may work as indicators of emphasis and that concentrate meanings drawn from cultural values or political discourses. Examining how themes are used through concordances and whole texts, and what framing and reasoning devices they may have in common, should therefore be revealing. Nodes have been identified based on the pre-existing knowledge generated by the literature and the empirical studies in the field.

While the software (Nvivo12) reduces subjective bias, it is also true that relying on automatic coding alone would have occurred at the expense of an empirical understanding of the post-2013 dynamics of power in Egypt, which requires a high degree of broad contextual interpretation for political and social events and a historical background from the 1990s until 2011. The analysis of the content has be based on selected key speeches and interviews of al-Sisi given between 2013 and 2019, which demonstrate the critical discursive transformations in order to generate an in-depth understanding of eventual gaps and discontinuities between discourses and policies. A critical analysis of possible discursive shifts will thus be analysed in connection to policy transformations and the transformative approach broadly taken with the book.

The application of thematic-content analysis, in combination with framing analysis, to the study of political legitimacy in post-2013 Egypt has built an original and interdisciplinary framework that sits at the intersection of political sociology with international relations theory for analysing from a domestic perspective the transformative activity of political legitimacy in systems that are captured as fluid, like Egypt under al-Sisi (Landau et al., 2009).

The book builds on an extensive and sophisticated collection of different categories of sources. The top-down approach has been combined with the integration of selected interviews with different profiles based in the UK, US, Lebanon and Europe. Qualitative sources have been analysed, taking both a qualitative and quantitative approach built in Nvivo with the goal of making the work impartial and reducing subjective interpretations and bias. The analysis of primary sources produced by the state proves itself significant, as such a combined content and framing analysis of Egyptian documents in combination of economic and political quantitative analysis of data produced by second and third parties like the World Bank, the IMF, the Corruption Perception Index (CPI), the International Labour Organization (ILO), the World Food Programme, the UNESCO Institute for Statistics, the World Health Organisation, the BTI, the ATP and Freedom House has been non-existent from updated studies and approaches interrogating the 'health' of governments in the broader Mediterranean area.

Primary sources consist of official governmental reports issued by the Egyptian state, ministries and the parliamentary cabinet. These include a selection of al-Sisi's public speeches and interviews delivered between 2013 and 2020; reports by the Cabinet (2006, 2008, 2014, 2015–2017); reports from Parliament (2005–2009, 2013–2019); the Ministry of Finance (2014–2020); the Ministry of Defence (2015–2019), content from the government's web portal, and presidential decrees and laws. Al-Sisi gave more than 16 public speeches between 2013 and 2020, some of them closer to short public statements than actual official speeches. However, three criteria determined the selection of primary material: (i) official public speeches which specifically attempted to verticalise the idea of consensus towards political authorities, and through discourse-infused optimism generate a political project previously overlooked by the army, which would have 'democratised' the socio-political domestic arena (top-down approach); (ii) official public speeches with suggested the authorities' will to broadly reconsider and rewrite the social contract between the ruler and the people, thus breaking with the draconian historical past (i.e. a programme that would deliver on the people's demand for the rule of law and reconsidered the role of the armed forces in the institutional structures); and (iii) speeches which emphasised the authorities' political will and agenda to recover the economic situation, thus considering social justice and social rights and implementing an economic programme that would have centralised these premises.

These three criteria more broadly reflect the four specific axes of analysis, or transformative phases, on which the entire book builds: the rule of law, charisma, religion and alliances, and economic performance. While this study acknowledges the existence of other public speeches equally relevant from a political and social perspective in the timespan considered in the book, these criteria more appropriately problematise al-Sisi's internal legitimacy and thus interrogate the transformative process and dynamics of leadership and authority-making and legitimation against a background of social, political and structural change in which the state's intra-relations were marked by fluidity. Unrestricted material on the EAF's website has also been examined. Other data analysed in the empirical chapters includes state-led Egyptian newspaper *Al-Ahram*, the BTI (2006–2019), policy briefs and reports. The documents have been divided into two categories: economic sources and political sources. Political material included the above-mentioned ministerial reports, the 2014 Constitution and its 2017 amendments with relation to the SCAF and the al-Azhar. The analysis in the book gives special attention to speeches delivered at the WEFs in 2006 under Mubarak, and again in 2014 under the new executive in Sharm El-Sheikh. Another crucial speech source of examination in the analysis is the one delivered by al-Sisi at the al-Azhar in 2014 and 2016, which called for a reformist agenda on Islam, identifying this as the basis for change in Egyptian society in order to purify it from radicalism. The analysis highlighted the political charge of the speech which reflects the socially different country Egypt became after July 2013.

A quantitative analysis has been employed in combination with the qualitative approach applied to the political sources mentioned above. Quantitative data was drawn from independent third party and ministerial sources, including the Ministry of Finance, the Central Bank of Egypt (CBE), the Ministry of Planning, the State Information Service and the Ministry of Military Production. The analysis of data included measurements of the variables of political and economic trust and social justice in Egypt from (i) the World Bank; (ii) the Global Economic Index; (iii) the World Food Programme; (iv) the World Health Organisation; (v) UNESCO Institute for Statistics; (vi) Freedom House; (vii) AB, WAVE III, WAVE IV and WAVE V (2011–2019); (viii) Polity IV and Polity V; (ix) CPI; (x) BTI and the Varieties of Democracy Project (V-Dem).

The approach of Freedom House presents similarities to that of the BTI. It assesses a range of conditions in any given region: whether the area is governed separately from the rest of the relevant country or countries, either de jure or de facto; whether conditions on the ground for political rights and civil liberties are significantly different from those in the rest of the relevant country or countries, whether the territory is the subject of enduring popular or diplomatic pressure for autonomy, independence or incorporation into another country; and whether the territory's boundaries are sufficiently stable to allow an assessment of conditions for the year under review, and can be expected to remain stable in future years. The goal is to focus not so much on possible separatism, but on the level of political rights and civil liberties. Specifically, the BTI and Freedom House data have not been generated over years from surveys involving members of Egyptian civil society, but are the result of knowledge in Egyptian politics, society and the legal system, of experts whose nationality is undisclosed in both cases of the BTI and Freedom House and for this reason results can be considered inductive. The analysis additionally draws upon the rich data provided by the EC-funded ATP (2011–2017), in relation to different determinants that can inform the study of internal legitimation in the post-2013 setting and the sub-variation in the regime, as a form of resistance to democracy, which impacted with making the state and its relations more liquid.[13]

Amongst the advantages of employing these combined data sources, and taking them at face value, lies the principle of political neutrality, which is one of the main prerogatives and principles of this book. These data have not been influenced by personal views or the active political engagements of experts (i.e. affiliation to Egyptian pro-regime or anti-systemic movements), which could impact the impartiality of data. The analysis additionally draws

Table 1.4 Vertical approach to the leadership's process of legitimation

Method(s)	Data
Content and framing analysis	Government documents, reports, al-Sisi's official public speeches, 2013–2019
Qualitative case studies	Mix of data sources: secondary data analysis, experts (academics, intellectuals, religious-political leaders), textual analysis
Other large-N data analysis	Data on performance, corruption, government spending on welfare, electoral process, debt, macroeconomic indicators

upon the rich data provided by the EU-funded ATP (2011–2017), in relation to different determinants that can inform the empirical analysis and the study of internal legitimation in the post-2013 setting.[14] Interviews also play a core function in the book. These were conducted with different professional profiles including Muslim Brotherhood members who had direct contact in Egypt with jailed or exiled members of the organisation after 2013. In addition, the book extends on interviews with EU-based scholars and experts of Salafism, London-based experts of Egyptian politics and economy, US-based former World Bank and Moody's experts of the Egyptian economy plus a renowned, MENA-based senior expert of militarism in Egypt and the broader MENA region. In order to maintain a balanced view of the data, and due to the impossibility of conducting research fieldwork in Egypt given the sensitive topic centred on al-Sisi and the sub-transformation in the regime and human rights violation in the country, semi-structured interviews were conducted with professionals in various political, economic, academic and institutional fields, who were not necessarily close to political authorities in Egypt.

The book includes selected interviews with heterogenous profiles, amongst whom (i) expert from the Chatham House policy institute; (ii) Europe-based experts on Egyptian Salafism and on the al-Azhar's affairs; (iii) UK-based member of the Muslim Brotherhood organisation; (iv) US-based World Bank and Moody's representative with expertise in Egypt's economy; and (v) MENA-based scholar and expert on Egypt's militarism and economy.[15] The interviewees were selected based on their professional profile, international reputation (all selected profiles which remain anonymous are authorities and have held policy positions as consultants for organisations, including the International Red Cross, the World Bank, Moody's, Chatham House, and the Carnegie Endowment for International Peace). Each category to which the selected interviewee belongs concerns the areas of the ruler's struggle to gain internal legitimacy: the legal foundations of the state and the significance of amendments to the penal code; army-ruler relations after 2013; the role of religion in post-2013 politics; the politicisation of Hizb al-Nour (the Party of Light); and economic and financial continuities and discontinuities by the post-2013 authorities, and their impacts on the World Bank's and rating agencies' classification of Egypt and the political-economic shifts they produced in Egypt.

The Muslim Brotherhood member was chosen based on his representativeness of the organisation in Egypt and internationally. The interviewee had contact not only with Mohammed Morsi, but also with non-Muslim Brotherhood Egyptian politicians such as Amr Moussa, and with exiled Muslim Brotherhood members who since 2013 have flown to Turkey. The individual provided information that cannot be found in written sources or gained from sources outside the Muslim Brotherhood, which remains a closed hierarchical network. Given this figure's international importance, the book gives him significant weight regarding issues such as the relationship between the military and al-Sisi, as he disclosed the persistence of a strict Muslim Brotherhood presence within the armed forces in a kind of wait-and-watch position, aspects that are considered in the empirical analysis in Chapter 6. The interviews with Europe-based scholar expert in Salafism and the al-Azhar's affairs, MENA-based expert in Egyptian militarism and US-based expert provided access to more specific information. Interviews focused on economic and financial aspects and in addition deepened the triangulation and fragmentation between al-Sisi, Salafis and the al-Azhar, empirically discussed in Chapter 6. Fieldwork gave this set of interviews an important weight. The interview with the Europe-based expert of Salafism elicited a novel explanation for the impacts determined in Egypt, after the vacuum left by the NDP, by the transformation of certain Salafi trends initiated in Gulf countries, amongst which the rise of 'pro-regime Salafism'. This information is not available in existing written works and as such the interview provided a more comprehensive and accurate explanation for the short-term alliance between al-Sisi and Hizb al-Nour in a contest in which political parties formed on religious premises were constitutionally banned, with the exception of the Salafi Hizb al-Nour.

In addition, this book gives significant importance to the interviews with the Middle East-based and US-based experts. These interviews have produced a more critical and independent analytical view, if compared to self-interested and strictly neoliberal-based views provided by the IMF and World Bank, on two crucial aspects: (i) on the societal and structural re-adaptation of

50   *Egypt and the rise of fluid authoritarianism*

the Egyptian military culture after 2013; and (ii) on the regime's economic performance and the consequent financial risks determined by the new economic model that started to emerge after the 2013 coup.

Notes

1 This conceptualisation is close Weber's but also recognises some limits to Weber's trilogy. According to Diamond and Plattern, political legitimacy is the moral title to rule (Diamond and Plattern, 2006). However, it should be mentioned that Diamond's concepts of morality and legitimation refer to democracies and the functioning of electoral systems (Diamond and Plattern, 2006). Many other theories of legitimacy exist (Beetham, 1991: 42; Booth and Seligson, 2009: 1; Easton, 1975: 278; Gilley, 2012, 2006; Hurd, 1999; Levi and Sacks, 2009; Linz, 1988).
2 The book mainly refers to the triangulation of the relations between the EAF, the Salafis and their political ambitions and the al-Azhar as more internally dominated by a Wahhabi trend, which eventually was externally projected in the sub-relations that still persist between the banned Muslim Brotherhood and the armed forces to whom the political authority remains detached and subjected at the same time.
3 David's Omnibalancing theory capitalises on a revisionist approach to Kennetth Waltz's structural realism exposed in the balance of power theory (1979).
4 Under this frame, Weber defined legitimacy as: an induction from experience that no system of authority voluntarily limits itself to the appeal to material or affectual or ideal motives as the basis for guaranteeing its continuance. In addition, every system of authority attempts to establish and to cultivate the belief in its legitimacy (Weber, 1947: 325).
5 According to Spencer (1973), Weber uses the concept of charisma in at least three senses: (i) the supernatural 'gift' of the leader, (ii) charisma as a sacred or revered essence deposited in objects or persons, [and] (iii) charisma as the attractiveness of a personality (Spencer, 1973; see also Weber, 1947: 352). There is wide agreement in the scholarship on Nasser's case of what Weber defined as 'charismatic legitimacy' as deriving from the attractiveness of his personality, despite being an autocrat. Expanding the classical Weberian interpretation, there is not necessarily any contradiction between despotic rule and legitimacy, as long as the latter is classified as either traditional or charismatic (Dusza, 1989).
6 The book corrects Würtenberg (1982) quoted in Gerschewski (2018), according to whom the etymology of legitimacy would be based on *legi-intimus*, translated with 'according to the law' while in the Latin etymology it would be *lex-timus*, where the suffix originates from the Proto-Italic.
7 From a historical perspective, the transformative and reactive approach of Sadat's open-door policies (*infitah*), and then Mubarak's post-1990s crony capitalism, demonstrate an ephemeral role of the popular masses and their consensus in the dynamics of rulers' legitimation, also due to failed economic projects (on an

Political legitimacy in fluid authoritarianism 51

economic explanation of the fall of Mubarak see Nagarajan, 2013 and Sabry and Levy, 2015). As a result, the centralised bureaucratic procedures and rules shifting legitimacy to a more legal-rational oriented model, were also strongly anchored to diplomatic and financial external support.
8 See on this Zhu's utilitaristic explanation of performance in the process of legitimation in China (2011: 124).
9 A further argument put forward, which in turn counters Mcloughlin's view on the connection between service delivery and state legitimacy, is that of Brinkerhoff et al. (2012), in whose view satisfaction with services does not necessarily equal increasing trust in the state.
10 In 2019 the US Congress introduced the Muslim Brotherhood Terrorist Designation Act despite the definition technically lacking the legal definition found in the US State Department's Bureau of Counter-Terrorism for defining the Muslim Brotherhood as a de facto terrorist organisation. Rather, the US decision ended up escalating a domestically politicised process in Egypt. See on this Dunne and Miller (2019).
11 At the theoretical level, omnibalancing draws upon the assumptions of the balance of power theory at the core of the mechanisms of alignments in world politics, while correcting some elements associated with it (Walt, 1985).
12 In the context of Egypt, this would relate to a selected Salafi party like Hizb al-Nour and the armed forces in opposition to the diffused circle of businessmen associated with the NDP's patronage.
13 The variables that were analysed include: (i) the state's spending in the military sector; (ii) spending in welfare programmes from 2011 to 2017; (ii) the government's performance from 2005 to 2017; (iii) attitudes towards politics and parties; (iv) the understanding of religion and politics; (v) perceptions of democracy; and (vi) electoral processes between 2014 and 2018.
14 Analysis for quantitative data has been software-assisted and expanded on variables like: (i) the state's spending in the military sector; (ii) spending in welfare programmes from 2011 to 2017; (ii) the government's performance from 2005 to 2019; (iii) attitudes towards politics and parties; (iv) the understanding of religion and politics; (v) perceptions of democracy; and (vi) electoral processes between 2014 and 2018.
15 See Appendix for alias assigned to profiles.

2

Not an Arab phoenix

The politics of non-partying

Since the 1970s up to the present day, and particularly following the frequently recalled *Third Wave: Democratisation in the Late Twentieth Century* (Huntington, 1991), what is normally referred to as transitology has kept questioning the notion of the exceptionalism of the Arab world regarding the conditions for moving towards more inclusive and democratic political systems in a climate of major political transformations that was spreading from Latin America to the Soviet Union (Dahl, 1971; Diamond, 2002; Gandhi and Przeworski, 2006; Levitsky and Way, 2002; Saikal, 2011). In its most basic and simple definition, a transition is defined as the ad interim period that separates two political executives. Using modern historical lenses of analysis, during the third wave a few countries successfully transitioned towards pseudo, though still defective, democracies, amongst which Ukraine and Nigeria (Carothers, 2002). Transition normally is a three-step process which involves a set of non-exclusionist phases, where the first step for transitioning towards democracies would imply a process of political openness. The second is followed by a breakthrough where the regime is believed to collapse leaving the transition open in favour of a gradual emergence towards a democratic political order. The third and last step implies the consolidation of the new-born democracy supported by a wave of economic liberalisation. This latter step, however, presents some major discrepancies as it generalises the consolidation paths of democracies, making them standard, while in fact paths are not. The non-linearity of the process, as argued in this book, is not subjected to the taxonomy of the non-democratic regime. In this general understanding, the book distances itself from the linearity of democratisation processes and rather gets closer to the distinction between controlled and actual democracies, which in turn is a reinterpretative definition of 'electoral authoritarianism', alias a façade form of democratisation in which the deep authoritarian nature of the government is hidden by recurrent elections (Schedler, 2002, 2006). Indeed, elections have long given authoritarian leaders a veneer of legitimacy, both at home and internationally. There is a shared agreement that elections in the context of purist military regimes serve a set of functions, including testing the party cadres and coopting opposition or other societal movements (Gandhi and Lust-Okar, 2009; see also Gandhi and Przeworski, 2006). In addition, by holding elections and setting rules regarding the eligibility of candidates and parties, dictators operate on *divide et impera* logic (Lust-Okar, 2005). As a third aspect, in multi-party systems, elections serve the information function (Magaloni, 2006; Brownlee, 2007). Thus, elections in autocracies next to elites and opposition control remain confined to the tactical realm and offer rulers the chance of exercising a direct control over risks of removal for office (Gandhi and Lust-Okar, 2009; on opposition and challenges see also Albrecht, 2007). Therefore, external support to multi-party elections as supported by Western state actors clashes with the understanding in comparative authoritarianism if we assume that there is a shared agreement on the fact that elections are not synonymous of regimes' instability, even when they are at their lowest.[1] This opens the debate concerning the connection between morality and democratisation. Democracy cannot be achieved through externally imported democratisation political and economic actions unless grounded on the moral commitment of citizens but, more importantly, on the citizens' capacity to structurally sustain forms of self-governance.

Although some Arab states strategically welcomed the endogenously driven wave of democratisation as primarily supported by the European Commission (EC) through the Euro-Mediterranean Partnership (EMP) and European Neighbourhood Programme Instrument (ENPI), they ultimately negotiated with it in the main and solo political interests of regime survival, in absence of de facto reformist approaches to politics from both parties (i.e. the EC and regimes).[2]

This political behaviour from Arab societies, and mainly youth, resulted in a form of pejorative framing of international actors due to the un-reformist and false moralist-liberal approach taken by the international community before societal requests (social dignity, right to access basic foodstuff, and support for political change).[3] The EU's relations with Egypt have remained governed by a series of bilateral and multilateral agreements, as well as by a set of policy frameworks, which aim to position relations in a strategic, transformed context. At the bilateral level, within the framework of the EMP, the Association Agreement entered into force in June 2004, forming the legal basis for EU-Egypt relations, which was and remains mainly economic in nature. In addition, as stated in the ENPI on the eve of the 2011 protests, amongst the goals of the instrument was the commitment by the European Commission to: (i) strengthening of participation in political life, including the promotion of public awareness and participation in elections; (ii) exchange of experience in the field of elections and jointly developing cooperation in areas of shared interest, including through providing assistance on registering electors and capacity building; and (iii) fostering the role of civil society and enhancing its capacity to contribute more effectively to the democratic and political process as well as to the economic and social progress in accordance with national legislation.

During recent decades, through the EMP, the EU has presented itself as a normative actor in its southern neighbourhood area, encouraging political change and supporting democratic principles and primarily the rule of law, human rights promotion and liberties, though the latter remained broadly undefined and the former unachieved. While the EU portrays itself as a promoter of reforms in the Mediterranean area, it is the European model of democracy as conceived that has entered a form of moral crisis, at least internally and amongst members. The Freedom House in 2021 and 2022 acknowledged a further decline in effective democracies around the world, in favour of a persistent and continuous rise in autocracies or what are labelled 'defective-democracies', which are spreading faster in Europe and Eurasia. Hungary and Poland between 2017 and 2021 experienced a steep decline in liberal democracy with suppression of the fundamental right to protest and, in the case of Hungary, the replication of a populist patriarchal state at the heart of Europe.

In the case of Mediterranean countries and Egypt, the celebration of opening to political parties by the EU and international actors should be read through this reactively oriented lens of economic opportunity and standardised approach to development and democratisation as stated earlier. If 'Egypt remains a maturing rather than a mature democracy' (Korany, 1998: 65; see also Feuille, 2011), thrown half way between its exceptionalism and transition in the Arab world (Perthes, 2008; Carothers, 2002: 6; see also Linz and Stephan, 2013; Pridham, 1995), after 2011 the debate on the transformation of states and the moderation of 'extremist' parties increased (Ahmed and Capoccia, 2014; Sokhey and Yildirim, 2012). In the case of Egypt, former jihadi parties such as al-Gama'a al-Islamiyya – a terrorist movement which grew in influence in the 1970s and was active from the 1980s up to 2003, and was blamed for the assassination of President Anwar Sadat in 1981 – participated in the 2012 democratic elections as a deradicalised and juridically recognised political party (Drevon, 2014, 2015a, 2015b). If on the one hand this fuelled further expectations on the process of transition and inclusivist approach to former Islamist and jihadist movements, on the other, it jeopardised the meaning of the concept of democratisation and the moral and ethical values it entailed, mostly found to be Western in their essence.

Existing works have tried to provide an understanding for political legitimacy the in pre-2013 setting. Mubarak's Egypt and the role of the elite in politics have extensively relied on the theoretical insights that started proliferating from the late 1990s onwards (Albrecht, 2005; Bellin, 2004; Weinbaum, 1985; Blaydes, 2008, 2010; Buehler and Ibraheem, 2018; Diamond, 2002; Fukuyama, 2013; Galal, 2011; Geddes, 1999b, 2014; Haber, 2006; Hinnebusch, 2006; Kelly, 2016; Levitsky and Way, 2002; Lust-Okar, 2005; Magaloni, 2008; Rutherford, 2013; Schlumberger, 2010, 2012; and Tullock, 1987). In comparison to previous years, the notion of political legitimacy has recently been called into question following the 2011 Arab uprisings. Given the implications of the 2011 uprising, there has been an initial return in addressing democratisation and party politics in a more consistent manner. Between 2011 and 2012, almost 50 new parties were institutionalised in Egypt (Al-Sayyed, 2011; Ahmed and Capoccia, 2014; Dodge, 2012; Tavana, 2013; Viney, 2011; Volpi, 2012), some of which already existed as social movements (Zollner, 2019a). In 2014 over 80 parties were created across the political spectrum, at least 50 of which were non-Islamist, but rather secular and founded on liberal democratic principles. The broader scholarship debate started looking at this formation of parties in 2012 as an important determinant in the construction of a more pluralist and inclusivist political system (Tavana, 2013; Zollner, 2019b).

However, the 2013 coup, and the gradual disappearance of the former parties under the wave of political repression, represented a critical juncture from which began a process of what is here theorised as an internal regime upgrade, involving the juridical foundation of the state and the premises of foundational legitimacy. After 2014, the regime worked to impose a new domestic political reality, dealing with political parties through interlocking methods such as banning, infiltration and subjugation. In addition, the regime – having dissolved those parties formed in 2011/2012 either directly or indirectly by freezing access to financial support like in the case of the Muslim Brotherhood and the Egypt Youth Party – supported the formation of a number of new parties through its sovereign organs. This was the specific case with the Future Homeland Party, established by the military intelligence agency, and For the Love of Egypt, formed by the general intelligence service, and the formation of the Nation's Future Block (NFB) or Mustaqbal al-Watan, which, more than a de facto political party, has ultimately represented a coalition supporting al-Sisi in the Parliamentary Assembly. All these pro-regime (in fact, part of the regime) political entities participated in the 2015 parliamentary elections under the transition-democratisation paradigm (Fouad, 2018).

The main argument that when an autocratic regime loses power and is replaced by a democratically elected leader, the latter may then at some point be replaced by a candidate from the former regime, was already outlined by Geddes et al. back in 2014, although no consolidated knowledge on why such a second shift occurred has yet been established, and this remains one of the limitations the scholarship still faces. With regard to post-2013 Egypt, the most interesting determinant in the shift from the democratically elected FJP back to a military-controlled regime lies in the traits of the transition itself. The absence of a regime party, replaced by the depoliticised and bureaucratised NFB in the Parliamentary Assembly, and the politicisation of former social-cultural actors such as Salafis, deserve mention when considering the key shifts from Mubarak to Morsi to the post-2013 coup setting and along the disconnection of this work's theoretical core foundations from existing works in the field arguing for a continuation of a Mubarakian-style emulated autocracy by Abdel Fattah al-Sisi.

Despite the post-2013 political authorities' references to an economic agenda on development that prioritises performance and good governance, political episodes and erosion of trust in governmental institutions (World Bank, 2017) suggest that the decision to rely on performance and prioritise social policies, could rather be embedded in a more complex state project fulfilled by the incumbent regime. This may aim to provide, at least externally and thus internationally, the idea of stability, although the opposite is revealed. It is unclear whether al-Sisi's decision to place emphasis onto social policies and performance may be embedded into a more ethical approach to legitimation, or is strategically connected to a project of self-perpetuation, which I further problematise in this book and in connection to government's economic reforms. The data for Egypt indicate that in early 2014, the people's level of satisfaction with economic development was 58.9 per cent while concern towards authoritarianism stood at only 2 per cent (ATP, 2014).

The effects of the 2013 coup: towards a liquid state

From the end of the 1980s until the early 2000s, Middle East regimes incorporated processes and institutions that jointly reflected both democratic and authoritarian aspects, resulting in so-called 'hybrid regimes' – a definition which happened to reflect limitation, if not application on the ground, due to the controversial/discrepant reference to democratisation processes (see Brownlee, 2007; Levitsky and Way, 2010; see also Morlino, 2009). In the early 2000s, roughly one third of the world's regimes could possibly be defined as hybrids (Diamond, 2002). The shift from the spread of military regimes from the 1950s to the 1980s towards more hybrid sub-categories of authoritarianisms found main theorisations as attributable to the post-Cold

War setting (Gilbert and Mohseni, 2011; Rutherford, 2018). One of the common trends in scholarship was the one treating hybrid regimes emerging in the early 1990s as incomplete or transitional forms of democracy. Yet in many cases expectations proved overly optimistic (Levitsky and Way, 2002: 51). Sharing Hinnebusch (2006) and Teti and Abbott's (2018) views, political pluralisation happened to be a substitute to democratisation mainly for structural reasons. At the level of the structure, so-defined hybrid regimes as a concept and category of systems may contain legislatures, independent judiciaries and civil society; do not allow the transfer of power through elections; and have been found to be unlikely to transfer to full democracies (Rutherford, 2018). A further approach to recall is Hinnebusch's school of 'new institutionalism', where autocracies found distinction in populist authoritarianisms and bureaucratic authoritarianisms (2006: 380; see also Ryan, 2001). In the case of bureaucratic authoritarianisms, military officers acted on behalf of the bourgeoisie and foreign capital and used authoritarian power to exclude segments of society in the name of capital accumulation.

A further category of regime remains the most undiscussed and these are personalist regimes. Fragmented views still question whether personalism forms a specific and distinct category, or whether it is rather a trait co-existing within other categories of regimes (Geddes, 1999b; Van den Bosch, 2016). However, discrepant views on personalist autocracies still dominate the field. The main divergences are found in Geddes et al. (2017), Svolik (2008, 2012) and Wahman et al. (2013), in whose view personalism is a regime trait rather than a distinct taxonomy. Regarding the parameter of temporality, in Hadenius and Teorell, personalist regimes tend to last longer if compared to military regimes defined as the most fragile (Hadenius and Teorell, 2007: 3). At the core of the longevity of personalist regimes lies the creation of clientelist networks and a pragmatic loyalty to the ruler. Similarly to Hadenius and Teorell, Geddes defines personalism as a category that is distinct both from military regimes and single-party states (Geddes, 1999b; Geddes et al., 2017; see also Lynch, 2013). The main source of difference attains to the strategies put in place for accessing office. The ruler can be an officer supported by a party, but neither the military nor the party exercises decision-making power in a personalist regime (Chehabi and Linz, 1998: 4–45; Snyder and Mahoney, 1999). A personalist regime arises when military intervention occurs to marginalise the rest of the officer corps, with power consolidated in a single individual (Geddes, 1999b: 124–125; see also Nordlinger, 1977). Geddes' definition of personalism exhibits the limitations of defining this category of regimes as a one-man show. Defining personalism as a trait existing within another category of regime means agreeing that personalism, irrespective of whether the system is based on civilian or military

Table 2.1 Table of leadership's polarised paradigm

Aspects of personalism	Transformational	Servant	Burns, bass model
Centrality of the ruler	x	x	
Subjectivity			
Human dignity			x
Participation			x
Community			
Autonomy			
Solidarity			x

Source: the author, modified from Whetstone (2002).

premises, is a component of all illiberal democracies. However, personalism can undergo different gradients, ranging from complete to a total absence. It follows as a result that, if personalism is considered a trait or component of other categories of regime, it can rise but also subside in the course of a regime's lifespan. The lack of agreement on how to classify personalism is possibly due to the lack of sufficient data (Wright, 2016). However, this book's analytical premises on personalism get closer to the scholarship which considers personalism in a more categorical sense (Colgan and Weeks, 2015; Davenport, 2007; Escribà-Folch and Wright, 2010, 2015; Fjelde, 2010; Geddes, 1999b; Geddes et al., 2014; Weeks, 2012; see also Reiter and Stam, 2003).

The paucity in defining personalist regimes can be seen in analyses of the way they seek to legitimate themselves and in the structure of their normative leaderships. Personalist leaders are found to be closer to the servant leadership paradigm, while the history offers abundant evidence of transformational leaderships (Whetstone, 2002). Shared and historical observations seem to suggest that the more transformational the leadership of a ruler is, the more it becomes subjected to a higher level of preoccupation associating this category of leadership to political characters like Hitler (see Whetstone, 2002).

Based on the triangulation of Whetstone's model and comprising Burns, Bass and Rost's leadership paradigms, the pejorative connotations attaining to the transformational leadership in the context of personalism highlight a high manipulative capacity, the exaltation of the ruler and face the risks tyranny derive. Otherwise, servant leaderships that attain to personalist regimes meet the definition for their being optimistic and subjected to the manipulation by followers (Whetstone, 2022). These features are inversely observable in the context of al-Sisi's Egypt with the exception of the connection between motivation and the recreation of values for the group the ruler is identified as being a member of.

Existing works have so far investigated the relationship between personalist regimes and political stability, concluding that personalism tends to be a cause of instability when compared to military regimes and so-called hybrid regimes (or semi-competitive autocracies). For decades personalist regimes have been associated with a short duration (Geddes, 1999b; Geddes et al., 2014), higher levels of state repression and domination (Davenport, 2007; Escribà-Folch and Wright, 2015; Weeks, 2012), and a higher probability of pursuing the acquisition of nuclear weapons (Way and Weeks, 2014). In addition, personalist dictatorships have been shown to be especially unresponsive to Western actors' attempts to incentivise them to democratise their regimes, including the use of both carrot and stick (Escribà-Folch and Wright, 2015). In Geddes' view, when personalist regimes do break down, these transitions are predominantly brought about by force rather than negotiation (Geddes et al., 2014). Besides, in the case of personalist autocracies, they are responsible for producing the worst policy outcomes and present a proclivity towards aggressive foreign policies and are least likely to engage in international cooperation (Frantz and Kendall-Taylor, 2021). On this latter aspect, the contention moved calls for a non-generalisation of personalist tendencies on the provocation that not all personalist rulers can be sacralised to the altar of political strength, despite megalomania. As this book demonstrates, in illiberal systems in which personalism is a nascent co-trait, international cooperation is employed as a device for reorganising consensus building around the ascendancy of the 'personalist ruler'. This is particularly the case of systems and regimes that organically emerge out of previously collapsed structures in response to political events.

The theoretical premises of this work share Van den Bosch's (2016) view of personalistic regimes as more eccentric autocracies in which the ruler operates with greatest freedom. Drawing on de Mesquita et al. (2003), unlike military regimes, in this category the selectorate is considered absent, while the winning coalition does not impact the legitimation of the system, as it is larger in size. Personalism, however, is not understood as a one-man show, but rather as a system in which the ruler chooses the cadre to assist them in governing, and with a balance of power tilted in favour of rulers. In personalist systems, loyalties are considered in terms of otherwise non-entities owing everything to the ruler (Van den Bosch, 2016: 15), without whom, in case of ousting, they risk losing their positions.

Membership in personalist cliques tends to be fluid, and somewhat difficult to identify when compared to membership in military regimes. During and after power seizures, personalist cliques are created from friendship networks or families' ties, while the power that emerges is concentrated in a strongman who tends to control both the military and the state apparatus (Geddes, 1999b: 130). However, this work contends that these factors are not fixed; rather, personalist rulers may go through phases of structural weaknesses, which can damage their control over the state and the military corps, with a consequent rise in internal fragmentation, which possibly risks exposing the ruler to failures. Structural weaknesses are theorised as more likely a result of internalised shifts by actors and their relations along power structures.

The focus on personalism is complexified if this category is approached not as a taxonomy per se, but as a sub-category that happens to emerge from within an already-defined regime category (e.g. single-party military, multi-party military). Thus, personalism can be identified as a regime category which defines elements more around the leader than the armed forces, although this study recognises the existence of the military in the infrastructure of a regime. In addition, it would be misleading to exclude the existence of sub-taxonomies of personalism which may be influenced by the historical state foundation of regimes and internal alliances along the domestic spectrum of politics. Therefore, there is a need to bypass reductive attempts of minimalising the structural complexity of personalist regimes and their structures confining them to the normative line. Amendments to the 2014 Constitution made by al-Sisi in 2019 projected the ruler's mandate through to 2034. It is contended in this chapter's historical analysis of the Egyptian state structure that next to the amendments to Articles 140, 185, 189, 193, 200, 204 and 234, which suggest an attempt at strengthening the role and figure of the ruler, there is the need to de-Westernise political analyses of the Egyptian state verticalising how amendments to the constitution, the introduced presidential decrees between 2013 and 2019, as well as the amendments to the penal code, created a rupture in the architecture of power captured as hegemonic and pyramidal and made power polarised for the first time since 1953.

The existing paucity of contemporary personalist regimes

Personalist regimes are broadly considered as a category of autocracy in which the absolutism of power is surrounded by a circle of loyalists subordinated to the ruler's political fears and projects (Geddes et al., 2014; see Leber, Carothers and Reichert, 2023). There is a need to go beyond this definition and fragmented views on this category of autocracy. Fragmentations principally question whether personalism can be still considered a de facto category of authoritarianism or a trait that eventually can emerge and coexist within a pre-existing regime category (Van den Bosch, 2015). Similarly, in the literature no agreement exists on their durability, as opposed to military regimes, for which there is a mutual agreement on longevity to a maximum of 25–30 years (Magaloni, 2008; see also Geddes, 1999b). In personalist regimes the construction of a clientelist network of sycophants represents the backbone behind the political construction of the machinery of governance. The question is: what does make personalist autocracies so different from other categories? Personalistic regimes can be considered more eccentric forms of autocracy in which the ruler tends to operate with greatest freedom. While a personalist ruler can be an officer supported by a party, neither the military nor the party can exercise power at the level of decision-making (Baturo and Elkink, 2015; see also Svolik, 2012 and Van den Bosch, 2015). In addition, the scope here is to go beyond the idea that personalism is a form of one-man show political system and to demonstrate that personalist regimes can also undergo different sub-taxonomies, similar to other most diffused autocracies (e.g. classical military regimes and juntas). Despite the eccentricity, personalism is not a one-man show system in which the ruler acts like a hero, but going beyond de Mesquita et al. (1999), it rather captures personalism as a system in which the ruler chooses the cadre to assist them in governing, and with a balance of power tilted in favour of rulers but the ruler has some limitations in ruling. Under these premises the book discusses loyalties in terms of otherwise non-entities owing everything to the ruler, without whom, in the case of ousting, they risk losing their positions (Van den Bosch, 2016: 15).

Even though personalism cannot be approached as a de facto 'one-man show' it still tends to concentrate power, and in some cases also the authority, within the person in political charge – at least from a representative trajectory. This leads to a condition in which the dictatorship is informal and in which political or economic decisions are not taken in consultation with the parliamentary assembly, as fictitious and non-representative of the society as these could be in all non-democratic orders, but with sycophants. Therefore, if personalism is considered as a trait or component of other categories of regime, then this means it can rise but also subside in the course of a regime's lifespan.

The paucity in defining personalist regimes is seen in the way they seek to legitimate themselves. An important aspect concerns how personalism contributes to militarism as a coup-proofing strategy. In autocracies rulers can reduce their vulnerability to being displaced from power by intentionally creating competing forces within the military that counterbalance each other, which both reduces the overall coordination capacity of the military and increases the probability that at least some segments of the military will remain loyal to the dictator in the event of a coup (see also Belkin and Schofer, 2003). In personalist autocracies, coup-proofing reduces military effectiveness through distorted command structures, non-merit-based promotions and reduced training (Reiter, 2020: 313).

The book demonstrates that from an institutional point of view, while personalist systems may present a strong bureaucracy, they also present a weaker organisation of the institutionalised sphere and, as such, of the state institutional power (as made by the weight of the state and the sub-national variation); they stand on precarious, fluid supports and on premises of hidden instability, which often remains neglected from an international perspective.

Trapped in orthodox debates: internal political legitimacy in Egypt

For decades, the existence of a hegemonic party in the Mubarak regime has been captured as an element of structural stability. In fact, if the existence of a party provides a source of stability to a regime ensuring its durability for over three decades, it is equally true that the regime party in Egypt became an element of structural destabilisation when dissent began to grow in the mid-2000s. This leads to a different argument, distancing itself from the claim that multi-party or hegemonic party systems are more stable as opposed to other forms of authoritarianism.

Expanding the critical lens of analysis, a limited number of studies have attempted to investigate the institutionalisation and legitimation of al-Sisi since his appointment to office (Ardovini, 2019; Caridi, 2015; Springborg, 2015; and more recently Yefet and Lavie, 2021) or provide an explanation for al-Sisi's ascendancy as a framed leader of Egypt, thus justifying such a perception of the ruler (El-Nawawy and El-Masry, 2016). El-Nawawy and El-Masry (2016) examine the iconography and cult of personality that characterised the 2014 election won by al-Sisi. While it is verified that al-Sisi conducted an unprecedented media campaign, with many posters celebrating himself, he did not gain an internal near-unanimous popularity, as human rights violations, routinised use of state violence (in this regard the book discusses state violence and the Raba'a al-Adawiya massacre in 2013), and an erosion in consensus fragmented the internal view of the ruler and downgraded consensus (Dunne, 2019; Stacher, 2020). Against the debate that al-Sisi 'won convincingly' in 2014 (El-Nawawy and El-Masry, 2016: 2276), this book proves that while al-Sisi won with 96.1 per cent of votes, this happened in the absence of a structured opposition as leftist parties had already disappeared from the political scene in January 2014, while the Muslim Brotherhood as a political-religious movement was constitutionally banned. In addition, while contributions report an excessive enthusiasm portrayed in the media and amongst al-Sisi's supporters (El-Nawawy and El-Masry, 2016), independent quantitative data provided by the Independent

Electoral Commission displayed a decrease in voter turnout from 50 per cent in 2012 to 41 per cent in 2014. Since turnouts can be considered indicative of a society's trust towards politics and politicians, a comparison of voter turnout between 2011 and 2014 indicates a process of gradually growing internal disaffection and mistrust of Egyptian society towards the evolution of the political process. Equally, the shift is indicative of a sense of disillusion towards the whole and promised process of democratisation (Stacher, 2020). Existing works converge on the fact that the strength and cult of personality for al-Sisi in 2014 remained closely attached to an unquestioned 'leadership' emerging out of a well-articulated media-constructed electoral campaign that emphasised references to symbols and signs to construct a leader. The produced idea of a strongman so far has been linked to al-Sisi's membership of the armed forces, and linked to the historical idea of the EAF as protectors from national threats. Hence, the ascendancy of al-Sisi as a leader is presaged on the portrayal of him as a military character who, in ascending to politics, saved Egypt from the risk of a cataclysm (El-Nawawy and El-Masry, 2016: 2276).

While this book acknowledges the societal view of the EAF as founders of the Republic, it posits that such an approach to the construction of a strongman in 2014 is only part of Egyptian society's view of the political authorities and the regime in the making. It neglects the existence of social dissent towards the ruler not necessarily being attached to those segments of the opposition targeted by al-Sisi's policies like Law No. 107 of 2013 – namely supporters of the Muslim Brotherhood. The present study contends that, considering the study and functioning of illiberal systems, there exist different taxonomies of coups, with varying societal support, which require careful consideration. This aspect is missing from contemporary views of societal support as a legitimising component of the 'counter-revolution' (i.e. the 2013 coup).

Taking a different approach from existing contributions to the study of the legitimation of political authority from an internal perspective, this book bypasses limitations posed by existing contributions in the field of Egyptian, Middle Eastern politics and regime change. Rather that providing an explanation for the institutionalisation of al-Sisi, or the construction of an 'uncontested' strongman in 2014 with similarities to the socialist 'Nasserian model', the work proposes a critical micro-structural, socio-political and economic analysis into the inner process of internal legitimation against a background of infrastructural, institutional, societal, cultural and political sub-change in the reorganisation of the political machine, which de facto problematises the construction of al-Sisi's legitimacy claim in connection to the sub-variation in the regime. It adopts a more comprehensive timeframe of study, including the micro- and macro-transformations Egypt underwent between 2013 and

2019, and not regarding exclusively the economic apparatus of the state but also the transformation in Islamism and the triangularisation between al-Sisi, the Salafi al-Nour party and the al-Azhar along the axis of religion and the 'ethics of development'.

While the book shares the view of the EAF as 'guardians of the state' – a function directly influenced by historical legacies – it contends that they have been repositioned in the state structure since 2013 with the same influence they had under Mubarak and Sadat going back to 1978. Thus it takes a different approach from more contemporary observers who instead share the historical continuum along the militarisation of the economic structures with the centralisation on the one hand, and a re-Nasserisation of the NSPO on the other (Dunne, and Bardos 2019; Yefet and Lavie, 2021; Mandour, 2019).

What remains relevant instead in the current and comparative debate in the field of democratisation, autocratisation and Middle East politics is the discussion around trust and institutional corrosion from below as premises for 'security sink-holes', alias dictatorships believed to be precarious and reliant on oppression, but in which contexts legitimation remains unaddressed (Teti and Abbott, 2018). This work shares the view that the discourse of trust and institutionalisation must be subjected to a deeper analysis, thus avoiding the reductivism views that the redrafting of law could be a source of legitimation in autocracies after shockwaves or that al-Sisi in Egypt is building a traditionally rooted eudaemonic legitimacy (Shahin, 2017), where eudaemonia stands for welfare. What this book problematises and deconstructs from within in connection with the sub-transformation of the regime is the unstainable non-modernist model of industrialisation and development as connected with the regime's idea of welfarised happiness as a source of internal legitimacy and consensus building. There is a deep vacuum in the way the discussion around legitimacy in authoritarian states after shockwaves, and legitimacy in the specific context of Egypt, both remain confined to an argumentative, rather than critical level of discussion that problematises forms of adaptation or, getting closer to Rutherford, the transformation of pacts (Rutherford, 2018: 165).

Maintaining the focus on the role of the military, drawing comparison between Algeria in 1992 and Egypt in 2013, as some have attempted, such as Yezza in 2013, blurs the contours of the debate on Egyptian sub-transformation and, broadly speaking, autocratic readaptation against the idea of democratisation. The argument that Egypt may today be drawing closer towards an upgraded strictly militarised system harmonises with scholarship which started predicting in Egypt a second Algeria in 1992. There are limitations and historical-structural discrepancies in this argument. The main difference between Algeria and Egypt finds logical explanation through the politics of rents (Beblawi, 1990; Smith, 2015; see also Beblawi and Luciani, 1987). In Arab regimes and monarchies rich in oil revenues, such as Algeria, legitimacy has not been necessarily or exclusively rooted in popular acceptance, but rather on rents, and this was indicated by the fact that during the 2011 Arab uprisings, in Algeria demonstrators demanded better working conditions and salaries, and lower taxes, but they did not seek regime change (Yazbeck, 2018; see also Dillman, 2000). This has not been the case in Egypt, where Rentier State Theory finds limited, if no chances of application at all. While in Algeria there has been a revolutionary portrayal of the army for the role it played in the country's anti-colonial liberation struggle, in Egypt the army has undergone a different transformative framing, from state-builders in the mid-1950s to praetorian guards, as a result of the neoliberal policies introduced and negotiated under liberal premises, and IMF loans accepted by Hosni Mubarak in the 1990s and 2000s. Their role is being renegotiated under al-Sisi's reinvention of authoritarianism. Thirdly, focusing on the locus of power, in Algeria power was and still is concentrated in the armed forces, although they have been pushed beyond the boundaries of politics. This latter aspect may show similarities to post-2013 Egypt, in which the EAF have been presented as an apolitical force committed to democracy and the rebuilding of the idea of the nation, through the lenses of the iconic past. It is in this regard that myths, symbols and memories in Chapter 4 see a specific applications. This book correspondingly asserts the existence of different gradients of militarised state along the taxonomy of authoritarianism. In addition, it is worth adding that from a juridical perspective, since 2014 in Egypt the number of civilian trials in military courts has dramatically increased, thus breaking with Art 204 of the constitution, which states that a civilian may not be tried in a military court, with the only exception of acts of aggression directed against military installations and bases (Khalid, 2020; Human Rights Watch, 2016). Despite this, theorising that Egypt is still a purist militarised state is deceptive. This book argues that the repositioning of the military and the elite in the power infrastructure has produced a variation on the process of 'hegemonisation' of state power in the hand of the NDP that saw an acceleration in 2007 and anticipated 2009 elections.

Conclusions

For at least three decades, the existing scholarship held that the durability of the Egyptian regime under Hosni Mubarak derived strictly from the army's role, which acted as a real selectorate, by which are meant the most influential constituency or those in the position to choose the leader, and the winning coalition in Parliament which, at least in the 1990s and early

2000s, was of significant size (de Mesquita et al., 2003). The collapse of a military-controlled regime party as a result of the 2011 protests, the transformation of the Islamist opposition, and a new relationship between Islam and politics, which emerged after 2012 following the FJP-Muslim Brotherhood experience in power, have structurally altered the mechanisms of durability formerly constructed around party politics since the creation of the ASU and then the NDP. Government control of the opposition, pyramidal clientelism, favouritism (mahsubeiyya politics) and the independence granted to the judiciary were externally oriented tactics to influence the view of the regime as possessing reformist inclinations. Recalling the main argumentation that legitimacy is a fluid concept, not an autonomous set of variables, and is in constant interactions with the circumstances, settings and socio-political contexts and structures in which governments operate, significative structural elements since 2013 (i.e. the absence of opposition or multi-party elections, and the absence of a regime party) in the case of Egypt, it is suggested that the former premises on which the NDP attempted to build legitimacy are no longer applicable in a structurally and ideologically transformed society, like the Egyptian one after 2013.

Under the NDP the mechanism of legitimacy became more externally rooted in a form of diplomatic survival and international acceptance, while that of durability was more domestically intertwined with the party's survival and society's acceptance or negotiation with an image of developmentalist state structures. Existing works have emphasised the perdurability of the military system and projected this analysis in considering the failure of the FJP government in 2012–2013.

A lacuna in the scholarship exists on authoritarian paths towards political legitimation and post-turmoil transformations in Middle East politics. While recent studies have achieved a detailed understanding of the functioning of Mubarak's NDP, they have equally argued in favour of the existence of a regime party as an element of stability in autocracies. In fact, a combination of theoretical and empirical perspectives allows a counter-argument contending that if the existence of a party can provide a source of stability to a regime ensuring its durability for over three decades like in Egypt (though this can be expanded to other nearby countries), it is equally true that regimes parties ended up being an element of structural destabilisation before societal dissent. This may lead to a different argument, distancing itself from the shared claim that multi-party or hegemonic party systems are more stable as opposed to other authoritarianisms.

The lack of understanding of the post-2013 authoritarian process of internal legitimation remains a notable gap in the scholarship on the sub-transformation of state and institutions in the post-2011 Middle East. In comparison to Egypt under Mubarak, when the regime's durability was granted through multi-party elections, cooptation of the opposition (Albrecht, 2005; Blaydes, 2006; Lust-Okar, 2009), and clientelist relations between the military and international state actors (Meital, 2006; Sharp, 2011), in the making of Egypt under al-Sisi the closed political and social panorama, the suppression and repression of all forms of opposition, and especially the lack of a regime party and its replacement with a technocratic Parliament, complicates the understanding so far developed on political legitimacy and regime durability (see Al Jazeera, 2014). Similarly, unlike the NDP, the NFB in Parliament today does not play a patronage role, nor it does provide straightforward support to the ruler. For the first time since 2013, Egypt has radically changed many of the state's structural assets and presents some features reminiscent of a more personalist authoritarianism.

Notes

1 On multiparty elections and electoral authoritarianism see Brownlee (2009), Posusney and Angrist (2005) and Schedler (2002).
2 For more than a decade the EU attempted to move away from its position of middle-power actor in the Mediterranean area and compete with super-power actors like the US and recently Russia after the military withdrawal of US troops and shifted interests from the Middle East toward the Pacific area and primarily Taiwan (on Russia and the uprisings see Malashenko, 2013). Despite this, looking back at the goals included in the European Commission's PfDSP (COM [2011] 200) in 2011 and the ENPI (2007–2013 and 2014–2020), much of the EU regional ambitions, despite revisions in the instruments, neglected to consider internal socio-political intra-structures (alliances, cultural variables, social morality). While the Partnership for Democracy and Shared Prosperity (PfDSP) presented itself as an effective instrument for answering the demands of the 2011 uprising and promised to invest in democracy; it in fact occupied a very marginal position (Hollis, 2012). To varying degrees, EU policies adopted were intended to effect change in Europe's neighbourhood and all had to do with regional and Western security cooperation rather than with economic and political stabilisation (Hollis, 2012; see also Teti et al., 2012).
3 The EU's pejorative exposition was accompanied by strategies promoted by Brussels. Through the Southern Neighbourhood Project the EU in 2018 launched 'Shoot and Share', a youth photo competition aimed at shedding light on EU-supported development in the Arab world (Dupire, 2018).

3

Reinventing a different political machine

The struggle for authority

Since al-Sisi took power as President in the aftermath of the 2014 presidential elections, the armed forces have exploited the political momentum of the coup to regain a great deal of territory and control – both lost in the late 2000s to the civilian business elite. Between 2011 and June 2012 the SCAF sought to shape the process of transition, bringing it to their side (Abul-Magd, 2018; Albrecht and Bishara, 2011; Atteya, 2013; Brown and Dunne, 2013; Roll, 2016). Despite the SCAF's declared commitment to guide the country towards a civilian government as a behind-the-scenes actor, in fact the army's influence in society expanded under the Muslim Brotherhood-backed FJP government in 2012, with what is known to be an alleged deal between the SCAF and the latter (Abul-Magd, 2018; Marshall, 2015; see also Middle East Institute, 2013). The relations between the EAF and the Muslim Brotherhood deserve careful discussion beyond the reductivism of state anti-system relations. Making use of Francois Bayart's terminology, they can be described as *la greffe de l'état* (state grafts), which Bayart employed to question the relations between religion and state formation in Africa and the Middle East (Bayart, 1996). The historical persistence of the Brotherhood's underground presence for five decades in the social-political domain might suggest that the movement is in many respects inextricable from Egypt's society and political culture. This is somewhat parallel to the EAF's position in Egyptian society: modern Egypt is difficult to imagine without the army at, or near, the centre, unlike many other Arab countries, such as Tunisia.[1]

In 2012, a deal with the FJP offered the SCAF the chance to increase its control over the AOI and the NSPO, whose power had decreased during the 1990s and 2000s.[2] This was made possible by backing from the Muslim Brotherhood (Marshall, 2015; see also Marshall and Stacher, 2012). It should not come as a surprise that under the FJP government, al-Sisi served as general, and represented the hand of the FJP within a SCAF hierarchy. Yet popular discontent was emerging with the government tendency to monopolise political power on religious premises, on top of protracted social dissatisfaction towards the inefficiency of the party's economic agenda. The creation of the protest movement Tamarrod, which has been viewed as linked to the SCAF's project, facilitated the EAF's organisation of a three-day anti-Muslim Brotherhood rally in Tahrir Square in late June and early July, which also benefitted from a diffused dissent coming from some leftist parties and movements asking for the departure of conservative ideologies as represented by the Muslim Brotherhood-led government. In this context of social disaffection, the Tamarrod movement emerged as a grassroots social reality, founded in 2013 by five Nasserite-oriented activists who had been part of the Kefaya movement in 2005, to oppose Morsi and force him to call early presidential elections, before it turned into a political party, which ultimately was short-lived (Achcar; 2016; Ahram Online, 2014a).[3]

The SCAF seized the opportunity to lead the Egyptian transition again and for the second time in two years, framing the popular contestations and rally in June 2013 as a legitimate act of resistance to what was considered an illegitimate power. On 1 and 3 July, al-Sisi delivered two public speeches, still in his capacity of SCAF general, proclaiming the FJP and Morsi's premiership as illegitimate in the popular will. In these speeches, the reinvention of the machinery of governance under the premise of the rule of law both started to unfold.

The SCAF statement given in the form of al-Sisi's 1 July speech initiated what was a strategic process of the persuasion of civil society and the international political system on the one hand, and a heroic framing of the armed forces for the political moment on the other. The speech found legitimation on historical state foundations, which linked the destiny of the armed forces to the Republic, thus associating the image of the SCAF with a function of reconciliation between the state and society, with the goal of pacifying the tumultuous relations in 2011 when the army and society entered a phase of confrontation that resulted in direct violence between citizens and the police in Tahrir Square. Politically and structurally, during the second half of the 2000s, with its liberalised politics and attempts to eradicate corruption, the army was internalised into a faulty and dissonant political model, in which the NDP was the highest guarantor of the pyramidal clientelist system; by 'dissonance' I here borrow from Glade and refer to a political system that creates a multipolar arena abetting competition and negotiation (Glade, 2005: 24). Dissonant politics found protraction under FJP rule, with a continuance of corruption and an escalation in authoritarian-theocratic tendencies.

Delivering Egyptian society's demand, the overthrow of the FJP, the EAF wished to present to the outside world a view of the army's intervention as a righteous act against the risk of theocratic and corrupt state in the hands of the Muslim Brotherhood, soon labelled as a 'terrorist organisation'. In fact, the coup signalled the start of a longer-term project envisioned by the Egyptian armed forces. To bring the envisioned project to reality, there was a need to redraw the bargained social contract between the army and the people. In this regard, it is noted that in 2012 the SCAF, under its then chairman Mohammad Tantawi, failed in providing a peaceful and unifying idea to bring together the army and the people with social divisions in Cairo. Part of my empirical observations in Cairo in 2012 included SCAF-produced advertisements in El-Nasr city (the SCAF's headquarters) in April of that year during the electoral campaign, portraying a soldier carrying a baby. The advertisements in such a time of transition drew criticisms, amongst foreigners and intellectual locals. The image was strategically thought-out and sought to purify the armed forces of their involvement in violence before 2011, and from their implication in the deep spiral of corruption under the NDP.[4] At the heart of the EAF's failure in capturing the social imagination lay the wave of police violence conducted against citizens during the 2011 protests, which the military had failed to condemn and had participated in until Mubarak's downfall became inevitable. After that, the armed forces in the country started to rebuild their lost momentum.

With the goal of purifying society's view of the EAF, at that time the SCAF's 1 July statement tried to manifest a strong emotional element, recalling feelings of hope, patriotism and the institutional moral integrity of the army's historical duty towards the homeland and the commitment to its resurrection. The statement became a clear attempt of emphasising the commitment of the SCAF to national stability and, above all, the restoration of the rule of law. Even though, at least thematically, the rule of law did not occupy a prominent role in the 1 July 2013 statement – indeed, greater emphasis was placed on the EAF's claimed commitment to democracy – it represented the main premise for al-Sisi's struggle for legitimation between 2013 and 2014. There are four main themes/nodes with which the legitimation of the SCAF's intervention against the FJP in late June and early July 2013 was justified. These principally attained to: nationalistic pride; EAF commitment to safeguard 'security'; EAF commitment to meet people's demand; and the armed forces' commitment to the process of democracy and apolitical mission.

However, adding a quantitative analysis (expressed in %) of the political weight played by the four nodes, it was nodes 2, 4 and, only in part, node 1, as shown in Table 3.1, that occupied a more prominent role, as opposed to node 3 which centralised the EAF's commitment to meeting the people's demand, with the goal of creating a new and corruption-free frame of the armed forces. Despite the EAF's references to democracy and its own societal importance at the anti-Muslim Brotherhood rally, democracy played a peripheral influence in the 1 July statement in 2013, while the attached

Table 3.1 Nvivo codebook and quantitative data for nodes coded for the EAF's 1 July 2013 statement

Node Number	Nodes	References	%
1	Nationalistic pride	1	2.65
2	EAF as committed to safeguarding security	3	7.17
3	EAF as committed to meeting the people's demands	1	1.05
4	EAF as apolitical force committed to democracy and apolitical mission	1	2.70

frame of the future apolitical mission of the army was emphasised next to the army commitment to safeguard the premise of societal security. What remains relevant is the priority that was assigned to the EAF's distance from politics. At least from a structural perspective, this represented a novelty and should provoke a new understanding of the role played by the SCAF compared to under Mubarak's regime. Al-Sisi's stated effort to maintain an apolitical role was made clear in his words that 'the armed forces have realised that the Egyptian people, who are calling on us to come to their support, are not in fact calling on us to assume power' (SCAF's speech, 1 July, 2013).

Going deeper into this issue and trying to make a clearer sense of the SCAF's apolitical promises, there are actually two distinct goals behind the al-Sisi/SCAF statement on the apolitical mission of the army and these were linked to the process of internal legitimation understood as a goal for non-fragmenting the societal consensus toward the armed forces. The first goal was cleaning the image of the army from the Mubarak era, deeply connected to the NDP-military politics of *wasta* and *shilla* (connections) on which Mubarak's political machine relied for three decades. Politically and structurally, this purification of the EAF's frame by al-Sisi initially resonated more easily at the level of civil society, due to 'the agreement of the latter with the military on the creation of the economic class in civil society. That, to many, was quite positive, despite the political and economic corruption and military oppression which always existed';[5] The second goal was facilitating Egyptians' recalling of collective memories of the army and its anti-imperialist function in the 1950s. Al-Sisi continued by delivering an ultimatum to the FJP government.[6]

The real importance of the 1 July SCAF statement was that it proved a prelude to the speech delivered two days later on 3 July, with which al-Sisi sought to legitimise the SCAF's intervention and the mandate by the people in the overthrowing of FJP rule. The 3 July 2013 statement attempted to justify and legitimise the SCAF's intervention in the form of the coup, in a counterrevolutionary frame. The principles of transparency and legality claimed by the army were connected to the necessity of a roadmap for supporting political transition and 'containing initial measures which ensure the construction of a strong and coherent Egyptian society' (SCAF statement, 1 July 2013). The EAF promised to be the guardian of this process, representing a first step towards the reinstallation of a rule of law, which the FJP – and, significantly, later the NDP – were accused of having broken. This first step ultimately underpinned a larger and more ambitious project of political and infrastructural reconstruction.

Through the recalling of the myth-symbol complex – theory previously aimed at capturing myths and symbols as guarantors of the preservation and the passing down to future generations of ethnic identity, but later revised to mean a more heroic mission (Smith, 1991, 1998) – the SCAF's statement attempted to create the moral premises of legitimacy by emphasising patriotism and their historic function in resetting the foundations of the state and the remaking of the idea of a great nation. This was an easy way through which it was possible to recall collective social memories among the protesters in Tahrir square demanding the departure of Mohammed Morsi in late June 2013. Cultural values embedded by the army and concerning the idea of the nation assured the moral-legal justification and legitimation for the orchestration of the coup. Egyptian society recognises the army as the real actor behind the state, and while not forgetting the systemic corruption in the Egyptian state, has tended not to target the army itself, thus avoiding direct confrontations with it, where and when that has been possible.[7] However, ties between the army and the people were more direct than expected due to the former's historical status as a major employer for youth in a country in which (as discussed in the final chapter) the unemployment rate constitutes a persisting social and policy issue and due to the loyalty shown to it by Egyptians who served in the military to get a salary as a main source of family income (GCDCAF, 2016). This could partially explain why in 2017, despite the 2013 Rabi'a massacre by armed forces, 85 per cent of Egyptians did not rise against the armed forces, according to data collected by El-Bernoussi (2021).

From a framing perspective, the claims of a close relationship between the army and the people, and the loyalty shown to the former by the latter, would make the qualifiers of *salience* and *cultural compatibility* most successful in the construction of the strategic frame of the armed forces as a coup-stager. Unlike the purpose of schemata which aim at altering the recipients' cognition (Scheufele, 1999), *strategic frames* can be considered as closer to the hoped operationalisation of a political change.

It follows that the detachment of the SCAF from the NDP and the Mubarak regime, the discursive act of recalling the historical function of the SCAF, and the commitment to restore the rule of law, worked as de facto strategic effects in the construction of the new top-down oriented frame of the EAF.[8] Empirically, the strategic effects from the speech were to persuade the anti-Muslim Brotherhood protesters of a political change and the definitive end of the authoritarian legacy of the EAF. Strategic effects, nonetheless, are found to have the function of also transforming *schemata*, recipients of a pre-existing cognition with cognitive links that can be activated or modified (Scheufele, 1999; Tuchman, 1978). The frame of the EAF attempted to alter the pre-existing cognition (schemata), thus attempting to propose a new mission for the EAF. The procedure created a more complex category of frame, the *strategic meta-frame* of the EAF and its role in protecting the political transition.[9]

Al-Sisi's reference to the SCAF's integrity, on the one hand, and commitment to restoring the rule of law by distancing himself from the pre-2011 power structures, also protracted under the FJP, on the other hand, have underpinned a broader, complex project, involving a redefinition of the premises for negotiating political power, and from which in al-Sisi's project would stem internal and top-down legitimacy.

When the implications for the coup speech are considered, comparing the themes coded in the 3 July coup-staging speech with those of the 1 July SCAF statement above, the common denominator was the recall of the SCAF's historical duty and the idea of a militarised nationalist identity that needed to re-emerge from the ashes of a historical past chaotically identified in Gamal Al-Abdel Nasser's legacy and Anwar Sadat's military industrialisation.[10] Al-Sisi's and the SCAF's references to the roadmap for transition were linked to a set of key phases, ranging from early presidential elections to the empowerment of youth and the parliamentary elections.

Promises represented, at least initially, the moral base on which the legal right to rule stood (Weber, 1978; Beetham, 1991).[11] These were framed in connection to node 4 (shown in Table 3.1) or the 1 July SCAF statement. The SCAF's calls for the people to take to the streets on 3 July, and for a military mandate to rule, were successful to the point that, following the appeal made on television, a personality cult began to emerge around al-Sisi. This culminated in much media excitement, with al-Sisi winning a popular vote to be named as *Time* magazine's 'Man of the Year' in 2013, food products being dedicated to al-Sisi, images of women kissing portraits of al-Sisi next to modern merchandise, and a monetarisation of the al-Sisi's

Table 3.2 Codebook for 3 July coup-staging speech

Node number	Nodes	References	%
1	Armed forces' duty towards the nation	6	6.12
2	Apolitical mission of the SCAF		3.72
3	Army involvement in leading the political transition as commitment to the stability of the homeland	3	4.04
4	SCAF's overlooking of the transition roadmap	1	1.04
5	Roadmap as instrument for a coherent Egyptian society	5	4.00
6	Early presidential elections	1	0.22
7	Free media and press	1	0.90
8	Empowerment of young people in the decision-making process	1	1.06
9	New parliamentary elections	1	0.76

myth-symbolism, through a process of heroification – though major fragmentations in public opinion started to emerge over the years.[12]

This acceptance derived not so much from al-Sisi himself or his political character still being formed, but from his capacity to initially flirt with symbols and memories and association with the armed forces, which despite the turbulence of relations with the civil society that manifested later in 2011 where the army intervened with violence to disperse crowds gathered in Tahrir, military-society relations remain pervaded by blurred countours simply for historical, economic and occupational reasons. The SCAF remains socially framed as an employer in a country in which the rise of the private sector and the model of market economy have been accompanied for years by a rise in the unemployment rate and where the gender gap remains unaddressed (Galal, 2022).

It is by taking a comparative approach to the modern political history of Egypt that the rule of law under Mubarak's last decade represented the only foundation on which the regime attempted to build a form and source of legal legitimacy. Indeed, the wide diffusion of corruption, the cooptation of the elite, and the manipulation of multi-party politics, all spread discontent towards the establishment. Responding to the external demand for democratisation in the MENA region, mainly by the EU, in the early 2000s Mubarak granted greater independence to the judiciary, with the purpose of providing the impression of greater transparency. The reality was different. In the absence of other qualifiers, amendments mostly to the electoral laws (e.g. in 2005), and a tactical independence granted to the judiciary, allowed the NDP to set a legal basis (albeit contested) for preventing the collapse of the regime in the short term. However, Hosni Mubarak's amendments to the legal framework and manipulation of the law raised parliamentary concerns and sparked institutional mistrust, decreasing the level of consensus to a minimum (BTI, 2010). A similar miscalculation was made by the FJP, when the introduction of martial law and the amendments to the Constitution granted far-reaching powers to the ruler, seemingly locating Morsi above the law, and thus eroding the legitimacy of the FJP (POMEPS, 2013).

Authorities' extensive reference to the commitment to the rule of law, and an inclusive roadmap for safeguarding the transition after the coup, correspond to the construction of what is here identified as a diagnostic frame (Benford and Snow, 2000).[13] The SCAF's distancing of itself from both the pre-2011 regime and FJP rule was symptomatic of an act of targeting predecessors for having betrayed the principle of ruling by law, thus presenting them as immoral. Borrowing from Noakes and Johnston's (2005) theory of frame resonance, and contextualising both Mubarak's and Morsi's manipulation of the rule of law, it is contended that interference into the civilian code worked as sub-qualifiers that helped the diagnostic framing of the rule of law by al-Sisi to resonate more effectively, due to consistency, which underpins the completeness of the beliefs, claims or actions promoted in the frame; and relevance, which relates to how the frame fits between the framing at the level of the cognition and political events.

Political violence in the liquid interregnum: state political violence and the struggle for legitimation

The political episodes of Raba'a al-Adawiya and al-Nahda in Giza in August 2013 – also known as the Rabi'a massacre (*Magazarat Rabi'a*) – with a total death toll estimated at 1,526 people, is remembered as the largest one-day loss of life caused by the state. The violent polarisation between the Muslim Brotherhood's resistance to the 2013 coup, the anti-coup alliance and the police in resisting both, alongside the new constitutional amendments by the interim President Adly Mansour, demonstrated a gap between words and deeds which weakened the 'counter-revolutionary' idea attached to the framing of the rule of law (Ardovini and Mabon, 2019) and the SCAF's role in safeguarding what was promoted as a peaceful transition. The political symbolism of Raba'a al-Adawiya, later known as Rabi'a, is represented by a four-fingered hand as the literal meaning is the fourth.[14] Raba'a al-Adawiya has found early mention with Tiananmen Square in 1989 and later with Andjan in Uzbekistan in 2005 (mentioned in *Middle East Eye*, 2018 and later found unquoted in Grimm, 2022: 133). When the shortcomings of the Anti-Coup Alliance, also known as the National Alliance Supporting Legitimacy (NASL), are recalled in the political event, works have stated that 'the fact that the Anti-Coup campaign failed to inspire even marginal support for its policies from within the military's ranks was indicative of the Muslim Brotherhood's political isolation by the time of Mursi's deposition' (Grimm, 2022: 180). The alliance's inability to inspire new forms of intra-army support is not so much a symptom of the Muslim Brotherhood's political isolation as indicative of the structural interest-driven shift which would have been initiated soon after and in which segments from the military ranks happened to be materially involved. The involvement did not happen on nationalistic-historical premises that since the 1950s have been portraying and sacralising the duty of the military to the 'protection of the homeland'. Smith's critique on the irrelevance of discoursive nationalist projections illuminates on the resources-opportunity nexus which structurally explains the no-impact exercised by the NASL on the military ranks. In 2013 the disengagement found justification in the pacted conditional support that tied the SCAF to the political character of the authority that would have been al-Sisi. Besides, there are some knowledge gaps behind the targeting of the anti-coup alliance for the non-influence exercised on the armed forces, while the pro-coup alliance known as 'Tamarrod' is acknowledged, as this book mirrors the national subjects who 'created' the movement.

Looking back at the Raba'a episode, beyond the symbolism of the event and its resonation at the level of activism, on a transnational and intraregional scale (Grimm, 2022), it introduced the institutionalisation of state violence as an everyday practice, which, however, fulfilled different purposes from the pre-2011 setting (see Stacher, 2020). Although state violence in Egypt was not alien under Hosni Mubarak's rule, nor during the 2011 protests, as also noted by Stacher who highlights that the SCAF committed torture in the Egyptian National Museum (2020: 96), before 2011, state violence was not considered a default or automatic response to social contestations.

Under the NDP, violence was processed as an 'effect' and not as a 'cause'. While this study shares Stacher's (2020) understanding of state violence under Mubarak as more sporadic if compared to its use under al-Sisi, it distances itself from existing approaches to state violence before and under al-Sisi (Stacher, 2020; see also Pratt and Rezk, 2019). Violence exercised by the armed forces over civilians in 2011 also underwent transformations (Ketchley, 2014).[15] A few years earlier, the relations between protesters and the SCAF underwent a kind of fraternisation (Ketchley, 2014: 52). This took the form of mass gathering in Tahrir and Abassiyah.

However, this work argues that the armed forces' and police's abandoning of violence against civilians, rather than being representative of the historical and economic relations that linked Egyptian society to a militarised identity, was tactically conceived at that stage. What Ketchley defined as the 'protesters-army fraternisation' was nothing more that the result of a calculated strategy through which the armed forces wanted to recall their historical duty in protecting the nation. In fact, the fraternisation happened to be intertwined with the long-term political and structural project by the EAF in regaining a key role in the new political system when the irreversibility of protests against Mubarak and the collapse of the NDP became clear to most. The historical institutionalisation of the armed forces here can provide a response for such behavioural choice, as clearly the armed forces became interested in their longevity, as a comprehensive entity, beyond the survival of the regime itself.[16] The SCAF turned their backs on the ruler, depriving foundational loyalty, a core premise for keeping the autocratic machine alive.[17] However, the concept of fraternisation should not represent a generalisation for what today could be understood as a historical misleading postulate, as the societal views of the army and the police was highly fragmented and divisive and it was walking down to Tahrir square that this feeling was noticeable in 2012 and in the actions taken by the military junta against protestors (Fahmy, 2012; see also Human Rights Watch, 2012).[18]

This book shares the reflection by Stacher (2020) and Pratt and Rezk (2019) that state violence after the 2013 coup aimed to dehumanise opponents (i.e. the Muslim Brotherhood) and presented itself as integral to the reconstruction of politics. Additionally is the argument that, between 2013 and 2014, attempts were made to link violence to a legitimation claim and the populist dominant frame of al-Sisi as a saviour of the country from civil war and the descent of Egypt into a theocratic authoritarianism, which was justified on seducing premises (as discussed in Chapter 5). Under this premise, the theory of 'emergency mentalities' (Abdelrahman, 2017: 9) embeds a short-term need, while in fact the political project initiated from within some military hierarchies was conceived along a longer temporal axis, at some point back in 2012.

State violence as it took place in 2011, 2013 and again in 2017 requires a different contextualisation as a result of the societal and political structures

3.1 Graffiti of Tahrir Square. A SCAF tank symbolically presented as suppressing social and political freedom. Picture taken by the author in Tahrir Square, Cairo 2012

that were in the making at the time and that shifted from a SCAF-led political transition in which violence became constructive in engineering the structure of politics, as recalled by Stacher (2020: 108), to a system which attempted to represent violence as legitimate for state security, and in which state violence became routinised, dehumanising not only political subjects, but also civilians. The connection between legitimacy and state violence underwent further deeper complexities and problematisations due to its protraction and intensification between 2015 and 2019, when consensus towards the emerging status quo started to become more evident, with purges not only of political opponents such as the Muslim Brotherhood, but also civil activists and children (Human Rights Watch, 2019). Taking a different approach from Stacher (2020) and Pratt and Rezk (2019), rather than an element of state formation, violence in the post-2017 setting became constitutive of deep structural-political phobias, rather than regime-making, stemming from the authorities' inability to fill the gap left by the legitimacy crisis caused by the coup. Amendments to the penal code and, more precisely Law No. 107 of 2013 and later Law No. 94 of 2015, attempted to construct a legalised framework that legitimated forms of violence as defensive before state threats. However, these amendments proved how some things are easier to legalise than to legitimise. Hence, it is possible to put forward the theory that state violence shifted from an 'effect', as it was conceptualised in the pre-2011 setting, to a 'cause' that stemmed directly from the enactment of anti-NGO, anti-protest and anti-terrorism laws after the 2013 coup, which internalised the Weberian conception of monopoly of violence as linked to the struggle of internal legitimation. Rather, the Raba'a episode introduced the institutionalisation of state violence as an everyday practice, which, however, fulfilled different purposes from the pre-2011 setting. The debate unfolding here gets closer to Stacher in defining 'effect' as the elite's inability to incorporate political demands from society, and thus the resort to state-exercised violence with the goal of maintaining what authorities defined as 'public order'. While this chapter problematises the sociological conception of the state from a Weberian perspective, which assumes that the state is a political institution that successfully claims the monopoly of violence (Weber, 1968), it contextualises differently the use of state violence before and after the 2013 coup, when the issues of political legitimacy and regime change are considered. In due course, state violence became a form of new governmentality, which indiscriminately targeted all forms of political dissent and participation to the point of including green movements that contested COP27, with Sharm El-Sheikh denouncing the hypocrisy and exclusionary approach of the regime to environmental ethics and politics.[19]

In July 2013, in the absence of the Parliamentary Assembly, Mansour issued a constitutional declaration, the 154th article of which ultimately granted the President extended legislative authority. This decision de facto provided the legal grounds for an extension of the emergency law (Ardovini and Mabon, 2019: 15), thus revealing the first discrepancies between the discourse and actual policy implementation.

Since its introduction in 1981, the state of emergency in Egypt has represented the legal tool at the core of securitisation policies and political repression, forbidding mass gatherings and denying the right to protest in public spaces. In a replication of Mubarak's strategy for countering opposition and for the securitisation of public spaces, Mansour's extension of the emergency in 2013 found justification through the discourses of counter-terrorism and societal security. The reintroduction and extension of the emergency law in the 2014 Constitution determined a severe crackdown imposed on civil society, under the same rhetoric of protection. However, the emphasis on protection clashed with the content of the 2013 statement, which emphasised a commitment to protecting the process of democracy, unlike (the SCAF claimed) the FJP. While the restrictions implemented in the emergency and anti-protest law determined a more central role for the armed forces in the societal fabric, they also accounted for the disappearance of political parties from the Egyptian political and societal domain, after the political opening of 2012 (Zollner, 2018).

If the 3 July 2013 coup-staging speech corresponded to the intention of creating a diagnostic frame in the emphasis on the rule of law, from a political perspective the speech matched with a set of policies that expanded the military's involvement in domestic matters, implemented through articles and decrees including Presidential Decree No. 136 of 2014, which provided further protection for government facilities.

Despite al-Sisi's attempt at purifying the collective imaginary of the EAF and the constant reference to the rule of law as a principle in governance to which the army would strictly adhere, a combination of qualitative and quantitative data in fact discloses a worsening domestic socio-political situation in late 2013, at the level of integration and social capital. In 2014 indicators of social-political integration drawn from data provided by the BTI scored at 5.3 out of a 0–10 score. By contrast, Egypt in 2016 scored 4.7 (BTI, 2014, 2016), indicating that social and political participation after 2013 were going in the opposite direction to the promises made in the 1 July and 3 July statement and speech. A further worsening was indicated regarding social capital, which in the 2012–2014 timeframe scored 6 (BTI, 2014). The data show how institutional trust in late 2013 almost equalled the level of institutional trust in Mubarak's last decade of tenure, 2000–2010; this raised concerns in terms of the rule of law and effective success of legitimation during this period, although it did not indicate what structural readaptations were occurring in the still-emerging new political system. Table 3.3 provides a simplified understanding of the function of the different categories of frames with specific reference to both the framing of the armed forces and the rule of law in the SCAF's statement on 1 July and al-Sisi's coup-staging speech on 3 July, which delegitimised the Muslim Brotherhood from power.

Al-Sisi's claims to the rule of law were not limited to the SCAF's statement and coup-staging speech in July 2013. References to it were also found in his 2015 interview with the BBC, and the speech delivered the same year at the WEF in Davos. However, a difference between the July 2013 statements and the 2015 interview and Davos speech lies in al-Sisi's positions and political functions before and the after the March 2014 election, and the candidacy of al-Sisi to the presidency – for the first time in the history of the country – as a presumed civilian figure, rather than as a de facto military leader.[20] There is a clear memory of al-Sisi standing in civilian uniform, declaring his renouncement to run as military. But there is also a memory

Table 3.3 Frames and qualifiers of resonance

Subject	Frame	Qualifiers of resonance	Frame effects	Frame purposes
	Benford and Snow (2000)	Noakes and Johnson (2004)		
Armed forces	Strategic effect (not exact frame)	Cultural compatibility	Strategic	Distance from the Mubarak regime
Restoration of the rule of law	Diagnostic frame	Consistency and salience	No effect attached	Distance from both the NDP's and the FJP's policies

Source: based on Benford and Snow (2000) in combination with Noakes and Johnston (2005).

of him standing, again, in military uniform during the inauguration of the Suez Canal branch. This is one example of what I mean by liquidity applied to post-2011 Arab states and authorities.

Nevertheless, a set of discontinuities can be identified in the way the rule of law was framed and defended when the 2013 speech is considered in opposition to the 2015 BBC interview, and the 2015 Davos speech. This triangulated comparison enables an empirical and discursive analysis of the fluidity of the way the rule of law was employed between 2013 and 2014/2015. While both the 2015 interview and Davos speech will be considered in depth below, their importance in connection to the study of the rule of law lies in the change of the agent supposed to implement the law. A combined analysis of frames for the three speeches revealed that the protectors of the rule of law shifted quickly over the years, from the army as found in the 3 July 2013 speech as discussed above, to al-Sisi himself as found in a March 2014 speech, to the 'government' as found in 2015.

If the claimed absence of a rule of law in Egypt under previous regimes formed a diagnostic frame, the roadmap for transition set forward in the 3 July coup-staging speech corresponded to the making of a prognostic frame, alias a frame which provided a solution to the diagnosed problem (i.e. the lack of the rule of law).[21] The construction of a diagnostic-prognostic axis behind the rule of law and the roadmap for democracy served an emphatic purpose of reconnecting the authorities to society, though it did not embed its own conception of political legitimacy.

A precarious trust and the roadmap for ascendancy: defence before a sceptical society

Societal trust towards politicians is generally considered as one of the determinants with the capacity to positively interfere with the sense of civic duty during elections, thus affecting the turnout. While this view has been primarily attached to the functioning of elections in democratic systems (Grönlund and Setälä, 2004), the theory is valuable in shedding light on the results of the 2014 presidential election, in which al-Sisi won with 96.1 per cent of the vote. Societal trust contextualises both the attempt of discursive charismatisation on the one hand, and the honesty-dominated discourse on the other. Appeals to a different model of social contract that did not reflect the 'social contract of informality' (Harders, 2009: 300), the honesty of the leader, the commitment to economic recovery, and the frame of a community working for the good of the homeland, fortified the perception of civic duty and built on the determinant of relevance (Noakes and Johnston, 2005). This in turn impacted the result of the elections and in the early stages after the July coup increased the perception of al-Sisi as a socially legitimated leader before the nation. This persuasion was further strengthened in the Constitution drafted between 2013 and 2014, which enforced the centrality of the people in determining the outcome of elections and selection of leaders.[22]

Unlike the July 2013 coup staging speech, in the speech which marked his candidacy for the 2014 elections, al-Sisi abandoned the rhetoric of the army's greatness, replacing it with aspects closer to legal-rational legitimacy, at least in Weberian terms (Weber, 1978), including the authorities' safeguarding of legality and transparency in elections. This was articulated as being closely intertwined with the fairness of the electoral process and the ruler's promises to deliver on an agenda built on social justice, which in 2013–2014 occupied a prominent role in al-Sisi's power and leadership-making process. Asserting his supposed democratic credentials, al-Sisi stated that 'my nomination for office should not deny others their right and duty to run if they regard themselves as competent' (Al-Sisi's March 2014 speech).

Quantitative data confirm that in 2014 consensus-building scored 5.2 (on a 1–10 scale), compared to 4.2 in 2012 (BTI, 2012). Moreover, the perception of possible national democratisation shifted from -21.2 in 2011 to 55.1 in 2014, which was indicative of a more global hope for democratisation (AB, WAVE III). Indeed, forecasts of potential transformation towards a more inclusive system shifted from −0.9 in 2011 to 69.8 in 2014 (AB, WAVE III). Nevertheless, despite optimism, indicators of performance and commitment to democracy shifted only slightly, from 2 out of 10 in 2012, to 3 in 2014, confirming the persistence of scepticism over the effective power to govern following a more inclusivist approach to politics and party politics (which was still calculated as 3 out of 10) (BTI, 2014).

In March 2014, al-Sisi officially announced his candidacy in the presidential election scheduled in September of that year. If the SCAF statement and the coup-staging speech created a strategic effect of the diagnostic frame of the rule of law and the prognostic frame attached to the SCAF's guardianship of the roadmap, the March 2014 speech corresponded to al-Sisi's attempt at authority-making in post-2013 Egypt. A great portion of the speech was addressed to the nexus between leadership and popular will and seeking societal consensus. The seeking of consensus was attached in the speech to the remark on honesty. However, despite the novelty of the civilian nature of his candidacy, al-Sisi discursively transferred the legacy of the SCAF, and the ethics and moral duty of the army as committed to respecting the people's will, from the level of the armed forces as established in 2013 to legitimise the coup or what the SCAF framed as a counter-revolution, to the level of an emerging and much desired idea of leadership, in a more personalistic and individualistic icon.

While al-Sisi was elected in 2014 with 96.1 per cent of the vote, the turnout was merely 47.5 per cent, compared to 51.7 per cent in the 2012 elections won by Morsi (Supreme Electoral Committee, 2012). There is a shared agreement that political disengagement is exercised by the most educated as a form of dissent on the one hand, but also to avoid incurring consequent costs on the other (Croke et al., 2016).[23] Judging from the 96.1 per cent figure alone, legitimation would seem to derive from the election, indicating citizens' general acceptance of the speech's premises. However, considering the background to the political campaign, discrepancies and concerns emerge, posing questions not concerning the legitimacy of the electoral victory as such, but the ruler's policy implementation before and after the electoral victory. The argument is that there was a lack of societal consensus and significant institutional mistrust, despite references in the speech to multi-candidate elections and the will to create a democratic Egypt. Building a framing analysis of the March 2014 speech – if the reference to the rule of law as the justification and legitimation of the coup was framed as diagnostic, with the roadmap presented as an instrument and framed as prognostic – al-Sisi's candidacy for the presidency symbolised the condition for putting into effect the rule of law and the roadmap.

The 2014 candidacy constituted the construction of a motivational frame which calls for an action to change the situation (Benford and Snow, 2000).

Table 3.4 Codebook of al-Sisi's motivations for March 2014 speech

Node number	Nodes	References
1	Relations between al-Sisi and the SCAF	3
1.1	Self-framing as a military hero	4
2	Civilian politics inspired by military values	1
3	Leadership attached to people's will	4
4	Seeking social consensus for the candidacy	3
5	Honesty	3
6	Promise for multi-candidate elections	1
7	Leadership's respect for roadmap	1
8	Consideration for the Egyptian people by political authorities	2
9	National cohesion	1
10	International respect for Egypt	2
11	Economic efforts	3
12	Candidacy for a democratic Egypt	1
13	Construction of a secularised salvation narrative	7

In practical terms, the election of al-Sisi as President would have represented in the imaginary a break from the past and the means to deliver on the people's demands. But despite his speeches and overwhelming share of the vote, al-Sisi's claims of legitimation clashed with the authorities' manipulation of the law following the amendments to the penal code, thus showing the short-term achievements of the motivational frame linked to authority.

In his March 2014 speech, Abdel Fattah al-Sisi presented himself as a national hero who had saved the country from what he labelled the risk of a 'civil war' under the FJP and the Muslim Brotherhood (al-Sisi's speech, 2014). However, some of the content dating back to 2013 found reiteration in March 2014 and impacted popular consensus to a limited extent in the first months after the 2013 coup, less after the events and massacre of Raba'a al-Adawiya in August 2013, which symbolised the Muslim Brotherhood's supporters' attempt at delegitimising the July coup. The mass media campaign praising the army for its 'heroic' role played in July 2013 was

Reinventing a different political machine 85

attached to a broader political project of power-building and the redefinition of authoritarian boundaries, which became evident after al-Sisi's decision to run in the 2014 presidential campaign as a civilian candidate, extensively supported by the interference of the EAF in the media and the press soon after July 2013 (*Guardian*, 2015b; Youssef, 2015).

In July 2013, the military gained control over the government's media policy (GCDCAF, 2016). The military's control over the media was the tool through which the discursive space of 'nation' was homogenised and policed. This led to an ever greater legal and discursive conflation between the 'nation' and the EAF-state (Rasha, 2012: 117–160). The military interference in the media, it is believed, was predicated upon a larger project of reshaping the SCAF's image (Abul-Magd, 2018; Bollinger et al., 2016). Furthermore, data from the independent Freedom House show that in early 2014, interference with the internet in Egypt exponentially increased, along with the military's extensive violation of users' rights. In addition, the legal framework which closed spaces for public gatherings, and the extension of the emergency law, ultimately led to the classification of Egypt as a partially free country, with freedom of the internet rated at 60 out of 100 (Freedom House, 2014). The BTI in the same year placed Egypt amongst the 'moderate autocracies', with an overall score of 4.9 out of 10 (BTI, 2014). The country similarly scored 4.1 in 2006 (BTI, 2006).[24]

The context in which the March 2014 speech was delivered was characterised by the sharp downgrading of the rule of law and the upgrading of the military's mechanisms of repression. This suggests the strategic and temporary function played by the rule of law in 2013 and early 2014, in positively framing the rising political figure of the ruler before the army to morally and legally legitimise the coup, though not al-Sisi himself before society.

The strategic frame effects of the armed forces in the immediate post-2013 situation did not only resonate through the qualifiers of salience and cultural compatibility with societal cognition. Rather, the frame and effects additionally impacted the military leaders, who saw in al-Sisi's ultimate end (*Gesinnungsethik*, German for 'ethics of virtue') a potential and apparently charismatic leader likely to succeed in a presidential role, and emerging from the within the army's hierarchy. Thus, the ruler's reference to the rule of law indirectly attempted to gain a form of indirect consensus from within the army. The reference to the rule of law disclosed a kind of mutual political courtship between the EAF and al-Sisi, still in his position of general. This was for a specific purpose, which at this stage remained undisclosed but in 2013 initiated a process of gradual authoritarian escalation, in which Egypt moved from a moderate autocracy under the FJP to a poorly functioning highly defective autocracy soon after 2013 (BTI, 2012–2014). Comparatively,

Egypt and the rise of fluid authoritarianism

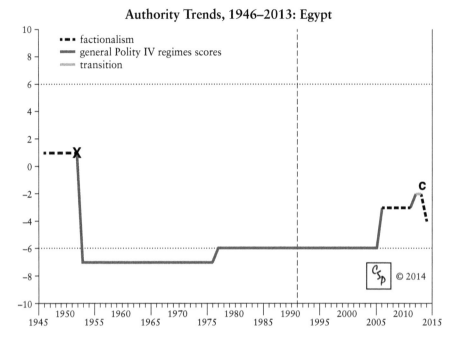

3.2 Trends in authority, 1943–2013; 2011–2013 transition to a closed anocracy.
Source: Polity IV (2013)

Polity IV tracked a change in regime in Egypt with characteristics placing the country closer to a closed anocracy or a system in which competitors are drawn from the elite. The status connotes factionalism, which according to Polity IV re-emerged after 2013 after having represented Egypt's politics between 2005 and 2010 (Polity IV, 2010; Marshall and Jaggers, 2013).

Hence, the desired effects generated at the level of discourse soon became tangible at the level of policy, and resulted in al-Sisi's escalation in terms of popular consensus – but not legitimation – in late 2013. In this regard, the BTI rated consensus-building in 2013 at 5.2, the highest score of the period (BTI, 2014), while Freedom House rated Egypt in 2012 with a 5.9 score, meaning the country was partially free (Freedom House, 2012). Comparatively, consensus-building in 2012 was calculated at 4 (BTI, 2012).

A different view of political transformation provided by Freedom House indicates how freedom in Egypt would have shifted from 5.5/7 in 2013–2016, to 6/7 in 2017–2018 (Freedom House, 2013–2018). Confirming the limits of the Weberian analysis of legal legitimacy, consensus-building (understood as approval to rule, preceding policies) proved itself to be short-lived, since it organically started dissolving as a result of the social context of repression

Reinventing a different political machine 87

that emerged in late 2013 and lasted until 2020. To understanding how the rule of law impacted, or sought to impact, the framing analysis of the post-2013 legal framework is valuable in illustrating the discontinuities and transformations between the principles of ruling by law, normative legitimacy and legitimation of the political authority. In this regard, the anti-protest law, the NGO and anti-terrorism laws, and the amendments of the penal code and the military court laws, deserve closer discussion and analysis, while considering al-Sisi's struggle for internal legitimation by referring to the rule of law. In addition, this analysis can potentially shed light on structural transformations as the implications of the post-2013 amendments to the penal code.

Al-Sisi won a resounding victory in the 2014 election, becoming President with over 96.1 per cent of the vote. While in theory this result would legitimate the victory and lend legitimacy to the ruler, in fact internal aspects complicate the nexus between elections and legitimacy in Egypt. Two factors deserve a mention. First, while it is true that al-Sisi conducted an unconventional electoral campaign, not based on the ground but instead more media-oriented, after the 2013 coup, media underwent a state consolidation and centralisation (El-Dabh, 2014). While the January 2014 Constitution contained clear protections for the media (including, under Article 71, bans on censorship and surveillance), many of the oppressive laws imposed under Mubarak remained in place (Mansour, 2015: 2). Data from Freedom House's 'Freedom on the Net' shows that state interference in internet freedom shifted from 54 out of 100 in 2011 to 60 in 2013 (0 being least free, 100 most free), impacting the view of the country as being free (Freedom House, 2013). Similarly, the number of journalists imprisoned shifted from 7 on a 0–25 scale in 2013 to 13 on a 0–25 scale in 2014, compared to 0 arrests in 2012 (Data from the Committee to Protect Journalists, 2000–2015, in Mansour, 2015). Secondly, the victory of al-Sisi also derived from state structures. Hamdeen Sabahi, the Nasserist opposition candidate of the Karama Party, struggled to fund his electoral campaign, and counted only on the support of a few parties, in opposition to al-Sisi who was supported by Hizb al-Nour and the Free Egyptian Party (El-Dabh, 2014).

The importance of the 23.57-minute BBC interview derived from the social and political context of tensions arising from the 2014 election result. The ruler's replies and discursive rhetoric in the interview with the journalist Lyse Doucet seem more self-defensive than state-persuasive, with attempts to decontextualise and divert the replies from the focus of the questions.

The promise of a more democratic and inclusive system additionally played a prominent, internationally oriented persuasive role, potentially due to the ruler's consideration of the domestic socio-political implications and restrictions on freedom deriving from the laws and presidential decrees

Table 3.5 Codebook of 2015 BBC interview with al-Sisi

Node number	Nodes	References
1	Al-Sisi's defensive argument of democracy	3
2	Anti-Terrorism Law as instrument of stability	1
3	Freedom of expression in Egypt	1
4	Human rights violations as equivalent with instability	1
5	Leader's benevolence	3
6	Leadership attached to people's will	1
7	Suggestion of future political inclusion of the Muslim Brotherhood due to their function in society	2
8	Rule of law	5
9	Acknowledgement that people asked for political change	1
10	Self-defensive arguments when journalist questions his capacity to control Egypt	1

introduced between 2014 and 2016. Thus, the emphasis on the defence of democracy and political inclusivism with regard to the function of the Muslim Brotherhood in the socio-political domain are more attached to the leader's benevolence, a positive framing of the authorities' agenda and the ruler's capacity to respond to demands for change, at least from an international diplomatic and political perspective.

However, the more neutral reference to the Brotherhood as socio-political force in the public speech, in contradiction to the harsh tones used in the past against the organisation, could possibly have been determined by the ruler's strategy of avoiding internal clashes with the EAF, while recognising the existence of direct contacts between the armed forces and the Muslim Brotherhood. The Muslim Brotherhood's ideology, influence and affiliation persists within parts of the army hierarchy.[25] Al-Sisi was evidently concerned over the possibility of disloyalty within the state forces, the basis of his regime: the *mukhabarat* (security agencies) had indeed undergone a split in 2014, between a pro-ruler military faction and anti-ruler paramilitary faction, contrasting with the strong centralisation of the *mukhabarat* under the NDP. The neutral and impartial framing of the Muslim Brotherhood, along with the encouragement of democratic hopes, sought to provide assurances about the short-term political future of Egypt and prevent possible internal defections, principally at the level of the army. This represented a strategy for maintaining internal order and creating internal cohesion at the level of the political apparatus.

The Nvivo-run quantitative analysis of word frequency indicated that the word used most frequently in the 2015 interview was 'organising' (0.53 per cent of reference coded in Nvivo), which in turn was connected to the pronoun 'we'. It is not clear whether the 'we' referred to the government coalition, that is, the NFB and the pro-Sisi party 'For the Love of Egypt', which was formed in 2014 in support of al-Sisi's candidacy, or the armed forces in light of the absolutism granted to them.[26] This view was also addressed by Springborg (2015), albeit from a different perspective. In Springborg's view, al-Sisi's regime may be described as simultaneously 'apolitical' and 'technical', referring to the anonymity of the government's close advisors and the non-existence of public political actors aside from the President himself (Springborg, 2015: 7). In terms of other thematic text frequencies, 'exceptional circumstances' and 'imprisoned dissenters' (both with frequency rated at 0.28 per cent), followed by 'confrontation' (with a frequency of 0.25 per cent) were also prominent in the 2015 interview with the BBC. Al-Sisi still attempted to portray the government as committed to democracy.[27] This rhetoric clashed with the reality on the ground: since 2014, Egypt has renewed and extended the emergency law at least 17 times, thus suppressing all forms of associations, manifestations and expression of civil society. The 2015 interview provides a case of the construction of *meta-frames*, which consist of *games* (politics) and *strategies* (tactics for winning and/or staying in power, but also strategies for emphasising personality) (Strömbäck and Dimitrova, 2006). Al-Sisi's discourse in the interview operated on at least three different levels (all quotations 2015 BBC interview with al-Sisi):

(i) *The EAF as guarantor of the security and stability of the homeland*: 'The key role of the army is to have control of Egypt';
(ii) *The full control of national challenges and will to implement democracy*: 'Democracy is about will and practice. Our will is to allow the Egyptian people freedom of expression and choice'; and
(iii) *The self-defence of claims of good perfomance in accordance with all presidential duties*: 'No, no of course it [the situation] is under full control. It is important that you know this'.

These rhetorical strategies may suggest al-Sisi's attempt to construct a complex meta-frame aimed at defending himself as a representative political leader, but ultimately defending the interests of the coalition keeping him in power. Despite this, the discursive struggle did not ultimately win social legitimation nor acceptance for al-Sisi, exposing the ruler to risks.

On another level, recalling Weber's argument that all those who exercise power have a psychological need for self-justification, and all those who are privileged must see their privilege as deserved or legitimate and not arbitrary (Weber, 1978: 549), al-Sisi's self-defensive reference to the leadership's capacity to perform, when contextualised in the 2013–2015 timeframe, suggests two levels of analysis.

Firstly, it is rooted in the authority's attempt to meet the expectations behind the reasons for his electoral victory in 2014, his image as a strong leader who can restore stability to Egypt, fight domestic terrorism, enforce law and order, ensure personal security, rebuild the failing economy which had declined since Mubarak's fall from power, and strengthen the country's damaged regional status (Utych and Kam, 2014). Secondly, however, as the BTI's data indicate, a degradation of consensus and social integration between 2014 and 2015, alongside the CPI's data, this work contends that the self-defensive approach for providing a positive image of a capable leader is linked more closely to the system imbalances indirectly emerging from al-Sisi's overemphasising of the SCAF's functions after 2013.

Authoritarian states both shape popular understandings of the 'rule of law' and construct an authoritarian 'rule by law' as positively associated with regime legitimacy (Ginsburg and Moustafa, 2008; Massoud, 2013; Rasha, 2012). In Weber's conceptualisation, legal legitimacy results when charismatic authority has undergone a process of routinisation (Weber, 1978).[28] However, the attempt of legitimating authority by legal premises in Egypt came as the *first* stage in the legitimation struggle of the post-2013 authorities, as a result of the collapsed infrastructures, that needed to be recreated in order to lay the foundations of the broad post-2013 political project. The rule of law occupied a particularly prominent position to redefine the triangularised contract between the ruler, the army and the people, and persuade the latter two parts of the desirability of this redefinition.

A precarious internal trust: a crack in the state foundation

The premises for legal legitimation of political authority soon began to justify and legitimise a set of legal provisions which created the structural-material conditions for coopting the state structures. On the surface, the government worked on reforming the Administrative Control Authority (ACA) on the premise of the authorities' response to the people's demands for ending systemic corruption, and achieving social justice, transparency and the end of military rule. Indeed, data provided by the ATP (2014) drawing upon surveys indicates that in Egypt, compared to other Arab countries, corruption counted as the main driver for the 2011 protests which toppled Mubarak. Thus, in the changeable post-2013 political conditions, the authorities struggled between reshaping the structural-material conditions in their inner circle on the one hand, whilst persuading society of their commitment to the homeland, and sincere anti-corruption efforts on the other.

The suppression of civil society's freedom corresponded with a first phase of persecution, initially directed against supporters of the FJP, capitalising on Presidential Decree No. 579 of 2014, which defined the Muslim Brotherhood as a terrorist organisation. When the Muslim Brotherhood was also designated a terrorist organisation by the Council of Ministers, thus making membership of the organisation prosecutable under Anti-Terrorism Law No. 97 of 1992 (later replaced with Law No. 94 of 2015), this persecution was placed within the jurisdiction of the intelligence and security agencies. The decree, which remains enforced, provides that any individual who promotes orally and in writing the membership or activities of the Muslim Brotherhood organisation will be punished according to the penalties established under the Anti-Terrorism Law No. 97 of 1992. The decree additionally calls for the punishment of anyone who finances or joins that organisation. Egypt's Emergency Law No. 162 of 1958 regulates the procedures followed when declaring the state of emergency, and the broader powers granted to the executive authority and its security apparatuses. The penal amendment ultimately was used as a catalyst for legitimising persecutions on normative premises.

With the amendments to Anti-Protest Law No. 70 of 2017, political repression was extended beyond the Brotherhood, and was accompanied by extensive power granted to the security and military apparatuses and military courts, to a far greater extent than the power allotted to the military under the NDP. Indeed, under the last decade of Mubarak's rule, military trials did not form part of the state's arsenal. Under Presidential Decree No. 136 of 2014, the EAF were assigned the power to assist law enforcement agencies in protecting government and public facilities. This found further enhancement ten years later in 2024. The government issued a new Law No. 3 of 2024, which amended earlier Law No. 136. The Decree No. 136 in itself was the first instrument that assigned the armed forces similar responsibilities to the police; and from a civilian perspective, the Decree created a danger of referring civilians to military trial, in violation of Article 204 of the 2014 Constitution (Council of Ministers Decree No. 579, 2014). While torturing and jailing dissenters was undeniably part of Mubarak's authoritarianism, under the NDP, military courts did not deal with civilian trials; this was rather a different development that violence underwent under the post-2013 authorities. Holding civilian trials in military courts can be considered a violation of the 1981 African Charter, which Egypt ratified under Mubarak in 1984.

Amendments to the penal code introduced between July 2013 and 2017 show how the legal instruments are twofold, strengthening securitisation similarly to the late 1980s and early 1990s, and underpinning political phobias which gradually emerged and intensified in post-2014 Egypt, concomitant with the legitimation and foundational making of a political authority. These two levels suggest imbalance regarding the armed forces as part of the *strategic effects* process (Benford and Snow, 2000), and al-Sisi as a still emerging authority but subordinate to the rule of law, presented and theorised here as a *diagnostic frame* (Benford and Snow, 2000), in turn linked to the necessity of implementing the roadmap presented by al-Sisi in 2013 as a 'prognostic frame', the tool needed to restore the rule of law. The following laws enacted between 2013 and 2017 offer an alternative understanding of how laws enacted after 2014 were indicative of a leadership struggling to emerge and to legitimate, in what may be defined as an unbalanced authoritarianism that remains in the making:

(i) Anti-Protests Law No. 107 of 2013;
(ii) Military Courts Law No. 136 of 2014 replacing Decree No. 5 of 2012 (Articles 1–8) and further extended in 2016;
(iii) Presidential Decrees No. 446 of 2015 and No. 128 of 2014;
(iv) Terrorism Law No. 94 of 2015 replacing Law No. 97 of 1992; and
(v) The NGO Law No. 70 of 2017.

Anti-Terrorism Law No. 94 of 2015 represented an escalation in authoritarianism, having expanded the definition of terrorist entities, when compared to Law No. 97 of 1992, and introduced the death penalty for perpetrators, as shown in Table 3.6. It was preceded by Law No. 107 of 2013, which regulated the suppression of freedom of dissent, importantly later extended to restrictions on academic freedom, which in Egypt have deteriorated since 2014 and when compared to other countries in the region (V-Dem Project data, 2022). While political and ideological freedom was underpinned by the specific desire of preventing mobilisation by the Muslim Brotherhood, the implementation of Law No. 107 was not a novelty in the history of Egypt, as similar crackdowns on Islamist opposition had previously and cyclically occurred (Wickham, 2012; see also Wickham, 2002). Rather, it is contended that the amendments to the anti-terrorism law and the introduction of Presidential Decrees No. 128 of 2014 and No. 446 of 2015 may be more valuable for understanding the post-2013 regime's structures. Compared to the 1 July and 3 July statements seeking to legitimise the SCAF's intervention and persuade audiences of the social commitment of the armed forces to transparency and democracy, the amendments to the penal code in the

Table 3.6 Extrapolated list of nodes for Law No. 107 of 2013 and Law No. 94 of 2015

Node number	Nodes	Sources	References
1	Terrorist entities	Law No. 94 of 2015	2
2	Nature of the perpetrator	Law No. 94 of 2015	1
3	Imprisonment for web-based terrorism	Law No. 94 of 2015	2
4	Freedom of expression connected to the securitisation of protests	Laws No. 94 of 2015 and No. 70 of 2013	4
5	Death penalty for perpetrators	Law No. 94 of 2015	3
6	Crimes	Law No. 94 of 2015	3
7	Confiscation of resources[a]	Laws No. 94 of 2015 and No. 70 of 2013	2
8	Armed forces and power	Laws No. 94 of 2015 and No. 70 of 2013	4

Notes: [a] Law No. 94 of 2015 asserted the state's right to appropriate all material and non-material assets belonging to organisations or entities labelled as terrorist.

considered laws go in the opposite direction. This suggests not only a process of authoritarian escalation but mainly of reorganisation of the state's legal foundations. Comparing Law No. 94 of 2015 to Law No. 97 of 1992 enacted under the NDP, the latter included a less all-encompassing definition of terrorist threats and crimes. Restrictions on civil liberties, and the extension of the definition of 'threats' and 'crimes', underpin a structural volatility and uncertainty in institutional infrastructure.

Juridically, Terrorism Law No. 94 of 2015 replaced Law No. 97 of 1992 enacted under the NDP. The law amended some provisions of the penal code, the criminal procedure code, the law establishing state security courts, the law on secrecy of bank accounts, and the law on weapons and ammunition, establishing a set of terrorism-related offences. The articles introduced, namely Articles 86, 86(a) and 86(b), drew criticisms for broadening the definition of 'punishable crimes' and 'terrorism' itself, which now included other forms of state-framed threats.[29]

Human Rights Watch accused the government of 'establishing an undeclared state of emergency on the pretext of protecting society and national unity' (Human Rights Watch, 2014). Claims of terrorism no longer necessarily referred to armed violence, but now included 'any threats or acts of intimidation used to disturb or interfere with peace' (Law No. 94 of 2015). The law also reinforced procedural requirements for political parties and compromised legal protection for peaceful political opposition. It additionally allowed the police to detain civilians for a period of up to eleven days without bringing any charges, under the claim that this time was necessary for investigation. As a result, the amendments to the pre-existing Anti-Terrorism Law No. 97 of 1992 ultimately legalised the persecution of non-violent political dissent, now perceived as a direct threat to the authorities.

A combined qualitative analysis of data of Law No. 107 of 2013 and Law No. 70 of 2017 on protests shows that the theme of jailing occupied a prominent weight in both texts, connected to the themes of crime, regime security and national security.

Like Terrorism Law No. 94 of 2015, which provided for imprisonment for online activity that supposedly undermined national stability, the law of association (Law No. 107 of 2013) enables jailing in violation of new legal prescriptions, including the formation or joining of trade unions, even though another law on trade unions was issued later in 2017 (Law No. 203). Trade unions in Egypt have been a complex matter since the first law regulating their activity enacted under Sadat (Abdalla, 2015; El-Shafei, 1995). Since al-Sisi took power, they have been labelled a subversive threat to national unity. Trade unions' activity became prosecutable under Laws No. 70, 84 and 203 of 2017. However, while the regime did not entirely suppress unions, unlike political parties despite Article 74 in the 2014 Constitution, they underwent a strict form of centralisation of state controls under NGO Law No. 70 of 2017.

Considering the modern history of Egypt, since the 1990s under Mubarak, Egyptian governments have been trying to tighten their grip on a growing civil society, including organisations involved in charity and development work. In 2002, Egypt issued Associations Law No. 84, which for a long period obstructed NGOs from acquiring legal status. The law also prevented NGOs, and other associations, from working independently, operating freely or receiving funds, in the name of preserving national security and public order. Under Mubarak's rules the regime used this Law to close down human rights organisations for 'security reasons'. As result of Law No. 84, human rights NGOs opted to gain legal status by registering as law firms or companies at the Ministry of Interior rather than associations or foundations, to avoid interference from the government. In 2017, Parliament approved new amendments with Law No. 70. A few years later, in 2019, Law No. 149

Table 3.7 Combined codebook for Anti-Terrorism Law No. 94 of 2015, Law No.107 of 2013 and Law No. 70 of 2017

Node /sub node number	Nodes	Sources	References
1	Terrorist entities	Law No. 94	2
2	Nature of the perpetrator	Law No. 94	1
3	Imprisonment for online terrorism	Law No. 94	2
3.1	Imprisonment for unlicensed NGOs	Law No. 94	1
4	Freedom of expression connected to the securitisation of protests	Law No. 94/ Law No. 107	4
4.1	Securing protesters' lives	Law No. 107	1
4.2	Academic freedom	Law No. 70	1
5	Death penalty for perpetrators	Law No. 94	3
6	Crimes	Law No. 94	3
6.1	Regime security	Law No. 94/ Law No. 107	2
6.2	National security, peace and unity	Law No. 94/ Law No. 107	4
6.3	Crimes committed against the economy, food and water, energy reserves or medical services[b]	Law No. 94	2
7	Confiscation of resources	Law No. 94/ Law No. 70	2
8	Armed forces and power	Law No. 70/ Law No. 107	4

Notes: [b] Law No. 94 of 2015 referred to acts which could have a negative impact on the national economy and trends. The law is vague in defining the nature of such acts.

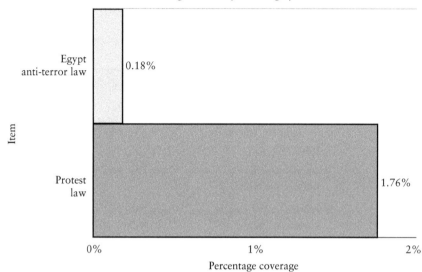

3.3 Quantitative analysis for sub-node 6.1

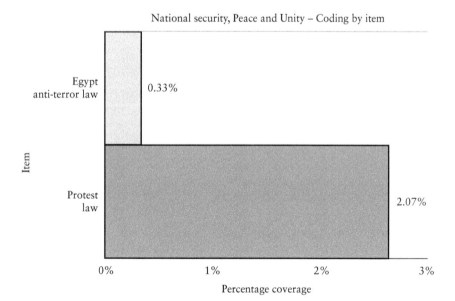

3.4 Quantitative analysis for sub-node 6.2

tightened restrictions implemented by Law No. 70 and undermined the humanitarian approach of civil society. The same type of centralisation by legal premises was followed by the legalisation of the Egyptian Federation of Independent Trade Unions and the Democratic Union of Egyptian Workers, under the control of the authorities by Law No. 213 of 2017 (ILO, 2017). Furthermore, Egypt retained a set of provisions in the penal code (in the chapter on offences by the press and others) affecting freedom of expression. The provisions currently in force criminalise insult or defamation of the President (Article 179), the judiciary, military and Parliament (Article 184), members of the prosecution and public servants (Article 185), and judges (Article 186). It follows that the legal framework introduced in 2015 and 2017 clashes with the provisions on political inclusion and freedom established in the 2014 Constitution, namely in Article 75 on the right to establish associations, and Article 65 on freedom of thought. This had the direct impact of downgrading social consensus on the one hand, and making the ruler appear pejoratively as a weak figure to the armed forces on the other.

Another aspect that needs to be considered and which marked the crack in the foundation, is the politicisation of the judiciary and the erosion of its independence. This does away with one of the primary features of a democratic state, namely the separation of powers, and the independence of the judiciary. Since the coup of 2013, the Egyptian judiciary has played a pivotal role in state repression. Most recently, in 2019, as part of a broad range of constitutional amendments, the government proposed amendments to a number of articles of the Constitution that eliminated the independence of the judiciary. The amendments enhanced the power of the presidency over the judiciary, giving the President the power to select the heads of the different judicial bodies, in addition to eliminating their budgetary independence.

The presidency's policies from 2014 to 2017 represented a form of populist propaganda, part of a struggle for the legitimisation of authority in an unbalanced equilibrium resulting from the SCAF's empowerment. The new regime aimed for the moral legitimation of its historical duty through strategic effects that resonated due to the qualifiers of compatibility and cultural salience. There nevertheless followed a fragility attached to al-Sisi's attempted construction of a legitimated leadership.

The introduction of Decree No. 128 and Terrorism Law No. 94 of 2015 represented a form of 'anti-vandalism act'. Under both legal instruments, as displayed in the codebook in Table 4.1 above, crimes against military and state infrastructure became punishable. The instruments in use in Egypt now resembled the Vandalism Act introduced in Singapore in the early 1990s. In *Authoritarian Rule of Law* (2012), the Vandalism Act was the first legislative instrument enacted in Singapore to prescribe mandatory corporal punishment. The state discourse of the time, directed at legitimising corporal punishment, was central to a particular construction of 'lawful' violence. Singapore used the Vandalism Act to demarcate certain expressions of opposition politics as criminal and anti-national, thus consolidating the state's power over the space of the 'nation', in both material and discursive terms. However, it additionally became a vehicle for state pedagogy, in that the citizen was instructed on what constituted a 'good' performance of citizenship and virtuous conduct. In Singapore, the principle of the 'rule of law' was transfigured into 'rule by law', providing legal legitimacy for state violence (Rasha, 2012).

Even though in Egypt in the 1980s crimes had been met with arbitrary punishments, such as forced eviction, Decree No. 128 and Terrorism Law No. 94 of 2015 put in place the basis through which the politics of punishment became the new attempted premise for ruling by law. However, in the context of Egypt's new political system, the attempt of ruling by law fell short at the level of political authority.

Now, both the protest and terrorism laws introduced by authorities after 2013 epitomised the content and apparent goals of the speech delivered in July 2013, which with its dominant frame of national security and protection of the homeland and diagnostic frame of military rule, attempted to purify the military ethos and convince the EAF of al-Sisi's suitability as representative and a political leader of the new government. While the first speech generated social trust, thus positively impacting consensus-building, a drop in consensus later stemmed from the contradictions and discrepancies enacted by the discrepant and non-socially accepted legal framework combined, with the intra-system imbalances. However, it would be premature to identify the system as dysfunctional in Foucauldian sense, at this stage.

Amendments to the penal code gradually increased forms of virtual domestic dissent, downgrading consensus towards al-Sisi, and impacting the authoritarian transformation of the state, though not Egyptians' identification with the state (BTI, 2014). The idea of a united Egyptian nation-state is accepted, with its millennia of history widely perceived as a source of national pride. 'We are all Egyptians' was an often-heard slogan during the 2011 revolution, an 'Egyptianness' that encompasses both Muslims and Christians. Nevertheless, over recent decades, scepticism has grown towards the state, ultimately leading to the 2011 Revolution and resistance against any policy threatening an usurpation of power in the post-Mubarak period.

Indicators have shown a rapid transformation in the Egyptian state towards authoritarianism in the first years of al-Sisi's leadership. According to the BTI, in 2014 Egypt was located among the hard-line autocracies, despite constitutionally remaining a parliamentary democracy (2014 Constitution). While Freedom House and BTI acknowledged a structural transformation, the identification as closed hard-line autocracy leaves room for debate over the nature of the system which came into being. De jure, the protection of civil rights in Egypt deteriorated under the 2014 Constitution, as the guarantee of such rights was restricted by a guiding Islamic culture. The 2014 Constitution provided for the separation of powers under the framework of a presidential system. While it gave Parliament the power to veto the appointed Prime Minister and their cabinet, this was only by a two-thirds or greater majority. Given the tradition of strong executive interference into parliamentary procedure in the past, it may also be considered important that Article 93 of the Constitution gives the President and the cabinet the right to demand that certain cabinet sessions be held in secret, without specifying whether Parliament has a right to reject this demand. In general, the Constitution leaves open many procedural questions, such as who has the power to nominate the head and judges of the Supreme Constitutional Court, and whether local governors are elected or appointed, and by whom.

Challenges at the level of the legitimation became more tangible in the shift from al-Sisi's inspiring speech of March 2014 to a more defensive approach to the external view of leader's performance found in the BBC interview a year later in 2015.

There is the agreement that legal legitimacy, at least by definition and following a linear path, results when charismatic authority has undergone a process of routinisation (Weber, 1978). However, in the context of Egypt but also in other North African countries that experienced recent transformations, the attempt of legitimating authority by legal premises came as the *first* stage in the legitimation struggle of the post-2013 authorities, as a result of the collapse of the former infrastructures, that needed to be recreated in order to lay the basis of the post-2013 political project. In this context, the reference to the rule of law occupied a particularly prominent position in the effort to redefine the social contract between the ruler, the army and the people, and persuade the latter two parts of the desirability of this redefinition.

It seems obvious that Weber's concept of legal legitimacy has limited application in the case of the post-2013 state transformation of Egypt. In detail, the weakness of Weber's legal legitimacy lies in the fact that when compliance is the result or consequence of coercion, it can be deduced that the society subject to the legal system is unlikely to accept it as legitimate. In this argument, the attempt of self-defending the legality of the political authority between 2014 and 2015 was intimately connected to the leadership's construction of a socially contested legal framework, inconsistent with the reference to the rule of law. Structural change in the political foundation, such as the absence of a regime party which was replaced by the coalition of the NFB, the strategy of giving a civilian nature to the government formed after the 2014 elections, and the downgraded consensus towards the leadership, as opposed to the social acceptance of the SCAF on historical premises, created imbalance in the political landscape, which interfered with the leadership's legitimation process. It is contended here that the reference to the rule of law under al-Sisi soon turned into the paradigm of ruling by law. Ruling on the basis of legal premises clearly shifted to a punishment-centred Weberian idea of bureaucracy and the state, indicating that the system was legitimated to a certain degree, but was nonetheless contestable, since Weber theorised the possibility of rebellion.

The legal framework that was introduced fulfilled the goal of regaining a form of institutionalised rule by the army, as opposed to the loss of control at the end of the 2000s. However, in the 2014–2018 timeframe, the rule of law set up mechanisms of societal detachment on the one hand, and fear on the other. In general, in 2013–2014 Egypt could be considered a *highly defective, poorly functioning moderate autocracy*, compared to 2012 data indicating the FJP government as a *moderate autocracy*, but with functioning flaws (BTI, 2014). By 2016 the situation had worsened, with data shifting to place Egypt among the *poorly functioning hard-line autocracies*. As for the rule of law, it underwent a repositioning, reflecting the implementation of a legal framework which ultimately aimed at reinforcing and legalising the ruler's and security authorities' powers. Quantitative data published by the BTI (2018) indicate that in 2014 the rule of law in Egypt was scored at 4.8 on a 1 (worst) to 10 (good) scale. By 2016 and 2018, this had declined to 2.6. The context of the legal framework introduced by the post-2013 authorities is both representative of a climate of draconian repression, and symptomatic of institutionalised attempts for a more flexible relationship of cooptation between the ruler and the armed forces, which seems to have favoured the latter.

With reference to the rule of law aimed at creating the premises and conditions for ruling by law after 2013, it is equally arguable that this framework may have 'legalised', but did not legitimate, the attempts towards the construction of a foundational legitimation claim. Compared with the pre-2011 context, if norms successfully provided a legal framework for consolidating the army's power in state structures, they did not fulfil the promise of al-Sisi's motivational frame of the army's leadership, a much-needed condition for the restoration of the rule of law. Rather, the boomerang effects of the amendments to the penal code interfered with the struggle for legitimation on legal premises, escalating the authoritarian nature of the system from 2013 onwards and leaving the legitimacy crisis following the coup de facto unsolved.

The implications of the penal code enacted after 2013, and the indirect sharp drop in consensus-building towards the executive in 2014 as opposed to the high support for the coup in 2013, directly created structural imbalance

Table 3.8 Transformation of authoritarianism in Egypt in the immediate post-2013 period

Timeframe	State transformation	Status of Parliament
2012–2013	Moderate autocracy	Parliamentary Assembly present
2013–2014	Highly defective, poorly functioning moderate autocracy	No Parliamentary Assembly
2015 onwards	Poorly functioning hard-line autocracy	Depoliticised Parliamentary Assembly

Source: BTI (2012–2022).

between the EAF, extensively celebrated for its historical anti-imperialist functions in the 1950s, and the emerging political figure of al-Sisi. While the difficulty of eradicating the deep military culture in Egypt should be acknowledged, amendments to the penal code, in combination with al-Sisi's announced civilian candidacy to the 2014 presidential elections, exposed al-Sisi to the risk of instability, embedded in the wave of popular dissent which emerged in 2014 due to the widespread perception of an escalation in authoritarianism and violation of international human rights law. This resulted in the reinforcement of former practices of state violence against civil society, rather than a promised empowerment and negotiation of boundaries.

Conclusions

If the reference to the rule of law initially created the popular impression of a basis of legitimacy to the SCAF's intervention into political affairs, it also left an internal vacuum that needed to be somehow filled, and structurally exposed the emerging figure of al-Sisi to risks. The triangulation of the frames into diagnostic, prognostic and motivational (Benford and Snow, 2000), served the purpose of justifying the SCAF's rehabilitation into the process of transition for safeguarding the restoration of the rule of law, the absence of which under both the NDP and the FJP was articulated as a *diagnostic frame*. The roadmap for security was presented as a *prognostic frame*, or the conditions which would have safeguarded the restoration of the rule of law. In this context, al-Sisi's candidacy, as a *motivational frame* in 2014, was presented to society as the necessary conditions for the operationalisation of the roadmap thus making the *motivational frame* inextricable from the *prognostic*. This showed signs of working perfectly, though limited to a rhetorical level.

Amended laws, and the promise of the restoration of a rule of law, created the conditions for the re-centralisation of the state under the EAF. It was hoped this would allow a regime upgrade, with the military seeing in al-Sisi a prospective leader who would had enabled the restoration of the army's role, after its marginalisation by Mubarak after 2005, which created internal divisions, weakened the NDP from within, and exposed it to social protests against corruption and demanding the end of the regime, with the historicity of the slogan *eshaab yurid isqat al-nizam* ('the people want the downfall of the regime').

The replacement of former legal articles with Laws No. 107 of 2013, No. 94 of 2015 and No. 70 of 2017, plus Presidential Decrees No. 128 and No. 579 of 2014, and No. 446 of 2015, apart from suppressing social movements, closing political platforms dating back to 2011, and suppressing civil society, thus undermining the culture of resistance, did not succeed in balancing coercion with consent (Moore, 2008). This resulted in a sharp drop in consensus towards al-Sisi, even before the escalation in the use of state force against NGOs and opposition forces, justified on the premises of 'ruling by law' and the amended penal code. This in turn, however, further compromised the ruler's position and stability in office in the eyes of the army, with dissent emerging virtually and remotely through social media, due to restrictions on public spaces and squares.

The political authority's attempt to simultaneously construct the diagnostic frame of the absence of the rule of law, the prognostic phrase of a roadmap to transition, and the motivational self-framing as a necessary political figure, represent an initial combination of strategies which would have justified the presence of the SCAF as intermediator and presented al-Sisi as a determinant variable for the restoration of the rule of law. However, the unsolved legitimation crisis, and the collapse in consensus towards authority, created structural political imbalances. While amendments to the penal codes, in particular the military court law and Law No. 107 of 2013 and No. 94 of 2015, strengthened the position of the armed forces in the state infrastructures and paved the way for a possible interference in the political domain, the amendments to the anti-terrorism law ultimately created a polarisation between state power and political representative power, with the former the domain of the SCAF, and the latter in the hands of al-Sisi, in the struggle to legitimise the 'civilian' face of the regime, classified in 2014 as a highly defective moderate autocracy (BTI, 2014).

Al-Sisi's attempt to gain legitimacy through a strategy based on the rule of law failed at that time. This initially pushed the EAF to sceptically reconsider al-Sisi's suitability for the role. The risk of seeing the collapse of the still-emerging structures of his rule, combined with the personal necessity for creating empathy with society, pushed the ruler to build a complex narrative of myths and symbols, recalling the social mythology around Nasser's legacy, at least in how rhetoric was used in connection to justifying, under social-welfarist premises, the central role enshrined by the army in the nationalisation of new developmentalist projects. I turn to this in the next chapter.

Notes

1 Author interview in London with PR1.
2 The AOI was founded in 1975 by Saudi Arabia, Egypt and the UAE with the main goal of supplying the army with training jets. The AOI is not monitored by the Central Auditing Authority, and its budget falls outside the purview of parliamentary scrutiny. The AOI is not governed by the Labour Law No. 137 of 1981 and subsequent amendments.
3 See also Mansour (2009).
4 Social perceptions of corruption (*fasad*), which grew from 32 on a scale up to 100 in 2012/13 to 36–37 in 2014/15, the highest public perception of corruption in Egypt since 2001 (Varieties of Democracy Project, 2023; see also BTI, 2013), as well as the lack of equal application of the rule of law and of social justice, drove al-Sisi to reframe his leadership in a more personalised and egocentric style. He tailored a complex narrative, according to which the entire country needed him. This attempt failed to capture the popular social imagination; in fact, behind al-Sisi's narrative exists a clear complex struggle for legitimacy combined with ambition. The story behind the struggle for legitimation is essential for providing a new understanding of the regime's structures, reconsidering the internal repositioning of domestic actors, principally the armed forces and Islamists along the taxonomy of the autocracy. This analytical perspective can reveal much about changes at the sub-system level and the connected fluidity of the autocracy, which in turn can inform the future trajectories of the country's domestic and foreign policy at international level.
5 Author interview in London with PR1
6 The ultimatum stated: The Armed Forces appeal to all parties concerned that if the demands of the people were not met within these 48 hours the Armed Forces will find themselves obliged, out of their national and historical responsibility and out of respect to the demands of the great Egyptian people, to announce a roadmap for the future along with measures that will be carried out under the Armed Forces' supervision with the participation of all the spectra and sincere national segments of society, including the young people who have been and are still the sparking plug of the great revolution, without any exclusion to any party.
7 Author interview in London with PR1.
8 Strategic effects are behavioural or attitudinal strategies concerning how a given piece of information is framed in public discourse (Tuchman, 1978).

104   *Egypt and the rise of fluid authoritarianism*

9   Unlike strategic effects, which work at the level of cognition and schemata, strategic meta-frames aim at generating a change not just in the political system, but also in the broader trajectories of state-business dynamics (Aalberg et. al, 2012; Fallows, 1997; Patterson, 1993).
10 On the Nasserian political economic model of industrialisation see Abdel-Fadil (1980).
11 In the critique of Weber's conception *Herrschaft*, Weber was not interested in whether *Herrschaft* was legitimate or illegitimate, but rather on the procedures behind it. In the legal understanding of *Herrschaft*, authority is considered impersonal (Beetham, 1991: 36; Weber, 1978).
12 The original Arabic hashtag 'al-Sisi leave' (*Irhal ya al-Sisi*) started trending on X (formerly Twitter) in 2022 on the anniversary of the military coup.
13 Diagnostic frames usually describe and explain a certain situation whilst also ascribing responsibility and blame. It is here argued that this category of frame, however, does not translate into a simplistic reading of the ruler as a hero who technocratised politics (see Storm, 2022). The hero-complex is not a single-level-built narrative, it attains to the interplay of the trilogy of frames' categories and is not society-oriented but intra-elites based.
14 'Arba'a in Arabic means four, where Rabi'a is the cardinal translation for 'fourth'.
15 It should be remembered that Egypt is a member of the United Nations and the African Union and has ratified binding international commitments to adhere to the Universal Declaration of Human Rights. In 1986 under Mubarak, Egypt was investigated for human rights violation under the African Convention against Torture.
16 On the institutionalisation vs the patrimoniality of armed forces see Bellin (2012).
17 See on this Albrecht (2012).
18 On 9 March 2012 the armed forces arrested women in a sit-in in Tahrir Square and forced those identified as unmarried to take a virginity test. In the following months the military exercise of power over civil society hit peaceful protests outside the Israeli embassy. Incidents at Mohamed Mahmoud Street also seem to lead back to armed forces involvement. See on this Fahmy (2012).
19 On COP27 and the exclusionary politics of environmentalism see Polimeno (2022).
20 On al-Sisi's announcement to run for presidency see also Haulslohner (2014).
21 Recalling Weber (1978), in legal legitimacy, norms are believed to set the bases for legitimacy, which in turn generates the idea of an authority. On this premise, authority strictly derives from norms and firmly stands on normative grounds. In turn, the incumbent derives their authority from the legal norms defining the sphere of jurisdiction of their office, and the legitimacy of legal-rational authority thus flows from the legitimacy of legal-rational norms. Just as the sphere of traditional authority is bound by traditional norms, the sphere of legal-rational authority is bound by legal norms.
22 The Constitution aimed at marking the sanctity of the social contract, stating 'The people are the source of power and safeguard their national unity that is

based on the principles of equality, justice and equal opportunities among all citizens' (Egypt government portal, 2019).
23 It is noted here, however, that the effects of education on political participation remains subjected to the contours of local geographies and illiberal systems.
24 The early 2000s connoted a period of an unprecedentedly structured social demand for democracy and demand for political and infrastructural reforms. Social activism demanding democracy developed amongst the intellectual and liberal elite in 2006 (see Ben Nefissa, 2007).
25 Author interview in London with PR1.
26 The 'For the Love of Egypt' party was formed by a merger of the Conservative Party, the Free Egyptian Party, the New Wafd Party, the Sadat Democratic Party, the Tamarrod Movement (which otherwise disappeared after 2013), the Modern Egyptian Party, the Nation's Future Party, the Conference Party, and the Reform and Renaissance Party. See also the report of the European Commission (2014).
27 A passage from the interview shows: 'Democracy is about will and practice. Our will is to allow the Egyptian people freedom of expression and choice. The will is there, is it being put into practise? Yes' (2015 BBC interview with al-Sisi).
28 Charisma, considered as the second input phase in the legitimating process, remains understood as occupying a subordinate position to norms. It therefore differs from a strictly Weberian understanding of legitimacy, in which the failures and limits embedded in charismatic authority routinise into normative legitimacy. On post-Weberian definitions of charisma and legitimacy see Tucker (1977). As Eisenstadt argues, the concept of routinisation is thus ultimately associated with non-charismatic leadership and takes the form of an appropriation of power of control and economic advantage by the followers or disciples of the leader (Eisenstadt, 1968: 58).
29 Law No. 94 of 2015 asserted the state's right to appropriate all material and non-material assets belonging to organisations or entities labelled as terrorist.

4

A hero in search of a political role: playing myths and symbols

Readapting power to structural polarisations

The conceptual connections between the army and the salvation narrative find some extensions in relation to the loyalty of al-Sisi to the SCAF and the construction of what this book calls a secular oriented salvation narrative. The construction of this narrative – a reference to salvation on the premise of economic prosperity rather than God-inspired projects – has occupied a certain emphasis from the perspective of the political authority making process since March 2014. The 2014 speech and the candidacy for the elections scheduled on the same year was largely built on the two main themes linked to economic recovery and societal struggle for achieving a form of economic and societal prosperity. Such a top-down approach in addressing the post-coup society fulfilled the purpose of triggering an initial wave of hopes in al-Sisi's longer-term project apparently promoted around the theme of the rule of law and a democratisation plan. There is one specific word that should be contextualised, and that is the word 'sacrifices' in the concluding part of the 2014 speech. It was constructed top-down in the way it attempted to reach and infuse a social diffusion of optimism regardless of the shift of the legal foundations of the country into a system based on ruling by law. However, there are substantial discrepancies that emerged in the ruler's framing of his loyalty to the SCAF, and this has to be processed as problematic given the promises of civilian leadership suggesting a process of demilitarisation. The self-identification by al-Sisi with the armed forces counted on a mutual loyalty between the EAF and al-Sisi. In addition, the self-framing as hero in initial speeches, saving Egypt from authoritarian repression on the one hand and economic devastation on the other, might have potentially protected the presidency from the emerging imbalance from his tendency of ruling by law, and the polarisation between the army as constitutive state power-holder with al-Sisi as a trustful representative figure. However, it is the self-framing as a required political figure for the country's stability and economic prosperity made the SCAF that can be considered a new though smaller, winning coalition rather than a new selectorate (de Mesquita et al., 2003). This shift in the EAF's role from one component of the state to another after 2014 begins to explain the gradual, soft and at time imperceptible variation in state structures, since in pre-2011 Egypt the SCAF under the NDP represented a de facto selectorate, or circle of elected people as alternatively referred to.

Hence, in these premises of tactical and structural transformation, the secularised salvation attempted to ensure al-Sisi's stability in office, which remains the central goal of all politicians regardless of the nature of the system (Downs, 1957; Riker, 1962). However, there is room for arguing there was also an immediate necessity to pacify the SCAF in the face of rising social dissent and mistrust towards the political authority, with support for the country's leader at its lowest since 2009 (BTI, 2014). This may have possibly exposed the political authority before the army, thus interfering with al-Sisi's envisioned long-term economic and political project.

Al-Sisi's attempt of charismatising his discourse by referring to redemption, prosperity, and a revised social contract between the ruler and the people, made his leadership after 2014 a phase of gradual collapsing support, after an initial peak in consensus reached in July 2013, which may had exposed the authority to the risk of dissent from the EAF itself. This, at least in theory, marks a cautious scepticism that the deep institutions seem to be projecting toward the figure of the leadership.[1]

The presidency's salvation narrative, built in concurrence of the 2014 presidential campaign, worked on the population's despair and hopes for redemption, through connecting economic hardship and 'sacrifices' to the promised 'prosperity and infrastructural social-economic recovery', while promising a reformist economic agenda and a civilian and social justice-oriented leadership, in fact primarily aimed at internally rebalancing power with the armed forces, after the imbalance emerged exposing the authority to greater risks by comparison and indirect confrontation with the SCAF. In this attempt, charisma plays a core function in the envisaged political project, in its employment to construct a political hero, by recalling collective historical memories and 1950s legacies, which still resonate with Egyptian society, and the memories of the nation and nationhood and in a Nasser-inspired reformist politics – though not oriented towards a reform of the industrial model, as Nasser instead did. However, al-Sisi's secularised salvation narrative was ultimately strategically reoriented towards a centralisation of religious-driven state aspirations which, in theory, left the role of Sharia in Article 2 of the 2014 Constitution constitutionally unchanged when compared to its role in Article 2 of the 2012 FJP-drafted text, and removed articles regulating the role of religion in public life, such as Article 219 and Article 4. However, Islam and Sharia in everyday life were centralised, with a

Table 4.1 Combined codebook for al-Sisi's speeches at the military graduation ceremony of July 2016 (1), commemoration of 23 July Revolution at the Military Academy in 2019 (2), and commemoration of the October War in 2019 (3)

Node number	Nodes	Sources	Coded references
1	Accusation of falling trust as attributable to terrorism	1	1
2	Al-Sisi as father of the army	2	2
3	Al-Sisi as guarantee for the nation's stability	1	3
3.1	Al-Sisi's position and army connections	0	0
4	Celebration of Free Officers	2	5
4.1	Al-Sisi's commitment to follow Naguib, Nasser and Sadat	1	1
5	Celebration of Nasser	1	2
6	Celebration of the army	3	9
6.1	Army and values	1	2
7	**Cohesion**	1	1
8	Support for democracy	1	1
9	Defence of economic revolution	2	2
9.1	Economic sacrifices and reconstruction	1	2
9.1.1	Reference to social justice	1	1
10	Revolution as drivers for political change	2	3
11	State formation	2	3
11.1	Citizenship and rights	1	1

regulation of moral conducts in public spaces and civil society in a way discrepant from al-Sisi's early promises of targeting the FJP-led state theocratisation. This further created a break with the 2014 Constitution and removed articles, but also between narrative and action on the side of the authority-making process.

After having presented himself to the international community as a determinant for stability, both for the region and domestically through the presentation of his structural and national necessity as a *motivational frame*, from 2016 to 2019 al-Sisi began delivering more public speeches, especially at the educational seminars of the Egyptian military academy in celebration of graduations and commemorations of the 23 July 1952 Revolution and the Yom Kippur or October War of 1973. There are three main selected speeches, which not only reveal how charisma worked as a second strategy of legitimation in a highly contested context that started to be determined from 2015 onwards, but also how al-Sisi began a failing Nasser-style militarisation of the state apparatus, despite the civilian nature of the new-formed government:

(i) The military graduation ceremony of July 2016;
(ii) Commemoration of the 23 July Revolution at the Military Academy in 2019; and
(iii) Commemoration of the October War in 2019.

Coding has taken place at existing nodes and primarily around the themes of the army and al-Sisi's loyalty to the EAF, which shows a magnification of the armed forces around the themes of the army and the royalty (or subordination) to the EAF. Furthermore, the generated codebook shows a celebration of the Free Officers who led the 1952 Revolution at nodes 4 and 5, and again of the SCAF in node 6. Drawing on data provided by the BTI, in the 2013–2015 period consensus was rated at 3.8 on a 0–10 scale, a decrease from 5.2 for 2011–2013. Thus, it follows that the embrace of a military rhetoric of patriotism and the recalling of the historic achievements and mythology of the armed forces in setting the modern Republic's foundations was a tactically reactive and defensive move against a social dissatisfaction with the government's performance (by this measure, al-Sisi's strategy was unsuccessful: consensus continued to decline to 3.2 in 2015–2017, and to a historic low of 2.6 in 2020) (BTI, 2015–2020).

Nevertheless, the references to the October War were not a novelty or exceptional for all presidents of Egypt. A similar reference to the conflict, in which Egypt and Syria inflicted significant damage on Israel, was made by Mubarak in an online appearance as the former President in 2019 (Maged, 2019). In this latter case, Mubarak's speech in the mid-2000s put emphasis on the army's involvement in the process of national defence, and the celebration of martyrdom was labelled as the price the army paid for national security (El-Amrani, 2005). However, from profiles closer to the Egyptian institutions it has been reported that the attempt of charismatising discourse through reference to such historical military victories has resulted in embarrassed reactions from the military elite and the broader political class.[2] From a strategic point of view, al-Sisi's 2019 speech for commemorating the October War can be split into two thematic groups, with the second part of it projected more towards emphasising the idea of democracy and promotion of democratic values. There is a political reason for this. The rapid shifts between themes in all three considered speeches was tactically tailored not so much with the goal of avoiding popular insurgencies, since Laws No. 170 of 2013 and No. 94 of 2015 had already dismantled civic freedoms

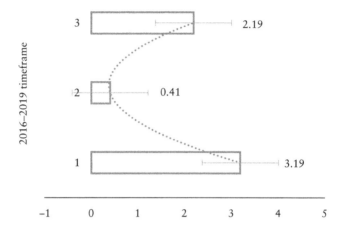

4.1 Extended quantitative analysis of the celebration of the army between 2016 and 2019 in a no-longer purely military regime. Source: the author

by legalising the suppression of most, if not all, forms of civic activism under the premises of enabling an anti-terrorism set of norms that would have protected society, though the addresser of the amended penal code remains the idea of the 'homeland' (or the institutions, to put it another way). Rather, based on a contextualised analysis of events, there is room for arguing that the shift was more externally oriented, with the goal of providing an externally and internationally acceptable face of the regime for Western actors, primarily the EU. Taking a triangularised approach to the three considered speeches (i.e. the military graduation ceremony of July 2016, the commemoration of the 23 July Revolution at the Military Academy in 2019, and the commemoration of the October War in 2019) the representation of the army and Free Officers by al-Sisi undergo some fluctuations. What emerged from the prism and the analysis set on the armed forces is that the celebration of the army was present more in the 2016 speech (percentage covered in the speech calculated in Nvivo at 3.19), with a substantial drop in 2019 (percentage calculated in Nvivo at 0.41). Instead, a further rise in the celebration of the armed forces was found in the 2019 speech.

Domestic political events that took place in 2018–2019 do not seem to account for the drop in reference to the military in 2019. What remains significant is the extensive celebration of the army in 2016, a moment which was crucial in al-Sisi's struggle for legitimation. Rather, the importance of the 2016 moment is complex as twofold, in the process of legitimation bifurcated with a military secular-oriented emphasis, and simultaneously personalisation of religion (as discussed in Chapter 5). While on the surface this bifurcation may appear discordant, in fact these two approaches worked in parallel to attempt to lessen the risks to the authorities, deriving from discontent with the worsened human rights situation. The 2016 speech at the Military Academy was specifically dictated by the need for counting on intra-army loyalty in a moment when the authority showed evident signs of intra-fragmentation, coming from determinant religious-state actors (i.e. the *Ulema* of the al-Azhar who, at some point between 2016 and 2018, opposed the political authority).

2016: a complex year

In a content-thematic analysis of the 2016 speech given at the cadets' military graduation, authorities' readapted the legitimation strategy which no longer magnified the army or the process of militarisation of the state, but rather inserted the idea of national stability as dependent on the preservation of (al-Sisi) authority, although this was still subordinated to the achievements of the EAF. The quest for credibility in the 2016 speech was twofold in the way it emphasised the EAF, but also attempted to build a clear narrative of self-perpetuation and much needed authority-making claim. While in 2016 the Fragile States Index (FSI) located Egypt on a level of alert for a second time after 2014 (FSI, 2016), the BTI rated governance performance at 4.9 out of 10 (0 poor, 10 strong), compared to 5 in 2014 (BTI, 2014, 2016). Data on governance performance continued to drop, from 4.9 in 2016 to 4.4 (out of 10) in 2018. This seems to suggest that over these years, in combination with the implementation of certain policies and economic manouvres, al-Sisi in fact ended up challenging a process of internal systemic difficulties while somehow stable in office.

The extensive reference to and celebration of the army in al-Sisi's discourse corresponded to a *tactical meta-frame*, which is a more complex category of frames (Dombos et al., 2009). Amendments to the military court law previously introduced in 2015 initially enabled the army to intervene in political affairs, contradicting the promises of the apolitical role of the army made in al-Sisi's July 2013 speech. A series of decrees from 2016 onwards elevated the army to a 'protected' position within the state infrastructure. To expand the EAF's influence and role in state institutions, Article 200 in the 2014 Constitution was further amended and, along with the definition of the military as the guardian of the state, the 'protection of the constitution, democracy, the state and its secular nature, and personal freedoms' were added to the army's roles. The 2014 constitutional amendments introduced what could be considered a new concept of sovereignty, where power moved from elected representatives to the military as the de facto guardian of the state.

Several years later in July 2018, the Egyptian Parliament, controlled by Mustaqbal al-Watan (the NFB), ratified Law No. 35 of 1979, first adopted by Sadat, on 'Treatment of Certain Senior Officers of the Armed Forces'. The use of Sadat's law by al-Sisi could be defined as an attempt to win the obedience of the armed forces. Article 1 states that the President can call upon senior army officers to serve in the military for life, even if they have already resigned their military posts. This effectively bars potential contenders within the top military brass from running for office and challenging al-Sisi. Article 5 forbids any investigation of these officers for acts committed in their official capacity between 3 July 2013 and 10 January 2016, unless permitted by the SCAF. Furthermore, Article 6 provides diplomatic immunity to these officers when travelling abroad, in an attempt to shield them from possible international prosecution. The law thus provided immunity to senior members of the military, while attempting to shield al-Sisi from their possible political ambitions. However, it is worth noting that laws protecting senior military leaders were previously enshrined in the Egyptian Constitution prior to 2018. Article 204 of the 2014 Constitution also granted higher levels of autonomy to the armed forces, though this should not be simplified as a signal of 'military continuation' on the one hand, or 'upgraded militarism' on the other (see Mandour, 2017, 2019).

In fact, the core complexities of the regime that gradually emerged after 2013, here captured as a moment of fluid transition in the cyclical phases of systems, are more sub-structurally oriented than descriptively captured under the simplicism of instability or restoration taking journalistic flairs.

Since 2015 observers have begun to theorise a 'Nasserisation' of al-Sisi's discourse and personalisation of charisma. Others asserted a 'Mubarakism without Mubarak', which would have started emerging since the army's overthrow of the NDP in 2011 (Goldberg, 2011). This indicates the persistence of some confusion over the political system(s) which emerged after 2011 and 2013 and still continue today. The armed forces' control of the mass media, and the resulting press freedom, facilitated the recall of Nasser's domestic politics, as the past leader had controlled the press with the aim of preventing the rise of intra-ASU and intra-army challengers (Crabbs, 1975; Diong, 2015; el Issawi, 2014).[3]

The Nasserisation of al-Sisi's personalised charisma, which contrasts with Weber's understanding of charismatic authority in *Economy and Society* (1978), also aimed to recapture the popular imagination of a much-desired strong leader, recalling al-Sisi's popularity in July 2013 when he was referred to as the *zai'im* (great leader). This view allowed him to win the popular vote in *Time* magazine, which defined the incumbent as the strongman of the world. This was somewhat similar to the visibility *Time* offered decades before to Nasser, but different from *Time*'s view of Sadat as 'man of the year', and Morsi as 'the most important man in the Middle East', limiting its view of the FJP's impact on the region.[4]

The SCAF's successful coup exercised a magnetic international pull, which ultimately had implications at a diplomatic level and in the external and international view of al-Sisi as an interlocutor for Western interests and priorities in the Mediterranean, primarily migration, military cooperation in the field of security with the EU and member states, and infrastructures. Recently, and with a certain emphasis since 2019, Egypt started to be reconsidered as a potential green energy partner and gas supplier due to Leviathan and Zohr offshore gas fields discovered in 2015 by the Italian oil and gas company ENI, but operated by Belayim Petroleum Company through a 50:50 joint venture between ENI and the state-owned Egyptian General Petroleum Corporation. Like Nasser, al-Sisi has been defined as striving for a comprehensive modernisation of Egypt's economic structures, and for taking an uncompromising attitude towards the Muslim Brotherhood. However, it should be noted that, historically, Nasser's sweeping crackdown on the Muslim Brotherhood in 1965 led to a period of renewed strategic debate within the organisation itself and between the dogmatic 'old guard' and the pragmatic 'conservatives' (Obaid, 2017; see also Joya, 2020: 166). On the contrary, the repression of the Muslim Brotherhood initiated in 2013 in fact gave the impression of being partly smoothed over in 2015; during al-Sisi's interview with the BBC, he defined the Muslim Brotherhood as part of Egypt's cultural fabric. The ruler's strategic moderation towards the Muslim Brotherhood derived from his need to consolidate a form of loyalty towards himself, especially from SCAF members sympathetic to the Brotherhood prior to the formation of its institutionalised offshoot, the FJP.

It follows that al-Sisi's 2015 moderation towards the Muslim Brotherhood discloses a continued existence of a pro-Brotherhood trend within the armed forces, and this despite the ban imposed on the organisation, which forced many to flee the country while other high-ranking members are jailed.[5]

The myth-symbol complex of national leadership

When macro structures in Nasser's Egypt and al-Sisi's Egypt are compared, it becomes evident that the two rulers' actions are set in completely different world orders, and stand on different premises regarding how they employed the idea of nations, nationalism and how symbols, memories and myths around the making of a national leadership and nationalist feeling of togetherness are being re-employed, albeit under different instrumentalisations and aimed at creating different truths about the nation and the idea of a greatness. Here Smith's perennialist approach to nationalism, defined as a modern expression of premodern ethnic identity which is rooted in a remote past (golden age) (Smith, 1998: 159–169), may be subjected to criticisms for being confined to a form of interpretative immobilism when applied to the transformation of Egypt in post-2013 setting. If post-2013 political authorities' nationalist model could be considered on theoretical premises closer to Ernest Gellner's nationalism, since more rooted into industrial and functionalist determinants, this work reiterates that there is not a cut off schism in the interpretation of nationalism in Egypt, neither from a Smithian nor Gellnerian perspective. In both cases nationalism finds a form of mixed application to the neomodernist and postindustrial idea of the nation, which in Egypt does not attain to discursive or ideological end goals but underpins a communality of interests related to the material field and mainly shared by the elite, rather than the ruler. Despite criticisms Smith's perennialism and Gellner's functionalist nationalisms can coexist in the transition period approached through Baumanian-Gramscian reinterpretative lenses (Gellner, 1983; Smith, 2009).[6] After 2013, the incumbent embarked on the celebration of 'spectacular' events and projects. A few years later, in 2021 the country hosted the 'Pharoahs Golden Parade' in central Cairo, which spectacularised pharaonic treasures being transferred on well dressed up military tanks from the old Egyptian Museum in Tahrir to the Grand Egyptian Museum on the Giza Plateau, adjacent to the Pyramids, as part of the new project of urban redevelopment opened in 2019. Here the recurrent use of symbols of ancient identity, mainly Pharaonic identity, remains of a high importance when political strategy and identity politics are mixed up through the playing of myths and symbols.[7]

Myths and symbols must be relatively stable and symbols must be extensive, though delimited in scope. Symbols affirm cultural resources capable of shaping collective responses to socio-economic and political circumstances, though they do not collapse the meaning borne by specific symbols in specific circumstances (Leoussi and Grosby, 2007: 7). Myths, instead, normally provide the collective with justification for distinctiveness, and while they lack any empirical verification, they still shape the moral conduct (Leoussi and Grosby, 2007: 7; see also Weber, 1978). Here ethnosymbolism tends to unify myths, memories and symbols in the process of marking a continuity between the premodern and modern idea of nations (Smith, 1986). While myths, memories and symbols are a complex set of elements they act as a chronicle of an ethnic past. In the context of non-ethnic nations, or nations in which the ideas of belonging and togetherness are not necessarily a problematisation of ethnic divide, an ethnosymbolism complex serves the purpose of elaborating, reinterpreting and evoking memories of a golden age while coping with problems of the modern era (Smith, 1991).

The power of nationalism in the making of nations does not reside merely in its political structure and principles, but above all in the large patrimony made of symbols and myths that the intellectual elites have often used, or invented, to confer a mass dimension onto political nationalism. What matters in the idea of myths is that they are, at some level, believed to belong to the realm of truth, which in turn is interconnected with a socially constructed post-truths culture, and no longer confined to abstract or mental productions. However, myths and symbols play differently in the process of a national identity and self-identification in the nation. Myths are a belief held in common by a large group of people that give events and actions a particular meaning (Edelman, 1971: 14). Symbols instead are emotionally charged shorthand reference to a myth (Kaufman, 2001: 16). Thus, the myth-symbol complex is the ethnic root for representing a nation and the process of reaching back into the past in order to provide the bases for the nation and the essential myths of common descent, homeland and golden age – a shared history, destiny and territory (Ghitens-Mazer, 2005: 28).

The political phenomenology of nationalism, at least in its original idea and project, is attached to a sense of identity and common purpose found in myths, symbols and collective memories from the past that, in some cases, stem from an ethnic past, and are mobilised in order to gain the congruence of the nation and the state, while simultaneously being a process which unifies individuals under the great banner of the nation (Ghitens-Mazer, 2005: 29).

The parallelism between Nasser and al-Sisi in the idea of the hero-complex can be found at two distinct levels: the level of the discourse and the level of myths, symbols and memories. In his 1955 work, *The Philosophy of the Revolution*, Nasser stated that there had been a role in Egypt for a hero, whilst promoting the secularised *da'wa* (proselytisation) of Pan-Arabism (Teti, 2004; Nasser, 1955). However, the system created by Nasser, unlike that of al-Sisi, was ideologically designed as a tool for decolonisation (Catusse, 2006: 218).

Since we know that discourses in politics are expected to generate a change at the level of policies (Newmann, 2004; van Dijk, 2001), al-Sisi's reference to updating the social contract proved itself to be politically fictitious in the way it disclosed a bureaucratised constituency of state institutions. Regardless of the ideology he represented, Nasser had the ability to influence through inspiring speeches. This basic quality is missing in al-Sisi's discursive capacities, which over the years have exposed the army itself to embarrassment, thus creating the potential for internal military disloyalties, possibly explaining the change in the heads of the military in 2016–2017, apart from the need of creating intra-family networks through which to exercise control, a practice of personalism (see also Geddes, 1999b).

Rather than a Nasserisation of post-2013 politics, the regime presented by al-Sisi has been identified as lying closer to a totalitarian structure[8] (see also Chehabi and Linz, 1998; Linz, 1975). According to my interviewee, 'For some analysts, al-Sisi wants to draw close to Nasser and be seen as a Nasser, and some constituencies in Egypt want to be able to portray him as a Nasser, because ultimately that can be used to legitimate their own broad agenda'.[9] These references to Egypt's historic national hero possibly link to the army's support of al-Sisi as the architect of structural transformation, though not political reform, in the 'Sisisation' of developmentalism. Thus, the significance of al-Sisi's image as a new Nasser lies in the eyes of the beholders and in the nature of al-Sisi's agenda and goals.

The incumbent regime shares features with Nasser, as he has responded to certain challenges in similar ways.[10] Nasser's model of state developmentalism also redefined the notion of politics in Egypt, as al-Sisi has attempted to do. The gradual dissolution of all political parties under Nasser, followed by the foundation of the ASU and voluntary associations, was not only a method for containing opposition and thus preventing intra-state and intra-army challengers. It rather related to a vision of politics as a divisive threat to the nation, to be replaced by a direct relationship between the leader and the nation, a corporatist and functional reorganisation of society, and the active role of the army in national protection and social modernisation (see Bianchi, 1989; Fahmy, 2002; Waterbury, 1983). The Parliamentary Assembly after 2014 instead eventually became subordinated to the developmentalist, neoliberal state model of the NFB, and was representative of the ratification, without debate and consultancy, of al-Sisi's decrees. While under al-Sisi the Parliamentary Assembly underwent a technocratisation and depoliticisation in which decisions were exclusively taken by al-Sisi and remained undebated in the parliamentary assembly. Nasser's idea and function of the Parliament was made up of the bourgeoisie, with a distributive function towards the population (Ben Nefissa and Arafat, 2005). Stepping away from works that build up a historical continuum between Nasser and al-Sisi (Yefet and Lavie, 2021), this could be acknowledged as perhaps the most significant difference between Nasser and al-Sisi in terms of the social basis of their regimes, the absence of reliance on the Egyptian bourgeoisie in the case of the latter.[11]

The existence of a deep-rooted military culture is at the core of understanding why rulers respond to social economic challenges with draconian, militarised political tools. This is the only shared similarity between al-Sisi and Nasser. Beyond this point, they present substantial differences. Expanding on the dissimilarities, at least two main discontinuities can be acknowledged:

(i) al-Sisi's lack of an ideological manifesto and thus the experience of a crisis in appealing to the nation and its identity; and (ii) differences in regional political challenges al-Sisi faces when compared to the 1950s.

From the discussion I had with interviewee SC2, al-Sisi's failure to inspire by proposing an original and reformist socio-political agenda, in addition to an alleged pre-existing embarrassment of some figures within the SCAF at al-Sisi's lack of charismatic discourse, made the armed forces more aware of the ruler's incapacity to perform as leader.[12] However, the post-2013 legal foundations discussed above had further subordinated the top brass to the President, who could quell the political ambitions of top generals simply by calling on them to serve for life within the military. According to another interviewee, this strengthened the President's grip on the military, and incentivised them to remain loyal to him in order to reap the individual benefits. By 2016, this had resulted in an ambiguous balance of power, with transformations in the relationship between political authority and the armed forces.

Nasser's motivation to construct a new national identity for Egypt was driven by several factors that cannot find a place in post-2013 authorities' political agenda. Arab nationalism evidenced considerable conceptual elasticity both historically and spatially (Barnett, 1995). Institutions were taken as consequential insofar as they have degree of permanence and shape the behaviour, if not the identities, of actors (Barnett, 1995: 485). Nasser's personal connection with his national audience became stronger due to the new identity which installed him as a father figure representing the nation's political identity. By participating in the construction of a new national identity, which had struggled to emerge between the 1920s and 1940s (Arif, 2017), Nasser generated a public dependency based on his personal emotions and his political – charismatic –actions at both domestic and foreign policy level, in a country and regional order quite different from that which emerged after 2011, in which al-Sisi was limited to a formula of diplomatic negotiation and military abstention in regional affairs, thus deciding not to involve the armed forces in regional conflicts on the ground. A notable example is al-Sisi's attempt at framing himself as regional mediator in the Libyan Civil War and international talks. Despite a number of statements announcing the possibility of the involvement of the Egyptian army in 2020, he never seriously considered a military intervention in Libya. In this, al-Sisi profoundly differs from Nasser who, in a significantly different regional order, involved Egypt in the North Yemen Civil War in the 1960s.

Nasser instituted what for some was a 'revolution from above', in which he brought about meaningful change which had very significant social impact in the 1960s, though it has been noted that this happened not necessarily with total clarity of ideology or belief.[13] Nasser had some desire to change class structure, which in addition would have the political purpose of creating legitimacy for the regime and winning social allies. He pursued radical economic policies, which had a profound impact on Egyptian society, ranging from land reforms, to Egyptianisation, expropriation and socialisation or redistribution. From a comparative point of view, al-Sisi has never shown such a vision for reshaping society or winning class allies, although he has attempted to exclude political parties, as Nasser did. This perhaps is the only variable on which both come together, in some respect. This form of response to the idea of political challenges suggests some similarities between Nasser and al-Sisi, but at the same time there are significant differences in how myths, symbols and memories have been differently employed and deployed behind the idea of a nationalist identity.

Most of al-Sisi's social interventions tend to increase his power in a limited sense, while prioritising personal political goals.[14] While a more independent view on the Nasserisation of al-Sisi's leadership highlighted the differences in terms of the leaders' political projects and their economic consequences, a more internal view to Egyptian politics disclosed a comparatively ineffective employment of the standard conception of charisma.[15] At the core of a rising intra-SCAF disappointment and embarrassment towards the authority in 2016–2017 was the emptiness of political speeches and the poor use of the Arabic language in itself.

Regarding the shift from the secular narrative of salvation employed by political authorities to the valorisation of the army along different lines and intensity, two novelties emerged: first, the celebration of the army's function in 2015 and 2016 moved from the level of politics and state construction to that of the economy. Secondly, the contribution of the army to the economic reconstruction of the country tactically served the double purpose of providing a sort of guarantee for the army regarding al-Sisi's leadership capacity, and the capacity of the latter in winning support from society by recalling memories of the social function of the army in the 1960s, when the NSPO, an offshoot of the military industry complex, was initially registered to meet civilian market demands (Sayigh, 2019), in a historical moment in which regional and domestic politics were oriented towards a form of socialist populism.

Middle East populism in the 1960s represented a variation of nationalism combined with socialist ideologies and, partially, Islam. Against this background, Nasser elevated himself to the role of saviour and protector of the people (Abdel-Fadil, 1980: 109). With the intellectual honesty and a more radical critical approach in rupturing with trends and traditions arguing for a certain continuum in the model of aspiration, one element of discrepancy between Nasser and al-Sisi relates to the sphere of nationalism and populism. Nasser's secular nationalism elevated itself above religion and clerical authority, to the point that the Islamic establishment was allowed no space for mobilising opposition against him (Al-Awadi, 2014). By contrast, since the election in 2014, al-Sisi has not attempted to gain a comparable position of a political, nationalist 'prophet'. From a rhetorical perspective, the power of Nasser's rhetoric was rooted in an ideological programme in which legitimacy was attached to state formation, and citizens' material interests were protected by the state (Arif, 2017; Barnett, 1995). These components elevated societal trust in the army and thus in the militarised leadership.

However, the decline in Arab nationalism in the broader Middle East made Nasserism closer to a utopian project, and resulted in a decrease in the importance of ideologies in the construction of political legitimacy. This shift became particularly tangible under Mubarak, when the rise of a liberalised military nationalism in the 1990s no longer represented a proper ideology, but a de facto finished political programme of the militarisation of the economic apparatus in a neoliberal order. The proposed hereditary succession of Gamal Mubarak coincided with the creation of a new civilian business elite, which ultimately threatened the military's economic empire created at the end of the 1990s. This finally led to clashes within the regime, and the army's acquiescence in the 2011 protests by not taking action against protesters, resulting in the deposition of Hosni Mubarak.

Concerning populism and popular autocrats, much of the existing literature revolved around the question of whether populism can be understood as inclusive or exclusionary (Canovan, 1984; Collier, 2001; Laclau, 1977) and what constitutes popular autocrats (Dimitrov, 2009). Conceptions of populism assert the possibility of its alignment with different fully-fledged ideologies, such as socialism, conservatism or even neoliberalism. The phenomenology of populism is largely defined as manipulative, irrational, anti-intellectual and easily accessible across sectors of society, including politically uneducated segments. Definitions of populism as predominantly exclusionary misconceive its inclusive typology, providing the chance for social subjects to become political, in opposition to a dominant bloc. Inclusive populism builds on political memories, but also ideas such as traditional religion, civilisational identity and nostalgia (Ritchie, 2019). Populist ideologies tend to glorify the common man and advocate the superiority of the masses over the elite (Canovan, 1981; de La Torre, 2019; Postel, 2007). On the contrary, exclusionary populism includes movements expressing reactions to social groups perceived as threats to identity or subjectivity. Furthermore, post-populism is approached as being both rupture and continuity with the populist tradition. Congruently with theories on populism and its irrational connotations, the combination of populist rhetoric with (post-populist) neoliberal policies, may create a basis of support among the lower classes for the leaders who combine elements of populism and post-populism.

To explore the issue empirically in the case of Egypt, Nasser operated a welfarist system, thus presenting himself as responsive to the demands for reforms and the rule of law (Dekmejian, 1972). In addition, after the mid-1960s, Nasser's attempt to gain a form of legitimacy abandoned the strategy of charisma, due to the limitations it presented domestically (Weber, 1978), and supplanted it with a more rational form, which relaxed the status of syndicates and suppression of different views which contradicted the regime's ideology. There was thus a certain degree of complexity within the Nasserian model of regime legitimacy, a characterisation of which as the politicisation of charisma would be a misleading simplification. Middle East populism in the 1960s can be considered as a variation of nationalism combined with socialist ideologies and, partially, Islam. Against this background, Nasser elevated himself to the role of saviour and protector of the people. As Abdel-Fadil writes, 'Nasser liked to look on himself as the representative of labouring masses and the people at large' (Abdel-Fadil, 1980: 109).

Al-Sisi also attempted to do this in 2014–2015, when benefitting from the initial popular trust towards him from a society disappointed by the FJP's poor economic performance and unable to address societal demands. However, al-Sisi has proposed a populist narrative in a neoliberalised and exclusive system. As World Bank and IMF loans have become contingent on the recipient countries' implementation of SAPs, as was seen under Mubarak's tenure, many countries in the developing world have privatised their economies, and dismantled state-owned enterprises, subsidies, and much of the social safety network often associated with classical populist economic models. Globalisation and the pervasiveness of free enterprise and market economies have made the classical populist rhetoric of economic autonomy and nationalist self-sufficiency meaningless (Weyland, 2001).

There could exist an agreement on some sort of continuum between Nasser and al-Sisi, based on the similarity of the positive emotions appealed to in the leaders' rhetoric, the specific challenges faced by the leaders, and – to an extent – the authoritarian styles of their periods of rule. In fact, this comparison is structurally and macro-systemically unsustainable, in the context of a country now subject to the logic of a strictly neoliberalised market. The rupture from populism in al-Sisi's discursive narrative results in the exclusionary character of his neoliberal economic project. Al-Sisi's appeal to subordinated classes' persistent loyalty to a revived populist identity through which they constitute themselves as political subject, demonstrates instead the post-populist element of his strategy. Al-Sisi thus demonstrates qualifiers that place him between a populist and a neoliberal post-populist logic. However, defining the system as a militarised technocratic populism – also taking intraregional comparative lenses – displays major inaccuracies (see Storm, 2022). At the core of the definition of Egypt's government as a technocratic populism – similar to Erdogan's Turkey and Saied's Tunisia – lies the argument of an erosion of core institutions legitimised as necessary to save the 'national project' (Storm, 2022: 4–5). This line of argument indirectly suggests and argues for a same-level intraregional comparative approach. The problem here is both structural and analytical. Structurally, speaking of 'erosion' (Storm, 2022) equals acknowledging the fact that before al-Sisi took power, institutions were 'legitimised', while in fact they were clearly not. Analytically, reducing institutional legitimation in Egypt to an erosive discourse simplifies the micro-structural intra-sophistication it deserves, as this book considers. The legitimacy of institutions was not eroded during 2012–2014, if this is what Storm meant. Rather, consensus-building, broadly speaking, identified with the forging of a legitimation process based on third parties' data (BTI, 2012–2014); comparing them with 2006–2013, governance index scored discontinuously, with a historical peak in 2014, followed a more gradual fall lasting from 2016–2022 (BTI, 2006–2022). Likewise, arguing that the process of erosion initiated under al-Sisi and protracted in the 2013–2022 timespan neglects major intra-determinants that attain to the study of the forging of a legitimation claim in a country that, as here argued, presents infrastructural and intra-societal aspects that gradually suggest a move towards a form of fluidity which in turn determined the sub-transformation in the regime's taxonomy and thus the an authoritarian rupture. Secondly, the vilification of opponents as 'foreign agents and enemies of the people' (Storm, 2022: 5) in the specific context of Egypt did not take place at the level of the society but at the level of the new idea of the nations that happened to emerge through the manipulation of myths, memories and symbols (Smith, 1991). Thirdly, the technocratic aspects of regimes that happened to be framed as populist did not aim to stifle the opposition; at least in Egypt amendments to the penal code normatively regulated this political reality. Rather, the technocratisation of politics in the parliamentary assembly (as the research associated in this work demonstrates in Chapters 4 and 6), marked the internal urgency by the executive to avoid political discussions around political and economic reforms which would have in turn further weakened the existing fragility of al-Sisi before the armed forces in a structural context which was being pushed away from an 'old-fashioned' militarised model.

However, in order to be maintained, both populist and post-populist logics require, next to the host-ideology, societal roots and the existence of a civil society. The idea of post-populism in post-2014 Egypt gradually emerged as an element triggered and diffused by the pro-ruler bloc, but in absence of a de facto civil society. Since the 2013 coup thousands of civilians have been imprisoned for their political or ideological beliefs and views, inclusive of children tortured and considered political opponents.[16] While this policy brings severe humanitarian consequences, it can act a potential driver for radicalisation, where the latter is not captured as a cause but as a direct effect. These policies have gradually suppressed all forms of civic activism, paralysing civil society. Thus, the idea of the hero and the creation of a myth-symbol complex behind neo-nationalism in the context of al-Sisi presents some discrepancies, different from the case of Nasser, in which civil society continued to exist in one way or another despite repression.

Military and economic rehabilitation in a no-longer military regime

After the 2013 coup, Egypt entered a process of restoration of military rule, particularly notable at the level of the military-industrial complex, as it was involved in a plethora of national projects linked to the redevelopment of infrastructure.

The remilitarisation of the state should not come as a surprise when events in the second half of the twentieth century are considered. The disempowerment of the traditional elite class between the 1950s and 1970s secured the military's long-term sway over land use. Since 1979, the peace agreement with Israel had secured US aid on the one hand, and made possible industrial expansionism of the military on the other (Marshall, 2015). Moreover, the second half of the 1970s witnessed the creation of the NSPO in 1979, while in 1975 the AOI was formed. The AOI was initially a joint venture between Egypt, Saudi Arabia, the United Arab Emirates and Qatar; Saudi Arabia and the UAE abandoned the venture in 1979 when Sadat made peace with Israel. Today the organisation is entirely owned by Egypt, with a leading role for the military: the conglomerates are under the control of the Ministry of Defence. Both the NSPO and the AOI were involved in the production of civilian goods at cheap prices, and as such the military-industrial complex was framed as a contributor to the civilian society and the economy. As Joya recalls, 'during the economic crisis escalated in Egypt in 2008 which increased discontent with the Nazif government, Mubarak called upon the army to increase bread production and distribute it to the poor' (Joya, 2020: 135). Nevertheless, having undergone a political-economic marginalisation under Mubarak and a fall in military expenditure in the 1990s and 2000s, in 2011 the army sought to regain lost influence by taking the lead in the political transition and in the civilian sector.

This change in sources of investments, projected more towards the civilian sectors and infrastructures, partially explains why in Egypt military expenditure from 2016 until 2020, when compared to the broader Mediterranean region, decreased to reach a historical minimum – data which are rated

A hero in search of a political role 123

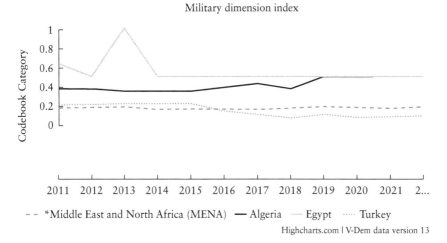

4.2 Military expenditure of % GDP in the broader Mediterranean region and the EU. Source: Stockholm International Peace Research Institute (SIPRI). Combined aggregated data obtained by the author

even below the score of the EU's military expenditure. However, arguing that the coup set up a process of demilitarisation of the state infrastructures is misleading. What the coup reinitiated is a process of neoliberal militarisation, also justified on national and moral premises, in a political system that underwent a gradual transformation at the sub-systemic level.

There is no available data on the army's precise budget; Article 2003 of the 2014 constitutional amendments did not grant transparency in that regard. This excluded the military budget from review by civilian entities and in combination with a parliamentary decision in 2021, accessing military data has become illegal in the country. The National Defence Council was additionally subject to reconsideration in the new Constitution drafted by al-Sisi, with the effect that the army, unlike under the NDP, could now be involved in national policy matters. Under al-Sisi, the army occupies appointments among Egypt's body of provincial governors, increased from 26 to 27, while the remaining 24 civilian governors share power with generals who serve as deputy governors (Marshall, 2015: 18).

Resources directed to the army have increased since 2014, peaking in 2015 (and then decreasing in 2018) compared to the state of affairs under Mubarak and Morsi. Between 2010 and 2019, Egypt's arms acquisitions also increased significantly compared with the previous decade, although Egypt's official figures showed an overall decrease in real-terms in its military budget. From around 3.1 billion USD in 2009–2010 to 3.2 billion in 2012, the figure reached 3.3 billion in 2014 and 3.5 billion in 2015.

These important facts have sparked debates about Egypt's return to a military state, but this claim remains subject to discrepancies and flawed attempts to draw parallels with the pre-2011 situation. There are, in effect, some features that reminiscent of the structure of Egypt post-2013 as a militarised system (Adly, 2016; Albrecht, 2005; Blaydes, 2006, 2008; de Mesquita et al., 2003; Geddes, 1999b; Geddes and Wright, 2014; Hadenius and Teorell, 2007; Levitsky and Way, 2002). Nevertheless, by expanding on the idea of the selectorate as a core theory, in combination with the EAF's empowerment in the business sector under al-Sisi, discrepancies emerge in relation to the theory of a purist remilitarisation of Egypt's state structures, which still today remains the most debated aspect. Similarly, attempts to establish a parallel with the Algerian militarised model additionally neglect the function of the military in the latter, as being highly involved in the political domain. Returning to the comparisons between al-Sisi and Nasser, both can be considered as having based their respective powers on the military, and at a later stage, on the consolidation of a military intelligence (*Idarat al-Mukhabarat al-Harbiya wa al-Istitla*).

However, unlike Nasser, under al-Sisi the consolidation of the military intelligence was soon followed by a fragmentation within the para-military sector. In Nasser's single-party system, the militarisation of the institution (*al-musasaa al-ashkariya*) served as a coup-proof tool to prevent the rise of a second strongman from within the army (Kandil, 2012; Quinlivan, 1999). However, Nasser never resigned from a military career, as al-Sisi did in March 2014 in order to run as a civilian candidate in the presidential elections; further, in the case of Nasser, the presence of Leninist-inspired institutions and structures made Egypt a more socialist country regarding wealth redistribution, eliminating the landowning elite and nationalising many businesses and services (Joya, 2020). These permitted Nasser to diffuse and coopt the political opposition (Cook, 2007: 76; Kandil, 2016).

A further difference between Nasser and al-Sisi relates to the function of the surveillance apparatuses and the ideological discursive reference to terrorism, as found in both rulers' discourses. The differences are evident when the themes of political violence and terrorism are historically contextualised. Indeed, attempts to establish a conceptual strategic continuum between Nasser and al-Sisi on the theme of terrorism are historically and socially inaccurate. While the concept of 'terrorism' emerged onto the world stage in conjunction with struggles in Northern Ireland, the Basque Country and around Palestine (Carlile, 2007), the term terrorism (*irhab*) was introduced in Egypt only in the 1990s (Edel and Josua, 2017: 2014); in the 1960s, references to it were in conjunction with *al-'unf al-syasi* (politically oriented violence). The threat coming from *jihadi* terrorism and opposition forces was differently conceived in Nasser's era, when political violence was more revolutionary in its goals and anchored to Sayyid Qutb's doctrines, before being influenced by post-Al Qaedist matrices that modified Qutbian thought. The term 'terrorism' also underwent a strict politicisation, which in turn justified the 2014 and 2015 anti-terrorism law which ultimately targeted social movements at a time when consensus had dropped. Framing protests as terrorism was a pivotal point for the anti-Muslim Brotherhood narrative. In July 2013, al-Sisi asked 'all honest and trustworthy Egyptians' to join state-sponsored rallies, 'to give me the mandate and order that I confront violence and potential terrorism' (Daragahi, 2013).

The Egyptian army remains the second-largest army in the region. Historically, it has perceived itself as the pillar of the republican establishment, but also the only source of authority over civilians (Moughira, 2015). After the uprising in 2011, the armed forces re-emerged as the dominant actor on the political scene. The 2013 coup provided the military with a *carte blanche* to strengthen its hold over the state in exchange for security, stability and an improving economy. Both under al-Sisi and the previous interim Mansour government, the regime's focus was on improvements in public services and the provision of basic commodities at an appropriate price (Khalil, 2017). In fact, the economic situation worsened because of prolonged instability that dried up foreign investments, with a sharp decrease from –3.891 billion USD in 2013 to –7.9 billion USD in 2016. The situation had marginally improved by 2017 with investments that shifted to –7.21 billion USD (World Bank, 2017).

The Egyptian army remains the only institution able to combine different sources of power in sectors ranging from business to major engineering and tourist companies (Sayigh, 2012, 2019). In terms of threats, it is not internally confronted by rival forces, as any security agency enjoys exclusive legitimacy (Brumberg and Sallam, 2012). However, it was only after the Tamarrod movement's demonstration in July 2013 that the SCAF decided to openly take the lead in politics, taking advantage of the emerging sharp social divisions. The formation of the National Salvation Front, which regrouped the left and liberal parties and names associated with the old regime, such as Sabahy, Muhammad el-Baradei and Amr Moussa, initially organised three days of street protests calling on Morsi to resign. Through a strategic labelling of Morsi's supporters as 'anti-patriotic', the EAF shifted the narrative of protests to its advantage, proposing itself as the only force able to restore law and fight 'terrorism' (Hussein and De Martino, 2019). This was also identified above in the framing and content analysis of al-Sisi's defence of the army in his July 2013 speech, the 2015 BBC interview, and the 2016 speech at the Military Academy.

When Abdel Fattah al-Sisi won presidential elections in 2014 with a significant majority of votes, the SCAF considered him the leader best suited to securing cross-national support. This loyalty in turn was repaid by the political authority, who granted the army complete independence with a set of presidential decrees. Constitutional changes enhancing army independence from civilian oversight broadened the army's capacity to influence political life. In this respect, the post-2013 micro-structures should not be compared to those of the 1950s, since Nasser himself kept the military under a form of strict control.

Under Nasser the SCAF began to occupy a role in providing an alternative source of welfare to the government and mosques (Gotowicki, 1999). The military's engagement in civil sectors and as a welfare provider put it in competition with Islamist forces active in society since the 1970s, particularly the Muslim Brotherhood, which had long been active in informal areas through a network of mosques, leisure centres and clinics, replacing the state and providing excluded communities with access to welfare and social services (Zuhur, 2007). The military's self-framing expanded its positive portrayal to the lower class as a secure job provider in a country plagued by 34.4 per cent unemployment (GCDCAF, 2016). The army capped prices for general civilian products, thus promoting the narrative of the EAF as a welfare provider, rather than requesting forms of military loyalty (Haulslohner, 2014). As a result, bridges, bakeries and water sanitation plants were 'framed' as gifts to society, partially evoking the rhetoric under Nasser, despite the systemic differences in the global economic order between the 1950s and the 1990s.

The US's pro-Egyptian stance led it to view the army as an instrument of socialisation and nation-building. However, this positive framing of the army was also connected to the generous aid and financial assistance provided from 2014 (i.e. after the military coup), following the suspension of military funding in 2013, after the election of the FJP. Clearly illustrating this change of attitude, two months after the 2013 coup, the US Department of State signed a new contract worth 300 million USD to deliver and coproduce military equipment with Egypt.

Following the ouster of Morsi in 2013, the army was offered greater opportunity to channel state funds into national projects. In 2013 the armed forces was expanded under Muhammed al-Assar, who in 2015 was promoted to Minister of State for Military Production by President al-Sisi. In 2015, several members of the Mubarak-era elite were reintroduced to the political and economic machine, including the businessman Muhammad Abou El-Enein, formerly accused of corruption in land projects and part of the mid-2000s circle of Gamal Mubarak (Cleopatra Group, n.d.).[17] Furthermore, the Panama papers revealed that Gamal Mubarak was part of Tahya Misr, the 'Long Live Egypt Fund', launched by al-Sisi (and taking the name of his supporting coalition in Parliament) and presented to society as a state-led charity for social development (the Tahya Misr Fund, established by Decree

No. 139 of 2014, on the initiative of al-Sisi to implement development projects). Presidential Decree No. 446 issued in May 2015 permitted the armed forces and the Armed Forces Land Projects Organization (under the Ministry of Housing and Land) to establish economic enterprises co-owned by the army and private foreign firms. This may open the door to further military financial engagement in areas where army involvement has already taken place, such as the Suez Canal project.

The Suez Canal Corridor Development Project deserves a mention next, as it clearly remains firmly in the hands of the military authority. The project involves the expansion of six Egyptian ports, the construction of tunnels in the industrial zone, and a canal, which was extended in 2015 by the EAF's engineering authority.[18] It was revised with the goal of creating 100,000 new jobs, with total costs estimated at 18 billion USD. Military firms were involved in constructing towers, gearboxes and solar panels. The fund for the project, created by al-Sisi in 2013 immediately after the ouster of Morsi, has financed several further massive infrastructure projects.[19] The fund benefitted from donations from the NSPO and other business entities. A total of 4.9 billion USD came from the UAE. Despite the politics of repression that persists in Egypt, EU countries have also played a role; since the start of 2015, Egypt has received over 7 million USD. The project of new administrative capital east of the desert of Cairo is a further project in which the army became involved after 2014. The military's involvement in other national mega-projects, as promoted on the EAF's website, includes other civilian services that ranged from housing to irrigation systems, education and health care (Ministry of Defence, 2020–2021). What may be understood as the monopolisation of the economic apparatus by the post-coup army was also aimed at reducing Egypt's dependence on military supplies and imports from other states. Immediately after 2013, Egypt changed its main trading partner, the US being replaced with EU states, namely France, Germany and Italy.

A certain intensity is observable in the way the military recaptured the state economic power it had lost after 2005. The private sector was in turn affected by al-Sisi's policy and monopolisation by the army of the state structures. The extensive involvement of the army in the economy under al-Sisi created the conditions for the shrinking of the private sector, dropping from 31.155 per cent of GDP in 2012 to 25.607 per cent of GDP in 2014 (World Bank data, 2012–2015). This was a noticeable decline from the situation before 2011. It is worth noting that in Egypt, the private sector employs more than 70 per cent of the labour force (Fedi, Amer and Rashad, 2019). Unlike the military sector, the extreme liberalising reforms introduced by al-Sisi impacted the inflation rate and increased social unrest, aspects that ultimately impacted private sector growth. The election of al-Sisi as

President in 2014 also coincided with a politics of centralisation of the army from a judicial perspective. By comparison, under Mubarak the responsibility for the protection of public facilities was held by the *shurta* (police) (Fahmy, 1999; see also Ismail, 2012); Decree No. 136 of 2014 transferred this power to the military instead, while the system kept arguing in favour of a depoliticisation of the military apparatus.

The death of charisma and the spectre of personalism

To better understand the military's repositioning in the state structures, the discontinuities in rule before and after the 2013 coup need to be fully appreciated. The NDP between 1978 and 2011 acted as the fulcrum of the loyalty of the elite (which also included civilian elites, not just the military ranks). The NDP also provided credible assurance in rewarding the regime's backers both in the medium and long term. These rewards were limited to members and high-profile supporters of the party, on condition of their demonstrating loyalty. In this mechanism of asset distribution, elections fulfilled a plethora of goals (Blaydes, 2006; Diamond and Plattern, 2006) including intra-party promotions, parliamentary immunity, and business influence in Parliament (Blaydes, 2010: 126–138). However, they also offered the opportunity to control and limit the opposition, whilst testing the regime's strength (Blaydes, 2006, 2010; Geddes, 2003; Sartori, 2001). Multiparty elections enabled the NDP to 'demonstrate' to the outside world the party's capacity to dominate and control the political arena. The manipulation of the judiciary and the electoral law of 2005, along with the pyramidal clientelism favoured by IMF's SAP, put in place the conditions by which the regime survived, though they did not provide a form of internal legitimation. The NDP's internal vacuum of legitimacy was compensated by strong external support which came through aid assistance, such as the US Agency for International Development. Continuing legal reforms and amendments under Mubarak attempted to contain authoritarianism within a certain level of legality, although the NDP was not immune from breaches of international legal standards, including on torture (Sherry, 1992).

Against the background set by the NDP, the post-2013 regime can be categorised in light of:

(i) the lack of opposition parties;
(ii) the role, power and game framing of the army in society;
(iii) the broadening of the military's function in the political domain through amendments to the legal code and presidential decrees;
(iv) the civilian nature of the presidency; and
(v) the system's more personalised orientation.

These arguments may be reinforced by the selectorate theory (de Mesquita et al., 2003). Building on de Mesquita et al.'s (2003) theory of the selectorate, Russett writes that the selectorate denotes the quality of characteristics institutionally required for choosing a leadership, or necessary for gaining access to private benefits doled out by the government's leadership (Russett, 2011: 15). Combining the selectorate theory with Aziz's (2017) argument of Egypt under al-Sisi as an 'electoral militarism', clashes emerge regarding the size of the new selectorate and the function played by the army in light of al-Sisi's 2016 decision to replace key figures with new appointments closer to him, a form of personal, rather than state, stabilisation.[20] If before 2011 the SCAF performed the function of selectorate, it had a larger role and possessed the capacity of determining the survival, or perhaps the collapse of, the regime, as confirmed in 2011. In non-militarised systems, while the incumbent remains in need of networks to maintain the loyalty of key parts of society, they do not need to maintain the loyalty of all. With the structural political transformations resulting, after 2013, in al-Sisi's Egypt the selectorate can be considered absent from the political scene, while the winning coalition underwent a process of strict depoliticisation, followed by a technocratisation.

Combining the findings of the framing analysis conducted in relation to the framing of the military with the existing theories of regime types (Arena and Nicoletti, 2014; de Mesquita et al., 2003, Gallagher and Hanson, 2013), it is suggested that Egypt under al-Sisi has moved towards a more *protected personalistic regime*, in which the military benefits in taking a more advanced role in society, making it both the selectorate and the winning coalition. It follows that while the military under al-Sisi is back in play, at least in Achcar's view of the role they played under Sadat, this work is more cautious, with Achcar's idea of al-Sisi's regime as 'old-new' (Achcar, 2016: 147) and Stacher's (2020) analysis of the regime which ended up obscuring possible faultlines between al-Sisi and military senior officers. This latter aspect found a systematic analysis and discussion, which benefitted from interviews with prominent senior figures about the internal transformation of the political machine after political and societal shockwaves.

As introduced earlier in the modified and hybrid framework at the core of this book, processes of charismatic legitimation are more likely to be overthrown by revolutionary waves, which in Weber's classical view are considered illegitimate in form (Weber, 1978).[21] Revolutions stemming from charismatic failures are replaced by new forms of legal-rational legitimacy, which in turn obey the same logic of being overthrown by popular protests and replaced by new sources of legitimacy, thus repeating a vicious circle. However, this Weberian circle of legitimation is only in part applicable to how different regimes in Egypt attempted to legitimate themselves from the

1950s to 2011. The charismatic component in Nasser's era was replaced in the first decade of Mubarak's rule by a legal-rational form of mutual top-down and bottom-up intra-NDP consensus towards the regime, strongly unified by political rewards and a certain independence granted to the judiciary. Egypt since the Free Officers' Revolution has always been built upon military involvement in all aspects of civil life, as demonstrated extensively above. Al-Sisi de facto offered himself to the military as being the manifestation of military influence in politics and civilian life. However, al-Sisi also worked tirelessly to build the power of the military for his own benefit, empowering himself through draconian reforms to the penal code, and attempting to portray himself as a pillar of political stability, not so much before society, but mainly before the army.[22]

Charisma was employed by al-Sisi principally as a strategic meta-frame (Dombos et al., 2009), which also combined some elements behind the idea of the nation, such as myths, collective memories and symbols from the past (Smith, 1991, 2009). These have been combined with and built on a 1960s-infused notion of the armed forces, which had been 'purified' from a corrupted legacy to the NDP both in the 1 July and 3 July 2013 speeches. This in turn has attempted to detach the EAF view from the FJP and the NDP's pyramidal cronyism in the eyes of the public. What might be theorised as the 'cultural compatibility' (Noakes and Johnston, 2005) of the way the army was recalled through the myths and symbols of Nasser's era has led the scholarly analysis to define Egypt's current authoritarianism as a restoration of a form of militarism. This is an argument from which this work prefers to take a considered distance.

Charisma and the attempt at its personalisation constituted a defensive and reactive tool to a structural need to build a more reform-inclined rhetoric, which (it was hoped) would reinforce, on the one hand, social perceptions of the ruler as a socially and industrially reforming leader, embracing a post-modern inclusive idea of populism in a decontextualised exclusivist post-populist global order, while on the other infusing hope and credibility among the military elite. This holds theories of authoritarianism as rooted in the military (Springborg, 2015), somehow inadequate in grasping the transformation of state structures and capturing the inner processes of the incumbent's strategy and struggle for internal legitimation.

In antithesis to the scholarly debate on the Nasserisation of al-Sisi's political discourse, which has been dated as early as 2014 (El-Nawawy, 2016), while political authorities since 2013 have attempted to summon visions of the army and Egyptian society in the 1950s and 1960s under Nasser, this was not accompanied by any substantive change at the level of social policies, since Nasser and al-Sisi have operated within very different social and political contexts (despite certain similarities between the challenges facing both leaders), hold opposing ideas of developmentalism, and have approached Egypt's social classes in very different ways.

Instead, the political authority deployed charisma as a reactive tool in response to his uncertainties and a potential fracture in the common interests between al-Sisi and the SCAF. The SCAF has always historically been more interested in protecting material (economic and infrastructural) assets, while al-Sisi has been more interested in legitimating himself and securing his office than in reforming the economic agenda on the tactical premises of welfarism and green sustainability in line with international actions on climate change, in antithesis to the global capitalist order which is finding a form of clear reproduction. This shift sufficiently illustrates the limitations of the existing scholarship's view of Egypt as a purely militarised state, in which the ruler and the army share the same priorities. They do not.

Conclusions

Recalling theories of authoritarianism, making a substantial difference in the structural imbalance in al-Sisi's Egypt and the leadership's desire for legitimation, are the absence of a regime party, the absence of a selectorate, and an unclear winning coalition. These structural differences point to a different organisation of political authorities, along different premises, in which the novelty lies in the strategic use of sources as legitimating foundations, and the impact they have concerning the armed forces, the rehabilitation of which should be noted as more than just a reductive notion of militarisation.

While the regime presented itself as stable, resting on the strong support of the military with its intimate connectedness to all levels of the state since the 1950s, the absence of a party-controlled political network, as had existed from the mid-1950s to 2011 in the ASU and then the NDP, structurally exposed the government to the risk of defection, as a result of a lack of political and career rewards from within the regime party itself. As a result, the premises and foundations of leadership stability shifted from an intra-party clientelist logic to being externally oriented and intertwined with al-Sisi's management of other resources, such as finance and large infrastructure projects. The absence of opposition parties, the beaurocratisation of the parliamentary assembly, the harsh crackdown on civil society, and last but least the dominance of the pro-Sisi coalition the NFB, are all indicative of a process of regime fluidity. Thus al-Sisi's attempt at legitimation through charisma ultimately led to an over-celebration of the armed forces, discussed in this chapter as a dominant (strategic) meta-frame, in such a way that does not offer a comparison with the 1960s. In this regard, the chapter argued that despite some parallels with Nasser in terms of similar challenges faced, al-Sisi differs significantly from Nasser. Nor can the process of legitimation as attached to the military in 2014–2015 be considered as durable as was the system of patronage under the NDP (or, for that matter, the ASU). The reasons for this derive from the different actors' diverging priorities and interests. The strength of the system under the NDP was connected to Mubarak's capacity to politically deliver on performance and enhance the economic agenda for reforms.

Judging from the debate entered above, scepticism towards the presidency has been building since 2015 amongst the newly appointed senior officers in the EAF, who seem to believe that al-Sisi's charismatic approach was lacking, and is likely to be ineffective in the longer term. To understand this attitude within the SCAF, it is necessary to consider the internal composition of the armed forces and its current intra-ideological fragmentations. There still exists a section of the SCAF sympathetic to the now-banned Muslim Brotherhood, and which may be in a position to exercise an influence over the religious establishment in the future, and it is suggested that this may expose al-Sisi to political risks, in the long-term, and problematise foundational legitimacy unless contingency measures are implemented. Chapter 6 considers these aspects.

Notes

1 According to the information emerged from a personal interview, from within the institution al-Sisi risked a mockery due the vacuousness of speeches. Author interview with PR1.
2 Author interview with PR1.
3 On media management by the armed forces see Bollinger et al. (2016).
4 Hosni Mubarak never won the popular vote in *Time* magazine.
5 Author interview with PR1.
6 Gellner's theory of nationalism was defined functionalist in the way it was explained for its beneficial consequences over the society (or societies) but for which it met criticism from O'Leary (1997).
7 To further complicate the sophistication of this picture, the celebration of Pharaonic identity and the idolatric greatness take place in a state constitutionally defined as Muslim, and in which pre-Muhammad practices (Pharaonic civilisation) are considered immoral.
8 Author interview with SC2.
9 Author interview with SC2.
10 Author interview with PR1 and SC1.
11 Author interview with SC2.
12 Author interview with SC2.
13 Author interview with SC2.

14 Combined information emerged from combined interviews between the author and PA1, PR1 and SC2.
15 Author interviews with SC2 and PR1.
16 Since 2013 until 2019, the number of children jailed in Egypt is estimated at 3,200. See on this Politics Today (2019).
17 Land projects dealt with the construction of housing and facilities in formerly protected lands. Cleopatra Group, founded in 1986, became involved in many such housing projects after 2015.
18 The project was approved in 2002 by Law No. 83, which was amended in 2015.
19 Sectors involved are textile, bunkering service, solar PV, pharmaceutical industry, agribusiness, petrochemicals.
20 Author interviews with PR1 and SC1.
21 While Weber considered charismatic legitimacy as emerging relatively spontaneously, legal legitimacy was defined as subject to people's confidence in the system. Indeed, to borrow from Weber, charisma is understood as subject to people's recognition, but it is also considered transitory, and is often transformed into legal-rational legitimacy (Weber, 1978). Hence, as opposed to norms, charisma can be understood as a transitory form of domination.
22 Author interview with PR1.

5

God, the political seductor

PHASE I: THE TRANSFORMATION PHASE: THE ASCENDANCY OF
PRO-REGIME SALAFISM

Religion, political power and legitimacy on the eve of 2013

Political authorities seek to instrumentalise religion, and call for a revolution in Islam specifically since September 2015. This delay suggests how religion was not contemplated from the very beginning as a tangible driver in achieving a form of top-down legitimation. Nevertheless, the decision to rely on the religious sphere must be viewed through the context of the ideological transformation resulting from both the 2011 uprising, and the 2012 Muslim Brotherhood's experience in power. The 2013 coup opened platforms of political negotiation from the perspective of politicised Salafis, who, having dissociated themselves from an early short-term alliance with the Muslim Brotherhood during the 2012 presidential election, saw in the overthrow of the FJP an opportunity to advance their own political constituency and influence into institutionalised politics. However, the presence of the al-Azhar in Egypt since 1961 has been of great importance for the formation of the state and the legitimation of regimes. In 2012, for the first time in the history of Egypt, the FJP conceded independence to the religious establishment after decades of control exercised by the government. However, it is worth noting that the al-Azhar is not unilaterally a religious institution, but rather embeds a high level of political symbolism, since in Egypt controlling the al-Azhar means being in full and total control of the political system at all levels.

The post-2013 authorities' reaction to the adaptation of Hizb al-Nour to the domestic setting after 2013 pushed the leadership towards a more conservative interpretation of society, with a direct reference to Islam as source of moral conduct. This, however, resulted in a strict personalisation of the divine, with a boomerang effect of fragmenting the al-Azharist *ulema*'s perception of al-Sisi. The discussion of al-Sisi's references to religion became particularly relevant between 2015 and 2018, with some implications still

Table 5.1 Transformation of Islamists after the 2013 coup and the leadership's corresponding transformative process

Transformative phase	Phenomenology of Islamist politics in post-2011 Egypt
Adaptative phase	
Reactive phase	Connection to the ruler's legitimation struggle
Isolationist and dissociative phase	

evident in 2020. Since 2011 the transformation of Islamists has become somewhat connected to the process of authority-making.

Religion has often been used as a source of political legitimation (Billings and Scott, 1994; Omelicheva, 2016: 146). From Turkey under the Young Turks and the Kemalists in the early twentieth century, to Iraq under Saddam Hussein in the 1980s and 1990s when the regime instrumentalised religion, particularly in foreign policy, the call for a 'true' Islam has been employed as source of state strength; over the decades, different interpretations of religion have bolstered rulers' credentials (Helfont, 2014). The instrumentalisation of Islamic ideologies has been both an instrument attempting to legitimise and to deflect criticisms, and alternatively to entrench political power and the claim of authority (Platteau, 2011: 248).

Nevertheless, religion's connection to politics has not always been an intimate relation in the broader Middle East. Going back to the 1950s–1960s, from Nasser's Egypt to the Ba'ath Party-dominated governments in Syria and Iraq, nationalist governments in Tunisia and Algeria sought to minimise religion's role in politics over the decades, one way or another, at least until 2018.[1] In this argument, the book shares El-Bernoussi's approach to decontextualising religion in post-2011 Egypt's political materiality while historically all rulers, even the most secular, presented themselves as devoted Muslims (2021: 41–42). These Arab states took their lead from Turkey, which had abolished the Sharia court system under Mustafa Kemal Ataturk, who was convinced that religious forces stood in the way of Turkish progress. In the 1950s, Turkey outlawed the Islamic veil for women, and imposed other moral regulations which directly opposed the injunctions of Sharia. Thus, state references to Islam morphed into an instrument for national identity-construction, employed by autocrats to build a form of internal societal consensus (Platteau, 2011).

After several decades of anti-colonialist independence movements influenced by Turkish Kemalism, from Egypt to Syria and Tunisia, in which political authority found legitimation in secular and nationalist premises, a change occurred in the late 1960s. The spread of Qutbism after 1964 as the core of new understandings of statehood and sovereignty also exerted an influence on the justification of political authority. After the failure of Pan-Arabism in the late 1960s, as evidenced by the defeat of the Arab states by Israel in the 1967 Six-Day War, the condemnation of *jahiliyya* – a clear and direct allusion to the secularism of the Nasserist regime – and its replacement with *hakimiyya* (governorship of God), supported the justification of *rububiyya* (dominion of God), the premise for an Islamic concept of statehood dissimilar to the Westphalian idea of sovereignty. Still later, by the early 1990s, Salafis' call for a return to a pure Islam of the Prophet Muhammad initiated a process of romantic nostalgia, with the goal of rectifying society from neoliberal capitalist-rooted policies and corruption, through an austere interpretation of religion. Religion has thus represented a source of institutionalised consolidation since the 1960s.

While some regimes in the MENA region have not perceived themselves as strictly Islamic-oriented, they still internalised different gradients of religious reference as a source of social acceptance, especially from religious establishments. Despite its secular basis, this was the case of Egypt under Nasser, a socialist-inspired model in which Islam, though not Sharia, nevertheless found a strategic place. This was introduced with the goal of exercising an influence over the al-Azhar, from which Nasser required some level of acceptance to see his reformist economic and political agenda implemented. Critics assert a crisis in the moral authority of the *ulema* long before the 1950s, although most historians locate the shift in Nasser's 1961 reforms to the al-Azhar. Once the religious establishment was deprived of both economic and political power, the *ulema* had no option but to submit to Nasser, issuing *fatawa* in support of the regime's reforms (Zeghal, 1999: 374). It follows that the process of legitimation in authoritarian states may opt for a form of instrumentalisation and reinterpretation of religion, which can be considered a form of 'soft power' exercised through the creation, dissemination and reproduction of belief systems (Beetham, 1991).

In Egypt, the 1960s began a more direct link between religion and the state, although the relations between religion and politics in Egypt remain a subject of debate. The display of Islamic piety in Egyptian politics is detected as far back as the 'Urabi Revolt of the late nineteenth century, which was particularly influenced by Jamal al-Din al-Afghani (Priewasser, 2014: 64). Unlike Syria or Tunisia, where presidents have considered religion a trap to stay away from, religion has historically played a different function and occupied a different role in the idea of a modern Egyptian culture and identity, and over the decades the influence of religion has been found at the level of the presidency, with presidents adopting the first name 'Muhammad' as official insignia (e.g. 'Muhammad Anwar al-Sadat' or 'Muhammad Hosni Mubarak'). When it comes to post-2013 authorities, al-Sisi's embrace of religious discourse has become clear in his use of the Islamic *bism Illah* at the open and close of most of his official speeches, as a way of publicly vocalising his personal faith in God, a feature not found in the key speeches of predecessors like Sadat, or even Mubarak. Some non-Egyptian observers from a more detached view noted how religion entered a phase of marginality from the perspective of leaders' legitimacy after 2012.[2] However, if religion became less relevant from a broader perspective, the same could not be argued regarding Salafism, which, particularly since 2011, has occupied an important position in transformations and remaking of the state foundations.

Before 2011 religion only marginally interfered with everyday life, and Egyptian society cannot be considered solely in reference to religious/Islamic factors, with a social perception of religion as a private matter to be kept separate from the political sphere. Recalling Weber and Bourdieu's *habitus*, in the early 1980s, reference to Islam fulfilled the instrumental purpose of justifying political agendas, though it never provided a de facto source of political legitimacy (see also Asimaki and Koustourakis, 2014). Hence, on the experience in power of the FJP, it is contended that the popular anti-Brotherhood sentiment in 2013 was not merely the result of missteps taken by the FJP, which generated social opposition to the mixing of politics and religion (Brown et al., 2013), but rather the FJP's failure to understand that the political function of religion worked best when limited to the operationalisation of 'reformist' policies.

In the 1970s, Islam in Egypt was mainly employed as a tool for political ends, countering leftist and nationalist opposition forces, and leading to a 're-Islamisation' of the country (Abaza, 2006: 17). While some Islamists attempted to enter the institutionalised domain after the partial opening to opposition forces, thus contesting the state on constitutional terms, others wished for a much more radical contestation. With the end of the 1970s, and Sadat's assassination by Islamists in 1981, Islamism entered a more direct confrontation with political authorities. This intensified for two decades in the 1980s and 1990s, due to the violent approaches to politics of the Gama'at al-Islamiyya and al-Jihad underground groups, impacting the Mubarak regime's pejorative narrative of Islamism (Singerman, 2009; see also Hafez and Wiktorowicz, 2004). The presence of these radical groups, which challenged the mainstream religious arena in the 1970s and 1980s, also spurred the al-Azhar's inclusion in public debates, and the increasing intervention of the religious establishment in the political domain (Zeghal, 1999).

Uniquely among Arab countries, the presence of the high religious authority the al-Azhar in the Egyptian panorama should be considered in discussions of relations between religion and politics. Since the 1950s, Egyptian regimes' durability was forced to confront the religious establishment, which had existed since the Fatimid Caliphate in 970 CE. The al-Azhar rose in importance in domestic politics only in the early 1970s, when it became the domestic node for autocrats' paradox of durability. To some extent this has made politics inextricable from the *ulema*s' *fatawa* in support of rulers. The instrumentalisation of Islam after the 1970s, tactically permitted by Sadat with the purpose of ending Nasser's cult, reintroduced the *ulema* as an aspect of socio-political Egyptian life, with an important role in the making of political legitimacy. Nevertheless, Eickelman and Piscatori (1996) noted a fragmentation in the al-Azhar's authority, with a growing influence of the Muslim Brotherhood and Wahhabi trends within it.

Relations between the state and the al-Azhar were changeable depending on rulers' concession to the religious establishment, although the durability of political rule has remained profoundly linked to the *ulema*'s acceptance of the political authority. This supports Meijer's evaluation of the relationship between religion and state in Egypt as an 'antagonistic interdependency', indicating frequent clashes but also the need for politicians to win moral approval by the *ulema* for proposed political reforms (Meijer, 2012).[3] The relation between religion and politics underwent further transformations in the wake of the 2011 protests due to an organic renegotiation of social and political platforms after the NDP's collapse (Hamid, 2017; Volpi, 2012). The renegotiation of social spheres and the inclusion of religion in the process led to different outcomes in both Tunisia and Egypt, with the former rooted in a state-based progressive reformism and the latter endogenously more likely to be influenced by religion.[4] While the Tunisian transition initially and before 2020 led to a form of more inclusivist political model, with the Ennahda Party, which distanced itself from the Islamist label (Koubaa, 2012; Lacroix, 2012; Meddeb, 2019; *Middle East Eye*, 2016; Voltolini et al., 2017; see also Blanc and Sigillò, 2019 and Schafer, 2015), the Egyptian experience certainly led to a different outcome, and this aspect comes as confirmation of the inextricability of religion from Egyptian politics.

The 2011 protests across the Middle East region have been marked by what can be considered a re-adaptation of relations between the state, Islam and Islamists (Volpi and Stein, 2015: 6). While some observers noticed that the spread of youth and secular movements and parties in the 2011–2012 transition period was leading towards a secular revival, the observations for this book posit that the authorities attempted to employ religion once again in connection to rulers' struggle to gain or consolidate political power. This led to forms of instrumentalisation of the term *karama* (dignity) (see El-Bernoussi, 2021), which happened to be politicised and combined with an intermittent and interchangeable reference to moral dignity on the one hand, and material dignity on the other. Differently from Egypt's 1971 Constitution, the 2014 Constitution revitalised the concept of state religion, with Article 2 strengthening the function of Sharia as the main source of consultation, a premise already found in the FJP-drafted Constitution of 2012. Writers of the 2012 Constitution disregarded intellectuals' arguments that the new Constitution should not identify a state religion, but rather emphasised the principles of citizenship in the idea of a 'hierarchical citizenship', as arising from the FJP's choice (Hamzawy, 2014).

The religionisation of politics produced further implications in the politicisation of doctrinal aspects, such as the dualism of *halal* (permitted) versus *haram* (forbidden) (Brown and Hamzawy, 2010). Support, acceptance and rejection of political, legislative and executive performance became based on religious premises, and entered the realm of the 'demand of salvation'. If, borrowing from Hamzawy (2014), the legitimation of Morsi and the FJP's authority was attached to Brotherhood-linked clerics and politicians due to the charisma exercised by the clergy over the community of believers, the concept of salvation now became expressly politicised and attached to voting for and supporting towards the FJP. However, the Muslim Brotherhood's approach to religion divided society, compromising Morsi's leadership and exposing the FJP to criticism in the debate on democratisation, initiated after the vacuum left by the dissolution of the NDP.

For at least four decades, Egyptian Islamism found in the Muslim Brotherhood almost the only form of political expression of Islam. The institutionalisation of the Muslim Brotherhood after the 2012 elections did not represent a complete novelty, considering the organisation's capacity to build a structured programme and conduct a long campaign of influence to access institutional politics since the 1970s. However, the politicisation and transformation of some Salafi trends in adaptation to post-2011 and post-2013 politics, and more precisely the rise of what can be identified as pro-regime Salafism, did represent a novelty (see El-Ashwal 2013; see also Drevon, 2015a, b; 2014).

The institutionalisation of Salafism dates to 2008 in Kuwait, when candidates from Salafi groups gained 10 out of 50 seats in the Parliamentary Assembly. Salafism gradually started entering the political domain in Bahrain in 2010, with the al-Asala al-Islamiya party, as a result of tensions between the Shia population and the Sunni royal family, in which Salafists supported the latter (Freer, 2019). The new wave of pro-regime Salafism, something which veteran Salafists of the 1970s, 1980s and 1990s absolutely rejected, resulted in a clash between hard-line Salafists and the neo-Salafists over themes like ideology or the use of the media. The new Salafism, coopted by regimes such as Egypt and Saudi Arabia, has sometimes occurred through connections with state intelligence agencies.[5]

In Egypt in the late 2000s, following a regional process of reform and revival of political Salafism, the first Salafi trends, such as al-Sunna al-Muhammadiyya, which originally emerged in the early twentieth century, gained increased visibility through Salafi TV channels (El-Sherif, 2014; Field and Hamam, 2009) such as Nilesat and Al-Nas (Al-Anani and Malik, 2013). Field and Hamam (2009) explain the phenomenon of 'Satellite Salafism' as a spread of the trend through mass media. In the late 2000s, Salafis returning to Egypt from the Gulf further benefitted from domestic tensions between the al-Azhar and the Mubarak regime. The religious establishment was accused by the NDP of lacking credibility and not representing the regime's view, thus contravening Nasser's Law of 1961.

Salafists in Egypt gained more visibility when Mubarak, with the goal of limiting the Muslim Brotherhood's influence, provided them with more venues to spread their views and expand their own network of charities, rivalling the Brotherhood's (Racimora, 2013). In this regard, the Ansar al-Sunna and al-Jameiya al-Shariyya were both registered at the Ministry of Social Solidarity. Egyptian Salafi groups produced an abundance of religious material, such as printed versions of the Qur'an and recorded tapes of radical preachers. They used a bottom-up strategy more oriented toward the Islamisation of society seen as a preliminary condition for the advent of an 'Islamic state'. In Salafist ideology, opposing the ruler remains prohibited as long as they are identified as Muslim. The politicisation of Salafism was connected to the *Sahwa* movement in the early 1990s in Saudi Arabia. This was when Salafists started to divide further and create political parties, especially in Kuwait. Salafis were more cohesive until 1992. The First Gulf War divided Salafis: some remained closer to the Saudi monarchy and were used by the Saudis to legitimise themselves; others opposed the Saudis and defended Iraq. They became very politicised and revolted against the monarchy, asking for reforms – conservative but desired reforms. Others became more jihadi-oriented, and used violence for legitimation. Amongst the second trend, when Kuwait was liberated from Iraqi occupation, some became involved in politics in Kuwait. There are debates on the Islamic Salvation Front in Algeria, whether it was Salafi or modernist, and to what extent they participated in the political process. When Salafis started to join the political process after 2013, their argument was similar. They justified political participation, although they did not believe in democracy. This became a pillar of a new phenomenology of Salafism that emerged just before 2010, and identifiable as 'pro-regime Salafism', a form of support regulated by doctrinal norms that does not contemplate rebellion against the status quo, in order to avoid *fitna*.[6] The phenomenology of 'pro-regime Salafism', believed to derive from the *Sahwa* movement, is specifically embedded in the Saudi project of the *al-Jamiyy'a*, while economically, Saudi petrodollars led to the diffusion of Salafism (Dau, 2012). *Al-Jamiyy'a* Salafism became known in Egypt as Madkhaliyya Salafism. Hizb al-Nour's support for al-Sisi, as discussed below, can be clearly identified as connected to the broader regional and Saudi-led project of the *Jamiyy'a* (see also Dau, 2012).[7] Despite the regional implications behind the politicisation of Salafism in the mid-2000s, Egyptian Salafis lack the flexible and, at times, more 'democratic' credentials that the Muslim Brotherhood acquired through decades of cyclical contentious and non-contentious opposition to the NDP. Hence, this work disagrees with Aziz (2017), according to whom al-Nour's objectives did not present much difference from the Muslim Brotherhood's. In fact, 'Tensions between the Salafis and the Muslim Brotherhood were over differences in the political project and understanding of religion, but they targeted the same population'.[8]

Unlike the Muslim Brotherhood, which produced a unified political vision of the state, Salafis do not share a unified political vision, although in theory there should be a common view of the identity of the state as strictly Islamic and based on the textual implementation of Sharia (Brown and Hamzawy, 2010). The Salafists adopt an eschatological view of the state as a vehicular instrument for the implementation of *tawhid* (oneness of God/monotheism), implying a rejection of the notion of equal citizenship for all (Meijer et al., 2020). This limitation has represented a source of dispute in societies which are ethno-religious mosaics. Superior access of civil rights, unlike the Muslim Brotherhood's understanding of citizenship (*al-muwatana*), is limited to the community of Muslim believers and thus dependent on creed. Salafis also place emphasis on the power of the ruler, rejecting the concept of the parliamentary assembly, though a Shura council may be temporarily tolerated.

On a practical political level, since 2011 Salafis have strategically, on a short-term basis, come together with the Muslim Brotherhood on issues such as the rejection of corruption and the rotation of power via regular elections (Ranko, 2015: 523). Since 2013, the authorities have been more aware of the boomerang effects determined by high levels of political and economic corruption as the main drivers behind the protests in 2011. Thus, governments following the NDP have attempted to shrink perceptions of corruption to avoid protests, including from the Salafis, though unsuccessfully considering that scores have ranged from 32 to 35 out of 100 (with lower scores indicating perceptions of greater corruption) between 2012 and 2019, with no significative improvements (Transparency International, 2020).

During the 2011 SCAF-led transition under al-Tantawi, Salafis, mainly represented by Hizb al-Nour, attempted to reconcile their ideology with some democratic principles. Their views, developed in the context of the 2011 uprising, to some extent approached the more moderate concept of a state ruling with reference to Islam, rather than a theocratic state. However, this moderation was underpinned by Hizb al-Nour's strategic goal, to win approval not so much from society or the regime as from the al-Azhar. The Salafis' interest in reaching out to and exerting influence over the religious establishment became the main source of contention between Hizb al-Nour and the Morsi government. The interest towards the al-Azhar and the desire to influence it became a common denominator between al-Sisi and Hizb al-Nour, especially after the FJP granted the al-Azhar's independence in 2012.

Phase II: The adaptive phase

Politicised but not political: the present, the past and the future of Salafism in Egypt

Egyptian Salafism emerged in 1926, the year of the creation of the Ansar al-Sunna al-Muhammadiyya (Followers of Prophetic Tradition), although it was quietist oriented. It was only eighty years later, towards the end of the 2011 protests, after having rejected participation in protests against the NDP due to appeals to avoid *fitna*, which discouraged political participation, that Salafis joined the uprisings in Tahrir, when the triumph of the uprising looked inevitable. Egyptian Salafism managed to convert its grassroots into an initial political machine, which, however, presented internal inefficiencies in its functioning as their entering politics was not supported by a political framework. Overall, the entering by Salafis into the socio-political domain was strongly dependent on the political openness following 2011. The vacuum created in 2012 encouraged Salafi movements to abandon the trend of quietism previously followed by Egyptian Salafism since the early twentieth century, and to search instead for a more political and institutionalised visibility. Nevertheless, in the domestic political scenario Salafists were regarded with suspicion by leftist groups during January 2011, and scepticism increased when some Salafi leaders publicly spoke out against Mubarak in the same year (Tammam, 2011).

Post-1970s Salafism (also described as neo-Salafism) in Egypt can be divided into three main trends: (i) the Alexandria-based al-Da'wa; (ii) non-violent but more political groups based in Cairo such as al-Salafiyya al-Harakiyya; and (iii) an Upper Egypt-based, more radical group closer to the Jama'at al-Islamiyya, although it should be remembered that Jama'at al-Islamiyya, having ceased-fire in March 1999, was reintegrated in 2012 into politics and participated in the elections, gaining 13 seats to the lower house of Parliament. When these three trends entered politics shortly after the 2011 uprising, their political identity found a more political representation in the initial trilogy represented by the al-Nour, al-Asala and al-Bina wal-Tanmiyya parties.

The most notorious neo-Salafi movement remains al-Da'wa, out of which emerged Hizb al-Nour. Politically, prior to 2011, the Da'wa was tolerated by Mubarak and enjoyed freedom not allowed to other Islamists, due to the NDP's strategy of emphasising its tolerance of Salafism to counterbalance the Muslim Brotherhood's presence in society through charities (Bayat, 2007). Unlike the Muslim Brotherhood elite, the Da'wa founders were mostly student activists (Mellor, 2018). They decided to apply the principles of organised activism to Salafism with a project that was, in a sense, borrowed from the Brotherhood's organisational playbook, although never reaching the Brotherhood's degree of institutional and financial sophistication. The Da'wa developed its own organisational pyramid headed by a *qayyim*, the functional equivalent of the Brotherhood's supreme guide, although no formal *bay'a* (pledge of allegiance) was required in the case of the *qayyim*. Lacroix notes that a network of branches and sections were established, and a council of scholars including the Da'wa's founders was tasked with running the organisation (Lacroix, 2013: 5). Similarly to the Brotherhood, also the Da'wa attempted to present itself as a charitable actor in Egypt's most disadvantaged areas (*ashwaiyyat*).[9] In the early 2000s, the NDP came to rely more on the social activity of the Da'wa, mainly by funding them as a counterweight to the Brotherhood's presence in disadvantaged urban places in Egypt. Once it entered politics in 2011–2012, the Egyptian security apparatus considered the Da'wa less of a regime threat when compared to the state perception of the Muslim Brotherhood, possibly as a result of Da'wa's previously apolitical stance.[10] Political Salafism in Egypt after 2011 found political representation in five main parties:

(i) al-Fadila, founded in March 2011;
(ii) Hizb al-Nour, founded in May 2011 by Imad al-Din Abd al-Ghaffour and led since 2013 by Younes Makhioun;
(iii) Hizb al-Bina wal-Tanmiyya founded in 2012, junior political partner of al-Nour;
(iv) al-Raya, founded in 2012 by the ex-Muslim Brotherhood member turned Salafi leader Hazem Abu Ismail, disqualified as a candidate in the 2012 presidential elections;[11] and
(v) al-Watan, founded in January 2013 by al-Ghaffour after his split with al-Nour.

Of these parties, al-Fadila, al-Raya and al-Watan have been the most ideologically conservative (Brown and Dunne, 2013). Nevertheless, the most representative political manifestation of Salafism remained Hizb al-Nour, which emerged out of the quietism of al-Da'wa. It was Hizb al-Nour's entry into the political realm which definitively altered trajectories in Islamist politics, dichotomising and restructuring the 2012 and post-2013 Egyptian Islamist scenarios and political campaign which led to the presidential elections in 2012 but which also influenced the aftermath. Its intra-party fragmentations accounted for reshaping intra-Salafi influences. Hizb al-Nour's success in the 2011–2012 general elections, as discussed below, can be considered as largely due to two factors: the social despair of large parts of the population, and the Saudi financial support it received (Cavatorta and Resta, 2019; see also European Parliament, 2013). It was not a shift in Salafis' interest towards money rather than morals, as argued by Cavatorta and Resta (2019), rather it was their electoral platform which was tactically oriented towards replacing the Muslim Brotherhood on the one hand, and putting together a sufficiently exhaustive political and economic programme which eventually might have challenged non-Islamist parties too on the other.[12] Al-Ghaffour asserted that the party was not subservient to the preachers, but intended to be a more pragmatic political actor (see Lacroix, 2016: 9–10).

This view demonstrates the distance between the Da'wa and al-Nour (Lacroix, 2013). Tensions between the Da'wa's spiritual leaders and al-Nour arose over the poll tax on non-Muslims or *jizya*, with al-Nour considering it inappropriate for the modern age, and Da'wa strongly supporting it. The party's spokesperson, who followed al-Ghaffour, Bayoumi, upheld that al-Ghaffour's position on the relationship between politicians and religious leaders was the main cause that forced al-Ghaffour's resignation as spokesperson of the party. Al-Ghaffour's resignation, however, did not substantially change al-Nour's approach to politics prior to 2013 (Lacroix, 2013; 2016). The influence of al-Ghaffour's new Salafi party, the Hizb al-Watan, has remained marginal, at least when compared with al-Nour's capacity to survive al-Sisi's depoliticisation of politics, as explored next.

Al-Nour became an exceptional case when the ban on religious political parties was applied in 2013 due to constitutional revisions of Article 2. Political Salafism should be examined in terms of its objectives before the Arab uprisings to see how they adapted to post-2011 settings. In pro-regime Salafism, Salafist movements, whether in Yemen, Saudi Arabia, Tunisia, Kuwait or Egypt all abide by a central rule: at the core of political Salafism, criticising and undermining the ruler is not contemplated.[13]

During the SCAF-led transition after the 2011 uprising, unlike the secular parties which emerged in that year, al-Nour decided to side with the SCAF on the issue of constitutional amendments, specifically concerning whether to keep or remove Article 2 on the role of Sharia. While secular and leftist parties argued for a secularisation of the Constitution, Salafi preachers aligned with the SCAF against it. The struggle over Article 2 accelerated the entry of Hizb al-Nour into the political establishment, at least initially. In the parliamentary elections of November 2011 to January 2012, al-Nour, al-Asala and the Building and Development Party formed a coalition under the guidance of al-Nour. Al-Nour contributed 87 seats, while the Building and Development Party and al-Asala won 3 apiece, the coalition thus gaining 93 seats, a quarter of the seats (European Parliament, 2012; see also Al-Jazeera, 2012). Together, they won a quarter of all votes and the same proportion of seats in the National Assembly, forming the second-most powerful political force in the country less than a year after their entry into politics. Secondly, the 2011–2012 parliamentary elections married Hizb al-Nour to politics, despite the fact that the main issues of the post-Revolution election did not deal with religion, and al-Nour, while representing the forefront of political Salafism, lacked experience in the political domain. However, the reason for the 2013 success lies in al-Nour's alliance with the army, to the extent that it represented the religious wing of the SCAF/EAF in 2013.[14]

Hizb al-Nour presented a pragmatic approach to domestic politics, half way between Islamism and the post-Islamism represented by Tunisia's Ennahda. Post-Islamist theory refers to a more fluid concept which recognises the failures of Islamist politics in the past, and pushes parties towards new sociological and political ways of interpreting their function. In post-Islamism, religion becomes employable for political purposes (Bayat, 2013; Imad, 2019; see also Abdul-Ghani, 2019, Al-Anani, 2014). Thus, al-Nour, differently to the Muslim Brotherhood, ended up symbolising, at least empirically, the manifestation of post-Islamism in Egypt.

However, al- Nour was not a champion of political and doctrinal coherence. The party did not maintain a coherent approach to politics in the 2012–2013 timeframe. Putting aside religious issues, it shifted from supporting to heavily contesting Morsi and the Muslim Brotherhood when it was realised that al-Nour would have no role under the FJP. Both al-Nour and al-Ghaffour's al-Watan opposed Morsi in the 2012 presidential election and supported Abdel Munim Aboul Fotuh, the ex-Muslim Brotherhood founder of the Strong Egypt Party (Lacroix, 2013). Al-Nour showed hostility to the FJP when Morsi decided to replace the heads of the major ministries in early 2013. In the broader understanding of the dynamics of state and religion in Egypt, this polarisation principally emerged in relation to two factors: the change in the Ministry of Religious Affairs, and the latter's capacity to exercise influence over the al-Azhar, a crucial aspect in the post-2016 dynamics of al-Sisi's legitimating process.

In early 2013, the FJP replaced Mazar Shaheen with a Muslim Brotherhood loyalist as the head of the Ministry of Religious Affairs (Fahmy, 2012). This was opposed by the al-Azhar, which, from this date, became critical of Morsi and the FJP (Morsy, 2013). Furthermore, the FJP's creation in 2012 of the Preachers' Syndicate 'for the sake of precious nation [sic] and stability', was considered by al-Nour and al-Da'wa as an attempt to isolate and push Egyptian Salafism out of the political game (Ahram Online, 2012). The antagonism also derived from the resignations of the former Minister of the Environment Khalid Alam al-Din and Morsi's advisor Basam al-Zarqa (El-Sherif, 2014). Thus, the perceived 'Brotherhoodisation' of the Ministry of Religious Affairs, other government departments, and the Preachers' Syndicate ultimately created a division in post-2011 Islamism, pitting the Brotherhood and al-Nour against each other. At the core of this contention were different views on religion and the political project and the question of who would be able to shape religion, but also the desire for influence over the same targeted population. This led to al-Nour joining the anti-Morsi protests in early 2013.[15]

After the 2013 coup, al-Nour decided to adopt an instrumental approach to domestic politics, which further altered the contentious al-Da'wa-al-Nour relations, and again turned al-Nour into a 'lobbying arm' of al-Da'wa (Lacroix, 2016). This shift was due to the sheikhs' consequent regaining control of the party, and reversing the gradual social marginalisation of the Da'wa in 2011 and 2012 when al-Nour was still under the guidance of al-Ghaffour. When the party's leadership passed to Younes Markhioun, following al-Ghaffour's split, major clashes resulted, with the former spokesperson related to the formation of alliances with political parties. Much of the contention concerned the view of the political authority as incontestable by al-Nour in order to avoid *fitna*, while it was opposed by secular and leftist parties.

Hizb al-Nour's initial closeness to al-Da'wa, with its doctrine of respect for authority, has been considered as a driver behind the pro-SCAF and then al-Sisi position taken by al-Nour between 2011 and 2013. During these years al-Sisi, although not referring to religion directly as a political matter, maintained an Islamic reference by presenting himself as a believer on the one hand, and defender of Article 2 of the Constitution on the other. A wider view is held by SC1, in whose view Hizb al-Nour's respect towards al-Sisi cannot be merely explained by Islamic juridical premises, but also by the party's struggle to control and shape religion, through the levers of the state if possible.[16]

The alignment of al-Nour with the political establishment, which is hated by many Egyptians, can be considered both beneficial and problematic for the party. Al-Nour's inclusion in the post-2013 setting, despite the constitutional ban on political parties founded on religious premises in 2014, was in the regime's best interests to maintain a façade of a certain view of religion. This shift in Salafi strategy has not been accepted by all within al-Nour's ranks. Divisions within the party emerged in the second half of 2012, during the campaign for the 2012 presidential elections in June. The political campaign in itself was a testing moment for alliances previously formed at street level, in particular the fragile and short-term support between the Salafis and the Muslim Brotherhood between February and April 2012. Intra-Salafi tensions led to the formation of al-Watan, which presented itself as being more moderate and distant from the Da'wa's doctrines. However, other Salafi factions' influence in politics has been minor compared to al-Nour's.

Under al-Sisi's presidency, al-Nour began to adopt an even stronger anti-Brotherhood position, in addition to the state crackdown conducted by Farid al-Tuhami after he was appointed Head of Intelligence (Kirkpatrick, 2013). Al-Nour's support for 'anti-terrorism' policies and discourses ultimately led to a strategic synchronism with the EAF on the one hand, and al-Sisi on the other. In 2015 al-Nour's spokesperson Makhioun proposed to al-Sisi a unified national agenda to combat terrorism, with a follow-up meeting with EAF generals (Olidort, 2015). However, despite possible shared interests between al-Nour, EAF and al-Sisi, there is a higher level of complexity in what is believed to be the army's dissatisfaction towards al-Sisi's capacity to act political leader, as discussed in Chapter 4.

Hence, the argument of a linearity in al-Nour-EAF relations, implying a synchronism between the EAF and al-Sisi as suggested by Olidort (2015), risks over-simplifying the configuration of internal alliances and actors after the 2013 setting. This chapter instead focuses on the politicisation of al-Nour in its goal to gain a form of control over society, like the Muslim Brotherhood had for decades, despite their cyclical existence.[17] This goal benefitted from al-Nour's return to sheikhs' policies, and al-Sisi's need to create a basis of consensus through reference to Islam, once both the rule of law and charisma had failed in bridging the gap in internal legitimacy. From the perspective of political leadership, however, the tolerance of al-Nour by al-Sisi discloses an additional level of complexity, intertwined with both actors' desire to exercise influence and gain control over the al-Azhar, which remains the fulcrum of today's political disputes on the one hand, and the attempt of the legitimation of authority on the other.[18]

Al-Sisi's tolerance of political Salafism, despite constitutional regulations prohibiting parties formed on a religious basis, can be explained by three factors:[19]

(i) Salafism's methodological and operational inability to exert effective control over the institutionalised political realm and pose a direct threat as political force like the well-structured Muslim Brotherhood;
(ii) Salafis as a strategic asset through which to assert an apparent societal consensus towards the political executive; and
(iii) tactical acceptance and inclusion of Salafis in order to divide Egyptian Islamists.

The institutional, and temporal, tolerance of al-Nour was not ultimately aimed at polishing al-Sisi's image as an unofficial representative of Islamism (Aziz, 2017). Aziz's claim is underpinned by the idea that Salafis benefitted from a widespread domestic social consensus, which might have helped the leader gain support and bolster his image before both the public and the al-Azhar due to his orthodoxy. However, this view is problematic. Immediately after 2013, and during the 2014 presidential election, al-Nour indeed temporarily mobilised social consensus towards al-Sisi in areas such as the slum of Ezbet al-Haggana in Cairo where there was previously a Muslim Brotherhood presence (Farah, 2009). However, according to SC1, 'it is not a matter of what al-Sisi says; what he wants is the control of religion, in order to align it to his political view', particularly the al-Azhar.[20] In fact, the sharply anti-Muslim Brotherhood direction of most of al-Sisi's post-2013 policies have reflected civil society's reaction against the official imposition of a Sharia-influenced moral code and the perceived Islamisation of society under the FJP. There was thus dissent raised when restrictions on moral conduct were introduced in 2016 by al-Sisi, under the indirect influence of Hizb al-Nour. Moreover, considering the al-Azhar as the official representative of Islam, the establishment *ulema* soon after the 2013 coup, and framing the al-Azhar as more-or-less supportive of Salafism, is a mistake, due to the al-Azhar's internal ideological diversifications, which are reflection of external political fragmentations.[21]

The toleration of Hizb al-Nour by the authorities was not strictly embedded in the ruler's need to polish his own image as a form of defence. Rather, recalling the implications stemming from the analysis into the legal framework conducted in Chapter 3 above, it is asserted that the Salafis were initially tactically employed by al-Sisi as counterweight to limit the spread of the Muslim Brotherhood on the one hand, and control possible army disloyalty and defections on the other.[22] The Muslim Brotherhood are seen even by secularist commentators as one of the most important social forces within Egypt, and possessing great influence among many people.[23] However, Salafism has presented itself as ideologically purist, but also adaptable to post-2013 circumstances, compared to the Brotherhood, which was not only insufficiently religious, and less adaptable to political platforms. This has made it possible for al-Sisi and al-Nour to balance their mutual support, with the primary purpose of targeting the Brotherhood.

Al-Sisi's tactical tolerance of Hizb al-Nour has not included his contemplation of a solid alliance, because al-Nour has proven to be an unstable ally and, after the initial moment of the 2013 coup, has been ineffective in winning significant support for the government.[24] Rather, al-Sisi's tolerance of Salafis has remained strictly within tactical boundaries. What the regime believed is that, if it targeted all the Islamists together, they would prove a stronger resistance. This could push the Islamists into a united front, making them stronger. The regime and al-Sisi were more intelligent in that sense. They only attacked the Muslim Brotherhood, and tried to include the other Islamists (i.e. the Salafis) in this attack. This prevented the Muslim Brotherhood from making the argument that the government was oppressing Muslims and Islam in general. It was in the regime's strategy to include some Islamists within its efforts, just to target the Brotherhood.[25]

On Salafi groups' part, there was a high level of diversity on the question of whether to play a political game. In early 2013, other Salafi parties (namely al-Watan, al-Bina and al-Fadila) initially expressed some solidarity with the Muslim Brotherhood and joined the anti-coup Brotherhood-led National Alliance, then stepped back from politics, returning to a form of quietism (Ahram Online, 2014b). Al-Nour seized the opportunity for exercising pressure against the Muslim Brotherhood by supporting al-Sisi's political actions. The pro-regime (or at least neutral) legacy of al-Da'wa and ideological influence of the thirteenth-century Islamic philosopher Ibn Taymiyya on al-Nour, plus its desire to exercise some influence on societal identity, explain why the party sided with military authorities in initially supporting the coup.

These experiences ultimately had a strong impact on al-Nour itself. Despite the lack of friction between the post-2013 authorities and al-Nour, the party won only one seat in the 2013 Parliamentary Assembly, and failed to achieve any other substantial benefit. Lacroix argues that the transformation of the political landscape, and al-Nour's reorientation towards politics over preachers, led al-Nour to be no longer strictly identifiable as an Islamist party, in purist terms. Lacroix refers to 'arguments of necessity' used to justify concessions which moved the party away from the Da'wa's theological roots (Lacroix, 2016).

After the coup, a gradual process of state marginalisation of al-Nour began when the party was not consulted by al-Sisi in the drafting of the 2014 Constitution. In SC1's view, the tactical toleration of al-Nour by al-Sisi turned into a threat when both actors found themselves in a position to shape religion and politics, because ultimately all the actors in the domestic political field are competitors.[26] Furthermore, the extent to which al-Nour ever substantially aided al-Sisi is an open question. While El-Dine (2014) argues that Hizb al-Nour was an important determinant of al-Sisi's legitimacy, this work contends that the Salafi party structurally did not add any form of legitimacy to the executive after 2014. The tolerance of the Salafis did not glorify al-Sisi in the eyes of the al-Azhar, considered a pillar for autocrats' durability since 1961. Rather, al-Sisi's intention of using Islam as a source of building legitimation with the religious establishment, including by flirting with the Salafis, in fact provoked tension with the establishment, including clashes which became sharper between 2016 and 2018. This chapter now turns in closer detail to the role of this establishment in providing the regime with legitimacy.

Here a focus on the nature of the leadership can explain why a government can make decisions regarding alliances which may not be beneficial for the state as a whole. The toleration of al-Nour in the domestic context after 2012 was short-term and fulfilled the need to provide ideological and moral support to the leadership for its survival, so as not to target the entire Islamist block and produce a counter-discourse of the regime's opposition to Islam itself. Internal realignments should also be considered in combination with a change in external patronage, in which a shift in the latter helps in balancing the internal threat. The apparent realignment with al-Nour coincided with an external change in Egyptian foreign policy and patrons, with the pro-Muslim Brotherhood Qatar, explicitly Islamist (within the bounds of international acceptability) in its discourse, with the much more moderate, pro-Western UAE. The alignment between UAE and al-Sisi enabled the Egyptian leadership to articulate a rhetoric of religious moderation (Cafiero, 2019). Hence, there could be room for arguing that al-Sisi's appropriation of religious discourse, initially with an alliance with al-Nour, and intensifying between 2015 and 2017, might have been an attempt, at least initially, at emulating the UAE's reference to moderate religion as platform of legitimation.

Phase III: The reactive phase

The religionisation of political discourses

In 2014, Qatar-based Egyptian Islamist Yussuf al-Qaradawi issued a *fatwa* encouraging Egyptians not to vote for al-Sisi in the presidential elections, declaring al-Sisi's path to institutional power as immoral and violent. If al-Qaradawi's *fatwa* attempted to discredit al-Sisi's leadership, it also represented a shift in the al-Azhar's view of the authorities. Recalling the contributions of Weber's *The Sociology of Religion* (1978) and Beetham (1991), the understanding of belief systems as an interpretative process stemming out of the interplay of material needs (exogenous level) and actors' goals (endogenous level), in al-Sisi's Egypt. This was materialised in the urgent material need of stabilising the political authority on the one hand, and adding another source of legitimacy to a deteriorating leadership, on the other – after the societal effects caused by the amended penal code that set the new foundations of the state and the short-limited role of charisma, which it is recalled was conceived as intra-hierarchical and addressed to

God, the political seductor 151

Table 5.2 Codebook of al-Sisi's December 2015 speech at the al-Azhar

Node number	Nodes' explanation	Coded references	%
1	Focus on the community of believers	2	40.98
2	Al-Sisi's self-location above religious authorities	3	23.20
3	Al Sisi as mandator of a doctrinal truth	2	15.64
4	Accusation to the Al-Azhar	1	10.31

the army, rather than being top-down, and as such oriented towards the societal materiality of the urban fabric.

It is within the context of these domestic social and spiritual attitudes that al-Sisi's December 2015 speech at the al-Azhar should be contextualised. In that context, al-Sisi called for revolutionising Islamic thought. However, the intention behind the speech also created a gap between al-Sisi and the *ulema*, which from a content perspective shown in Table 5.2 becomes tangible at nodes 2 and 3 respectively. However, al-Sisi's more aggressive tone used against the religious establishment (the al-Azhar) remains minimal, at least from a merely textual reference, as node 4 shows, though it was not with regard to the political actions.

This shift in the political authority's relocation above the religion authorities resulted both from the presidency's attempt to amend the FJP's 2014 Constitution Article 4, which specifically focused on the al-Azhar, and from the episode of the Raba'a massacre of 2013 which remains the most ferocious mass murder in the modern history of Egypt, after which Ahmad al-Tayyeb, Grand Imam of the al-Azhar, called for an end to the aggression against supporters of the FJP, with the goal of 'protecting the sanctity of blood and preventing the country from falling into a civil war' (Ahram Online, 2013).[27]

The political authority's displeasure with the al-Azhar's 'lack of action' on renewing Islamic discourse, however, was anticipated at the Ministry of Awqaf in January 2015 on the day of the birthday of Prophet Muhammad, in which al-Sisi targeted the *ulema* for the first time since he achieved the presidential mandate. This is something that did not happen in the country under predecessors, and when confrontations took place, political tones were previously more subdued. On that occasion he ordered the *ulema* to view Islam 'from a more enlightened perspective', and threatened that he would 'argue against you before Allah' on Judgement Day, if they did not begin the process of discursive reform (al-Sisi's speech at the Ministry of Awqaf, January 2015).

From a combined quantitative perspective, the reference by al-Sisi to the community of believers occupied a prominent role and was covered at 40.98 per cent in node 1 (Table 5.2), although coded references (three in total) in the speech were more in line with al-Sisi's firm assertion of his location above the religious authorities coded at 23.20 per cent of the entire speech and his self-framing as mandator of the doctrinal truth, coded at 15.64 per cent. The direct blaming of the *ulema* was coded just once in the speech, despite a significative coverage calculated in Nvivo at 10.31 per cent in node 4.

Arguments in the January and December 2015 speeches found reiteration in March 2018 (A) and March 2019 (B) (see Table 5.3), at the celebration of Laylat al-Qadr during the month of Ramadan. However, the two speeches revealed discoursive differences in the references to Islam and, broadly speaking, to its function, both ultimately linked to a form of justification through moral and ethical religious inspired values of the ruler's domestic political agenda, as coded in node 1 of Table 5.3 below. In both, the al-Azhar and the Ministry of the Awqaf were identified as beacons against radical ideologies and extremism. In the mind of many Egyptians, the al-Azhar is part of Egypt's political identity, having stood at the forefront in the fight against colonialism since Napoleon's attempted invasion at the end of the eighteenth century. It is believed that Napoleon failed to take control of Egypt because he failed to take control of the al-Azhar (Moustafa, 2000). In recent times, the al-Azhar *ulema* have attempted to distance themselves from the political establishment and political decisions, but in 1961 the religious establishment underwent a nationalisation through Law No. 103, which transformed it into a state arm. This imposed absolute political power not over the daily running of the institution per se, but was rather targeted at the politicisation of *fatawa* supporting Nasser's attempt to bolster his legitimacy and win consensus for his socialist reforms.

The spread of *jihadi* threats in the mid-1990s resulted in the leveraging of the al-Azhar, which was put at the forefront of fighting violent extremism (Moustafa, 2000). In turn, the regime provided more concessions to the institution, politically and financially. Budgets in support of the al-Azhar's expansion were approved by the state (Bano and Benadi, 2018; Moustafa, 2000). Under Mubarak, the regime–al-Azhar relations underwent further change with the appointment of Muhammed Sayyid Tantawi as Grand Imam, known for being theologically progressive, and who symbolised the strength of the regime over the *ulema* (Moustafa, 2000). Under Mubarak, the al-Azhar cooperated with the *mukhabarat* (security apparatuses) to support the NDP in the fight against radicalism, as part of the post-9/11 project of fighting violent ideologies. The al-Azhar re-emerged as an important player in the political and social vacuum created by the 2011 uprising. It

Table 5.3 Combined codebook of al-Sisi's speeches at the Laylat al-Qadr celebrations, 2018 (A)–2019 (B)

Node number		Source	Coded references	%
1.	Religious-economic agenda	A	4	11.10
2.	Ref. to religious discourse	B	1	
3.	Ref. to interfaith dialogue	B	1	
4.	Need to reinterpret religion	B	1	
5.	Conduct guided by the Prophet	B	1	
6	Al-Azhar/Ministry of Awqaf as minarets of Islam	B	1	
6.1	Al-Azhar/Min. Awqaf as actors rectifying misconceptions	A	1	7.52
6.2	Al-Azhar as minaret against radical ideologies	B	1	

took progressive steps forward by bringing together Coptic leaders, Islamists, opposition figures, women and youth, and sponsoring several consensus-building initiatives in a way that the SCAF failed to do.

The juridical dependence of the al-Azhar on the state remained unaltered until 2011. In 2012, the religious establishment gained constitutional independence from the FJP. Politically, this was finally made possible for two reasons: firstly because of the democratic platforms created in 2012, which made it possible to negotiate the al-Azhar's independence, and secondly because Morsi, unlike his predecessors, was never in control of all the levels of state of the Egyptian regime.[28]

The religious establishment still continued to play a central role soon after 2013. However, views of the al-Azhar's role in the scholarship and among the analysts I interviewed vary widely. Some consider the al-Azhar as close to the Muslim Brotherhood ideology, while others pointed out internal fragmentations and divisions within the institution, making it impossible to identify a hegemonic ideological trend over the others within the religious establishment. PR1, while acknowledging the existence of competing internal trends within the religious establishment, identifies the dominant one as close to the Brotherhood. Al-Sisi and the SCAF understood that pro-Morsi and pro-uprising sentiments had emerged early within the al-Azhar, and an anti-regime hub could coalesce in the al-Azhar.[29] According to SC1, defining the al-Azhar as monolithic would be erroneous: 'There are different leaderships inside the al-Azhar, with competition between Salafis and the Muslim Brotherhood. The competition between religious actors outside the al-Azhar is reflected within the al-Azhar'.[30]

The polarisation in al-Azhar–al-Sisi's relations in 2015 did not prevent al-Sisi's insistence on the role that a variety of political institutions can play in shaping religion, and thus no longer identifying the al-Azhar as the only actor in the position of calibrating religious dogmas. Unlike the March 2018 speech (A), which was more focused on the need to rectify misconceptions and apply a religious ethics to the economic agenda, coded at nodes 1 and 6.1, in 2019 (B) covered more aspects of the function of religion. Although the Ministry of Awqaf's function remained unaltered and institutionalised, as an actor in the position of shaping religion alongside the al-Azhar, the speech returned to the call for revolutionising and reinterpreting religion, similar in terms of its goal with the December 2015 speech at the al-Azhar. Both can be explained by evolution in the political domain after 2015: if on the one hand al-Sisi was forced to seek approval for his reforms, he additionally faced the *ulema*'s resistance to his appropriation of tradition, on the other.

In the March 2018 speech, the context of Laylat al-Qadr required a discursive emphasis on Islam as a pillar of civilisation, science and progress, with the latter requiring 'work'.[31] The triangulation between progress, development and citizens' sacrifices is not a novelty in al-Sisi's speeches, and such an argument was used in his March 2014 speech announcing his candidacy to the presidential elections. However, the words 'sacrifices and hard work' in 2014 also presented a promise to society, based on the belief that the 2011 uprising was driven principally by economic inequality and institutionalised corruption (Teti and Abbott, 2016), and acted a legitimating driver supporting al-Sisi's candidacy. Indeed, after 2014 al-Sisi found himself with the structural need to build societal consensus that would have made the leadership look more reliable before the armed forces.

The reference to religion and economic progress and reforms played a more relevant function than al-Sisi's focus on the al-Azhar as found in node 1 and sub-node 6.1 (Table 5.3), despite the significant tensions with the religious establishment in 2018. The reference to economic progress is explained by the economic reforms and IMF stimulation package accepted by al-Sisi after 2014, which initiated cuts to energy and then food subsidies, amongst other adjustments. Similar cuts, which involved the depreciation and devaluation of the Egyptian pound, can be found in 1977, though under different structural premises from those presented in 2014–2017 (see Momami, 2003). This in turn exposed the fragilities of a society with an unemployment rated estimated at 13.4 in 2014 (ILO, 2014), unable to react to the rise in food stuff but also unable to contest the legitimation of the status quo and the undertaken economic reforms due to the anti-protest law enacted in 2014.

There is a significant shift from 'sacrifices and hard work', as a condition of necessity justified by the neoliberal market, and which served the purpose of providing a form of justification for the militarisation of megaprojects, to the conceptualisation of progress and economic development as reached by work attached to a correct interpretation of Islamic economic values and tradition in 2018. This was a highly strategic move with the goal of preventing waves of dissent instigated by cuts to fuel subsidies introduced in July 2014, which fulfilled the expectations of the IMF and ratings institutions and rid the state budget of a heavy burden, but transferred this to millions of consumers. As discussed in depth in Chapter 6, this raised prices for fuel in the framework of fuel subsidies reform. Petrol and butane increased by 22 to 25 per cent between 2014 and 2017. After the local currency was floated in 2017, fuel prices increased by 34.6 per cent for Octane, by 30.6 for diesel and by 45.5 for natural gas.[32] Hence, religion in 2018 was tactically employed in the ruler's narrative in connection to economic reforms and the reform to fuel subsidies to repay yet another IMF loan of billions USD. Ideologically and morally, there was an intensification in tensions between al-Sisi and al-Tayyeb, initiated in 2015 over the modernisation of the religious establishment. This accounted for a shift in the Laylat al-Qadr speech in 2019, emphasised the need to re-interpret Islam, and to live by the example of the Prophet (as found in nodes 1, 2 and 4 of Table 5.4), and the importance of interfaith dialogue and the acceptance of 'secular views' in the country, as found in node 5.

Yet again, this was tactical and politically connected to the process of legitimation, but certainly did not envision a political programme based on secularised visions. Religious minorities in the country have been at the core of contentions and critical discussions which exposed the regime's domestic modus operandi. Al-Sisi had previously presented himself as a devout Muslim believer, and had vigorously rejected atheism as a threat to national security (Darwish, 2015; Kingsley, 2015; 2014). He continued to portray himself as a devout Muslim, with photos from his Umrah pilgrimage to Mecca appearing on his Twitter account in May 2019 (al-Sisi's Twitter account, 2019). The al-Azhar's disobedience to al-Sisi was tactically played by the latter, who claimed to consider an opening to other religions in the country, playing the strategic double game of both the conservative and reformist, potentially recalibrating internal support towards the leadership, rather than the religious establishment. The dispute between al-Sisi and al-Tayyeb represents a discrepancy in the former's strategies of internal support, considering that historically that since the 1970s the al-Azhar has determined the political durability of the different regimes that succeeded in

Table 5.4 Codebook of al-Sisi speech at Laylat al-Qadr, March 2019 (B)

Node numer		Coded References	%
1	Conduct guided by the Prophet	1	7.24
2	Need to reinterpret religion	1	3.27
3	Al-Azhar/Ministry of Awqaf as minarets of Islam	1	4.56
3.1	Al-Azhar as minaret against radical ideologies	1	10.71
4	Ref. to religious discourse	1	9.95
5	Ref. to interfaith dialogue/ acceptance of secular views	1	6.65

the country. The poor relations between al-Sisi and al-Tayyeb represented tensions over access to power and the consequent capacity to shape religion, as claimed by SC1. In 2016, al-Tayyeb rejected an Islamic conference in Chechnya, hosted by Egypt and the UAE. The conference aimed to impose a strict leadership over religious institutions and pushed for an effort to isolate radical ideologies. Politically, the conference attempted to target Salafis and the already-banned Muslim Brotherhood, and called for the backing of the religious establishment, a call which however remained unheeded. Recalling the dynamics of internal re-balancing (David, 1991), according to one of the interviewees, al-Sisi's shift from tolerating to countering Salafism demonstrated the Salafists' irrelevance as either a political threat (despite their politicisation) or a basis of support.[33] Al-Tayyeb adopted an opposing position to that of al-Sisi and the UAE.

The conference did not lead to the result the incumbent hoped for, an official theological declaration against the Muslim Brotherhood and Salafism, but generated major difficulties at a foreign policy level, with Saudi Arabia declaring the conference as a Russian-Iranian conspiracy against Sunni Islam. Al-Tayyeb and other Sunni Institutions expressed solidarity with Saudi Arabia. From a political perspective, al-Sisi's goal of controlling the spread of Salafism and the Brotherhood negatively impacted the al-Azhar's perception of and trust in al-Sisi. This left the gap in internal legitimacy unfilled, while compromising al-Sisi's capacity to exercise control over the state structures in a Nasserian manner. The shift in the religious establishment's view of the leadership, and its refusal in providing a form of legitimation by traditional premises, explain the inclusion in a new law in 2019, of preventing the al-Azhar's

Grand Imam, among other high authorities of state, from travelling outside Egypt without prior approval from the President (Middle East Monitor, 2019). The law was introduced following constitutional amendments in 2018, aiming at the further centralisation of presidential powers.

However, there have also been sights of rapprochement between the two. By comparison with the December 2015 talk, the 2018 statement by the Ministry of Awqaf on behalf of al-Sisi, while remaining focused on Islam and its need of reform, was strategically premised towards moderation, which may have been a precondition for a return to a dialogue between the two parties (Yehoshua, 2020). Once again, this shift is considered closer to the construction of a *strategy* for revolutionising Islam, out of the previous not so much failures but implications left by the failure in referring to rule of law and charisma in fixed and readapted structural-political boundaries.

When understood as a tool for improving Egypt's image as a regional pillar of tolerance, al-Sisi's reference to and re-appropriation of religion reveals a more domestic level of complexity, around the re-evaluation of the state and the battle over tradition and legitimation of the political authority. Even before 2013, al-Sisi portrayed himself as strongly pious; his apparent religiosity was so well known that Morsi appointed him as Commander-in-Chief in August 2012. However, between 2015 and 2016 al-Sisi's religiosity began to impact on political trajectories. Rather than applying religious dogmas to the governmental domain with the purpose of rectifying political conduct and proposing a specific form of government, al-Sisi's reference to dogmas attempted to incorporate an older style of politics with religion. This resulted in al-Sisi's attempt at appropriating religion for personalised ends. This appropriation of religion protracted to 2022.

Weber defined religious dogmas as both contextualised to the system in which they find reproduction, and conditioned by external factors (Weber, 1963). In the case of al-Sisi's Egypt, the personalisation in the interpretation of dogmas was conditioned by the internal necessity to reduce the leadership's exposition to structural risks (e.g. disloyalty or disaffection) while presenting himself as the holder of political solutions and the protector of the masses. Combining data gathered by the BTI from 2014 to 2018 with the implications of the reactive phase discussed above in this chapter, the parameter of 'interference of religious dogmas' shifted from 4 on a 0–10 scale in 2014 to 6 in 2016, and remained at this level in 2018 (BTI, 2014–2018). The improvement derived from constitutional reinterpretations and the roll-back of the influence of Sharia by the Supreme Constitutional Court. However, the BTI's data show gaps in inclusion of the sub-parameter of 'no interference of religious dogmas' in the taxonomy of stateness. Data gathered between 2016 and 2018 suggest a popular optimism about the presidency's response to the call for religious freedom (BTI, 2018; see al-Masry al-Youm, 2018).

However, the official policy of religious freedom began only in 2018, and arguably did not emerge organically from al-Sisi's agenda, but was strategically tailored out of the President's failure to negotiate a pact with Islamic religious authorities in the 2016 tensions with the al-Azhar and al-Tayyeb (*Egypt Independent*, 2017). As hinted at above, religious freedom and pluralism were more determined by a socio-political 'condition of need' rather than by a political project of inclusivity.

Returning to al-Sisi's 2015 speech at the al-Azhar, it represented, at least in part, a kind of reappropriation of Nasser's Law of 1961, which declared the preaching of unregistered imams illegal but also replaced the Council of Senior Scholars (Ha'yat Kibar al-Ulema) with a new body controlled by the Ministry of Endowment, thus giving power to the ruler to directly nominate the Grand Imam of the al-Azhar. In 2015, the centralisation of imams and control over mosques were issues on which, internally, al-Sisi's regime was closer to the Mubarak era than to Nasser, due to Mubarak's comparative reluctance to implement reforms. Al-Sisi's 2015 speech at the al-Azhar thus took a different approach to his recent predecessors in the struggle for the legitimation of the leadership in particular, rather than the broader authoritarian machine. The speech, for the first time, harshly blamed the *ulema*'s weakness in countering 'radical ideologies', attributing responsibility for the spread of what al-Sisi defined as 'misinterpreted Islam' to the theological authorities. He began by blaming the 'thinking' of the religious establishment, embodied in a 'corpus of texts and ideas that we have sacralised over the years', which had the impact of 'antagonising the entire world'. To his audience, he had accused 'You, imams, are responsible before Allah [...] because this *umma* [the Islamic nation] is being torn, it is being destroyed, it is being lost – and it is being lost by our own hands' (al-Sisi's speech at the al-Azhar, 2015). The accusation was reiterated with greater intensity in 2018, with the condemnation issued by the Egyptian presidency on the Supreme Council of the al-Azhar for not issuing statements on gender equality in inheritance (*Daily News Egypt*, 2018).

The presidency's self-portrayal as omniscient in the political domain is also reflected in the spiritual field; PR1 stated 'the ruler [al-Sisi] wants to provide an example of what Islam should be'.[34] This attitude clashed with domestic religious actors' interpretation of religion and the political project, exacerbating the existing competition over traditional power and projecting it into social, spiritual and political domains. PR1's view of al-Sisi's behavioural conceit is confirmed in the protraction of tensions between the presidency and al-Tayyeb over the issue of *talaq* (divorce) a few years later in 2017 and from 2019 onwards.[35]

The polarisation in al-Sisi–al-Azhar relations, it is thought, would have had implications on internal alliances and realignments. In this regard, PR1

God, the political seductor 159

argued that the polarisation brought together the army and the religious establishment in opposition to al-Sisi. In 2015, the al-Azhar shifted from initial support toward al-Sisi, to condemnation and distance from the political leadership. The shift in the al-Azhar corresponded to a critical phase at the level of the leadership and al-Sisi's call for revolutionising Islamic thinking. In this regard, PR1 notes how the Sheikh of the al-Azhar made a public comment against 'Islamic revisionist thinkers. He was really responding to al-Sisi's call. The sheikh essentially criticised some of the premises of al-Sisi's regime, indicating the dynamics of where the al-Azhar stands'.[36]

Al-Sisi's speaking in the name of religion was not limited to the public-political sphere, but also now expanded to the ethical domain. This contributed to his pushing for a more inclusive form of religious populism, which is considered below. From 2015 to 2019 religious superiority claimed by the ruler corresponded to a *tactical meta-frame*. Unlike the frames attached to the rule of law and charisma, as analysed earlier in this book, the tactical meta-frame of religion provides meaning to the interaction. Tactical framing has been defined as a method of achieving a strategic goal (Dombos et al., 2009). In addition, tactical frames operate at the micro-level of framing. Thus, al-Sisi's attempt at revolutionising Islam is considered a *strategic meta-frame*, an effort to construct a discourse within which different political actors occupy a centrality in the process of reconstruction of the state's identity, poised between a nationalistic historical past and neo-reinterpretation of cultural symbols. Politically, the call for revolutionising religion translated into the will to push for a change in citizens' attitudes to Islamist actors on the one hand, and reshape the role of religious authorities on the other, with the ultimate tactical goal of strengthening anti-Muslim Brotherhood trends within the al-Azhar – this after the consolidation of a centralised influence over Dar al-Iftaa, which endorsed the regime's policies towards the Muslim Brotherhood but also the regime's Grand Ethiopian Renaissance Dam, which was contested by the al-Azhar and framed as a tyrannic appropriation of a public good (i.e. water). This division and different framing of the regime resonates a deep polarisation that does not facilitate the overall process of internal consensus and faith, as externally projected.

Recalling specific and internal support, al-Sisi's struggle in finding a base of support over religious matters shifted from an internal and specific (Easton, 1975; Gerschewski, 2013) strategy built on charisma and the rule of law, to an external and more diffused axis of international consensus-seeking. On the occasion of the 70th Session of the UN General Assembly in 2015, al-Sisi delivered a speech in which, apart from updating the international community on Egypt's programme of development and economic innovations, delved into diffuse understandings of Islam. In doing so, al-Sisi did not recall the moral and doctrinal role religious institutions should play in

Table 5.5 Strategic and tactical frames attached by al-Sisi to religion and revolutionising Islam as attached to the reconstruction of the state

Object of the frame	Category of frame	Function
Religion	Tactical meta-frame	Specific method of achieving strategic goal
Call for revolutionising Islam	Strategic meta-frame	Construct discursive conditions in which actors are central

'purifying' religious dogmas from radical ideologies, as he did in 2015. Rather, an analysis of the content of the 2018 statement demonstrates that al-Sisi's discourse was less aggressive than his address in December 2015 at the al-Azhar. This moderation in tone demonstrated a discursive strategy placing a greater emphasis on actors (Dombos et al., 2009).

Al-Sisi's speech at the General Assembly in 2016 in New York was centred on the ruler's struggle to find a source of justification for the leadership's actions not domestically, but rather among the neutral external actors among UN-member states attending the UN General Assembly, as coded at node 1 and sub-nodes 1.1 and 5.1 in Table 5.6. Despite this, at node 4 al-Sisi's attempt to justify his position as real mandator of the doctrinal truth – the purification of Islam from radical ideologies, ultimately connected to the framing and labelling of the Muslim Brotherhood as a terrorist organisation – before the international community, has the goal of framing himself on an international level as a key point of reference for the so-called 'war on terror' in the Mediterranean area.

The process of coding has been expanded to include three more themes:

(i) the search for international consensus towards al-Sisi's leadership for domestic policies;
(ii) the search for international consensus (diplomatic level) for foreign policy; and
(iii) a self-framing of the leader as driven by a sense of domestic and international responsibility.

From a quantitative comparison with the December 2015 speech, which was more internally oriented and aimed at presenting al-Sisi as a religious authority in the position of redefining the boundaries of religious interpretation, the September 2016 speech at the UN General Assembly prioritised the search of consensus, more on external and diplomatic axes. Furthermore, in a context

Table 5.6 Codebook for the December 2015 (A) speech at the al-Azhar and September 2016 (B) speech at the UN General Assembly

Node number	Nodes	Sources	Coded references	%
1	Search for international consensus on domestic policies	B	3	2.36
1.1	Search for external consensus toward the leadership on regional issues	B	5	40.98
2	Community of believers	B	5	23.2
3	Al-Sisi's self-location above authorities	B	3	23.2
4	Al Sisi as mandator of a doctrinal truth	A-B	4	12.22
5	Accusation to the Al-Azhar	B	1	15.65
5.1	Al-Sisi's self-framing as religious and responsible leader	B	2	0.99

of growing tensions with the al-Azhar, the collapse in the reciprocal attempt at legitimation with Hizb al-Nour, and signs of initial dissent against the repression of civil society, in October 2016 the ruler held the first Youth Conference in Sharm El-Sheikh. On that occasion, al-Sisi centralised the fight against terrorism and religious radicalism. This double-shift urges reflection on the structural effects determined by the tactical framing of religion, and the leadership's capacity to reach out to all segments of society (*The Economist*, 2017).

PHASE IV: DECLINING RELATIONS

A dissociative phase: on the army's internal realignments

Regarding the internal transformation of the nexus between politics and tradition, the theorised isolationism of the political leadership became highly politicised in 2016 when al-Tayyeb rejected the Islamic Conference in Chechnya, intended to be under the direct authority of al-Sisi and the UAE. The conference aimed to impose a tight leadership over religious institutions, and pushed for a joint effort in isolating radical ideologies. Politically, the 2016 Islamic Conference attempted to expand the targeting to Salafists, as well as the already-banned Muslim Brotherhood, and sought the backing of the religious establishment, a call which, however, remained unheeded. Recalling omnibalancing theory (David, 1991) and the dynamics of internal rebalancing, and expanding on the remarks of PR1, al-Sisi's shift from tolerating to countering politicised Salafis was representative of the Salafists' inability to represent a political threat (despite the politicisation of the trend) or win a broad base of support.[37] Al-Tayyeb differed from the positions of al-Sisi and the UAE, adopting a broad definition of Islam which would also include those hostile to the model of political authority in Egypt and the UAE (al-Tayyeb, Grozny Islamic Conference, 2016). The Islamic Conference did not fulfil al-Sisi's hopes of achieving an official Sunni condemnation of the Brotherhood and Salafis, and in fact generated major foreign policy implications, with Saudi Arabia declaring the conference as a Russian and Iranian conspiracy against Sunni Islam. This declaration was joined by other Sunni institutions which, expressing solidarity with Saudi Arabia, left Egypt and the UAE isolated.

From a political perspective, al-Sisi's goals of controlling the spread of Salafism on the one hand, and preventing the reorganisation of the Muslim Brotherhood on the other, led to boomerang effects which negatively impacted the al-Azhar's perception of and trust towards the incumbent and the symbolic and political meaning the religious establishment plays. This left the gap of internal legitimacy unfilled and compromised al-Sisi's capacity to exercise control over the state structures, at least in a mythified Nasserian manner as hoped.

Conclusions

After three decades of partial marginalisation, religion returned to play a more central function in the dynamics of regime durability in Egypt. The opening to political platforms in 2011, and the entrance into legal politics by the Muslim Brotherhood, followed by a politicisation of the Salafis, helped forge new bonds between religion and politics. However, the new trajectories in Islamist politics fuelled competition over political projects and over control of the religious establishment (i.e. the al-Azhar), and ultimately resulted in new power struggles. This struggle persists today, though it has entered a phase of paucity.

Al-Sisi's reference to religion and attempted positioning himself as a reformist thinker corresponded to a political *tactical frame*, in turn an extension of the *motivational frame*. The tactical meta-frame of the call for a revolution in religious thought aimed to locate al-Sisi above the al-Azhar, with the goal of subordinating the religious establishment to his political authority. This signified a partial reversal of the independence previously granted by the FJP to the religious establishment.

The strategy of cultivating, at least initially in 2015, a pro-incumbent support from the Salafis to counter the risk of the Muslim Brotherhood (Gerschewski, 2013), was also inscribed into deeper mechanisms of societal cohesion. Indeed, it has emerged that the short-term toleration of the Salafi party Hizb al-Nour in 2015–2016 was a wise move from al-Sisi, with the goal of maintaining a certain role for Islam in the new state infrastructures. Due to the unbridged gap in legitimacy left by the failure of the rule of law and charisma, there was a strategic need to keep an Islamic-rooted identity for the state foundations, to minimise the risk of social revolts. Al-Sisi's later call for religious reformism between 2016 and 2019 acted as both a *tactical* and *stategic meta-frame*, but antagonised relations between al-Sisi and al-Nour, since both ultimately aimed at exerting their own control of the al-Azhar. In certain authoritarian systems, mostly personalist illiberal regimes, controlling the church or the religious sphere results in a form of symbolism for the entire system, to the point that controlling or exercising a form of control and influence over religious endowments corresponds to controlling the entire political apparatus.

Al-Sisi's struggle to gain control over the al-Azhar was in fact at the core of relations with internal actors and their views of the executive. As emerged from interviews and data, al-Sisi's self-presentation as reformist thinker was perceived by the *ulema* as an arrogant attempt deriving from al-Sisi's personality. Despite the existence of multiple trends within the religious establishment, the dominant Wahhabism of the al-Azhar has worked as a counterweight to al-Sisi's project of religious reforms, which aimed to marginalise pro-Muslim Brotherhood and Wahhabi attitudes within the al-Azhar. The ideological shift within the al-Azhar reflected domestic political realignments amongst actors and a new view of the executive, which took shape between 2015 and 2019. Internal struggles over reformisms in Islamic thought protracted however as part of the al-Azhar's attempt of exercising and safeguarding independence from the political executive (see on this Yehoshua, 2020; State Information Service, 2020a).

The failure in emulating Nasser's ability to control the al-Azhar has resulted in two more discrepancies. The first relates to the continuing influence of the Brotherhood's ideology in the state structures; the second concerns the theorised intra-SCAF disloyalty, in turn possibly emerging from a penchant within the military hierarchy for Wahhabism. As PR1 noted, a SCAF realignment with the Brotherhood, facilitated by the al-Azhar, is not beyond the bounds of possibility in the future of Egypt: 'If the military become sufficiently displeased with al-Sisi, they might open the door for some sort of channel of communication with the Muslim Brotherhood. The conditions are being created for some sort of opening. The Brotherhood itself, in recent years, has been going through a process of regional regrouping'.[38]

If the political ruler's 'seduction through God' still failed in providing a source of legitimation to political authority, it did in fact lead to a significant redefinition of internal alliances. Two implications have emerged in this regard. It pushed the al-Azhar and the government apart, despite some attempts in late 2019 by al-Sisi in smoothing relations. Al-Sisi's moderation suggests a recognition of the continuing relevance of the institution within political boundaries. In addition, the enhancement of the Wahhabi trend within the al-Azhar marginalised Salafis' ability to exercise influence and play a role in politics and in the EAF (as they had done in 2013, acting as the religious wing of the SCAF), and thus downgrading the relevance of the trend within the al-Azhar. Yet shifts in the rebalancing of alliances with internal actors, and al-Sisi's attempt to rely on the support of the Salafi party Hizb al-Nour, were major failures which left the legitimation void unfilled.

Alternately, the call for revolutionising Islam was intended to distance the state from the Wahhabi-Muslim Brotherhood trend. However, this chapter found that its results risked reinforcing the link between the Wahhabi al-Azharist tradition and the SCAF's pro-Brotherhood/Wahhabi trend. The September 2019 protests against the regime, while not aiming at al-Sisi's complete overthrow, had a highly symbolic importance, publically disclosing the fragility of the army's loyalty to the President.[39]

While religion has had a determinant function since the 2011 uprising, and over the past nine years has been used in an attempt to influence and shape the trajectories in domestic politics, the role it ultimately played has been confined to the protection of a national cultural identity as represented by the al-Azhar, with no actual capacity to interfere in the political sphere, nor add much to the legitimation of political authority, despite the incumbent's attempts. While religion has not been as marginal in the political process as it has been in Tunisia, its relevance in politics nevertheless declined after 2017. In this regard, the religionisation and personalisation of the political discourse, and the ruler attacks on the *ulema*, became perceived in some circles as an assault on the country's historical cultural identity. It risked the fragmentation of SCAF internal loyalty, and the revival of the Wahhabi ideology, which could bring the al-Azhar and some sections of the SCAF closer to the Muslim Brotherhood. The mismanagement of the reference to religion and its personalisation again in recent years has exposed the authority to major structural risks, which still persist today as despite the ban and exiles of Muslim Brotherhood's member in Turkey, the Muslim Brotherhood remains intertwined with some internal trends that still exist within the al-Azhar and some segments from the armed forces.

Notes

1. On Tunisia after the 2019 elections see Blanc and Sigilllò (2019).
2. Author interview with SC1.
3. Author interview with SC1.
4. Author interview with PR1.
5. Author interview with PR1.
6. Author interview with SC1.
7. Author interview with PR1.
8. Author interview with SC1.
9. Egypt's *ashwaiyyat* are not 'free-standing' urban spaces (Dorman and Stein, 2013: 6), they are porous areas that the central authority started to be unable to penetrate from the 1990s, and the failure to effectively control the periphery ended up with a state framing of areas as dangerous due to the Jamaat al-Islamiya.
10. Author interview with PR1.
11. Although popular amongst some young Salafis, protests against him in May 2012 erupted, when his house in the Dokki neighbourhood was set on fire (personal observations by the author).
12. This marked a point of agreement amongst views. Author interviews with PR1 and SC1.
13. Author interview with PR1.
14. Author interview with PR1.
15. As this passage clearly states in the text: 'There will be no good without work; this is the principle upon which the deep-rooted Islamic civilisation was founded' (al-Sisi's speech on Laylat al-Qadr, March 2018).
16. Author interview with SC1.
17. See Munson (2001: 499) on the tactical survival of the Muslim Brotherhood despite attempts at suppressing the organisation, which happened in 1948.
18. Author interview with SC1.
19. Author interviews with PR1 and SC1.
20. Author interview with SC1.
21. Author interview with SC1.
22. Author interviews with PR1 and SC1.
23. Author interview with PR1.
24. Author interview with PR1.
25. Author interview with SC1.
26. Author interview with SC1.
27. The al-Azhar's cooling towards al-Sisi corresponded with the declining social consensus towards the presidency and, in light of the 2015 speech, can be read as a reaction to al-Sisi's hyperbolising.
28. Author interview with SC1.
29. Author interview with PR1.
30. Author interview with SC1.
31. A year later in 2020 at the al-Azhar Conference on the Renewal of Islamic Thought, al-Sisi pushed for a modernisation of the religious establishment using

the following metaphor: 'I love my father's house, but I would not like to live there. [Similarly,] I appreciate our ancient heritage, but I want to create a new one to live by'.
32 See the Ministry of Petroleum's portal. https://www.petroleum.gov.eg/en/gas-and-petrol/Pages/info-indicators.aspx.
33 Author interviews with PR1 and SC1.
34 Author interview with PR1.
35 Author interview with PR1.
36 Author interview with PR1.
37 Author interview with PR1.
38 Author interview with PR1 in London.
39 Author interview with PR1.

6

The political economy of resurrection: power and nature as a critical ecosystem

Challenging societal and economic expectations

Political turmoil is often triggered by poor economic performance and created disequilibria, which has existed in developing countries since the adoption of the Washington Consensus back in the 1990s (Carothers, 2015; Diamond, 2002; Kurer et al., 2019; Shadmehr, 2014; see also Abu-Odeh, 2009) This is combined with of a mafia-style politics, which emerged from a pyramidal circle of corruption and cronyism in systems in which foreign aid was channelled in absence of structural, political and, primarily, societal reforms. The tale of the Arab uprisings, which erupted at a moment of widespread economic recession in 2011, is just one part of this story, in which the issues of economic corruption and intra-elite distribution of resources in a strictly clientelist manner must be considered. Economic data on Egypt collected from the mid-2000s to the early 2009 protests against the NDP show that unrest can also be sparked at a moment in which macro indicators on labour productivity and income per capita had increased, with a fairly strong real GDP growth rate value: in Egypt it was estimated at 5.1 per cent in 2009/2010. This 'economic success' of late 2000s Egypt is, however, histoirically and financially attributed to the IMF's second wave of reforms initiated earlier in 2004, in which the private sector was promoted as the engine of job creation and growth. However, taking different analytical lenses beyond data provided by the IMF, the appearance of Egypt's economic success and boom in jobs can be accounted for by growth in the self-employed category, while 46.1 per cent of the population just prior to 2011 were living below the two-dollars-a-day poverty line. Demands for resource redistribution triggered workers' strikes as early as 2005–2008, initially in the historical area of Mahalla al-Kubra and then spreading across Cairo (Beinin, 2007; see also Shenker, 2008).

Economic challenges remained badly managed under the Muslim Brotherhood's party (FJP) in 2012, due to Morsi's miscalculation on the IMF's delay of structural packages, which he wanted to avoid. In 2013, by the

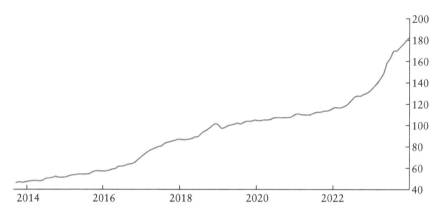

6.1 Egypt consumer price index 2014–2022. Source: Central Agency for Public Mobilisation and Statistics (CAPMAS), 2022

time of the coup, 26.3 per cent of the Egyptian population lived below the national poverty line, with 4.4 per cent under the extreme poverty line (CAPMAS, 2013; Nelson and Sharp, 2013: 4). While poverty was reduced between 2011 and 2013, the unemployment rate did not decrease until 2020, leaving Egypt above the regional average with a peak between 2013 and 2019 (World Bank, 2011–2020; see also Mansour, 2016). The situation worsened in the context of the COVID-19 pandemic and economic-financial crisis, to improve in 2022 and 2023 when the rate dropped to 6.96 per cent (State information Service, 2023), while the number of permits issued to Egyptians to work abroad steadily increased in 2021 and in 2023, along with Egyptians who applied for a foreign citizenship (CAPMAS, 2022 see also CBE, 2023). This additionally implies considerations at the level of remittances, on which Egypt has been dependent, next to deals with GCC countries, amongst which the UAE deserve a mention, to finance national projects. However, remittances drastically decreased in 2023 (CBE, 2023). Equally, amongst other discrepancies in policy labour, a significant gender gap persists in the job market.

Welcoming these data with success obfuscates the persisting economic challenges the country faces. Part of the success story has been determined by development projects which, since 2016, pushed the regime to invest borrowed money. However, gaps persist as the creation of new jobs, mainly if not exclusively through the NSPO, has not been accompanied by an economic revival as amongst all the other aspects, the pound in 2023 lost 50 per cent of its value, and 40 per cent of budget services its debt. This does not concrete over the incumbent-armed forces relations.

Taking a broader, though critical, explanation, between 2004 and 2010, growth remained constrained by the insufficient quality of employed labour and lacklustre gains in productivity, which grew by a mere 0.8 per cent per year (IMF, 2015). The apparent economic consolidation of Egypt in the late 2000s, and when the initial protests broke out, thus, can be read more as a by-product of the boom in the oil market, although domestically Egypt suffered from a persistent structural debt and a deficit amounting to 90 per cent of GDP, and a sharp increase in internal debt (World Bank Group, 2014–2019). The hike in oil prices between 2005 and 2007 directed significant revenues to the MENA region, including Egypt, but food prices remained high (World Bank, 2009). The financial and economic situation continued to worsen after 2013, with unemployment rising by 16 per cent in 2014; so too did the budget deficit, with GDP growth at 1.9 per cent after a drop of –0.4 in 2010–2011 (CBE, 2011).

These persistent economic trends are products of policies designed by the IMF to support growth and sustain low incomes with generous subsidies, which often, as history proves, led to large public deficits and short-term achievements. This demonstrates the limits of development intervention on the principle of the 'conditionality of aid'. Amongst the limits of the IMF's SAP imposed on Egypt in the 1990s was its inflexibility; however, in 2016 the IMF stimulus package accepted by al-Sisi showed itself as slightly less rigid.[1] The FJP, from 2012 to early 2013, sought to embrace social liberalism, with the pursuit of social justice and the redistribution of resources and incomes, whilst pushing for FDI. However, the concept of social justice in its reference occupied a more prominent position in the FJP's 2012 Constitution, compared to the 1981 and 2014 Constitutions ratified under the NDP and al-Sisi respectively. Despite an early approach to welfarism, the FJ Party's economic choices ultimately rolled back to neoliberalism, through structures defined as emulating Mubarak's economic model, which made the original economic goals unachievable.

After the January 2011 Revolution, political instability had a strong negative impact on the economy, not least because of a sharp decline in tourism revenue and non-oil investment, mainly due to security concerns. Security uncertainties derived not unilaterally from terroristic threats, but also from the level of repression and state use of violence and intimidations that started manifesting more consistently since 2015 and exponentially increased from 2016 onwards. As result, both the public deficit and debt widened, the latter growing from 8 per cent of GDP in 2010 to 14 per cent in 2013, and the former rising from 73 to 89 per cent of GDP (World Bank, 2020). Instability additionally increased the size of the informal economy, accounting for to up 70 per cent of the country's economy (Chatham House, 2011). However, the expansion of the private sector's profitability by 2013 triggered frustration, and an increase in the perception of corruption (CPI, 2013; Saif, 2013). Both corruption and the informal sector remain a source of concern alongside the national economic spectrum, and in 2023 the informal economy absorbed up to 62.5 percent of the skilled labour force (Mohammed et al., 2023). The overall status of subsistence, however, was followed by a Western-led constructed narration of what is in fact a passive/semi-defensive and loans-dependent 'policy success' in providing a responsive system in support of the poor.[2]

As a former World Bank expert on the Middle East economy told me directly in our meeting, 'Egypt could no longer shirk its structural deficits'.[3] FDI dropped to a net outflow of 482.7 million USD, and the CBE restricted capital transfers due to the political and economic situation (World Bank, 2011). The economic effects of political instability eroded foreign currency reserves used to purchase foreign commodities, putting pressure on the CBE, which spent even more of its reserves. These moves forced the country to seek out new debt; however, Egypt could not gain access to foreign debt markets, as credit agencies such as Moody's downgraded Egyptian debt to Caa1 form B3 due to to risks of default (Moody's, 2013).[4] The reclassification to B persisted in 2016 (Standard & Poor's, 2016). However, Moody's upgraded Egypt's rating from negative to positive and then classified it as stable in 2018, and it remained as such (as a B3) in 2019 (Ministry of Planning and Economic Development, 2019–2020; Moody's, 2018). In 2023 ratings underwent major fluctuations and in 2024 shifted to positive. However, much if not all has to be linked to foreign investments committed by the UAE in early 2024 (Moody's, 2024; see also State Information Service, 2024). Yet again, the monetary and positively constructed frames by Western' agencies are smoke and mirrors in the way it excludes the criticality of the social and policy economic machinery and the unsustainability of loans and deals politics.

Gulf funding, mainly from the UAE, has attempted to cover most of the imbalance (World Bank, 2011). The Gulf package allowed the international reserves to rise to 18 billion USD, which in turn put the CBE in a position to cut interest rates. As result, in absence of a clear economic policy, foreign borrowing represented the main source of income and this permitted al-Sisi to mitigate the intensification of discontent from the circle of people in a position to select or confirm the appointment of the ruler. In the fiscal year 2012, net public debt stood at 85 per cent of GDP.

The IMF loan delay

A year later in 2012, the IMF pushed the FJP to implement a structural reform of the subsidy system. However, at the time, Morsi refused the IMF package, with the conviction that a cancellation of the subsidy system would have contributed to reducing corruption, and seeing IMF structural reforms as implicated in the development of cronyism under the NDP, (as earlier established in Chapter 2) (Hamid, 2018). Theoretically, while removing subsidies may result in a positive social outcome and a better allocation of resources in the long-run, the potential losses from particular interest groups prevent the efficiency of and the capacity to introduce reforms (Verme, 2016: 6). The FJP's economic manoeuvres contradicted the military's interests. The reforms of subsidies remained difficult, as Morsi pulled back from agreements with the IMF between 2012 and early 2013. However, influxes of investments from the Gulf, and especially Qatar, allowed Egypt under Morsi to remain solvent for some time.

The delayed structural reforms under the FJP, in addition to lower revenues and rising subsidies and wages, led to a rapidly growing budget deficit, which before 2012–2013 was close to 13 per cent of GDP. According to the IMF, this in turn created the risk of pushing up borrowing costs (Muasher, 2013). In the same period, due to capital outflows determined by domestic political insecurity and instability, the CBE supplied larger amounts of foreign currency as a means to stabilise the exchange rate. While this allowed the Egyptian economy to survive, it drained Egypt's international reserves, which fell from 35 billion to 14.5 billion USD (African Development Bank Group, 2013). While former Minister of Investment under Morsi, Yahya Hamid, has acknowledged the mistakes made by the FJP, these macroeconomic indicators and economic stagnancy were behind the societal dissatisfaction with the government's performance. While Morsi's popularity was initially boosted based on his government's foreign policy choices (though these drew the concern of the West), the FJP's economic project of developmentalism rather than subservience to the IMF failed when the idea of Morsi as *za'im* crumbled on internal premises. Morsi's miscalculations left a gap from which al-Sisi gradually emerged (Hamid, 2018).

The economy al-Sisi inherited was still in a precarious condition due to the shock of the 2011 uprising. The first phase of the transition period was marked by volatile economic circumstances associated with political and market uncertainties, with a GDP growth of 2 per cent. Two broad, structural themes can be identified in post-2013 government performance in the economy: financial and monetary policies, and developmental agenda.

The removal of the FJP from power in 2013 clearly had regional political repercussions, transforming the map of political and economic alliances. Under the FJP, the main donor state was Qatar, which offered Egypt a form of economic survival with 5 billion USD in the touristic sector, while Turkey promised a 2 billion USD aid package. The SCAF and al-Sisi's subsequent ban on the Muslim Brotherhood interfered with the block of regional alliances and interests, and contributed to the growing isolation of Qatar. Not long after July 2014, economic support had amounted to 12 billion USD – 5

Table 6.1 Two levels of post-2013 economic reforms as attached to stateness

Government performance (stateness)	
Financial and economic measures	Fiscal policy reforms GDP Reforms of VAT Free floating of the Egyptian pound
Development agenda	New administrative capital Infrastructural projects ranging from the Suez Canal Zone to the housing units project: a total of 12 development projects under the NSPO and SDG-16 agenda, green energy transition projects

Source: Compiled by the author from World Bank data.

billion in grants and loans from Saudi Arabia, 4 billion from the UAE and 3 billion from Kuwait – in addition to a package offered by Bahrain (Isaac, 2015). Most of this money took the form of cash grants and oil and gas donations, which partly contained the repercussions of the cut in energy subsidies introduced in July 2014. Thus, more than the policies introduced by al-Sisi after the 2014 elections, these packages allowed Egypt to buy a few months to avert a balance of payments crisis by boosting foreign reserves. However, the package did not solve the economic growth per se.

Austerity measures did not improve the economic situation, although the IMF and ratings agencies such as Standard & Poor's and Moody's celebrated the fiscal reforms, and Egypt's loan requests were accepted. The IMF's expectations, highlighted by Lipton in the Egypt-IMF conference in 2018 that 'now would be a good time for Egypt to shift growth and job creation into a higher gear' (Lipton, 2018), was not reflected on the ground. Unemployment grew to 13 per cent in 2013 compared to 9.3 per cent in 2010. Equally, the poverty rate rose to 26.3 in the same year, with youth poverty estimated at 42 per cent (CAPMAS, 2013). Citizens in Egypt do not object to state intervention in the economic arena, but do object to an inept state which 'accepts economic prescriptions that do not guarantee jobs and essential services' (Teti et al., 2018: 108). In 2011, surveys reported that only one in ten Egyptians believed the country's economy would decline over the next few years, while over half believed the government had managed the economic crisis relatively well (Teti et al., 2018: 97). These expectations had sharply dropped by 2014, when the political leadership was exposed to social and political volatilities, including resistance to the enactment of

Anti-Protest Law No. 70 of 2013, cuts to fuel subsidies in July 2014 – which spread dissent, especially amongst taxi drivers – and the Raba'a massacre of August 2014 (BTI, 2014, 2016).[5]

Along with these short-term economic figures, social security had substantially declined over time, as Egypt's turn to neoliberalism was not accompanied by compensatory reforms to fight social risks. This had undeniable repercussions in the social sector, including the expansion of the Muslim Brotherhood, which for decades represented the only social and health services provider which most Egyptians could benefit from, regardless of ideology or faith.[6] The healthcare system deserves particular consideration too. Healthcare is a key component of sustainable development, and ineffective and insufficient healthcare systems create negative economic consequences through losses in worker productivity. The Egyptian government's withdrawal from the health system, when compared to previous years, became more evident after 2013. Its spending of 2 per cent on healthcare broke with Article 18 of the 2014 Constitution, which established minimum healthcare expenditure at 3 per cent of GNP (2014 Constitution). In 2014, the level of public satisfaction with al-Sisi's government performance in the healthcare system was below 50 per cent (ATP, 2014; Teti et al., 2018).

It would be wrong to consider economic performance as a tool for gaining a normative mandate to rule, since al-Sisi's rule has shifted into a ruling by law. However, governments' awareness of the 2011 uprising made ruling by violence and coercion an unstable option. Thus, performance in the government's economic and social agendas could provide the idea of a socially oriented developmentalist model of industrialisation. However, given the context of Egypt, in which the necessity for legitimation was embedded, it is theorised that the regime believed that economic performance was a tool for preventing an internal anti-Sisi alliance between the SCAF, the Muslim Brotherhood and the al-Azhar, which could grant a SCAF-led coup normative legitimacy, and for constructing the myth of developmentalism in a consolidated neoliberal and unsustainable order. This is explored further below.

The pro-ruler block: youth militancy and education

Moving away from the *karama* (dignity)-faith paradigm (El-Bernoussi, 2021), al-Sisi's rhetoric of 'sacrifices' and commitment to 'hard work' was introduced in his third speech of March 2014, under the premise of relaunching what he framed as a welfarist economic model of development and social reforms, which would have led to a more diffused form of socio-economic dignity. The narrative returned in many more speeches, including those at the WEF in Davos in 2015, the Youth Economic Forum at Sharm el-Sheikh in 2016, and at the Laylat al-Qadr celebrations in 2018 and 2019. In the March 2014 speech, the narrative of hard work and sacrifices was instead attached to the leadership's promises, and thus to the construction of the motivational frame explaining al-Sisi's candidacy for office. Here sacrifices were distanced from more ethical and moral interpretation confined to the sphere of religion (see El-Bernoussi, 2021). While the intervention at the WEF in 2015 was more externally presaged on magnifying the Egyptian authorities' commitment to changing the social contract and revising the overall conception of social justice as 'redistributive', from a domestic perspective, in the first Youth Conference held in 2016 due to declining social consensus towards al-Sisi, the authorities attempted to persuade new segments of society identified as potential bases for a pro-Sisi social class that would magnify the image of the leadership, and the overall stability, abroad. The formation of the National Youth Conference and its respective logo from 2016 onwards found articulation also around the politics of environmental reforms, when the platform was discussed in the context of the COP27 Summit in 2022, during which green social movements contested the Summit itself and were replaced by pro-regime green movements celebrating national green ambitions.

The historical relationship between state and youth in Egypt has been complex. Since the 1960s, the state's view of youth has undergone various phases, at times being viewed as a resource for development, and at other times being considered a political threat due to their political activism. Egyptian youth can be split into two categories. A first group presents more malleable features and are, therefore, more inclined to be coopted politically, economically and culturally in the measure they accept the boundaries of state laws. The second constitutes young people who want to move beyond the so-called 'authoritarian block' in favour of more democratic negotiations (Sika, 2012, 2019).

As displayed in the codebook of the 2016 Youth Conference speech in Table 6.2, the politics of persuasion occurred through promises for a better education for youth, investments in the public education sector, and setting the conditions for youth political inclusion.

It is posited that youth involvement in politics was underpinned by the logic of a top-down controlled reinclusion of youth, after the revolutionary youth movements in early 2013 were suppressed, and experienced a structural inability to shift from the street to a political constituency (Abdalla, 2013).

The promise for a renegotiation of the social contract between the ruler and the people occupied a central position in the content of the speech, alongside the focus on reforms to the education sector, as emerge at nodes 7, 2, 1 and 2.1 (Table 6.2). However, it was in fact the 'rectification of religious discourse' which returned to an important function in the October

The political economy of resurrection 175

Table 6.2 Codebook of the Youth Conference speech, October 2016

Node number	Nodes	Coded references	%
1	State coordination of youth in politics	1	3.47
2	Rectification of religious discourse	1	4.93
2.1	Promise and sacrifices for a better education	2	4.84
3	Political and religious inclusivism	1	1.93
4	Father-figure tones (revision of the social contract)	4	2.23
5	Economy, development and challenges	1	3.14
6	Discrepancies between fiscal reforms and education	1	2.29
7	Democratisation in favour of youth's voice in the political and public sphere	2	5.34

2016 speech, immediately after the promise for a more democratic political system, which would provide a space for involvement in politics for youths and underrepresented social classes such as peasants. The importance of this element is linked to the presidency attempt at appropriating religion with the goal of creating a self-perpetuation narrative around beliefs and creeds. This shift to religion by the political authority in 2016 represented an attempted strategy of clearly marginalising the Muslim Brotherhood not so much as religious actor but as political actor, in order to try to exert the regime's full control over the al-Azhar as the religious establishment in Egypt symbolically enshrining the unity of the regime. The focus on religious reform, now presented to youth, was an attempt at capturing a small base of support from below, after the ruler's attempt at exercising control from above, over the al-Azhar, which failed, and in absence of a larger civil society, which still remains harshly repressed. Looking at the daily challenges of citizens and the hardship of life in Cairo as dictated by raised poverty levels despite economic reforms, education and employment opportunities remain higher priorities for young Egyptians not so much in terms of enrolment as in terms of quality of the education system and in line with Social Development Goal 4 (SDG-4) found in Agenda 2030. However, education and reforms in the sector, at least in non-liberal systems, are normally undertaken with the main goal of propagating regime's values rather than national values. If in liberal democracies education is considered a major driver of political participation, in illiberal countries education is pursued by institutions under indoctrination premises, while it is proved that political participation reduces (Blaydes, 2006).[7] Indeed, since 2014 Egypt has been investing in the education sector, one of the persisting key challenges for the regime besides the health sector.

However, despite investments, educational equality in the country scored the lowest in the region (V-Dem Project data, 2000–2022). It should be added that investments in the education sector took place in the private sector, at the expense of the public, in line with the authorities' continuum in reinforcing the country's neoliberal turn, despite the shortcomings under Mubarak and despite the constitutional regulations incorporated into the 2014 draft. In 2022, in an article that appeared in the *Middle East Eye*, Springborg argued how investing in education is a convenient and non-threatening subject that allows the public to vent political steam and does not mobilise masses (Springborg, 2022). While this work convenes with Blaydes and Springborg on the fact that in some illiberal orders education does not lead to political mobilisation, it is equally true that there should be a specific acknowledgement of the structural constraints that prevent such a connection. Egypt undertook reforms in the education sector after 2015, once the penal code was amended with the enactment of Law No. 107 of 2013 in combination with Law No. 94 of 2015.[8] Both offered the regime the juridical foundations for suppressing forms of dissent under the rhetoric of national security. Thus, it follows that Springborg's position finds a validation in combination with Blaydes if the re-adaptation of the juridical structures of the state are contextually considered.

From an economic perspective, the state of the higher education sector in Egypt is considered responsible for both high unemployment rates and the incremental growth in the unskilled job market, in turn absorbed by the informal sector estimated at 34.8 per cent and which constitutes up to 50 per cent of GDP thus providing approximately 68 per cent of new jobs (Fedi et al., 2019; Soliman, 2020). Since 2013, the literacy rate in Egypt has dropped by 3.89 per cent (World Bank, 2017), with no real state plans to recover this. In 2014, the Education and Technical Education Minister Tareq Shawki announced the presidency's priority in education and announced the initiative 'towards a community that learns, thinks and innovates'. In theory, the initiative would have supported the right to an education. In fact, educational equality in Egypt scores the lowest between 2015 and 2018, and again started to decrease in 2020.

In 2019 al-Sisi announced the 'Year of Education' during the sixth national youth congress that took place a year before in 2018. The occasion was captured as an opportunity to launch the reform of the educational system.

However, in authoritarian systems, education is also political and capable of playing various political roles within societies where politics and power are intimately entwined (Apple, 1995). As shown in Figure 6.1, campus integrity in Egypt still remains poor, when compared with other countries in the broader Mediterranean area. The manipulation of education can therefore remain a practice for maintaining regime legitimacy and in the dissemination of a certain knowledge with the goal of sustaining the status quo. The government-led initiative to reform education, when analysed from a macro-structural perspective, should also be read through these analytical lenses. Let us now return to the politics of fiscal reforms. Fiscal reforms introduced in 2014–2015, then protracted up to 2016, tended to centralise the regime's goal to bolster growth by reforming fuel subsidies with gradual cuts, which inevitably meant a rise in fuel prices up from +40 to +48 per cent in 2019 (Ministry of Petroleum, 2020).[9] Thus, from a political perspective, the Youth Conference speech al-Sisi gave displayed some tactical goals which clashed with the weakness of the government's economic reforms, and ultimately did not improve the image of the leader, as instead hoped.

The speech addressed to youth in 2016 was indicative of al-Sisi's double game in tactically forecasting citizens' societal grievances deriving from austerity measures, and thus trying to psychologically prepare them before the impacts of the structural reforms were fully felt, while still attempting to portray himself as the saviour of national stability. Political developments between 2014 and 2016 had by October 2016 taken an opposite course to that desired by the leadership, and acted as the drivers for the disengagement of youth from a pro-regime and pro-leader state-sponsored youth platform, which would have limited the political effects of the isolationist phase into which the leadership entered in 2016. This was shown in the social media reactions to the second Youth Conference – held with the official government hashtag on Twitter – 'We need to talk', which proposed itself as a platform for discussions about peace and inclusivity, but which drew remarks about the need to talk about political repression. The politics of fear and the lack of change to the social contract, the latter of which was promised in the speech in July 2013 during the coup, remained at the core of al-Sisi's domestic struggles.

Despite the youth conferences held over the years, speeches on pluralist youth inclusivism became increasingly abstract, rather than oriented to actual facts (see the speech by President Abdel Fattah al-Sisi in the Closing of the World Youth Forum, 2018). Youth participation was soon translated into a pro-al-Sisi block of students, with features similar to the movements of the 'Youth Fascists' formed in Italy in between the mid-1920s and 1930s, which tried to represent a form of youth militancy sacralised to the personality of

Benito Mussolini. This pro-regime youth movement did not bridge al-Sisi's vacuum of internal legitimacy, but rather pushed the system towards a return to an exclusivist and exclusive-populist manifesto. The protracted lack of internal acceptance thus pushed the authorities to build a defensive form of state, and shift to an external strategic framing of state functions while reshaping the politics and economics of assistance (Hallahan, 2008). While the debate on this latter aspect remains fragmented, the simplistic association of the mid-1960s establishment with the one that emerged in the post-2015 setting regarding the remaking of a Nasserite-inspired socialist economic mold is erroneous in the way it neglects, in a historical and transnational comparative approach, the socialist inspired economics of Italian Fascism based on central planning, heavy state subsidies, protectionism, nationalisation, cronyism, large deficits, high government spending on massive social welfare programmes, and high levels of national debt. These are components that find a form of replication under the post-2013 political establishment, with the exception of the social welfare programme, which remains faulty and inadequate, and subsidies whose efficacy remains questioned.

A rapid shift in legitimation approach in 2018: seeking international diplomatic consensus over the enhancement of developmentalist ambitions

A combined content and framing analysis of the WEF in which al-Sisi participated in person in Davos in 2015, highlights the shift in the government's priorities when compared to the March 2014 speech. Narratives of salvation and sacrifice, extensively framed as tools of emancipation behind the 2014 election, no longer held any function in 2015. While the March 2014 speech had emphasised the poor economic situation of the country and the need for societal sacrifices, the Davos 2015 speech predominantly attempted to project the image of a legitimate and well-performing government to the outside (e.g. international state actors), reassuring state and non-state actors about the country's performance and relevance for long-term regional stabilisation. From a thematic content analysis, this has been coded at node 1 and sub-node 1.1 in Table 6.3, with a coverage percentage calculated at 3.95 and 1.08 respectively. This was followed by a reference to policy and legal reforms as coded at node 2 (3.40 per cent). Social justice (1.57 per cent) for the first time was clearly mentioned in intimate connection to monetary and policy reforms, as coded at node 9, though in the speech it occupied a less prominent importance when compared, for instance, to the frame of al-Sisi as an inclusivist leader supporting moderation and interfaith dialogue, as coded at sub-node 1.2 (2.19 per cent). However, the state's

Table 6.3 Codebook of al-Sisi's speech at the World Economic Forum in Davos, 2015

Node number	Nodes	Source	References	%
1	Public self-reference as legitimate leader in opposition to the NDP and the FJP rules	1	7	3.95
1.1	Leader representative of a government trusted for the economic performance	1	1	1.08
1.2	Inclusivist leader supporting interfaith dialogue and religious moderation	1	2	2.19
1.3	Leader as committed to create a civilian state	1	2	1.49
2	Policy and legal reforms	1	6	3.40
3	Monetary policies	1	1	1.49
4	Support of investments to the private sector	1	2	0.68
5	Support to the public sector	1	2	1.07
6	State's goal in bolstering the economy and fighting political and economic corruption	1	1	0.10
7	Defence of Egypt as committed to the respect of the International Law, the UN Charter and international legitimacy	1	1	0.68
8	Seeking support for the Suez Canal	1	1	1.72
9	Social justice through economic reforms	1	6	1.57

goal in bolstering the economy and fighting political and economic corruption, as coded at node 6, occupied an irrelevant role in the speech at that time (0.10 per cent).

Viewed though a critical analytical lens, the state efforts to portray Egypt as a regional pillar in economic and political-diplomatic affairs became extensively centralised a year later in the UN General Assembly in 2016. In fact, despite constant reference to regional issues, and the public speeches positing Egypt as a pillar of regional stability, as found in the thematic analysis

Table 6.4 Codebook for al-Sisi's speech at the 71st UN General Assembly, 2016

Node number	Nodes	Coded references	%
1	Trust toward authorities	1	0.63
1.1	External obstacles to the leadership	1	0.60
2	Responsible leadership	3	2.44
3	Egypt commitment to fight terrorism	1	3.72
4	Egypt as pillar of political stability in the region	13	18.22
5	Development agenda	4	4.44
6	Commitment to social justice and growth	3	0.26

of the BBC interview in 2015 and the UN General Assembly speech in 2016, the Egyptian authorities' influence over regional and area issues has remained minor and constrained to a merely discursive predication. Egypt has not played an important role in the resolution of political and social crises that emerged between 2014 and 2020 like in Syria and Libya, to mention two of the most problematic countries in the area, despite announcements more than once of military intervention in the latter country, which at that time was economically unaffordable and would have exposed the authority towards non-preconceived outcomes. The persuasion of reforming the instability of the economic system and tackling corruption proved itself weak as scepticism remained in the WEF in 2015 towards these two mentioned determinants.

Combining framing analysis of the 2015 WEF talk with the evolution of domestic politics, the positive self-framing of the authorities' performance remained, at least in 2015, part of what I call here the *strategic* meta-frame complex. From a political perspective, the framing of the state's commitment to pursue an infrastructural and socio-economic recovery reflected international actors' demands for democratisation and de-militarisation of the state functions, with the goal of defusing pressure over human rights abuses and jailing of opponents, activists and academics, and winning international actors' support for al-Sisi as a trusted international interlocutor for the stabilisation of the Mediterranean area. From an internal perspective, international support for the leadership would have helped to recalibrate the domestic view of al-Sisi, bolstering his position in the new infrastructures of power. The WEF in Davos in 2015 therefore offered al-Sisi the chance to provide a positive image of a trustworthy and legitimate political system, dedicated to reforming the entire economic and business sector while proactively supporting the fight against climate change and the idea of a green economic transition, which is being developed in the country and remains at the core of the political establishment's priorities.

As all discourses are a projection of politics, a political justification can be traced in al-Sisi's Youth Conference and WEF speeches behind the economic reforms introduced after July 2014 and cuts to food and energy subsidies imposed by the IMF to reduce the debt level, which kept increasing. The myth of the return of state developmentalism in reality clashed with the state's return to an economic conditionality as based on international loans and dependency, meaning the continuing subordination of a political existence to international Western donors and financial institutions. If this on the one hand laid the basis for receiving Western support, on the other it enabled the establishment to benefit from the IMF-recommended reforms (e.g. cuts to subsidies) to operationalise the politicisation of the developmental model as dominantly based on a beautification of the capital and the idea of a sustainable economic system, in line with the environmental framework established in the UN Agenda 2030 as needed to improve human development. Despite international hopes and expectations, the new capital city and, broadly speaking, new developmentalist model addressed to urbanise military-owned desert lands remains socially unsustainable in a political system that displays uncemented cracks at the inner level, under environmental premises, such as water and resource scarcity in association to climate change-related effects.[10]

The politics of subsidies after 2016

The government's application of fiscal reforms, such as the cuts to fuel subsidies, was justified in early 2014 by the necessity of attracting foreign investment after years of capital flight out of the country as a result of political instability. From a macro-perspective, in November 2016 the government initiated a project of fiscal reform to meet the IMF's conditions for a loan of 12 billion USD (IMF, 2016).

Subsidies play the role of both stabilising prices and providing a form of social protection. However, subsidies and state grants/loans in authoritarian political systems tend to create barriers to social growth. Broadly speaking, although the politics of subsidies, at least initially, was aimed at price stabilisation, later – at least in the view of international financial institutions like the IMF and World Bank – three main problematic aspects emerged: (i) the nominal price tends to increase in the long run; (ii) subsidies become politicised by governments as an instrument for consensus-building; and (iii) interest groups are generated by the existence of subsidies, which could be viewed as a form of corruption (Verme, 2016: 3). From the IMF's perspective, energy subsidies are a significant price distortion. They keep fuel costs well below the market price, which encourages inefficient use of energy and overinvestment in capital-intensive industries to take advantage of low fuel costs. A partial removal of subsidies may hurt citizens' welfare in the short-term, yet at the same time can be indicative of a political will to introduce reforms in a narrative of salvation and social dignity. In addition, cuts to wheat subsidies found justification in the government's battle over the black economy, which in Egypt, it is estimated, counts for up to 35 per cent and falls outside of GDP, attracting approximately 10 million workers (World Economics, 2022). Unused subsidised bags of wheat at bakeries are sold on the black market (Barnes, 2022). Al-Sisi's move to cut fuel subsidies should thus be primarily viewed as a move seeking to satisfy the IMF and present the economic foundation as a model of neoliberal fiscal responsibility. The following provides an overview of the political and socio-economic-related implications behind the policies of implementing or cutting subsidies. However, while tackling the black economy constitutes a priority, it has still absorbed

Table 6.5 Political implications behind subsidies

Reasons for removing subsidies	Reasons for keeping subsidies
Economic	*Economic*
Distortion of consumption • Distortion of production • Distortion of investments • Delaying of energy decisions	Reduction of production costs • Reduction of price volatility, financial risks and uncertainty for households
Social	*Social*
Costly for taxpayers	• Compensation for incremental increase in prices • 'Social protection' • Benefits all social classes
Political	*Political*
Supports authoritarianism and populist governments	Buys political consensus Benefits established monopolies/ oligarchies connected to the politicians

Source: Modified by the author from Verme (2016: 6).

around 10 million people since its beginning back in the early 1970s, and in the neoliberal system continues to be a key replacement to the government in terms of employment.

According to a 2017 report by the Institute of International and Strategic Relations, there was initially 90 per cent popular support for the political authority's reduction of fuel subsidies, and simultaneous investment in the expansion of the Suez Canal Zone which bought an initial consensus (IRIS, 2017). The reliability of this statistic, however, is questionable: general consensus towards the government in 2013 was estimated at 4.5 on a 0–10 scale, and decreased after July of that year after the coup and the enforcement of Law No. 107 of 2013 (BTI, 2014, 2016). Support for the Suez Canal's expansion was also highly contested and meant initial losses of real revenues. A behavioural realist approach and the theory of system justification can provide reasons why, despite contestations of the leadership, disadvantageous fiscal reforms did not immediately lead to an upswing in active dissent against the regime. Easton's (1975) theory of belief systems is an integral determinant of 'system justification theory', in which citizens are rationally likely to accept negative consequences to remain consistent with the dominant system of belief (e.g. sacrifices as necessitated by the economic project of recovery) at the time reforms take place (Blasi and Jost, 2006). Framing is closely connected to the theory of system justification, and actors' acceptance or refusal of reforms sheds light on the opportunistic structures of the model which emerged after the 2013 coup, rather than being a reliable indicator of its success.

Unlocking loans does not necessarily lead to a form of legitimacy by outputs, rather, it is likely to contribute, amongst other implications, to the oligarchisation of the productive model (Verme, 2016). Thus, reforms to the economy and monetary agenda do not necessarily buy bottom-up leadership legitimation.

Starting from July 2014 the government introduced cuts to fuel subsidies, followed by food and energy cuts. The reform package was technically tailored to improve state-level economic indicators, due to decreased remittances caused by falling oil prices. In addition, the fact that CBE reserves almost dried up in 2013, creating a foreign-currency black market, made reforms urgent, since the trade deficit of 7 per cent of GDP and a budget deficit of 12 per cent of GDP closed off possibilities of organic recovery (Bloomberg, 2016).

The decision to cut fuel subsidies in July 2014 came soon after al-Sisi's election as President. This was not surprising, given the straightforward connection of such cuts with the narrative of hard work and sacrifices discussed above from a thematic and framing perspective. In July 2014, the government announced an increase to the price of all fuel apart from

LPG. Overall, fuel subsidies fell from 3.3 per cent of GDP in 2016 to a forecast 2.7 per cent the year after, with a prediction of a further decrease in 2018 to 1.8 per cent of GDP (although the exact financial costs of energy subsidies are not transparent in the budget, complicating estimations) (see on this World Bank, 2014–2019). While from the IMF's perspective the cuts were small, they still drove protests against the government soon after they were announced. Given the political structural premises discussed in Chapters 4 and 5, it is likely that these manoeuvres were first negotiated with the military, which initially had reason to oppose the reforms, given that subsidies always tended to benefit military-led oil industries, such as the Gulf of Suez Petroleum Company, formed in 1965 as part of the Egyptian General Petroleum Corporation.

Politically, the decision to reduce energy subsidies, which followed the fuel cuts, was supported by a 'technocratic' cabinet and principally by Prime Minister Ibrahim Mehleb and Minister of Finance Hany Kadry Dimian, close to the IMF after having served as alternate governor at the Arab Monetary Fund and the IMF itself. According to Gad (2014) and Esterman (2014), al-Sisi had pushed for higher cuts than those eventually approved, with the intention to further reduce the deficit below 10 per cent of GDP. Government energy subsidies declined from 0.7 per cent of GDP in 2017–2018 to 0.3 per cent in 2018–2019, with the intention of elimination by 2021.

According to the anti-subsidies attitudes of the World Bank, the July 2014 initial cut would result in a reduction of the budget deficit by more than 20 per cent, real consumption would fall by 1.4 per cent, and investments would increase. Additionally, the cut would have benefitted the employment sector and significantly redistributed incomes (World Bank, 2014b). In fact, despite the cuts to 'corrosive' subsidies (World Bank, 2014b), the unemployment rate has not significantly reduced and has remained high, especially amongst youth, while the poverty rate has continued to increase since 2014, from 28 per cent in 2015 to 33 per cent in 2019 (see *The Economist*, 2019; Nasralla, 2014; Korany, El-Sayyad and Sarag, 2016). FDI in 2014 remained flat, due to major political uncertainties and instabilities such as the Raba'a massacre in August 2014, which impacted foreign investments in the country.

Post-2013, political authorities started working on alternative energy sources specifically on solar power plants in Aswan and, in 2018, on constructing a nuclear power plant with Russian financial support. The former attracted foreign investors, including the Norwegian Scatec Solar, Germany and France. The plan attracted up to two billion USD of FDI; it involved 100 Egyptian companies and was proposed as a job creator. In fact, divergences persist on the positive effects of FDI in developing economies (see Heshmati and Davis, 2007). While an initial trend established a connection between FDI and economic growth, a second school of thought has argued against the positive effects of FDI, instead claiming that FDI may determine negative impacts on economic growth, employment, research and development, and entrepreneurial opportunities. This critical view relies on the theory that industrialists and foreign corporate lobbyists influence host governments. The project was based on solid theoretical foundations: the use of alternative energies (e.g. solar and wind) implied a reduction in the import and consumption of oil and gas (the prices of which increased by 2–4 per cent due to the cut in subsidies), thus favouring the internal market, and an environmentally friendly economic ethics, in line with the United Nations Development Programme (Bohl et al., 2018; see also UNDP, n.d.). However, there is another side of the coin, in connection with the political issue of strengthening and legitimating the leadership.

Combining the political perspective of al-Sisi's green economic ethics with framing (Benford and Snow, 2000; Bondes and Heep, 2013; Entman, 1993; Minsky, 1977; Scheufele, 1999; Tuchman, 1978), the ruler's attempt to rely on input legitimacy left the void severely unfilled. Thus, the government's expansion in its development agenda, followed by a massive intensification of national infrastructure programmes such as green energy sources, was connected to two main frames: (i) the *dominant frame* of the army, and (ii) the *motivational frame* attached to the personalisation of al-Sisi's leadership (Benford and Snow, 2000; Minsky, 1977). The dominant frame of the armed forces was strategically constructed and presented to society in a moment of leadership volatility and exposure to structural risks. Thus, the militarisation of infrastructure was part of a project of reinforcing the political authority of a new government, ostensibly presented as civilian, and a ruler presented as a charismatic leader before both Egyptian society and international actors. It follows that the motivational framing of al-Sisi soon became inextricable from the state's economic agenda, oligarchically controlled by military companies. This provided sufficient stability to the regime, despite existing social dysfunctions.

Behind the authorities' apparent enthusiasm for environmentally friendly development lay the regime's awareness of the potential implications of the cut to subsidies and the need to control floating of the Egyptian pound. Organically, this produced a widely positive result regarding the army's satisfaction with the leadership's economic performance, since the centralisation of the EAF's role in social projects impacted with the positive view of the armed forces, thus detaching the former from the corrupt NDP club. It additionally contributed to a positive and optimistic framing of the ruler, able to satisfy Western-imposed neoliberalism and capitalist market logic, whilst raising the EAF's optimism. If in the late 1980s–1990s neoliberal policies in the medium term revealed the faulty circuits of pyramidal capitalism, due to the spread of corruption and weakness of economic performance, after 2015 the adaptation of neoliberal manoeuvres by al-Sisi to Egypt's political and economic needs paradoxically added a form of short-to-medium-term financial stability to Egypt. This functioned as a mechanism for building a form of output legitimacy based on performance in the economic-business agenda, which satisfied foreign investors and rating companies. From a top-down perspective, it also placated citizens' animus in the short-term, by not forcing them to pay higher prices for energy and basic foodstuffs. This in turn provided the apparent image of a government responsive to citizens' needs.

The complexity of this threefold mechanism lay in the ruler's capacity of lowering prices by investing in the green economy, in turn attracting foreign investors and externally communicating the strength of a reactive, responsive and responsible political leadership, also reflecting positively on the AOI both endogenously and exogenously. This demonstrates what PR1 said, that the manoeuvre returned the military to the function of state-builder, making the idea of the Egyptian state and its existence inextricable from the EAF, but without implying a wholesale return to a militarised system.

A new state ecology of political power

Since the end of the 1960s, overpopulation and the depletion of natural resources have played a central role in political discourses in the context of neo-Malthusian environmentalism, where overpopulation and ecological challenges found discussion (Malthus, 1798). A decade later, in the 1970s, the writings of Heilbroner and Ophuls inspired the rise of eco-authoritarianism, understood as an authoritarian response to environmental issues and on the management of environmental crises (Heilbroner, 1973, 1972; Ophuls, 1977). More recently, environmental activism has undergone an intensification and centralisation on a regional scale, from Tunisia to Lebanon, and this despite the political repression – supported by a routinised use of violence, though in different forms – across countries. Movements in the region represent a hope for outcomes and some countries, in collaboration with NGOs, are trying to move in the direction of innovative, independent, sustainable society-rooted projects, such as in Lebanon with the LWM (Lebanon Waste Management) where solid waste management represents a chronic problem in a structurally corrupted complex political system which has facilitated predatory state-building practices.[11] In the context of closed autocracies, like Egypt, environmental policies are strictly operated from above: green movements and urban grassroots mobilisations are curtailed, undergo similar procedures applied to political movements, and are prevented from receiving foreign funding under amended Law No. 84 of 2002. Likewise, environmental politics in Egypt undergoes exceptionalism in the way that from 2019 nature became strictly neoliberalised and presented in a propagandistic perspective that supports the gears of the internal legitimation complex in a system that transformed at the sub-structural level and became more fluid in its organisational and relational capacity.

Since 2019 nature has become institutionalised and deeply intertwined with the process of legitimation claim, albeit that this started happening in an unconventional way distorted by the scope of eco-politics. In 2016, at the African Ministers Conference on Environment (AMCEN), Egypt launched a national strategy aimed at enhancing the green economy, providing clean sources of energy, and advancing quality of life (Ismail's speech at AMCEN, 2016). The partnership found support in the United Nations Environment Programme. However, it is from 2019 onwards that the legitimation struggle and the organisation of the new political machine intersected with the altering of the core foundational premises of environmental politics, which happened to be readjusted with the main scope of supporting the overall paths of making an internal legitimation claim. In order to be effective, environmental politics requires a degree of multilateral inclusivism, flexible institutions and, on theoretical premises, to be feminist (Capra and Spretnak, 1986: 21). As unpacked previously in this work, from a more contemporary perspective, amendments to the penal code and the revision of anti-protest law also interfered with green movements in the way gender, environmental security, socio-economic and violence have taken a 'high moral ground' and patriarchalised Egypt, thus recalling the policies of pre-2011 period with regard to practices of state centralisation. Even though developmentalism started playing a core role in the overall forging of a legitimation claim after 2018, authorities from 2016 started putting the structural conditions for massive inequalities and abuses over resources and wealth redistribution, which when analysed through the state narrative are dystopian as the historical process of development in the country remains inextricably class-oriented, subjected to forms of direct or indirect control by state authorities. Thus, the most essential pillars of environmental politics are antithetic to the historical conformation of politics in Egypt, regardless of the regime mandate. In the complexity of this context, the internal legitimation vacuum, in combination with the previous steps undertaken by post-2013 authorities (i.e. reorganisation of the rule of law, symbolism of charisma and the playing of memories and myths complexes), created a set of sub-systemic gears which, once attached to environmental politics, turned the latter into a financialised political device. In this framework, environmental activism and green movements happened not to be suppressed, like in other illiberal structures, but embedded into the political machine's environmentalist manifesto, of which youth movements, and youth climate movements, are instrumental to greenwashing and which convey the paradigm of legitimacy. Concomitant with COP27 in Egypt, next to a non-transparent participation of civil society's representation at the summit, new pro-regime green movements celebrating the public image of the authority and the state's framing of the institutionalisation of nature were created. Indeed, since 2019 the state narrative has accelerated regarding environmentalism. While this work does not argue that this marked a shift in the way the struggle for the forging of a legitimation claim was previously crafted, it is the contention of this work that previous phases constituted pivotal stages for a revised idea of foundational legitimacy, while nature and environmentalism could be reinterpreted through the lenses of contingent legitimacy.[12]

In addition, while it is empirically observable that from 2016 the government became active in promoting the 2030 vision, the black economy remained unresolved, thus impacting the overall GDP.[13] However, when environmental politics is intertwined with human security, it is the ambitious project of the housing complex, which has been long debated, in terms of prices set for each unit. The value of these properties goes beyond the reasonable line of the market in the context of the country's economic deterioration and increased relative poverty, thus marking the dystopian conception of life security in an economic system on the brink of the balance of payments.

Concurrent with fuel subsidies and food reforms, the political establishment announced, a few years earlier in 2014, the construction of what would be new administrative capital, with the promise of increasing the minimum wage from 700 LE to 1200 LE in the public sector, bolster private sector growth, and lower the unemployment rate with the creation of new jobs (Al-Ahram, 2019; see also State Information Service 2020b). These measures underwent revisions in the following years as it was agreed that the minimum wage would be periodically increased. Revisions, however, should be read as the continuum of a dependency on the IMF system, which on principle, it is reiterated, does not contemplate forms of social protection. Yet, the project ultimately resulted in a further bureaucratisation of military enterprises, since the company in charge of developing the project was formed by the New Urban Community Authority linked to the Ministry of Housing, Utilities and Urban Communities, the NSPO and the Armed Forces National Lands Projects Capital. All three enterprises are registered under the AOI.[14] The project reflected the initial broader reforms of food policies. The measure in the short term produced some effects that reflected on the annual unemployment rate, which from 13.1 fell to 7.8 per cent (ILO, 2014–2022) and further decreased to 6.96 in 2022. However, in the mid-term it produced a new increment in unemployment, which increased up to 9.3 per cent of the total labour force and created a vacuum in terms of gender balance in the job sector.

The politics of cuts to subsidies, discussed in the next section, was accompanied by the administrative capital project, which was anticipated by the Suez Canal Zone plan, presented by the government as an epic task and 'Egypt's gift to the world'. It was predicted that the number of ships passing through the canal would increase from 49 to 97 for daily average transits by 2020, and therefore the expansion was much needed to cope with the demand. If financially, the Suez Canal was presented as an opportunity to replenish capital at the moment when Egypt's reserves dried up, it attempted to serve the purpose of magnifying al-Sisi's personality before the NSPO and to stabilise the new infrastructural relations underway between the SCAF and the ruler, beyond the here contested theory of the 'protection path'. The project was inserted into pervasive and persuasive nationalist sentiments, and presented as an epic continuation of Nasser's project that would make 'Egypt great', as al-Sisi asserted in the official launch of the project (State Information Service, 2015). In fact, the project was just an extension of existing branches of the canal built between 1955 and 1980. In addition, the Suez Canal Zone project replicated a project already proposed by Morsi and the FJP and before that by the NDP, which in turn originated in a 1991, 1995, 1998 and 2001 concept and which was at the core of a large project for North Sinai's agricultural development (Sayigh, 2019).

The project cost 80 billion USD; despite the investment certificates stating that the founders were companies and individuals, the government sold 64 billion LE in bonds to raise money for the project, and borrowed 850 million USD from local banks. The EAF started working on the canal in 2015 and in May 2021 the Suez Canal Authority received approval from al-Sisi for expanding the southern section, thus making the canal up to 40 metres wide, 82 metres long and 72 feet deep.

Technically, in 2014–2015 the canal was forecasted to contribute up to 10 per cent of GDP, the authorities' top priority, and also to the international image of national credibility and performance. Revenues were expected to be a third source of national income behind remittances and tourism. Additionally, the project was expected to generate FDI and restore the value of the Egyptian pound through the IMF's Special Drawing Right Unit (an international reserve asset created in 1969 to supplement the IMF's member countries' official reserves) and contribute to food security through the cultivation of an additional four million acres and the establishment of a fishing company on the eastern side of the canal, also contributing to support the employment sector and rate (El-Beblawy, 2014). By December 2018, Vice Admiral Mohab *Mamish*, chairman of the Suez Canal Authority, claimed that 30 billion USD had been invested since 2015, 75 per cent of which came from foreign investors led by China (Sayigh, 2019: 244). In fact, four years after the conclusion of the Suez Canal Zone project, in 2019, the economic and industrial performance of the canal remained flat, despite the state's optimistic views. Once again, the project in itself served the purpose of magnifying not so much the political authority, but the resurgence of nationalistic projects promoted through a post-modern symbolism of a glorious Pharaonic. Yet, what remains at odds in the model and idea of the newly forged Egyptian nationalism are the historical discrepancies that, as previously found in this book, would not permit parallelism with the idea of a restored Nasserism. Data shared by the Ministry of Planning display a curve, with a slight GDP contribution calculated at 10 kilometres a year after the completion of the project. GDP grew between 2017 and 2018, before it started falling again in 2019 and recovered only between the end of 2021 and 2022.

Despite positive data registered between 2017 and 2018, the government's expectations on the growth rate have to be considered unrealistic, taking into account that global trade growth is rated at 3 per cent of GDP, and in the 2000s during the trade boom it grew at 7.5 per cent. Given the current average of growth, and despite investments in infrastructures, it is unlikely that the Suez Canal can contribute 9 per cent of GDP by 2023.[15] In 2022, the political establishment celebrated the economic success of the Suez Canal, with revenues reaching a record of 7 billion USD in the fiscal year 2021/2022, in strict reference to July 2022. However, while the news resonated across local and transnational media (al-Ahram, 2022; Reuters, 2022) a closer look at the fiscal year 2022/2021 shows that overall the Suez Canal's revenues contributed to 1.5 per cent of the total GDP (Ministry of Planning and Economic Development, 2022). While the Suez Canal's profitability can find a form of acknowledgment, it does not account for the health of the national economy or for the level of internal consensus towards the status quo as the extension of the Canal, and the following dispossession of lands, could set ignite society-authority relations. Furthermore, from a broader economic perspective, Egypt has become a net importer of fuels, and therefore does not profit on balance from the export of oil and gas. In the fiscal year 2022/2021 imports of goods and services estimated at 40.8 per cent exceeded imports, which reached 59.2 per cent of GDP (Ministry of Planning and Economic Development, 2022).It follows that, yet again, the politics of the industrialised spectacle is at odds with micro-indicators on national economic recovery, but served the purpose of strategically preserving, internationally, the financial and economic image of the nation and the presidency.

Politically, and problematising the internal legitimation claim, the Suez Canal project fulfilled the double structural need of firstly providing to the outside world the images of a government performing well economically in the neoliberal market, of al-Sisi as a trustworthy leader trying to reduce fiscal imbalances, and of a stable Egypt which would have increased the traffic along the canal, and establishing the EAF, through the SCA as the main business actor in the entire project. This was a much-needed manoeuvre, which al-Sisi was, to an extent, forced to undertake, in opposition to an exponential increase in social dissent towards the executive, visible online in 2014 and 2015 as result of long-term implications determined by Law No. 107 of 2013 and Law No. 94 of 2015. Consensus towards the executive dropped sharply from 5.2 in 2014 to 3.6 in 2016 (BTI, 2016). Thus, the project was strategically oriented towards fulfilling the EAF's desires and buying its support in light of the energy cuts and reduction of Egypt's reliance on fossil fuels. Another move with the goal of increasing growth rates and meeting the IMF's neoliberal expectations is the cut to food subsidies. However, the economic and developmental manoeuvre did not fix the fracture on consensus building, which in 2022 reached the lowest score since 2006 (BTI, 2022).

Reforming and negotiating the 'right to food'

The debate on subsidised politics is dominated by fragmented views on the effective benefits linked to them in connection with the nature of political structures in which they find application. As a general norm that backs the IMF's views, cuts to subsidies find justification on the premise that subsidies discourage investments in the energy sector, encourage the black economy, and introduce distortions instead. As a result, this would dampen the effect on growth (Sdralevich et al., 2014). Thus, their removal and replacement with more transparent social safety instruments in the long term is still defended as a measure that can positively impact the elimination of distortion, the rationalising of energy use, and the increment of export revenues in oil so positively affecting growth (Sdralevich et al., 2014). Yet subsidies remain at the core of social contracts, that is, the agreements between all groups and the authority as defining rights and obligations towards each other (Loewe et al., 2020: 3), which in turn could be connected with the internal premises of legitimacy.

In the economic history of Egypt, food subsidies were early introduced between 1910 to provide affordable bread and 1941 to cope with scarcity in times of war. The measure was extended in the 1960s. In the 1970s the rise in the price of wheat led to an extention of subsidised food which, in turn, impacted a proportion of the government expenditure. Under Nasser, in the post-1970s setting, subsidies became a benefit for all Egyptians regardless of their income level, a non-targeted social transfer to the poorest, and a mechanism for the political establishment to buy consensus while withholding political freedoms (Lorenzon, 2016: 108). The Mubarak regime attempted to first cut overall expenditure, which declined from 14 per cent in 1980–1981 to 5.6 per cent by the end of the 1990s (Ibrahim and Lofgren,

1995; see also Adly, 2011; Ahmed et al., 2001). However, despite cuts, in the 1990s the discrepancies between policies of political exclusion and the regime's commitment to provide for the basic needs of the population ultimately translated into a form of 'societal support' (See Gutner, 1999; Singerman, 1996). The regime then introduced reforms in the mid-2000s, with a presidential decree to assist the Ministry of Supply and Internal Trade with administrating subsidies and manage the introduction of a ration card system as a measure to 'avoid' malnutrition. In fact, the measure was tactical in the way it attempted to 'buy' a form of political stability. In the run-up to the 2012 elections, the Muslim Brotherhood adopted a discourse of the *democratiyyat al-khubz* (democracy of bread) to gain votes for the FJP. In 2012/2013, the FJP government spent 32.5 billion LE on food subsidies; in 2013 under the FJP, *baladi* bread absorbed 86.6 per cent of the food subsidy budget, namely 3.1 billion USD, accounting for 1.2 per cent of GDP. Subsidised bread in Egypt, where food subsidies constitute up to 2 per cent of GDP, also constitutes a tool through which to address nutritional needs; Egypt, next to Yemen, in the 2000s period, concomitant with subsidies reform, experienced a rise in malnutrition amongst children (Brown, 2017; IFPRI, 2013).[16] In 2013/2014, the last year before al-Sisi announced the subsidy reform, the cost amounted to 35.5 billion LE. Nevertheless, food subsidies comprised a small fraction of the total subsidies, meaning that their targeting had a marginal impact on the monetary budget (Springborg, 2017).

Wheat production and selling are connected to the political domain, as they occupy important positions in the country's import bills and external debts. Wheat importation grew significantly from 5 per cent under Nasser to 90 per cent in 2013 (Hamza et al., 2013). Related to the limits and implications of subsidies, food (mainly bread) subsidies have been part of the remaking of internal networks of corruption which contributed to economic distortions (Verme, 2016). This does not only occur in connection to the international market and price of wheat. Over recent decades with regard to the politics of the NDP, local political actors such as bureaucrats and civil servants have been involved in the *baladi* supply chain, creating the sources for political instability. Food subsidies in Egypt can be classified into explicit and implicit categories. While the former relates to public spending, which is recorded in state budgets, the latter does not explicitly appear in the budget, but nonetheless contributes to the spending deficit. In this second category, *baladi* bread – Egypt's most commonly consumed foodstuff, eaten by all social classes – is central in the food subsidy system and it is in turn linked to the making of a bread politics and the politicisation of wheat import/export.[17] From a historical point of view, bread subsidies have been an explosive issue in the country since the late 1970s, when 70 million people received state rations (Abdalla and Al-Shawar, 2017). In

1977 riots in Cairo and other major cities, including Suez, under the slogan *Intifadet al-Khobz* (Intifada of bread) were triggered because of an increment of commodities' prices after a cut of up to EGP 500 million by Anwar Sadat which cancelled subsidies of basic foodstuff.

Despite the attempt to resolve the logistics systems to build more efficient wheat reserves before possible crises, the Mediterranean risks destabilisation for a combination of economic and unresolved political reasons, primarily food prices, which after a decline in 2020 started soaring again in 2022 up to 23.9 per cent as a result of a constant increment in the inflation rate and of the implications determined by the Ukraine conflict, in combination with resource and food scarcity towards which Egypt and, more broadly, the region is exposed to (see CPI, 2022).[18] Beyond the neoliberal explanation, there is a need to de-Westernise and decolonise the approach to economic reforms. Egypt faces the challenge of a rising poverty rate despite the magnification of economic and industrial reforms and data on decreased unemployment rate in urban areas, thus cuts to foods subsidies, rather than downgrading corruption and tackling the black economy where subsidised wheat bags are re-sold, may risk reorganising forms of structured dissent in consideration of the fact that consensus building continued to decline after 2014 and shifted from 5.2 out of 10 to 2.2 in 2022 (BTI, 2022), at the expense of consolidated cooperation, which however remains confined by a very exclusivist and elitist unreformist logic. After 2011, the FJP implemented reforms for various fuels, among which were petrol and natural gas, though reforms did not arrest the soaring of subsidy costs, which between 2002 and 2013 shifted from 2 per cent to 22 per cent, counterbalancing the dried state revenues since 2011 and resulting in fiscal instability, which still persists despite protests in the country being muted. When it comes to food subsidies, they account for 1–2 per cent of national GDP.

The reforms introduced in 2015 by the Ministry of Supply overhauled the bread subsidy scheme, shifting it towards a points-based system which, it was planned, would be integrated with the previously existing ration card system, which benefited 80 per cent of Egyptians, formerly accounting for 39 per cent of the subsidies. While the ration card system has been presented as an effective measure for managing cuts, in fact it presents non-revised structural inefficiencies. The reform introduced in 2015 pushed for two programmes, the first, a cash transfer system through Takaful and Karama programmes. As part of the rationale, these programmes would have increased cash liquidity to households by enabling them to spend more on necessary goods. In fact, this logic impacts the inflation rate. The second sub-programme of food subsidies is the ration card system, initially introduced by Nasser as a social protection measure, to then grow under Sadat but ultimately reformed under the first decade of Mubarak's rule.

To be eligible, the revised system introduced in 2015 requires that ration card holders obtain the ration on a daily basis without the possibility of taking the bread all in one go. In addition, the reform made the bread no longer universal, thus limiting loaves to 150 per month per person/per household (MSIT, 2014). In 2022 the ration card increased up to LE 100 for a six-month period to reflect inflation and the rise in wheat and food prices, as also exacerbated in 2022 by the global economic crisis.[19]

However, this extension of the ration card in late 2022, presented as state capacity to increase bread, sold up to 10 per cent – thus framing it as a measure supporting social security. In theory the measure suggests being overall in line with outcomes 1–5 set in the strategy country report through which Egypt would contribute to the United Nations partnership development framework, SDG-2 and SDG-17 (World Food Programme, 2018–2023).

In addition, following the cut to subsidies, the armed forces paved an intense return in the economic field, although it would be reductive and misleading to view the armed forces' involvement in the economy as a reproduction of the Nasserian or even Mubarakian strictly economic model type. To control food prices and thus limit the risk of unrest, the EAF returned to an active role, representing a main pillar of the economy through the NSPO and the centralisation of the food and commodities sector (Sayigh, 2019). According to the World Food Programme, 13.7 million Egyptians suffered from food insecurity in 2011. Increasing resource scarcity, the worsening of the economic environment, and the corrupt and unsustainable food subsidy system have all contributed to making malnutrition endemic in the broader Mediterranean area and are all drivers which historically have fuelled protests, like in Egypt in 1977 where the bread riots erupted, and diffused to other North African countries in the late 1980s.

With regard to the cuts to subsidies from 2014 to 2017, at the core of the government's defence, Minister Moselhy argued that the reduction of subsidies to those without the smart card introduced in 2005 would have curbed corruption. Indeed, targeting corruption remained at the core of most of al-Sisi's discourse and stated goals between 2015 and 2017 compared to the preceding years, although this still pertained to strictly infrastructural aspects and the 'Sisisation' of religion, for political purposes. Yet as a result of the government's struggle to attract foreign investments, partly through its strategy of slashing subsidies, as well as the shortage in foreign currency due to the reduced flow of remittances, the black market between 2015 and 2022 enjoyed an expansion. Likewise, similarly to the Algerian scenario where a parallel circuit to the banking system to exchange dinars with other currencies is preferred and tolerated by the Algerian government as it was worth nearly five billion dollars in 2018,[20] the Egyptian pound in 2022 kept falling on the black market exchange rate ahead of the approved IMF loan, as hard currency shortage persists. The wheat crisis perpetuated the system

The political economy of resurrection 195

of indebtness, and in 2022 authorities obtained a new 3 billion USD loan from the IMF to preserve 'macroeconomic stability'. Both the cuts to energy and later food subsidies created the additional social implications of a rising internal (though virtual) dissent towards the political executive and no alternative measure thereafter found a theorisation. As per corruption, trends do not go in the same direction as promoted by authorities; macrodata indicate no oscillations between 2020 and 2022, rather cuts to subsidies pushed for an exponential rise in corruption between 2014 and 2015 and again between 2018 and 2019 (Transparency International, 2022).[21]

From a pro-Sisi view, the post-2013 authorities' approach to food subsidies revealed itself as being more generous than the FJP's: subsidies increased by 19.6 per cent in 2015/2016 compared to 2014/2015, but then decreased by 8.95 per cent in the fiscal year 2016/2017 (Ministry of Finance data, 2015–2017). This two-stage approach was a reaction to the severe tensions emerging between 2014 and 2016, when al-Sisi's position seemed extremely unstable as a result of the tensions with the al-Azhar and an angry civil society, and the ambiguous attitude of the SCAF, which enjoyed the power of political interference until 2021.[22] A heavy cut to food subsidies all in one go would have contributed to further social dissent and compromised the security of the authorities, despite the difficulty of social mobilisation due to the legal restrictions previously introduced by al-Sisi, and the block on funding for oppositional movements due to the enforcement of Law No. 70 of 2017, which regulated the channelling of money from outside Egypt to Egyptian NGOs.[23] Hence, al-Sisi's consensus-buying did not intend to work very differently from the FJP's rhetoric of the democratisation of 'bread politics'. However, an exponential growth in basic food prices was accompanied by increasing inflation by 34 per cent in 2017, which reached 38 per cent in 2022, scoring the highest peak since 2007–2008. Cuts to food subsidies and rising inflation in turn created a similar social reaction to that witnessed in July 2014 after the cut to energy subsidies.

According to a view somewhat sympathetic to the regime, al-Sisi's acceptance of the IMF's recommendations enabled the floating of the currency and the market's determination of the value of the currency.[24] This situation was worsened by the lack of need to raise reserves due to the aid flows from the Gulf, and the depreciation of the Egyptian pound, which lost 30 per cent against the US dollar between 2014 and 2015. The currency's instability protracted in 2022 when the pound lost half of its value. As noted by Springborg (2017), the policy of saving the Egyptian pound by restricting access to foreign exchange resulted in collateral damage to the market, to confidence, and to business in general – damage that intensified in 2015 in tandem with the Central Bank's further tightening as foreign reserves slipped further (CBE, 2016). Egypt's largest steel producer, Ezz Steel, reported a first-quarter net loss of 19.5 million USD, up from 2.7

million USD in the same period in 2014. The company's chairman attributed the downturn to Ezz's inability to 'source sufficient foreign currency, due to a major change in the regulations of the banking sector' (Springborg, 2017: 4). Russell Investments' reclassification of Egypt followed a series of downgrades, since 2011, of Egypt's sovereign credit rating by Moody's and Standard & Poor's, taking the country to junk bond status (Springborg, 2017: 189–190).

Against this backdrop, the authorities at that time were unable to intervene in the job market, with population growth exponentially on the rise. Despite more optimistic views provided by the UNDP and the IMF in terms of growth, with a projection of cuts to the poverty rate from 1.3 in 2015 to 0.66 by 2030, projections on unemployment by ILO remained less positive, with Egypt forecasted to hit the highest score in the region since 2010 (Fedi, Amer and Rashad, 2019). Now, projects of industrialisation managed to attract the labour force, providing the impression of a significant reduction in the unemployment rate. However, the celebration of data needs to be contextualised against the societal and economic background. If SCAF-led projects in the construction sector have generated a few more jobs, the gender-based gap has remained unchanged. Contextually, Egypt's labour market has been dominated by the public sector, a product of policies beginning in the 1950s and 1960s that promoted public sector employment and guaranteed a government job for university graduates (Richards, 1992). Nasser's policies conversely harmed the development of the private sector, which has been damaged by the lack of a strong entrepreneurial culture, limited available financing options, opaque licensing regulations, and weak anti-trust laws that favour large firms and politically connected companies, while failing to protect small and medium-sized firms (Al-Ghafar, 2016). The goal of boosting state revenues was then followed by amendments to the VAT tax law, which was introduced and approved in 2016. The VAT tax law wanted to replace the 10 per cent Sales Tax. Despite these reforms, the long-term implications clashed with an erosion in the global economy aggravated by external shocks (i.e. conflicts) which, on top of unsustainable costs for 'mega-projects' put the national economy under pressure. While these financial challenges did not spark protests, at least in public spaces in a conventional way, societal dissent found a more marginal manifestation in virtual spaces.

Nature as a critical political system

Food and natural resources in illiberal structures in the context of the globalised dimension of environmentalism constitute the essential dimension of political legitimacy, and Egypt is not immune from the nature-legitimacy syllogism. However, beyond the obsoletism of 'inputs' and 'outputs' legitimacy as a two-dimensional concept (Scharpf, 1970), the politics of reforming subsidies can be internalised into the politics of reimagining nature as a new political ecology of both power struggle and authority's political legitimation in a fluid autocracy like Egypt. Here, what could be more broadly contextualised as environmental and food politics have ended up playing new core functions in the process of political legitimation. In this shift, outputs play a different function. While the fundamental component of output legitimacy has always referred to citizens' satisfaction with the concept of government policy, this happens if anticipated by a recognition of citizens' political preferences and decisions (Hoekema et al., 1998). Now, in the context of environmental crisis, the institutionalisation and financialisation of nature as interlinked with the process of legitimation, it is no longer dictated by government policies towards which citizens are called to express a form of acceptance of identification, as necessary for the output-driven legitimation process. Rather, output legitimacy has become critically interconnected with the critical ecosystem.

While 'critical ecosystem' borrows from Acheampong (2020), the early model was theorised to reconcile the sociological and political dimension of political ecology, for which criticisms still persist regarding the lack of a moral ground or the emphasised political, over ecological, dimension (Zimmerer and Bassett, 2003; Vayda and Walters, 1999). Here, critical ecosystems, in the context of sub-transformed autocracies that internalise a strong fluid component, is employed in reference to the categories of power dynamics that the ecosystem replicates. As such, reforms to subsidies, in the context of sub-transformed structures which additionally implied a redefinition of power hierarchies, is not exclusively captured through financial and economic axes and needs to be determined by neoliberalism. Rather it is through the new categories of power that critical ecosystems embed when intertwined with the overall struggle for internal legitimation. In the context of Egypt, announced subsidies and food reforms in 2014, and their gradual applications soon after, aimed at relocating NSPO-related industries of the 1970s–2015 as producers of basic commodities along a new, differently non-Nasserian, societal imaginary by taking high moral ground in the protection of the environmental ecosystem. This was also consolidated through official discourses that, between 2019 and 2022, aimed at consolidating the authorities' position with regard to environmental actions and policies. This was particularly evident in official speeches as the country accelerates towards green transitions with a clear cut-off emphasis on the national infrastructural transition, including solar, hydrogen and wind energy projects. As it is possible to see from the coded codebook and chart in Figure 6.2,

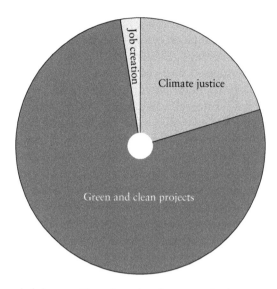

6.2 Combine-coded data on Egypt's national strategy in the sector of sustainable development and milestones. Data obtained from a combination of coding of: Major Economic Forum on Energy and Climate (MEF); Middle East Green Initiative 2022; Summit Opening of Cairo Water Week 2022; UN Climate Change Conference 2021 and COP27 in 2022

despite the overall narrative on fighting climate justice from a transversal perspective, the domestic focus remains set on the profitability of the new green capitalist model and rather marginally centred on the domestic implications this shift will determine in the field of the employability, which constitutes just a mention.

The making of a non-pyramidal corruption: a diffused network

The creation of patronage networks over decades represented one of the means for autocrats to stay in power, though this interfered with the selection of bureaucrats in charge of conveying rent extraction, thus setting up a loss of welfare in the system (Mueller, 2015; see Blaydes and Rubin, 2008). These practices characterised Egyptian politics under the NDP from the early 1990s, and were closely connected to cronyism and vote-buying practices during the phase of opening to multi-party elections (Blaydes, 2008). Indeed, pyramidal cronyism and clientelist networks for three decades represented the engine that allowed the NDP to buy durability, although they did not provide any internal legitimating claim to the regime. While the mechanism of cronyism was apparently (at least until 2011) 'perfected' under Mubarak,

The political economy of resurrection 199

it may be argued that the strength of this system disincentivised the search for legitimacy, at least in purist Weberian terms (Weber, 1978). Thus, the emphasis on regime durability became associated with large mechanisms of corruption, of which the NDP and high-ranking generals under Mubarak were part; this may have led authorities to ignore the necessity of reform of the ACA (ACA, 2020).[25]

Although the nexus between state corruption under the NDP and the eruption of the 2011 protests was straightforward, under al-Sisi tackling corruption did not initially appear as a top priority in 2014. However, it became a necessity in early 2015, and was connected with the process of legitimation-building between 2015 and 2017. The regime's anti-corruption strategy has been organised on three broad levels: precautionary measures, initiative policies, and public awareness of corruption-related problems (ACA, 2019–2022). Al-Sisi's self-framing as a 'reformer' expanded to many sectors of the state, and included the notion of purifying a corrupt state, interwoven with the restoration of the rule of law and shadow interests. In December 2014, the authorities launched the National Anti-Corruption Strategy, planned to last four years. In theory, at the core of the rationale was the idea of prioritising integrity, social justice and transparency. The same promotion of anti-corruption laws found a place in the fifth governmental pillar presented at the WEF in Davos in 2015, next to the reform of the pension system.

In fact, a deeper focus on the undertaken reform of the ACA suggests that the ACA merely reinforced specific tasks, such as the work of the National Security Agency, founded in 2011, the Committee on Terrorism and Extremism, the National Payments Council, and the Supreme Council on Investments. These, in combination with the legal reforms such as Laws No. 107 of 2013, No. 94 of 2015, and No. 70 of 2017, created what can be considered a 'strategic continuum' between the assurance of the EAF as protector of the state while limiting its power, and al-Sisi's obsession for government economic-based performance. Of crucial importance is the transformation of the ACA into a strictly civilian state body. This significantly differs from the ACA's original Constitution dating back to 1964, although at all times the ACA has been exempt from undertaking investigations into the military.

Al-Sisi's regime cannot be compared to the 'classical' corruption under Mubarak and the NDP, a pyramidal form of clientelism closely tied to the survival of the regime party, and neither is it an oxidisable mechanism interlinking society with business and politics. Rather, after 2013, the system of corruption underwent a shift from being hierarchical (pyramidal) to being more diffused. While corruption has not decreased – quantitative data show that society's perception of state corruption increased from 23.0 in 2011 to 49.5 on a 0–100 scale in 2014 (Teti et al., 2018: 91).[26] It is here argued that corruption cannot be considered as the exclusive determinant for analysing performance and its connection to regime stability.[27] In 2014, both the World Bank's Worldwide Governance Indicators and the CPI reported failing governance in the seven macro areas (World Bank, 2014a; CPI, 2016). Despite al-Sisi's reforms to the ACA and his economic agenda, government effectiveness scored improvements between mid-2014 and mid-2015, only to fall again between mid-2015 and 2018. Similarly, corruption underwent fluctuations, with state control calculated as stable at 37 out of 100 between 2014 and mid-2015. State capacity to control corruption increased between mid-2015 and mid-2016, to downgrade again from 2016 to 2018 (World Bank Worldwide Governance Indicators, 2018). This has to be interpreted in light of the reforms to the fuel and food subsidies, which sparked disaffection, at the level of monetary policies to the free floating of the Egyptian pound, and in terms of the development agenda to the economic illusions of the Suez Canal Zone, which served the purpose of strengthening the EAF's hold on business.

Expanding on the structural conditions behind the construction of a political leadership, until 2015, and prior to al-Sisi's ACA reform, the ACA was in the hands of General Erfan. In 2018 Erfan was removed and promoted to the position of Presidential Advisor for Government Affairs (Noll, 2019). Not surprisingly, the same mechanism applied to the rotation of heads of intelligence services and military ranks which took place in 2016. This rotation of influential figures and their promotion up the hierarchy is reminiscent of Nasser's technique used to prevent the rise of potential challengers within the ASU and neutralise others' prospects for mobilisation, with the goal of building non-state related power bases. Yet, between Nasser and al-Sisi exist more dissimilarities than similarities.

Although al-Sisi's regime has not based itself on a political party, the changes in the heads of security apparatus and military are nevertheless embedded into the failure of the legitimation of the political leadership. Thus, the close centralisation of the network under al-Sisi is here interpreted as an attempt at the leader's securitisation, aimed at infusing an apparent sense of regime stability, with all the limits posed by the concept of securitisation as opposed to security and durability.[28] The control of the ACA under Seif al-Din (Erfan's successor) acted as an extension of al-Sisi's control over the agency, which was then passed to al-Sisi's son Mahmoud before his removal in 2019. Confirming the argument of the leadership's need to create a protective state structure around it due to the organic failure of the input legitimating process (discussed in previous chapters), since 2017 the ACA has been tightly controlled by the President's direct authority (Noll, 2019). Amendments introduced in 2017 to Law No. 54 of 1964 attempted to strengthen al-Sisi in the broader power structures, while strategically framing the goal of the policies as tackling corruption and achieving political honesty

(ACA, 2019–2022). In an attempt to demonstrate the transformation of the social contract and the new state transparency, some arrests followed the reform of the ACA, including those of al-Labban and Shalaby, accused of receiving huge bribes in foreign currency. However, many officials still seem to enjoy immunity from such investigations, for reasons that appear unclear: there is no transparency to the operations of the ACA under al-Sisi (Noll, 2019).

The exception of the military from undergoing ACA investigation suggests that al-Sisi's regime is not precisely a pyramidal cronyism with power confined to the military elite level with a de facto military ruler on top of the state and the government, but is more diffused and operates through a logic of 'ruler favouritisms' that still rely on networks. This is unlike the mechanisms of corruption between 1991 and 2006, but nevertheless lacks the premises of transparency and honesty emphasised by the ACA and at odds with al-Sisi's July 2013 and March 2014 speeches and 2015 interview with the BBC. In addition, it is in disagreement with Noll (2019), that the administrative exceptionalism of ACA, while a tool for the management of networks to secure resources, also generates support and legitimacy for the regime to a limited extent. While this latter argument indicates how clientelist networks in non-democratic systems act as a mafia circle – the more the network is favoured the less likely it is to expose the regime to instability shocks – it is equally true that societal consensus towards government performance also plays a role in influencing networks, although this is often neglected. Hence, if the ACA reform in 2017 and the shift in power from the Prime Minister to the President in 2017 were designed for regime protection, neither will provide legitimacy to the regime, should social dissent rise again in the long-term under unpredictable structures.

Ultimately, while corruption constituted a form of guarantee to the Mubarak regime's durability, it also contributed to its overthrow in 2011. In the case of al-Sisi and the different governmental machine created between 2014 and 2019, this book has not analysed corruption as a determinant that, if taken in isolation from other factors, can contribute to social dissent, mistrust and ultimately shocks to the regime, which are otherwise limited by the new legal framework enforced by Laws No. 107 of 2013 and No. 94 of 2015 and the disappearance of political parties. In this regard, according to the scenario hypothesised by Noll, the anti-corruption campaign under al-Sisi was misguided, with possible counterproductive effects, since 'the agency lacks sufficient transparency, accountability and independence from the centres of power (Noll, 2019: 4). However, despite mistrust in the institutions, a bad management of the anti-corruption campaign and the failure in input legitimacy, the political system is likely to endure as long as the economic sector and its mega-projects meet the military's desire to exercise its influence. However, it is argued that the system of corruption since 2013 has shifted from being pyramidal and tied to the NDP into being more diffused, due to the absence of a regime party and the system of *wasta* around it, and attached to mega-projects.

The present and the future of Egypt's economic performance

Empirically, despite deep and structural economic problems, especially concerning social inequality, the Egyptian economy has been viewed as improving in recent years, with government policy moving in the right direction.[29] Macroeconomic indicators in 2019 compared with those of previous years were good, showing improving GDP, growing foreign currency reserves and reasonable FDI rates. In 2017, after the CBE liberalised the exchange rate, the stock exchange recorded 550 billion USD (CBE, 2017). However, almost all investments have been in the rebuilding of the energy sector, with a stronger state interest towards renewables, with little investment in any sector other than construction, which according to views expressed by PA1 and ER1 is not likely to generate significant new economic activity.[30]

In the government's own view, reforms introduced since July 2014 have had a significant impact on restoring confidence in the economy and improving macroeconomic indicators. Data from the Ministry of Finance highlight the decrease in the deficit from 4.2 to 3.8 per cent of GDP between 2017 and 2018, and a rise in revenues from 4.2 per cent of GDP in 2017 to 5.3 in 2017/2018 and 5.6 in 2018/2019 (CBE, 2019; CBE, 2017, 2018, 2019). However, real GDP growth dropped to 2 per cent in 2020 to slightly recover in 2022 and decrease again in 2023 (CBE data, 2023; IMF, 2018). From the IMF's perspective, subsidy reforms initiated in 2014 and continued over the years contributed to reducing the budget deficit, and made available more resources for social programmes to support the most vulnerable.

It cannot be denied that the government has performed quite well on gradually reducing both domestic and external debt, which initially underwent an incremental decrease in 2017 to 3.097 trillion LE (89 per cent of GDP). However, external debt in 2018 further increased to 4.315 trillion LE (35.2 per cent of GDP), peaking in the first half of 2019 at 4.801 trillion LE, then decreasing to 4.655 trillion LE in the second half (CBE, 2019). In June 2019, external debt was calculated by the CBE at 92.6 billion USD, while in September of the same year it was 93.1 billion USD. External and national debt eventually increased again from 2019 to 2022 (Central Bank of Egypt data, 2022).

In the Ministry of Finance's narrative, inflation also declined markedly; however, data demonstrate an increase from 11 per cent in 2015 to 29.6

in 2017, the highest peak since the early 1980s, followed by a decrease to 20.9 in 2018 and 13 per cent in 2019 (IMF, 2015–2019; Ministry of Finance, 2015–2019). However, inflation remains stubbornly high when compared to the MENA region (IMF, 2020). In 2022 consumer prices rose to 2.21 per cent while in February the percentage was scored at 1.61 per cent. This increment primarily affected food. Inflation jumped to 10.491 per cent in March 2022 and was above the upper bound of the CBE's target which was rated at 5.0–9.0 per cent for the first two and a half years (CBE, 2022).[31]

In terms of general taxes on goods and revenues, in 2016 VAT on imported and domestic goods recorded 107.8 billion LE, an increase of 51 billion LE. However, the benevolence of the legal framework introduced after 2013 exempted the military from VAT, problematising the government's claims of transparency. Such favourable moves for the military, since al-Sisi came to power in 2014, have meant that military enterprises have flourished after a decline in the 1990s and the 2000s, with all national infrastructure projects now led by the army, and factories associated with the army involved in the production of goods and facilities for the civilian market. Income tax revenues increased by 56.9 billion LE, while taxes on salaries generated a liquidity of 14.0 billion LE.

Comparatively, revenues from the Suez Canal Zone project in 2017 contributed only 10.6 billion LE, with collected dividends amounting to 12.2 billion LE (Suez Canal Authority, 2021). Despite the authorities' emphasis on the project, and its costs amounting to 80 billion USD, data on revenues confirm that the Suez Canal Zone had not raised significant revenues until 2021; although politically and strategically it provided the leadership with some reassurance vis-à-vis the armed forces, it did not provide the regime with legitimacy before society, at least in terms of economic expectation versus effective performance. Under a façade of nationalism, the expansion of the Suez Canal met the support of the EAF, being the contractors of the project, though wider society and economic forecasters were sceptical in terms of its contribution to growth (Deknatel, 2019).

The Egyptian economic miracle continued in 2018 and 2019. Strong programme implementation and generally positive performance has been instrumental in achieving macroeconomic stabilisation, but also to show the post-2013 authorities' commitment to social and economic promises. External and fiscal deficits shrank, inflation declined, and growth accelerated. The authorities' celebration of Egypt's economic recovery was apparently vindicated by the speech given by then First Deputy Managing Director of the IMF David Lipton at the Egypt-IMF conference in 2018, in which he stated that in Egypt macroeconomic stability and market confidence were restored, growth had resumed, inflation had fallen, and the public debt ratio was expected to fall for the first time in nearly a decade, and he congratulated the Egyptian people for having played a role in the economic and financial success with 'patience through a disruptive time' (Lipton, 2018). The macroeconomic data shared by the Ministry of Finance in its bulletins since 2015 aimed at polishing government performance, engendering society's trust in the authorities, and attempting to convince the world of the promises made by the leadership in the March 2014 speech, in which 'hard sacrifices' were linked to a communal effort at improving the domestic economy in a 'salvation' narrative.

The Ministry of Finance's emphasis on the country's repositioning in the eyes of international credit ratings agencies, such as Standard & Poor's, Moody's and Bloomberg, confirms this chapter's argument that government economic performance has become more externally, rather than internally, significant. The World Bank's data suggest that government performance in 2014–2018 improved (WGI, 2018), while Fitch Ratings in 2017 upgraded the outlook for the economy from stable to positive, along with Standard & Poor's. The same celebrative line was followed by the economic international media (Zhukov, 2015; see also *Guardian*, 2015a), which predicted that the discovery of the Zohr Field of natural gas would be of high importance for making Egypt the main road for the Eastern Mediterranean's export of gas to Europe. It should be noted, however, that Zohr was discovered by the Italian company ENI, which by agreement owns 80 per cent of the entire field, with only 20 per cent designated to Egypt, insufficient to satisfy the country's energy needs.

Based on data reported by the government, there is an agreement that al-Sisi managed to improve the financial condition of Egypt for the good of the neoliberal market, though the human cost remained uncalculated by the IMF and World Bank.[32] Comparatively, there have been some real achievements made over recent years in terms of economic recovery and looking at the macro indicators.[33] Broadly, this book does not try to deny that, under al-Sisi, Egypt has performed reasonably well on a set of macroeconomic indicators, and that revenues have exponentially increased for the first time since 2004. However, these data require a political and social contextualisation in order to be properly understood, especially regarding – as ER1 agrees – the social distribution of resources and wealth.

A critical investigation of the macroeconomic indicators involves a consideration of investments in different sectors. Since 2014, the Egyptian economy has become oriented towards the construction sector. Construction is an important part of any economy, though its capacity to generate new economic impact once construction work is complete is only conditional, and in Egypt is dominated by the military and its subsidiaries. With regard to growth, while it is true that there was a nominal increase of a total of 303 billion USD in 2018/2019, 2–3 per cent of GDP out of a total growth rate calculated at 4.3 per cent in 2017, 5.3 per cent in 2018 and 5.6 per cent in 2019, it is mainly represented by military revenues. Historically, Egypt performed better in 2005–2010 under Mubarak, with a GDP growth rate of 6.2 per cent, compared to 5.6 per cent under al-Sisi in 2019.

While the authorities have seemed to expend significant effort on building a functioning economy, this remains based on selling Egypt as an attractive market for middle-class or foreign investors, which is a gamble. The political authorities' strategy is to bring in as much FDI as possible, but to spend these funds on projects the government (and the military) sees fit. One problem with relying so heavily on foreign investment is that Egypt does not possess its own capital and is returning to a high level of debt, even though this has so far been sustainable. In addition, foreign currency reserves are dependent on constant injection of capital from sympathetic foreign governments and organisations (e.g. Gulf Cooperation Council, IMF). It follows that while in the simplistic views of the IMF and ratings agencies the macroeconomic indicators show the government's performance in a positive light, from a more critical perspective the economic outlook for Egypt is not so reassuring.[34]

A hybrid model of developmentalism

Egypt's successful economic performance at a macro level was definitively not the first time that economic improvements were celebrated as 'miracles', but left structural issues unsolved, particularly concerning foreign debt. External debt rose from 79 billion USD in 2017 to 92.6 billion USD in 2018, the highest since the 2000s, after the depreciation of the Egyptian pound reached its first peak in 2019 (CBE, 2019; see IMF, 2019). Arguably, the IMF manipulated Egypt's economic structures, with the country's foreign currency reserves amounting to over 40 billion USD, consisting of borrowed money and thus a form of (external) debt. In 2019, the authorities allocated 38 per cent of the budget to paying off the interest on this debt; along with paying off other loans, 58 per cent of the budget was ultimately spent, and thus was not invested in civil society.

In turn, investment in education did not increase while in health it sharply decreased from 2017, despite the growing population, which reached 98.4 million people in 2018 (V-Dem, 2023; World Health Organisation, 2021). Furthermore, salaries did not significantly increase until 2020, clashing with al-Sisi's discourse on economic social justice.[35]

The growing role of the state in economic reconstruction during 2016–2021, through the interventions of monetary and fiscal policies, was in line with the making of strategic and tactical frames which sought to recalibrate the role of the army in the government's mega-projects (i.e. the Suez Canal Zone, the project of greening desert lands, and investing in vertical agriculture to reduce water consumption and rebalance exportations), and counteract the implications of the austerity measures introduced to meet the requirements of ratings agencies and the IMF. In practical terms, the IMF pressure on Egypt to cut subsidies further pushed al-Sisi to go to the international money markets for capital, relying on the IMF's willingness to provide a multitude of loans to reassure new investors of the Egyptian market's stability. Considering the country's lack of capital, this economic behaviour is unsustainable in the long run.

Cuts to fuel and food subsidies played a double function in meeting the IMF's requirements. They provided the image of a highly responsible government to the outside world (and investors), but they also favoured the internal mechanisms of structural upgrading. The elimination of subsidies allowed the armed forces to play an even greater role in the production of low-quality civilian goods, normally sold at low prices, and thus implementing mechanisms for bypassing the negative effects of the removal of subsidies such as price rises through local production.

The response to pre-existing problems linked to the deterioration of services and posing a challenge to the quality of life, such as access to water and housing, has become nationalised under al-Sisi and centralised under EAF authority, similarly to the involvement of the armed forces in the Suez Canal Zone project. In 2014, 91 per cent of Egypt's population had access to water; the remaining 9 per cent, most of them from urban slums or rural areas, was isolated from easily obtaining this essential resource (see Mohammed, 2015).

This made the project of urban upgrading inextricable from the government's propaganda on social justice and the right to a dignified life, extensively found in al-Sisi's March 2014 speech, the 2015 interview with the BBC, the speech at the WEF in Davos, and the address at the UN General Assembly in 2016. In the fiscal year 2018/2019, the government announced the replacement of slums with 80,000 housing units, which had already been part of the NDP's unfulfilled agenda in the early 2000s and which aimed at the relocation of Cairo's slums on desert land in order to provide a solution to the demographic boom (Sims, 2003, 2012).[36] However, al-Sisi's developmentalism also marked an increasing role for the EAF as a business actor, especially concerning the sale of state land through Presidential Decree No. 446 of 2015, which gave the Land Project Agency authorisation to engage in commercial activities. Presidential Decree No. 57 of 2016 then created a public limited company between the Land Project Agency, the New Urban Community Authority, and NSPO, with the goal of planning construction projects.

The 'military nationalisation' of development projects corresponded to a historical repetition of the regime militarisation. Social and structural development programmes re-launched by the government soon after 2014 and backed by non-state Western actors (e.g. the UNDP) and regional allies (such as the UAE) – including the projects of upgrading slums, building a new administrative capital, and water sanitation, amongst others – are fertile ground for the reconsolidation of the military into the sustainable business sector and transformed state infrastructure. This neatly dovetailed with the transformation of Egypt's economic foundations, aimed at bringing in more money for mega-projects and serving the purpose of bolstering al-Sisi's 2013–2014 discourse on making Egypt socially and environmentally sustainable, democratic and inclusive. In fact, despite green projects addressed to green desert lands and supporting the sustainability of the agricultural sector, which accounts for 28 per cent of all employment and remains the major component of the Egyptian economy but also the sector more exposed to external shocks and crises (i.e. wheat crisis as mainly determined by the principle of dependence on imports), consensus building in 2022 further dropped to 2.2 from 2.6 in 2020 and 3.2 in 2018, while the perception of sustainability remained unchanged when compared to the pre-2011 setting under the leadership of Morsi and even the latest year of Mubarak rule (BTI, 2022).[37]

Conclusions

As a general norm, the Egyptian idea of environmentalism as elite-centrist remains profoundly at odds with the definition of green politics and economic industrialisation. Environmental politics calls for social responsibility and requires flexible institutions and practices, participatory democracy, decentralisation, and for political parties to be feminist- and religion-inclusive (Polimeno, 2022). These are political and societal determinants that find no replication in Egypt, despite the huge investments that push for an acceleration towards logic of economic and industrial sustainability that predict a new model for the economy. The enforcement of Law No. 107 of 2013, in combination with amendments to the penal code undermining freedom of association and any form of societal activism, regardless of the its nature (civic and non-necessarily political), have produced an exclusivist domestic panorama that further centralises the elite's role in the domestic realm. At the core of this model of development, elites are considered as the actors that capitalise on the global economic market failure of capitalism in order to regain the lead of economic and developmentalist system, thus making the environmental less exploitable in terms of resources.

The political ecology of new job generation is accompanied by old practices of privatisation. In the medium term, in the absence of strategies of legitimation and economic performance (a drop in the debt level which rose in 2020–2021), it will undermine Egypt's already precarious economic and financial situation. As a main obstacle, state-owned enterprises define the notion of nature and practise exclusionary, unsustainable forms of development. The departure point this book wants to expose is that environmentalism and green politics in Egypt have become new tools to reorganise political power and resilience over human lives and nature in service of global capitalism (Polimeno, 2022). All this raises major concerns about the risk of bio-autocracies developing in the Mediterranean area, which are likely to be at the core of future debates and works.

The rehabilitation of the army in the industrial and business complex, which has accelerated in recent years, has been also facilitated by the Cleopatra Group. However, this book's definition of the military traits of al-Sisi's authoritarian rule, and the militarisation of the economic and industrial sector, differs from the mainstream reading of the role of the army in the industrial complex.

The rehabilitation of the EAF in the economic sector has sparked academic theories on the remilitarisation of the regime, diffused by osmosis into journalism and other fields (see Mandour, 2017; 2019). Recent contributions recognise an increased and centralised role of the EAF in the economic-industrial complex forming a paternalistic force (Noll, 2017; Sayigh, 2019, 2020; Springborg, 2020). However, in this book I contend that the effective domination of the Egyptian economy by the EAF does not come as a novelty. Since the 1980s, the SCAF began to emerge as the key actor in the economic sector, expanding from the military to the civilian market (Abul-Magd, 2013). The SCAF's control of more than 44 per cent of Egypt's national resources and revenues, and status as the main investor in hotels on the Red Sea (i.e. in the Hurghada area) is nothing new; neither is the secrecy of the military's operations in the economy, despite the demand by the IMF reported by Human Rights Watch for the transparency of military-owned firms (Human Rights Watch, 2020).

From an economic perspective, access to loans and the politics of indebtedness, on which foundations the Egyptian system lies, leave serious questions about the affordability of the country's economic behaviour, despite its current stability brought by financial influxes from Saudi Arabia and UAE, and the capacity to rebalance imports with exports. Since 2016, the IMF has lent 20 billion USD to Egypt, with the goal of promoting more transparent reforms. However, the data which this chapter has cited suggest a discrepancy in al-Sisi's economic performance which, from an economic perspective, may impact on the struggle for top-down legitimation by output drivers.

There are four specific main risks to the Egyptian economy: the steady decline in value of the Egyptian pound; the depletion of national reserves, especially in foreign currency; the country's overreliance on foreign investors, who could withdraw their capital at any point; and the desperate need for further investment in healthcare services, which could have serious economic as well as social ramifications, especially during crises such as the COVID-19 pandemic of 2020–2021.[38]

From the political and structural perspective, in relation to the market and economic risks outlined above, there are formidable challenges in the way of al-Sisi's struggle for legitimation by outputs. First of all, despite some achievements, such as obtaining bonds and the macroeconomic indicators from IMF and World Bank sources, the gap in resource distribution, the high poverty rate, and the relatively slow GDP growth rate despite the massive investments in the military-led Suez Canal Zone project, may ultimately have serious effects on al-Sisi's search for legitimacy (Sayigh, 2019; see Suez Canal Authority, 2022).

What does authorities' attempt to rely on a 'greening' of the economy and washing of the armed forces from Mubarak-era corruption – related to both a struggle for legitimation through economic performance, and the effort to frame the EAF as possessing a socially oriented developmentalist function – reveal about the inner process of legitimation and about the stability of the regime? It has been found in this book that rather than a return of the function of the EAF to the Mubarak era, or its adoption of the Algerian military model, the military's involvement in the economy through the EAF, AOI and NSPO, in combination with a supposedly civilian political leadership, displays more similarities to the Sudanese model since the ouster of Omar al-Bashir in 2019, in which a civilian component has existed within a deep structural military culture.

The emphasis on large infrastructure projects, and the remilitarisation of social-urban developmentalism, along with the replacement of subsidies with the marketisation of military-produced civilian goods has attempted to strategically defuse social dissent, while asserting a social developmentalist function for the EAF in line with the United Nations' SDG-17 and the broader Agenda 2030. Broadening the analytical lens, this political behaviour suggests reconnection to the return of the phenomena of environmental autocracies and the rise of eco-populism. This way of acting, in the absence of a restoration of public trust driven by inputs, fuelled scholarly debates, according to which Egypt after 2013 moved from a provision pact to a protection pact, in which the elites would back the incumbent in order to get protection from internal and external threats (Rutherford, 2018; see also Slater and Fenner, 2011). As demonstrated in this book, the structural architecture of al-Sisi's regime underwent sub-transformations and different phases between 2013 and 2020, which impacted on the repositioning of internal actors, mainly the armed forces, in the state infrastructures and followed by a polarisation between state power versus political representative power.[39] However, the armed forces have not been the only actor impacted by the sub-variation, despite repressive politics over opposition movements, mainly the Muslim Brotherhood – ties between the two sides still exist at the inner level. The army capacity to protect the incumbent is not determined by the risk political Islam poses in Egypt, as Rutherford argued in 2018 but rather, by al-Sisi's capacity to protect the interests of the armed forces in a system that shifted towards a personalism that, for historical reasons, became non-exclusionary. Hence, the idea of protection remains subjected to divergences as the army and the ruler do not share same interests.

Against this backdrop, Egypt's economic model, extensively built on premises of indebtness from the IMF or GCC countries, cannot be considered sustainable, since it is based on a more intensified form of neoliberalism than that put in place by Mubarak, exposing Egypt to high financial risks. However, apparent achievements in macroeconomic indicators, despite internal challenges concerning GDP, unemployment rate, unequal distribution of resources, and rising external debt, plus the image of security projected by Anti-Terrorism Law No. 94 of 2015, was sufficient to win al-Sisi a form of diplomatic consensus, mainly from European states The economic and particularly industrial ties between Egypt and EU member states regarding power plants and gas fields (with the involvement of European firms like ENI) have been consolidated since 2014, and indirectly benefit the role of the EAF in the industrial plan.

However, to appreciate the current state of the country from an independent perspective, it is important to note that al-Sisi and the EAF do not share all the same interests, and that from the analysis of the legitimation struggle and state structures, al-Sisi can be considered a political civilian delegate in a system undergoing a sub-variation towards what is called a non-exclusive personalism, alias a shift that is consolidating at the inner level of the militarised state and which is attached to the development of the internationalised business and green developmentalist network in which nature represents the new locus of political and contested power.

Notes

1 Author interviews with PA1 and ER1.
2 The rise in the poverty rate, however, at least between 2015 and 2018 was a direct result of the devaluation of the currency.
3 Author interview with PA1.

The political economy of resurrection 211

4 Caa1 next to Caa2 and Caa3 is a speculative rating category which related to poor quality and implies a high credit risk, thus discouraging investors.
5 Violence between police and protesters at al-Nahda Square in Giza in August 2014 should also be mentioned.
6 Author interview with PR1 and SC2.
7 By indoctrination the book here expands on Diwan and Vartavona and means the reproduction of beliefs and behaviours that serve the purpose of the political regime (Diwan and Vartanova, 2020: 2).
8 For an account of private education in Egypt and its post-2014 challenges see Sabry and Levy (2015).
9 Fuel prices increased in 2015 to +37 per cent. A drop of 18 per cent was registered in 2017, although an exponential rise by +40 per cent was seen in 2019 (Ministry of Petroleum, 2014–2020).
10 On former early effects determined by capitalism on urbanism in Egypt see Chaichian (1988).
11 See Parreira (2020).
12 Foundational and contingent legitimacy as theorised by Mittiga (2022) are here reinterpreted through a naturalistic-complex of protection.
13 In early 2023 the authority gave a speech which acknowledged the black economy but the speech itself failed to address policies for tackling it.
14 In 2015 a new NSPO-related enterprise was founded: the National Company for Fishery and Aquaculture. According to a view somewhat sympathetic to the regime, al-Sisi's acceptance of the IMF's recommendations enabled the floating of the currency and the market's determination of the value of the currency. However, in a country where the black market is large in size and remains dominant or the first choice to banks' rates due to financial gains, the pound started being traded at a rate of 70 per dollar between 2022 and 2023.
15 See Tamer (2017) on false economic expectations from the Suez Canal.
16 On neoliberalism and the moral economy of bread see also Frerichs (2016).
17 On the incumbent's sliced bread subsidies see Shahira (2021).
18 A similar trend in food prices persisted in 2024. See on this FAO (2024). Available at https://www.fao.org/faostat/en/#country/59. Accessed May 2024.
19 It is added that in the second part of 2023, the inflation rate reached the historical peak of 38.0 per cent (State Information Service, 2023), spurring the government debt to GDP ratio to 97 per cent.
20 See on this Belkaid (2018).
21 In concomitance of the cut to subsidies, 2014 was the year in which corruption reached its historical peak since 1995 (see Transparency International, 2022).
22 In 2020, al-Sisi amended Law No. 232 of 1959, limiting the SCAF's interference in political issues, thus constraining the legal amendments introduced in 2014–2015.
23 The existing scholarship has noted that aid volatility has a negative welfare impact for aid-receiving countries (Arellano et al., 2005). A similar view on aid volatility and its impact on the level of economic growth is put forward by Ramey and Ramey (1995).

24 Author interview with ER1.
25 The ACA enjoys the legal status of a civilian authority involved in countering corruption. However, Noll (2019) argues that it shares important features with security institutions for the post-2013 regime. In Noll's view 'the main purposes of the ACA under al-Sisi: punishing some officials for corruption while protecting others, enforcing his 'rules of the game' in the state bureaucracy, and helping to bolster Egypt's reputation and attract foreign investment needed to deliver the economic turnaround that he has promised' (2019: 4).
26 Data provided by the Transparency International Index show that corruption in 2011 was scored at 27 (on a 26–38 scale) and in 2014 at 37. The level of corruption scored higher again in 2018 and 2019 (Transparency International Index, 2020).
27 In 2006 and 2009, transparency in Egypt was scored at 29 and 28 respectively, the lowest scores since 1995 and in the timeframe up to 2020. Despite the drop in corruption, the NDP's regime remained weak on other structural premises (i.e. elite fragmentation, military division (see Gerschewski, 2013), social repression and lack of social justice) (Egypt Corruption Index, 2011–2020).
28 According to forecasts, inflation in the country will increase over the entire 2022/2023 fiscal year.
29 Author interview with ER1.
30 Author interviews with PA1 and ER1.
31 SDG-16, promoted by the UN Department of Economic and Social Affairs, had the purpose of promoting peaceful and inclusive societies for sustainable development, providing access to justice for all, and building effective, accountable and inclusive institutions at all levels.
32 Author interviews with PA1 and ER1.
33 Author interview with ER1.
34 Author interview with PA1.
35 The government started introducing minor revisions to the minumum wage in 2014. However, the manouvre was criticised for the associated inflationary risks than for a boost in production.
36 Similar projects, aimed at the eradication of slums from urban areas, can be found in Morocco and in projects dating back to the mid-2000. See Bogaeert (2012).
37 Under the flagship of SDGs and mega-projects, international cooperation in the country was boosted in 2022; this happened at the expenses of 'political' credibility after 2014 (see BTI, 2014–2022).
38 Author interview with ER1.
39 See Chapter 4 on this.

Conclusion

Political legitimacy has for so long been a misused concept in the context of non-democratic systems, regardless of their geography, and beyond the Middle East. Accused of attaining to philosophical abstractions, its internal axis has never found empirical in-depth discussions in the micro- and macro-understanding of the MENA region before and after the 2011 upheavals, which straightforwardly impacted with the redefinition and reconstruction of governmental machina. The 2011 grassroots protests did not produce significative structural change, at least in terms of redistribution of resources and change in state–society relations as demanded by social protesters. Rather, the process of autocratisation underwent a form of sneaky restoration under the distorted banner of political change and democracy, as also internationally supported with all the limitation of moral exportation embedded. Yet it revealed the paucity and fragility of self-sustainable autocracies and the need to reconsider the vacuum and relevance of internal legitimacy as a condition for staying in power, in one way or another, to contain class struggles and the spread of new societal dissent. Thus, the 2011 major shockwaves exposed the dependent relation of rulers on a form of consensus, diverting the external axis of legitimacy as mainly based on diplomatic bargain, corruption in the economic sector and loyalties and the incapacity by the neoliberal system to repay them financially, towards a more internal and societal core determinant: the capacity of reproducing shared beliefs, memories and myths that would unify the idea of the nation under new nationalist- and populist-rooted propagandas. In other words, the capacity to seduce. This shift in the premises for accessing and maintaining political power impacted by flattening previous neoliberal infrastructural power dynamics and in turn pushed the focus on what mechanisms are put in place to create forms of consensus from below, with the goal of resisting democratisation. In the specific case of Egypt, the reshuffle in internal alliances between al-Sisi and the armed forces and some Islamists, as well the consequent internal rebalance of power and disequilibria amongst them, constituted one of the core pillars to deconstruct the Egyptian political machine from within, a key factor in understanding how this complex process can impact or redefine the stability of the system on the one hand and the rule on the other.

The economic and developmentalist variable remains the main source of societal, internal – and in turn international – seduction, albeit under different premises when compared to the classical neoliberal turn exposed by Hosni Mubarak in the 1990s and early 2000. International programmes and policy initiatives on green transition and in support of a more ethical developmentalist model as proposed by the international actions under the SDGs and the EU Green Deal – where the latter is promoted as a benchmark committed to an action plan towards sustainable development and circular economy by 2050 – are occupying prominent importance in the entire Middle East. Equally, behind these premises is the risk that policy actions are likely to be weaponised by autocracies in Egypt and beyond, with the goal of renegotiating the premises of consensus. However, differently from the classical conception of eudaemonic legitimation translated as the search for moral legitimacy and the production of 'happiness', in transformed systems in the region – and Egypt as shifted towards a non-exclusivist personalist regime – this side of the legitimation process is intertwined with the new power structures that have sub-systemically emerged in the liquid interregnum (transition period). Hence, green policy initiatives risk producing a conception of green developmentalism which will remain exclusively based – and unredistributive – for addressing industrial elites' needs on the one hand, while pleasing Western political and financial actors on the implementation of policy directions on the other. This discourse undergoes further complexities and problematisation when the paradigm of food security-rising insecurity is considered in the context of external shocks (e.g. climate change-induced effects, wars or conflicts external to the region). A closer look at Egypt's programme of nationalised sustainable development, which is claimed to be implemented under the SDGs, in fact is centralising intensive-based urban and extra-urban projects – promoted as a new chapter in economic development (see General Authority for Investments and Free Zone, 2023) – and which suggests going in the opposite direction of sustainability and redistribution as based on premises of distributive social justice and social integration in a civil society that remains in stand-by mode. Despite this, the government is succeeding in producing an external narrative of economic growth and monetary stability which clashes with the main four financial challenges the currency faces, as discussed in the final chapter of this book, to the point of gaining diplomatic trust from EU member states (i.e. France and Italy) regarding future economic growth and stability.

Ultimately, and more broadly speaking, these kind of domestically adapted policies in combination with the tariffs the EU could impose in the long term on reducing gas emissions could lead to a destabilisation of rentier societies in the area, which premises already underwent a major change in 2019–2020, like in Algeria with the Hirak movement of 2019 which led to the removal of Bouteflika in April the same year, rather than accepting material concessions from the army (El-Naggar, 2022; Ouaissa, 2020).

Despite the limitations dictated by the unpredictability of the political scenario in Egypt, this book posited the existence of a persistent vacuum in top-down internal legitimation for al-Sisi's regime, despite some support from the army, which, however, remains subjected to strictly economic and industrial conditions and internal fragmentations. Much will depend on al-Sisi's capacity to impose a presence along the international business network and here the idea of modernisation of the industrial and developmentalist sectors will play a seductive role in the future domestically, regionally and internationally in the way the reinvention of eudaemonic legitimacy can be effectively translated into 'welfarised happiness'.

The deconstruction of the struggle for internal legitimation after the deep crisis in legitimacy left by the 2013 military coup allows the de-structuring of the existing inner gaps in the politics of Egypt and the risks that the perseverance of structural gaps and discrepancies in the socio-economic agenda associate with it, not unilaterally from a local perspective, but also and primarily from a regional and eventually international trajectory. This book has for the first time challenged the prevailing scholarly views according to which, since the removal of the Muslim Brotherhood from power, Egypt has undergone a restoration of the military apparatus along trajectories that replicate the militarised and structural scenario under Mubarak, though with some Nasserian elements of leadership and approach to the socialist-oriented view of the economic model. In fact, the legitimacy crisis left by the 2013 coup has reshaped and rewritten the present of ruler-military relations, boundaries and respective political and business areas of influence, differently from those which regulated the state under Mubarak's NDP and earlier from 1953. While the system under al-Sisi remains deeply anchored to an extreme neoliberal market logic, the future of such relations should be considered less taken-for-granted or optimistically oriented. While both the identity of the state and the nation remain deeply rooted in a form of militarism, the armed forces play a different role in the incumbent regime, which is primarily connected to the internationalisation of the business network between EU states actors and non-EU actors, such as China, Korea and mainly Russia, which since 2014 have captured the moment of transformation to reshape and re-define a more economic presence and neo-imperialist interests towards the broader and transforming Mediterranean region and a compelling presence in the Gulf.

The EU, for the time being, will remain challenged by two distinct scenarios: on the one hand reorganising its political presence in the wider region under new premises, which seem projected towards environmental politics; on the other, rediscussing the main goal of its foreign policy in the wider regional area, which remains fragmented due to intra-member states' interests and conservatism. Indeed, the issue of environmental challenges and the connection with political ecology, as introduced in this book, may have repercussions at the level of the regional political authorities and their dynamics of resilience.

The distinction between input and output sides of the legitimation process in al-Sisi's system due to the state foundations exposed the persistence of internal discrepancies in the new system that gradually emerged after 2013, with some consolidations only achieved between 2018 and 2020. The output side of the legitimation process, instead, focused on a new plan of economic-business performance – also committed towards more environmental beneficial reforms – impacted with the reframing of autocracies as committed to the respect of the Paris Agreements and a new political ecology that it is expected will play a role in coming decades.

Introducing a comparative approach to the debate on Anthropocene-related effects and political power, autocracies have tried to repropose themselves as oriented towards sustainable and ethical developmental actions. These aspects in turn do not end the debate on the ecology of authoritarianisms as connected to the UN SDG-17 and the broader Agenda 2030. Despite the persistency of fragmentations in criticisms on the risks eco-authoritarianisms pose to the liberal system, the relocation of autocrats as international diplomatic interlocutors for the sake of the planet's health remains at odds in the Westernised and neoliberal idea of development, which remains subjected to the persistency of Orientalist and neocolonial logics in how growth is understood under the premises of preventing migration, where the latter remains conceived under the label of security and threat to identity (Hollis, 2016).

While the scholarship since 2013 has focused on Egypt's authoritarian drift, questioning what went wrong with post-2011 democratisation processes, this book instead inquires how, in contexts undergoing social, political and cultural transformation, the strategies of internal legitimation also undergo alteration, not so much in the way they are employed, as in the purposes they are meant to fulfil, and their implications determined on power structures.

By employing a modified Weberian conception of political legitimacy, combined with David's omnibalancing (1991), Gerschewski's internal support (2013) and Easton's specific support, as linked to the theory of cohesion (1975), this work has established a new and hybrid framework for analysing political legitimacy in political machina after major shockwaves which provoked a structural collapse in those premises which kept systems together: clientelism, pyramidal corruption, external aid. While the latter will remain an essential component for impeding defaults, it does not add to forms of internal legitimation of highly indebted status quo. This conceptual framework is suited to a politically, socially and ideologically transformed system like Egypt after 2013, but also embeds the value to find application beyond the case study of Egypt and the MENA as a region. Intellectually, while there has been in this work a recognition of other intellectual approaches to debating political legitimacy, the approach in this book represents a novelty in the way first of all it has permitted an empirical observation of legitimacy, detaching it from abstract and purely theoretical dimensions confined to strictly sociological explanation rooted into a Weberian classicism combined with Scharpft's idea of output legitimacy (see Barker, 2007; Scharpft, 1970). Second, the hybrid and modified framework that has combined Bauman with Gramsci demonstrates the speed of sub-variations that can happen in post-transition autocratic structures. The fluid approach articulated as the results of the structural implications determined by the four step strategies of legitimation, as well as by the consequent internal repositioning of actors along the domestic political and economic spectrum, reiterates the liquidity of the cycles to which autocracies are exposed after shockwaves (on cycles see Khaldun, 1958). If this rationale goes against traditions on authoritarian restoration, in this fluidity of cycles, nature has ended up constituting a critical political ecosystem for power where consensus is negotiated.

Post-2013 amendments to the penal code, the holding of civilian trials in military courts, and principally the enforcement of Laws No. 70 of 2017, No. 94 of 2015 and No. 107 of 2013, created a twofold effect. First, amendments to the penal code provided the army more authority to intervene in the political process, diverting from the promises made in July 2013 about the apolitical commitment of the EAF. The wide-ranging powers given to the armed forces did not meet the people's expectations, though this was not surprising, considering the militarism of modern Egypt since 1953 (Croissant and Eshcenauer, 2018). The role of the army since the 1960s in providing employment and a livelihood to a large sector of Egyptian society has been key in preventing large-scale popular dissent. However, it has also been found that the initial trust and consensus around al-Sisi in 2013–2014 was attached more to his identification with the armed forces and his rank of general. His resignation of his military career and dissociation from the army, and the decline of his promise to restore the rule *of* law into the principle of ruling *by* law, influenced the falling consensus after his election as President in 2014.

Secondly, the application of the rule of law has created a polarisation between real state power and political representative power as represented by al-Sisi, which persists. This polarisation has been the result of boomerang effects of amendments to the penal code, which aimed at setting the new legal foundations of the state under new premises, goals and ambitions. The polarisation between political leadership state power (ultimately in the military's hands as the guardian of the Egyptian republic's foundations) exposed al-Sisi to structural risks linked to the drop in consensus (BTI, 2014, 2016). Furthermore, while the experience of the claimed restoration of the rule of law did not help to induce a top-down legitimation, it weakened al-Sisi not only in the eyes of society, but also the army itself.

Therefore, the gap in legitimation left by the strategic reference to the rule of law in 2013–2014 underwent a routinisation into charisma until early 2016. Charisma represented a structural necessity for rebalancing power and preventing a coup in the short-term; this would have exposed not so much the presidency as the armed forces to a premature capitulation of nurtured international interests. The strategy of self-portraying as a hero, charisma and the personalised style of rule represented a tactical-transitional phase, rather than a will to build them as a proper source of long-term legitimation behind the idea of a Nasserisation of myths, symbols and memories of a golden age.

Despite portraying himself as a hero for the country, al-Sisi's attempt at projecting charisma internally failed in capturing the imagination of both wider society and the EAF. The Brotherhood and the SCAF are both powerful and deep-rooted structures in Egyptian society and politics, able to influence the financial and industrial sectors of the state. The reintegration of the Brotherhood in the economy, including the CBE and Islamic banks such as the Faisal Islamic Bank of Egypt, would have been more in line with the EAF's own interests. Indeed, it is not necessarily a strong communality of interests linking the army, concerned with maintaining its determinant role in the industrial sector, to the incumbent, more oriented towards remaining in office. For at least four decades, the relation between politics and religion in Egypt has been shaped by the interference of the former in the latter, although religion has not represented a source of political legitimation as it has done in some MENA countries. Islam still plays a role in forming Egyptian cultural identity, and the al-Azhar's role in shaping the identity of the community of Muslim believers is still influential, despite the presence of a large Copt and Christian minority.

The initial toleration of the Salafi party Hizb al-Nour, despite the 2014 constitutional ban on parties formed on a religious basis, should be analysed in the regional context of change within Islamist politics and the antagonism between Salafis and the Muslim Brotherhood. However, initial tolerance towards al-Nour was tactically intended to prevent the emergence of societal antagonism resulting from the perception that al-Sisi was targeting all devout Muslims and Islam itself, given his offensive against the Brotherhood.

The government's imposition over the *ulema* was at the core of major disputes between al-Sisi and the al-Azhar from 2016 to 2018. The ruler's call for revolutionising Islam and his personalisation of religion, while aiming to minimise the risk of support for the Brotherhood within the al-Azhar, created the opposite effect. The polarisation between al-Sisi and the *ulema* reinforced the Wahhabi (pro-Brotherhood) trend historically existing within the al-Azhar, and eventually marginalised the Salafi one. This in turn was projected externally, to the alignment of pro-Brotherhood/Wahhabi elements of the SCAF with the religious establishment. This has not exactly led to a wider repositioning of the EAF but has impacted the perceptions some of the SCAF hierarchy hold of al-Sisi. Nevertheless, it is important to remember that religion in post-2013 Egypt has not had a significant role in influencing political legitimation.

While al-Sisi's references to collective struggles in the economic domain for the good of the homeland and to restore economic and social dignity occupied a great prominence in official speeches from 2014 to 2018, the chapter found that this discourse anticipated the 2014 cuts to fuel and energy subsidies. Economic reforms inaugurated by Egypt on the one hand contributed to strengthening the country's performance as far as the macroeconomic indicators show (i.e. FDI, internal debt and bonds), yet on the other remain entirely built on dependency on international loans and a logic of indebtness that requires to be repaid. Influxes of investment from Saudi Arabia and UAE further enabled the regime to survive after the cuts to fuel and food subsidies initiated in July 2014. Macroeconomic indicators infuse a certain optimism among international actors, who remain persuaded that Egypt is apparently stable after several years of turmoil but failed in creating bottom-up social legitimation of the regime, as challenges including unequal distribution of resources and increasing poverty and unemployment rates remained unaddressed. Equal access to the healthcare sector, which for decades was filled by the Muslim Brotherhood as a social services provider, remains another challenge for the regime as well as the education sector, which equality remains unguaranteed and significantly below the regional trend (see data on education equality, V-Dem Project data, 2023).

Of relevance is political propaganda connected to the struggle for legitimation by output of social developmentalism, around the housing construction industry and the infrastructural sector (i.e. water sanification, solar and recently nuclear power plants as funded by Russia), gilded with references to an environmentally friendly economy. These projects enabled the rehabilitation of the SCAF, through the AOI and NSPO, in the real estate industry, as detached from the image of the Mubarak era's corruption based on pyramidal clientelism; however, it has not totally succeeded in purifying the army's image as a form of circle with upgraded ambitions in the international economic network and the network with the EU. Along this framework the architecture of corruption has been transformed, becoming more diffused and linked to the new ecology of political power as represented by the institutionalisation and financialisation of nature. The project of the army's involvement in ambitious, socially oriented infrastructure projects attempted to justify the deep presence of the military, beyond the cultural sphere. However, there is an internal balance of power between al-Sisi and the SCAF that remains fragile, and which is determined by the fragility of the President.

Thus, what remains a challenge for the time being, at least in the mid-term, is the protracted fragility of the economic ties between the army and the political ruler, also in light of intra-army persistent legacies. In this regard the book discussed the persistence of a Muslim Brotherhood's presence within some military factions and their communality of interests.

Structurally, the absence of a regime party, the tight control of non-competitive elections and suppression of parties, the absence of the selectorate, and the bureaucratisation of the Parliamentary Assembly and the pro-Sisi NFB, form the pillars of the authoritarian model that has emerged under al-Sisi, identified in this work as *personalism*. However, the regime of al-Sisi is not completely a one man show. The system led by al-Sisi can be defined as a civilian leader guiding a coalition with the military, with the ultimate task of institutionally safeguarding the army's business interests along the agenda of green development. This definition suggests that the army, while rehabilitated in the state infrastructures and granted more centrality in the economic and real estate sectors than the EAF achieved in the last decade of Mubarak's rule, is not – at least directly – involved in political affairs.

The personalisation of the government and its structure will imply, for the time being, a reconfiguration of the system at the regional and international political, economic and diplomatic level, with a massive interest projected towards the based on international pillars as set in the SDG-17, primarily goal 15 aimed at blocking deforestation. Despite projects under the umbrella of the Agenda 2030, the regime's foundations are built on anti-ecological attitudes which, however, are dominated by a no-longer strictly pyramidally organised corrupted military apparatus that is attempting to remerge in the international system as:

(i) the mandator of, and being committed to, a form of strategic security on ethical premises in the broader Mediterranean area
(ii) a societal oriented actor and an interlocutor

What this book defined as a non-exclusivist personalist diktat, in relation to post-2013 dynamics of legitimation, the armed forces under al-Sisi seems moving closer to the model of post-Bashir Sudan, rather than Algeria or a return to Egypt's predecessors Mubarak or even the overmentioned Nasser. However, while in Sudan the Sudanese Armed Forces' guarantees may include an amnesty for abuses committed under Bashir's rule, in the case of Egypt under the incumbent regime the SCAF's priorities concern their business interests and their involvement in profitable infrastructural projects that are projected more towards the expansion of the civilian industries and production sector with a focus on infrastructures (mainly highroads) intensive fishing, farming, and the strengthening of the agricultural sector under Agenda 2030.

Stability ... but at what cost?

Despite the unbridged gap in internal legitimacy from both input and output factors, the political leadership as represented by al-Sisi has succeeded in staying in power and has survived periodic waves of dissent so far. This includes protests in September 2019, led externally and virtually by Mohamed Ali, a former government contractor and critic of al-Sisi, exiled in Spain, who accused the regime of mismanagement of funds and corruption (BBC, 2019). On theoretical premises, if a new regime – regardless of its taxonomical form – survives for several years, the chances of a coup significantly decrease, although internal legitimacy may remain contested on the ground (Quinlivan, 1999). The fact that the government survived the 2019 protests, however, does not mean that it inherits a stable political machine, though externally perceived as such on several key points that remain dearer to Western state actors, than to Egypt (i.e. an unsustainable model of development).

According to different interviewees' perspectives, even though the 2019 protests against the government did not destabilise authorities, they were highly symbolic in that they indicated the existence of an internal opposition to al-Sisi, despite purges and a penal code that outlawed opposing political parties and NGOs. Externally triggered protests by the exiled Mohamed Ali undermined the view of a strong and reliable regime and may indicate disloyalty among some segments of the armed forces believed to have indirect ties with the Muslim Brotherhood. This is the aspect which at this stage remains neglected: while the Muslim Brotherhood remains pejoratively framed at international level and designated a terrorist organisation in the US, Austria, Russia amongst the principal countries, and while EU interrogations on the Muslim Brotherhood's infiltrating the European Parliament has been conducted, what remains neglected is the hidden deep and historically inextricable connection between the armed forces and the Muslim Brotherhood under the incumbent regime. What, then, enabled the survival of the regime despite internal fragilities? There are four reasons which have prevented the fall of the regime in Egypt thus far:

i. The government's ruling by law which, expanding control over the judiciary, has made possible tight control of the whole state apparatus and normalised its state of exception.
ii. Changes among the heads of the military, with appointments made through family ties, a common practice amongst personalist regimes to ensure loyalty (Geddes, 1999b). However, due to the fragile stability of the inner structure of the establishment, the practice additionally reveals al-Sisi's lack of trust in the broader SCAF constituency.
iii. Armed forces' interests in the industrial sector and need of al-Sisi as a 'civilian' face and interlocutor for the reinvention of their interests under the Social Development Goals agenda.
iv. External diplomatic support to the incumbent, as shown by EU member states to counter a more consistent interest shown by Russia in the Mediterranean area, which has strategically relocated itself in the region since 2011 as key-trader projected more towards the construction of renewable energies, including on desert lands managed by the armed forces.

While the process of top-down legitimation has undergone contestations and boomerang implications in the reorganisation of power balances, as long as the political presidency is in a position to prove to his internal audience (the army rather than society) that he enjoys international diplomatic 'trust', and will be a reliable deliverer of economic and market interests, it is unlikely that bottom-up dissent will meet EAF support. As seen in the 2011 uprising, unlikely other regional countries and for reasons strictly attained to the realm of state foundations, sympathy from within the military is a determinant of success for protestors against an Egyptian regime.

Thus, Egypt's system and fluid machine of governance, which emerged in the interregnum, while perceived as a pillar for stability in the Mediterranean and a key trading partner by the EU and its member states, including Italy and France, is in fact a highly indebted and financially high-risk model. The politics of aid on which the regime has heavily relied can, in the long term, impact administrative capacity, straining and undermining the governability of domestic institutions and thus decreasing government performance.

I have argued that while from the internal perspective the system can be considered brittle, the regime from a short-term perspective presents some traits of stability, though subjected to expensive conditions, determined by al-Sisi's capacity to present the image of an internationally trusted delegate, rather than authority, before the army's eyes. This will in turn depend on the ruler's capacity to meet Western actors' economic and political needs. The more al-Sisi's presidency is in a position to reinforce his diplomatic and economic position, the more EU and non-EU states view Egypt as a pillar of stability in the Mediterranean, thus ratifying trade deals (mainly in the energy sector and industrial developmentalist projects), through which the army can consolidate interests and positions; and the more bottom-up dissent is likely to be suppressed before it visibly emerges, on the simple premise put forward in this work that Egyptians tend to avoid direct confrontations with the armed forces.

However, there are some limitations and questions that emerge out of this. The first limitation deals with a new popular consciousness in the capacity to overthrow systems, despite suppressions which emerged in the post-2011 setting.

One of the main implications of the 2011 uprising on a regional level was rulers' growing awareness about the fragility of the political authorities as they became more dependent on a form of societal acceptance. Despite this, the political transition in Egypt after 2013 marked a return to authoritarianism, with some elements of totalitarianism, if the dynamics of 'support' and the importance addressed to the construction of a 'belief system' are considered. From a broader perspective of the trajectories of the post-2011 MENA region, the return to authoritarian politics broke with the 2011 demand for social justice and democratisation. On this premise, this book has opened the way for studies on democratisation and what went wrong with democratisation as a concept exogenously infused and based on Western EU moral premises and values. In this regard, looking beyond Egypt to Tunisia, the democratic performance of the government in 2018–2019 displayed limitations in its satisfaction of youth and civil society, due to the continuance of corruption in all its different forms (pyramidal or diffused along the spectrum of business and industries). A similar discourse can be expanded to other countries in the region beyond Egypt as a single problematisation of the debate.

In 2019, Freedom House found that global freedom was in its fourteenth consecutive year in decline around the world. In the MENA region, lack of consistent international leadership from democracies has encouraged authoritarian powers to engage in proxy wars and in sweeping oppression. People have taken to the streets to express discontent with existing systems of government and demand changes leading to more democratic outcomes. However, protests have frequently foundered in the face of resistance from defenders of the status quo.

Future applications of the framework

In combining classical approaches to the study of political legitimacy with an intradisciplinary model based on theories rooted in international relations and comparative politics, the multi-level framework analysis designed in this book adds new perspectives on the complexities of the study of internal political legitimacy, not unilaterally in the context of the liquid Middle East and Egypt. Rather, the theoretical premise set out in the book, which expands on a brand-new taxonomy of regimes, theorised as fluid authoritarianism, alias a form of autocracy in which the coexistence of features belonging to traditional personalist regimes (e.g. Pinochet in Chile, Chavez in Venezuela, Saddam Hussein in Iraq, Erdogan in Turkey, Ortega in Nicaragua, Kim in Korea, and Putin in Russia) is submerged in state foundations with primordialist cultural identity and the identity of the nation grounded into military traditions. This conception can additionally express transformations that do not necessarily move from a more pluralistic to a more closed illiberal panorama, but which also go in the opposite direction, like in the case of Tunisia after 2022, which is sliding back into a new form of autocracy. The country moved from an overcelebrated model of constitutional pluralism and political inclusivism to the risk of meeting a new authoritarianism in the making once Saied seized control. Beyond the MENA region, fluid authoritarianism, as conceptualised in this book, however, goes a step further in the way it can be additionally exported to systems that do not necessarily present a militarised institutional foundation but in which the military component – either in the form of police or intelligence services – is centralised or over-represented in the nationalistic imaginary, beyond the MENA region to find application in other geographies in the Global South or in contexts in which internal shifts recentralised the functionalist role of military or police actors.

The multil-level based approach has been designed with the main goal of providing a new model for digging into the inner functioning mechanisms of illiberal systems in times of transition. The model permits the destabilising of early (conventional) convictions and knowledge about the functioning of post-shockwaves illiberal machina of power, like those that happened to emerge in the Middle East. In addition, it pushes for reconsidering comparative approaches with ambitiously drawn lines neglecting the micro-structural readjuments entered by autocracies in post-shockwave contexts for the purpose of forging new internal legitimation claims supported by new nationalistic waves also infused by a discrepant and fit-for-purpose use of populist narratives in post-populist settings. Once again, neglecting the intra-repositioning and intra-readjustment of actors along the sub-transformed state infrastructures risks counter-impacting the production of political knowledge.

Not least, the framework challenges political legitimacy, highlighting how structuring effects need to be micro-structurally considered over more intraregional comparative approaches. The applicability of the framework will go beyond the Middle East to find future and potential applications to the Global South but also to non-Western contexts exposing the reality of autocratic transition on the one hand, and elites' attempts of negotiating their own acceptance.

Outlook

To conclude, one of the fundamental motivations which inspired and motivated this book was to provide a different and more radical understanding of the dynamics of internal legitimation in post-shockwave contexts, building on the argument that in the case of Egypt, the coup, captured as a major shockwave, has upgraded power infrastructures, creating a distance from the pre-2011 Egyptian authoritarian model based on militarism. The book expanded the theory of a selectorate, which has been captured and employed in a non-orthodox way and as a model through which to distinguish different sub-categories and identities of contemporary autocracies. Contemporary autocracies can be observed by looking at the size of a group (i.e. the selectorate) vis-à-vis the size of the dictator's inner circle (i.e. winning coalition) and the rules of their internal organisation, such as political membership and distribution of assets. The book demonstrated how by re-engaging with two distinct categories of selectorate (the nominal and the real), there is room for differently understanding obsolete conceptions of personalist systems that present more as a form of new-born hybrid autocracies and in which exist contours that are reminiscent of a militarised system. The focus on the selectorate in combination with the foundations of the state and identity of the nation has in fact enabled a new and fresher explanation of the selectorate, which in the book has been fused with international business connections. Thus, personalist regimes exist and are able to resist principally because of their well-structured international business network and neoliberalised political ecology.

Returning to the theory of sub-variation, the book demonstrated that this change at sub-systemic level will be projected along the international system, politically and economically making the country a more liquid political entity, including from a diplomatic and business perspective. The concept of state liquidity discussed in this book refers to the new attitude that has emerged from within Arab countries and states in playing double-games in the international system, in absence of stable societal and economic oriented policies. Looking at the broader transformation of the region and Mediterranean area, the theoretical and intellectual insights emerged from research conducted for this book provide a combined framework for reconsidering the internalisation of political legitimacy against a background of structural societal and infrastructural transformations and intra-systemic upgrade as based on a reorganisation of alliances at the inner level and against traditional trajectories.

The decline in democracy around the world and the rise in dysfunctional systems beyond the considered region, frequently driven by freely elected leaders who narrow their concerns to nationalist interests, has been responsible for providing autocrats with the structural conditions in which they can build a persuasive rhetoric based on which democracies constitute a source of structural instabilities as subjected to societal will. The debate and existing knowledge have not yet fully considered or established how, in a regional order transformed by shockwaves and in which democracy is still highly defective if not deterred, social-economic developmentalism – as supported mainly by the UN Social and Economic Affairs Unit as part of SDG-17, and Western actors like the European Bank for Reconstruction, the EU's Neighbourhood Development and International Cooperation instrument, and FAO – could interfere with the liquidity of states, thus leading to new forms of moralised institutional resilience combined with forms of high ground morality in political ecology in financial systems, which, however, will remain confined to high levels of financial indebtness. The complexity of these intertwined determinants that intersect nature with critical ecosystems of power while legitimacy crisis remains in the background are core axes, not so much in the transformation of the regime, where new structural fluid identity has entered a phase of consolidation, but in interfering with the trajectories of elite's acceptance in a non-exclusivist and non-pyramidal personalist system. Political ecology has ended up representing a programmatic new critical political ecosystem where internal legitimacy remains intimately intertwined with the institutionalisation of nature.

Appendix

Integrative interviews

This book has ensured the safety of participants through safeguarding anonymity and confidentiality. Participants have been assigned an alias which reflects their professional backgrounds:

(i) PR1: London-based, political-institutional profile, member of the Muslim Brotherhood.
(ii) PA1: Independent/non-partisan London-based researcher and analyst of Egypt's politics and economics.
(iii) SC1: Independent/non-partisan Geneva-based scholar and expert on Salafism in Egypt.
(iv) SC2: Independent/non-partisan Beirut-based expert on Egypt's military economy.
(v) ER1: Independent/non-partisan Washington-based former employee of the World Bank in Egypt and close to Moody's; expert on Egypt's economy.

Ministerial data and reports

CBE (Central Bank of Egypt) (2014). *Economic Review* Vol. 54, No. 4. Available at: https://www.cbe.org.eg/en/economic-research/economic-reports/economic-review.

CBE (2015). *Economic Review* Vol. 55, No. 4. Available at: https://www.cbe.org.eg/en/economic-research/economic-reports/economic-review.

CBE (2016). *Economic Review* Vol. 56, No. 4. Available at: https://www.cbe.org.eg/en/economic-research/economic-reports/economic-review.

CBE (2017). *Economic Review* Vol. 57, No. 4. Available at: https://www.cbe.org.eg/en/economic-research/economic-reports/economic-review.

CBE (2018). *Economic Review* Vol. 58, No. 4. Available at: https://www.cbe.org.eg/en/economic-research/economic-reports/economic-review.

CBE (2019). *Economic Review* Vol. 59, No. 4. Available at: https://www.cbe.org.eg/en/economic-research/economic-reports/economic-review.
Ministry of Defence, *National Projects* (2019). Available at: https://www.mod.gov.eg/ModWebSite/Default.aspx. Accessed November 2019
MoF (Ministry of Finance) (2014). *Executive Summary Financial Bulletin.*
MoF (2015). *Executive Summary Financial Bulletin.*
MoF (2016). *Executive Summary Financial Monthly Bulletin*, December.
MoF (2017). *Executive Summary Financial Bulletin.*
MoF (2018). *Executive Summary Financial Bulletin.*
MoF (2019–2020). *Executive Summary Financial Bulletin.*
Ministry of Planning (2018). *Monitoring and Administrative Reforms: Egypt's Voluntary National Review*. Available at: https://sustainabledevelopment.un.org/content/documents/20269EGY_VNR_2018_final_with_Hyperlink_9720185b45d.pdf.
UNFCC (2022). 'Egypt's First Updated Nationally Determined Contributions'. https://unfccc.int/sites/default/files/NDC/2022-07/Egypt%20Updated%20NDC.pdf.pdf. Accessed April 2024.

Data and macro indicators

AB (Arab Barometer) (2018). 'The Arab Barometer Technical Report WAVE V'. Available at: http://www.arabbarometer.org/wp-content/uploads/ABIII_Technical_Report.pdf. Accessed February 2019.
Al-Ahram (2022). '7 Billion US Dollars: The Suez Canal Achieves the Highest Annual Fiscal Revenue in its History'. Available at: https://gate.ahram.org.eg/News/3592232.aspx (in Arabic). Accessed September 2022.
BTI (Bertelsmann Transformation Index) (2012). 'Transformation Atlas'. Available at: https://atlas.bti-project.org/. Accessed October 2019.
Corruption Perception Index (n.d.) Available at: https://www.transparency.org/en/news/cpi-2023-middle-east-north-africa-dysfunctional-approach-fighting-corruption. Accessed May 2024.
ENPI (European Neighbourhood Programme) (2013). 'Country Progress Report 2013 – Egypt'. Available at: https://ec.europa.eu/commission/presscorner/detail/en/MEMO_14_223. Accessed February 2021.
FSI (Fragile States Index) (2016). 'Egypt'. Available at: https://reliefweb.int/sites/reliefweb.int/files/resources/fragilestatesindex-2016.pdf. Accessed March 2020.
Global Economy (2019). 'Egypt: Political Stability Index'. Available at: https://www.theglobaleconomy.com/Egypt/wb_political_stability/. Accessed February 2021.

Global Forest Watch (2022) 'Egypt Deforestation Rates & Statistics'. Available at: https://www.globalforestwatch.org/dashboards/country/EGY/. Accessed May 2022.

Human Rights Watch (2014). 'All According to Plan: The Raba'a Massacre and the Mass Killings of Protesters in Egypt'. Available at: https://www.hrw.org/report/2014/08/12/all-according-plan/raba-massacre-and-mass-killings-protesters-egypt. Accessed August 2020.

Human Rights Watch (2018). 'Egypt: Events of 2018'. Available at: https://www.hrw.org/world-report/2018/country-chapters/egypt. Accessed February 2021.

Human Rights Watch (2019). 'Human Rights Watch Country Profiles: Sexual Orientation and Gender Identity'. Available at: https://www.hrw.org/video-photos/interactive/2019/02/28/human-rights-watch-country-profiles-sexual-orientation-and. Accessed February 2021.

IMF (International Monetary Fund) (2005–2019). 'Inflation (annual percentage) in Egypt and the MENA region'. Available at: https: //data.worldbank.org/indicator/FP.CPI.TOTL.ZG?end=2019&locations=EG-ZQ&start=2005. Accessed December 2020.

Politics Today (2019). Available at: https://politicstoday.org/tortured-and-imprisoned-children-are-unsafe-in-sisis-egypt/.

Polity IV (2010). 'Political Regime Characteristics and Transitions, 1800–2010'. Available at: http://www.systemicpeace.org/polity/polity4.html. Accessed May 2024.

Reuters (2022). 'Egypt's Suez Canal Revenue hits $7 Billion Record Peak'. Available at: https://www.reuters.com/business/egypts-suez-canal-revenue-hits-7-bln-record-peak-2022-07-04/. Accessed September 2022.

Suez Canal Zone Project (2022). 'Suez Canal Economic Zone'. https://sczone.eg/. Accessed January 2023. Accessed April 2024.

Trading Economics (2020). 'Egypt Corruption Index'. Available at: https://tradingeconomics.com/egypt/corruption-index. Accessed February 2021.

Transparency International (2017). 'Corruption Perception Index'. Available at: https://www.transparency.org/news/feature/corruption_perceptions_index_2017. Accessed February 2019.

UNESCO Institute for Statistics (2023). 'Government Spenditure on Education Total of % GDP'. Unesco Institute for Statistics. Available at: https://data.worldbank.org/indicator/SE.XPD.TOTL.GD.ZS?locations=EG. Accessed March 2023.

World Bank (2014). 'Worldwide Governance Indicators'. Available at: http://info.worldbank.org/governance/wgi/Home/Reports. Accessed April 2020.

World Bank (2017). 'Egypt Literacy Rate 1986–2017'. Macrotrends. Available at: https://www.macrotrends.net/countries/EGY/egypt/literacy-rate. Accessed April 2020.

World Bank (2018). 'Worldwide Governance Indicators'. Available at: http://info.worldbank.org/governance/wgi/Home/Reports. Accessed April 2020.

World Bank (2020). 'Inflation, consumer prices (annual %) – Egypt, Arab Rep., Middle East & North Africa'. Available at: https://data.worldbank.org/indicator/FP.CPI.TOTL.ZG?end=2019&locations=EG-ZQ&start=2005. Accessed February 2021.

World Bank Worldwide Governance Indicators (2018). Available at: https://databank.worldbank.org/reports.aspx?Report_Name=WGI-Table&Id=ceea4d8b. Accessed February 2021.

World Food Programme (2018). 'Egypt Strategic Country Plan 2018–2023'. https://docs.wfp.org/api/documents/8e97bc6add374c9ab811e5a0cedfe7b1/download/. Accessed February 2023.

World Health Organization (2000–2010). 'Global Health Expenditure Database'. Available at: https://apps.who.int/nha/database. Accessed March 2023.

References

Aalberg, T. and T. Brekken (2007). 'Når spill og enkeltepisoder blir viktigst [When games and single episodes become most important]'. In A.T. Jenssen and T. Aalberg (eds), *Den medialiserte politikken* [The mediatised politics]. Oslo: Universitetsforlaget: 177–196.
Aalberg, T. et al. (2012). 'The Framing of Politics as Strategy and Game: A Review of Concepts, Operationalizations and Key Findings'. *Journalism*, 13: 162–178.
Aalberg, T., J. Strömbäck and C.H. de Vreese (2012). 'The Framing of Politics as Strategy and Game: A Review of Concepts, Operationalizations and Key Findings'. *Journalism*, 13: 162–178.
Abaza M. (2006). *Changing Consumer Cultures of Modern Egypt*. Cairo: AUC Press.
Abdalla, M. and S. Al-Shawar (2017). 'The Tamween Food Subsidy System in Egypt: Evolution and Recent Implementation Reforms'. In The World Bank (ed.), *The 1.5 Billion People Question: Food, Vouchers, or Cash Transfers?* The World Bank: 107–150.
Abdalla, N. (2013). 'Egypt's Revolutionary Youth: From Street Politics to Party Politics'. Stiftung Wissenschaft und Politik, German Institute for International and Security Affairs SWP. Available at: https://www.swpberlin.org/fileadmin/contents/products/comments/2013C11_abn.pdf. Accessed May 2024.
Abdalla, N. (2015). 'The Neoliberal Policies and the Egyptian Trade Union Movement: Politics of Containment and Limits of Resistance'. In E. Akcali (ed.), *The Limits of Neoliberal Governmentality in the Middle East and North Africa*. London: Palgrave Macmillan.
Abdalla, N. (2016). 'Youth movements in the Egyptian transformation: strategies and repertoires of political participation'. *Mediterranean Politics*, 21 (1): 44–63.
Abdel-Fadil, M. (1980). *The Political Economy of Nasserism*. Cambridge: Cambridge University Press.
Abdelrahman, M. (2017). 'Policing Neoliberalism in Egypt: The Continuing Rise of the "Securocratic" State', *Third World Quarterly*, 38 (1): 185–202.
Abdul Ghani, I. (2019). 'Post-Islamism: Ideological Delusions and Sociological Realities'. *Contemporary Arab Affairs*, 12 (3): 3–20.
Abu-Lughod, J. (1971). *Cairo: 1001 Years of the City Victorious*. Princeton, NJ: Princeton University Press.
Abu-Lughod, L. (1989). 'Zones of Theory in the Anthropology of the Arab World'. *Annual Review of Anthropology*, 18: 267–306.

References

Abul-Magd, Z. (2013). 'The Egyptian Military in Politics and the Economy: Recent History and Current Transition'. *CHR Michelsen Institute*, 2 (1): 6.

Abul-Magd, Z. (2018). *Militarising the Nation*. New York: Columbia University Press.

Abu-Odeh, L. (2009). 'On Law and the Transition to Market: The Case of Egypt'. Available at: https://core.ac.uk/reader/70375510. Accessed May 2024.

Abulof, U. (2016). '"Can't Buy Me Legitimacy": The Elusive Stability of Mideast Rentier Regimes'. *Journal of International Relations and Development*, 20: 55–79.

ACA (Anti-Corruption Authority) (2019–2022). 'National Anti-Corruption Strategy'. The Sub-Coordinating Committee for the Prevention and Combating of Corruption. Available at: https://aca.gov.eg/Media/News/2022/2/28/2022-637816447925630469-563.pdf. Accessed March 2021.

ACA (Administrative Control Authority) (2020). 'National Anti Corruption Strategy Report'. The Sub-Coordinating Committee for the Prevention and Combating of Corruption. Available at: https://aca.gov.eg/Media/News/2022/4/11/2022-637852900183154098-315.pdf. Accessed March 2021.

Achcar, G. (2013). *The People Want: A Radical Explanation of the Arab Uprising*. Berkeley, CA: University of California Press.

Achcar, G. (2016). *Morbid Symptoms*. Stanford, CA: Stanford University Press.

Achcar, G. (2021). 'Hegemony, Domination, Corruption and Fraud in the Arab Region'. *Middle East Critique*, 30 (1): 57–66.

Adly, A. (2009). 'Politically-Embedded Cronyism: The Case of Post-Liberalization Egypt'. *Business and Politics*, 11 (4): 1–26.

Adly, A. (2011). 'When Cheap is Costly: Rent Decline, Regime Survival and State Reform in Mubarak's Egypt (1990—2009)'. *Middle Eastern Studies*, 47 (2), 295–313.

Adly, A. (2014). 'The Future of Big Business in the New Egypt'. Carnegie Middle East Center. Available at: The Future of Big Business in the New Egypt – Carnegie Middle East Center – Carnegie Endowment for International Peace (carnegie-mec.org). Accessed December 2020.

Adly, A. (2016). 'Egypt's Regime Faces an Authoritarian Catch-22'. Carnegie Endowment for International Peace. Available at: http://carnegieendowment.org/files/EgyptRegimeFacesandAuthoritarianCatch22.pdf. Accessed May 2024.

African Development Bank Group (2013). 'Egypt Economic Quarterly Review'. Available at: https://www.afdb.org/sites/default/files/documents/publications/egypt_economic_quarterly_review_-_volume_3_-_april_2013.pdf. Accessed January 2020.

Ahmed, A. and G. Capoccia (2014). 'The Study of Democratization and the Arab Spring'. *Middle East Law and Governance*, 6: 1–31.

Ahmed, A.U., T. Gutner, H. Lofgren and H.E. Bouis (2001). 'The Egyptian Food Subsidy System: Structure, Performance, And Options For Reform'. Research reports 119, International Food Policy Research Institute (IFPRI).

Ahram Online (2012). 'Preachers Syndicate Offers to Supervise Egypt's Constitution Referendum'. Ahram Online. Available at: http://english.ahram.org.eg/NewsContent/1/64/59684/Egypt/Politics-/PreachersSyndicate-offer-to-supervise-Egypts-cons.aspx. Accessed February 2020.

Ahram Online (2013). 'Al-Azhar Grand Imam Threatens Retreat if Bloodshed Continues'. Available at: https://english.ahram.org.eg/NewsContent/1/64/76030/Egypt/Politics-/AlAzhar-Grand-Imam-threatens-retreat-if-bloodshed-.aspx. Accessed April 2024.

Ahram Online (2014a). 'Tamarod Movement to Turn into a Political Party after Presidential Elections'. Ahram Online. Available at: http://english.ahram.org.eg/News/100104.aspx. Accessed February 2021.

Ahram Online (2014b). 'The Salafist Front Withdraws from the National Alliance to Support Legitimacy'. Ahram Online. Available at: english.ahram.org.eg/NewsContent/1/64/117222/Egypt/Politics-/The-Salafist-Front-withdraws-from-the-National-All.aspx. Accessed February 2020.

Al-Ahram (2019). 'Salary Increases Promised to Egypt's Government Employees'. Available at: https://english.ahram.org.eg/NewsContentP/1/337712/Egypt/Salary-increases-promised-to-Egypts-government-emp.aspx. Accessed May 2024.

Al-Anani, K. (2014). 'Book Review. *Post-Islamism: The Changing Faces of Political Islam*'. *Sociology of Islam*, 2: 347–365.

Al-Anani, K. and M. Malik (2013). 'Pious Way to Politics: The Rise of Political Salafism in Post-Mubarak Egypt'. *Digest of Middle East Studies*, 22 (1): 57–73.

Al-Awadi, H. (2014). *The Muslim Brothers in Pursuit of Legitimacy Power and Political Islam in Egypt Under Mubarak*. London: I.B. Tauris.

Albrecht, H. (2005). 'How can Opposition Support Authoritarianism? Lessons from Egypt'. *Democratization*, 12 (3): 378–397.

Albrecht, H. (2007). 'Authoritarian Opposition and the Politics of Challenge in Egypt'. In O. Schlumberger (ed.), *Debating Arab Authoritarianism: Dynamics and Durability in Nondemocratic Regimes*. Stanford, CA: Stanford University Press: 59–74..

Albrecht, H. (2012). 'Authoritarian Transformation or Transition from Authoritarianism? Lessons from Egypt'. In Bahgat Korany and Rabab El-Mahdi (eds), *Arab Spring in Egypt: Revolution and Beyond*. Cairo: The American University in Cairo Press: 251–270.

Albrecht, H. and D. Bishara (2011). 'Back on Horseback: The Military and Political Transformation in Egypt'. *Middle East Law and Governance*, 3: 13–23.

Albrecht, H. and D. Ohl (2016). 'Exit, Resistance, Loyalty: Military Behaviour during Unrest in Authoritarian Regimes'. *Perspectives on Politics*, 14 (1): 38–52.

Albrecht, H. and O. Schlumbeger (2004). 'Waiting for Godot: Regime Change without Democratization in the Middle East'. *International Political Science Review*, 25 (4): 371–392.

Aldrich, H.E. and C.M. Fiol (1994). 'Fools Rush in? The Institutional Context of Industry Creation'. *Academy of Management Review*, 19: 645–670.

Al-Ghafar, A.A. (2016). 'Educated but Unemployed: The Challenge Facing Egypt's Youth'. Brookings Doha Center. Available at: https://www.brookings.edu/wp-content/uploads/2016/07/en_youth_in_egypt-2.pdf. Accessed May 2024.

Al-Jazeera (2012). 'Muslim Brotherhood Tops Egyptian Poll Result'. Available at: https://www.aljazeera.com/news/2012/1/22/muslim-brotherhood-tops-egyptian-poll-result. Accessed May 2024.

Al Jazeera (2014). 'Egypt's Parliament Left Ramshackle in the New Constitution'. Al Jazeera. Available at: https://www.aljazeera.net/news/reportsandinterviews/2014/1/4/الجديد-الدستور-في-للسقوط-آيل-مصر-برلمان. Accessed May 2024.

Al-Masry al-Youm (2018). 'Egyptians Have the Right to Worship What They Want or Not to Worship at all: Sisi'. *Egypt Independent*. Available at: https://egyptindependent.com/egyptians-have-the-right-to-worship-what-they-want-or-not-to-worship-at-all-sisi/. Accessed March 2020.

Al-Sayyed, S. (2011). 'Egypt Political Parties Coalesce in Readiness for Parliamentary Elections'. Ahram Online. Available at: https://english.ahram.org.eg/NewsContent/1/64/20471/Egypt/Politics-/Egypt-politicalparties-coalesce-in-readiness-for-.aspx. Accessed September 2011.

al-Sisi's Twitter account (2019). Available at: https://twitter.com/AlsisiOfficial/status/1134472849023016960. Accessed March 2020.

Andersen, M.S. (2012). 'Legitimacy in State-Building: A Review of the IR Literature'. *International Political Sociology*, 6 (2): 205–219.

Acheampong, M. (2020). '"Critical Ecosystems" as a Concept in Political Ecology – Developing a Comprehensive Analytical Framework'. *Journal of Political Ecology* 27 (1): 190–212.

Apple, M.W. (1995). *Education and Power*. New York: Routledge.

Arab Barometer (2018). 'Arab Barometer Wave V Technical Report'. *Arab Barometer*. Available at: https://www.arabbarometer.org/wp-content/uploads/ABV_Methods_Report-1.pdf. Accessed February 2019.

Ardovini, L. (2019). 'Institutionalising Authoritarianism in Egypt: al-Sisi's struggle for Power', ISPI. Available at: Institutionalizing Authoritarianism in Egypt: al-Sisi's Struggle for Power | ISPI (ispionline.it). Accessed December 2020.

Ardovini, L. and S. Mabon (2019). 'Egypt's Unbreakable Curse: Tracing the *State of Exception* from Mubarak to Al Sisi'. *Mediterranean Politics*, 10 (4): 445–454.

Arena, P. and N. Nicoletti (2014). 'Selectorate Theory, the Democratic Peace, and Public Goods Provision'. *International Theory*, 6 (3): 391–416.

Arendt, H. (1965). *On Revolution*. New York: Viking.

Arif, M. (2017). 'Constructing the National Past: History-Writing and Nation-Building in Nasser's Egypt'. Alexandria, Egypt: Bibliotheca Alexandrina, Futuristic Studies Unit. Available at: https://www.bibalex.org/Attachments/Publications/Files/2017121114173047484_ShorofatEnglish1.pdf. Accessed February 2021.

Asimaki, A. and G. Koustourakis (2014). 'Habitus: An Attempt at a Thorough Analysis of a Controversial Concept in Pierre Bourdieu's Theory of Practice'. *Social Sciences*, 3 (4): 121–131.

ATP (The Arab Transformations Project) (2014). *Listening to the Voice of the People: Policy Briefs on Democracy, EU-MENA Relations, Security, Migration, Socioeconomic Development, Corruption*. Ed. A. Teti and P. Abbott. Available at: https://assforum.org/ar/wp-content/pdf/Combined%20Policy%20Briefs%2020170410.pdf. Accessed April 2024.

ATP (The Arab Transformations Project) (2017). 'Key Findings from the Arab Transformations Project. Arab Transformations Working Paper 16'. *The Arab*

Transformations Working Paper Series. Ed. A. Teti and P. Abbott. Available at: https://www.researchgate.net/publication/314034104_Key_Findings_from_the_Arab_Transformations_Project_Arab_Transformations_Working_Paper_16. Accessed May 2024.

Atteya, A. (2013). 'Armed and dangerous: Egyptian court gives military the vote'. Al-Monitor. Available at: http://www.al-monitor.com/pulse/originals/2013/05/egypt-voting-rights-army-officers soldiers.html&num. Accessed March 2020.

Ayubi, N.N.M. (1995). *Over-Stating the Arab States: Politics and Society in the Middle East*. London: I.B. Tauris.

Aziz, S.F. (2017). 'Military Electoral Authoritarianism in Egypt'. *Election Law Journal: Rules, Politics and Policy*, 16 (2): 280–295.

Babbie, E. (2004). *The Practice of Social Research*. Belmont, California: Thomson/Wadsworth.

Bâli, A.U. (2009). 'From Subjects to Citizens? The Shifting Paradigm of Electoral Authoritarianism in Egypt'. *Middle East Law and Governance*, 1: 38–89.

Bano, M. and H. Benadi (2018). 'Regulating Religious Authority for Political Gains: Al-Sisi's Manipulation of al-Azhar in Egypt', *Third World Quarterly*, 39 (8): 1604–1621.

Barayez, A.F. (2016). 'This Land is Their Land': Egypt's Military and the Economy'. Jadaliyya. Available at: https://www.jadaliyya.com/Details/32898/%E2%80%9CThis-Land-is-their-Land%E2%80%9D-Egypt%E2%80%99s-Military-and-the-Economy. Accessed March 2020.

Barker, R. (2001). *Legitimating Identities: The Self-Presentation of Rulers and Subjects*. Cambridge: Cambridge University Press.

Barker, R. (2007). 'Democratic Legitimation: What Is It, Who Wants It, and Why?' In A. Hurrelmann, S. Schneider and J. Steffek (eds), *Legitimacy in an Age of Global Politics*. New York: Palgrave Macmillan: 19–34.

Barker, R.A. (2012). *Political Legitimacy and the State*. Oxford: Oxford Scholarship Online.

Barnes, J. (2022). *Staple Security: Bread and Wheat in Egypt*. Durham, North Carolina: Duke University Press.

Barnett, A., B. Yandle and G. Naufal (2013). 'Regulation, Trust, and Cronyism in Middle Eastern Societies: The Simple Economics of "Wasta"'. *Journal of Socio-Economics*, 44: 41–46.

Barnett, M. (1995). 'Sovereignty, Nationalism, and Regional Order in the Arab States System'. *International Organization*, 49 (3): 479–510.

Baturo, A. and J. Dornschneider-Elkink (2015). 'Dynamics of Regime Personalization and Patron–Client Networks in Russia, 1999–2014'. *Post-Soviet Affairs*, 32: 1–24.

Bauman, Z. (2012). 'Times of Interregnum', *Ethics & Global Politics*, 5 (1): 49–56.

Bayart, J. (1996). *La greffe de l'État*. Paris: Karthala.

Bayat, A. (1997). 'Un-Civil Society: The Politics of the Informal People'. *Third World Quarterly*, 18 (1): 53–72.

Bayat, A. (2000). 'From "Dangerous Classes" to "Quiet Rebels": Politics of the Urban Subaltern in the Global South'. *International Sociology*, 15 (3): 533–557.

Bayat, A. (2007). 'Radical Religion and the Habitus of the Dispossessed: Does Islamic Militancy have an Urban Ecology?' *International Journal of Urban and Regional Research*, 31 (2): 579–590.

Bayat, A. (2013). *Post-Islamism: The Changing Faces of Political Islam*. Oxford: Oxford University Press.

Bayat, A. and E. Denis (2000). 'Who is Afraid of *Ashwaiyyat*? Urban Change and Politics in Egypt'. *Environment and Urbanization*, 12 (2): 185–199.

BBC (2019). 'Egyptians Protest Against President Fattah al-Sisi'. BBC News. Available at: https://www.bbc.co.uk/news/world-middle-east-49777287. Accessed February 2021.

Beblawi, H. (1990). 'The Rentier State in the Arab World'. In Luciani, G. (ed.), *The Arab State*. Berkeley and Los Angeles: University of California Press.

Beblawi, H. and G. Luciani (1987). *The Rentier State*. London: Croom Helm.

Beetham, D. (1991). *The Legitimation of Power*. London: Macmillan.

Beinin, J. (2007). 'The Militancy of Mahalla al-Kubra'. *Middle East Research and Information Project*. Available at: The Militancy of Mahalla al-Kubra – MERIP. Accessed October 2020.

Belkaid, A. (2018). 'Algeria: A Thriving Black Market in Currencies'. Orient XXI. Available at: https://orientxxi.info/magazine/algeria-a-thriving-black-market-in-currencies,2319. Accessed May 2024.

Belkin, A. and E. Schofer (2003). 'Toward a Structural Understanding of Coup Risk'. *Journal of Conflict Resolution*, 47 (5): 594–620.

Bellin, E. (2004). 'The Robustness of Authoritarianism in the Middle East: Exceptionalism in Comparative Perspective'. *Comparative Politics*, 36 (2): 139–157.

Bellin, E. (2012). 'Reconsidering the Robustness of Authoritarianism in the Middle East: Lessons from the Arab Spring'. *Comparative Politics*, 44 (2): 127–149.

Ben Nefissa, S. (2007). 'Hereditary' Political Succession Scenario Becomes Consolidated'. IEMed, Yearbook 2007. Link available at: https://www.iemed.org/publication/egyptian-politics-2006-democratic-mobilisation-wanes-and-the-hereditary-political-succession-scenario-becomes-consolidated/. Accessed September 2019.

Ben Nefissa, S. and A.D. Arafat (2005). *Al-Intikhabat wa-l-Zaba'iniyya al-Siyasiyya fi Masr* [*Elections and Political Clientelism in Egypt*]. Cairo: Cairo Institute for Human Rights Studies.

Benford, R.D. and D.A. Snow (2000). 'Framing Processes and Social Movements: An Overview and Assessment'. *Annual Review of Sociology*, 26: 611–639.

Benjamin, N. et al. (2014). 'Informal Economy and the World Bank'. The World Bank. Available at: http://documents.worldbank.org/curated/en/416741468332060156/pdf/WPS6888.pdf. Accessed February 2021.

Bensman, J. (1979). 'Max Weber's Concept of Legitimacy'. In Arthur J. Vidich and Ronald M. Glassman (eds), *Conflict and Control: Challenge to Legitimacy of Modern Governments*. Beverley Hills, CA: Sage Publications.

Biancthi, R. (1989). *Unruly Corporatism: Associational Life in Twentieth-Century Egypt*. New York: Oxford University Press.

Bicchi, F. and B. Voltolini (2013). 'EU Democracy Assistance in the Mediterranean: What Relationship with the Arab Uprisings?' *Democracy and Security*, 9 (1–2): 80–99.

Billings, D. and S. Scott (1994). 'Religion and Political Legitimation'. *Annual Review of Sociology*, 20: 173–202.

Blanc, T. and E. Sigilllò (2019). 'Beyond the "Islamists vs. Secularists" Cleavage: The Rise of New Challengers after the 2019 Tunisian Elections', Issue 27. *European University Institute*. Available at: https://cadmus.eui.eu/bitstream/handle/1814/65592/PB_2019_27_MED.pdf?sequence=3&isAllowed=y. Accessed January 2021.

Blasi, G. and J.T. Jost (2006). 'System Justification Theory and Research: Implications for Law, Legal Advocacy, and Social Justice'. *California Law Review*, 94: 1119–1168.

Blaydes, L. (2006). 'Electoral Budget Cycles under Authoritarianism: Economic Opportunities in Mubarak's Egypt'. Available at: https://www.researchgate.net/profile/George_Tsebelis/publication/228342108_Electoral_budget_cycles_under_authoritarianism_economic_opportunism_in_Mubarak's_Egypt/links/0c96052782bdbda3f7000000.pdf. Accessed May 2024.

Blaydes, L. (2008). 'Authoritarian Elections and Elite Management: Theory and Evidence from Egypt'. Prepared for delivery at the Princeton University Conference on Dictatorships.

Blaydes, L. (2010). *Elections and Distributive Politics in Mubarak's Egypt*. Cambridge: Cambridge University Press.

Blaydes, L. and L. Rubin (2008). 'Ideological Reorientation and Counterterrorism: Confronting Militant Islam in Egypt'. *Terrorism and Political Violence*, 9 (18): 461–479.

Bloomberg (2016). 'Egypt's Failing Economy is Sisi's Fault'. Available at: https://www.bloomberg.com/opinion/articles/2016-08-16/egypt-s-failing-economy-is-sisi-s-fault. Accessed February 2021.

Bogaeert, K. (2012). 'Cities without Slums in Morocco?' In T.R. Samara, S. He and G. Chen (eds), *Locating the Right to the City in the Global South*. New York: Routledge: 41–62.

Bohl, D. et al. (2018). 'Sustainable Development Goals Report Egypt'. University of Denver/United Nations Development Programme. Available at: https://www.undp.org/sites/g/files/zskgke326/files/migration/eg/Sustainable-Development-Goals-Report.-Egypt-2030.pdf. Accessed March 2021.

Bollinger, R., M. Elmenshawy and R. Weilandt (2016). 'The Military, the Media and Public Perceptions in Egypt Communication and Civil-Military Relations'. The Geneva Centre for the Democratic Control of Armed Forces. Available at: https://www.dcaf.ch/sites/default/files/publications/documents/Egypt_Civil_Paper3_ENG.pdf. Accessed May 2024.

Bondes, M. and S. Heep (2013). 'Conceptualizing the Relationship Between Persuasion and Legitimacy: Official Framing in the Case of the Chinese Communist Party'. *Journal of Chinese Political Science*, 18 (4): 317–334.

Booth, J.A. and M.A. Seligson (2009). *The Legitimacy Puzzle in Latin America*. Cambridge: Cambridge University Press.

Bourdieu, P. (2005). *For the Science and its Social Uses*. Athens: Polytropon.

Brinkerhoff, D.W., A. Wetterberg and S. Dunn (2012). 'Service Delivery and Legitimacy in Fragile and Conflict-Affected States: Evidence from Water Service in Iraq'. *Public Management Review*, 14 (2): 273–293.

Brown, N.J. and C. Bardos (2018). 'Power Politics or Principle?' Carnegie Middle East Center. Available at: https://carnegie-mec.org/diwan/77928. Accessed February 2021.

Brown, N.J. and M. Dunne (2013). 'Egypt's Draft Constitution Rewards the Military and Judiciary'. Carnegie Endowment for International Peace. Available at: http://carnegieendowment.org/2013/12/04/egypts-draft-constitution-rewards-military-and-judiciary. Accessed January 2020.

Brown, N.J. and A. Hamzawy (2010). *Between Religion and Politics*. Washington: Carnegie Endowment for International Peace.

Brown, N.J., A. Hamzawy and M. Ottaway (2006). 'Islamist Movements and the Democratic Process in the Arab World: Exploring the Gray Zones'. Carnegie Endowment for International Peace. Available at: https://carnegieendowment.org/research/2006/03/islamist-movements-and-the-democratic-process-in-the-arab-world-exploring-gray-zones?lang=en. Accessed February 2021.

Brown, T. (2017). 'The Role of Food Subsidies in Egypt's Rising Malnutrition Problems'. International Food Policy Research Institute. Available at: https://www.ifpri.org/blog/role-food-subsidies-egypts-rising-malnutrition-problems. Accessed March 2023.

Brownlee, J. (2007). *Authoritarianism in an Age of Democratization*. Cambridge: Cambridge University Press.

Brownlee, J. (2009). 'Portents of Pluralism: How Hybrid Regimes Affect Democratic Transitions'. *American Journal of Political Science*, 53 (3): 515–532.

Brumberg, D. and H. Sallam (2012). 'Survival Strategies vs. Democratic Regimes: The Politics of Economic Reforms in Contemporary Egypt'. In Henri J. Barkey (ed.), *The Politics of Reforms in the Middle East*. New York: St. Martin's Press.

BTI (Bertelsmann Transformation Index) (2006). 'Egypt Democracy Status'. Available at: https://atlas.bti-project.org/1*2024*CV:CTC:SELEGY*CAT*EGY*REG:TAB. Accessed October 2019.

BTI (Bertelsmann Transformation Index) (2010). Egypt's Country Report. Available at: https://bti-project.org/fileadmin/api/content/en/downloads/reports/country_report_2010_EGY.pdf. Accessed November 2019.

BTI (Bertelsmann Transformation Index) (2012). 'Egypt Governance Index'. Available at: https://atlas.bti-project.org/1*2024*CV:CTC:SELEGY*CAT*EGY*REG:TAB. Accessed October 2019.

BTI (Bertelsmann Transformation Index) (2012–14). 'Egypt Governance Index'. Available at: https://atlas.bti-project.org/1*2024*CV:CTC:SELEGY*CAT*EGY*REG:TAB. Accessed May 2024.

BTI (Bertelsmann Transformation Index) (2014). 'Egypt Democracy Index'. Available at: https://atlas.bti-project.org/1*2024*CV:CTC:SELEGY*CAT*EGY*REG:TAB. Accessed November 2019.

BTI (Bertelsmann Transformation Index) (2014). 'The Governance Index". Available at: https://atlas.bti-project.org/1*2024*CV:CTC:SELEGY*CAT*EGY*REG:TAB. Accessed May 2024.

BTI (Bertelsmann Transformation Index) (2014–2022). 'Egypt Democracy Status, Stateness'. Available at: https://atlas.bti-project.org/1*2024*CV:CTC:SELEGY*CAT*EGY*REG:TAB. Accessed May 2024.

BTI (Bertelsmann Transformation Index) (2016). 'The Governance Index'. Available at: https://atlas.bti-project.org/1*2024*CV:CTC:SELEGY*CAT*EGY*REG:TAB. Accessed May 2024.
BTI (Bertelsmann Transformation Index) (2018). Egypt Country Report. Available at: https://bti-project.org/fileadmin/api/content/en/downloads/reports/country_report_2018_EGY.pdf. Accessed April 2024.
BTI (Bertelsmann Transformation Index) (2022). 'Egypt Governance Index'. Available at: https://atlas.bti-project.org/1*2024*CV:CTC:SELEGY*CAT*EGY*REG:TAB. Accessed May 2024.
Buehler, M. and A. Ibraheem (2018). 'Regime Resilience and the Arab Uprising in the Southern Mediterranean: Four Emerging Approaches for Explaining Authoritarian Persistence'. In Gillespie, R. and Volpi, F. (eds), *Routledge Handbook of Mediterranean Politics*. London: Routledge: 207–218.
Burnell, P. (2006). 'Autocratic Opening to Democracy: Why Legitimacy Matters'. *Third World Quarterly*, 27 (4): 545–562.
Bush, R. and E. Greco (2020). 'Egypt under Military Rule'. *Review of African Political Economy*, 46 (162): 529–534
Cafiero, G. (2019). 'Islam in the UAE's Foreign Policy'. *Politics Today*. Available at: https://politicstoday.org/islam-in-the-uaes-foreign-policy. Accessed March 2020.
Canovan, M. (1981). *Populism*. New York: Harcourt Brace Jovanovich.
Canovan, M. (1984), '"People", Politicians and Populism'. *Government and Opposition*, 19: 312–327.
CAPMAS. (Central Agency for Public Mobilisation and Statistics) (2013). Press release 2012/2013. Available at: https://www.capmas.gov.eg/Admin/News/PressRelease/20151110143133_955_e.pdf. Accessed May 2024.
CAPMAS (Central Agency for Public Mobilisation and Statistics) (2022). Annual Bulletin of Egyptians who Obtained Approval for Emigration and Egyptians who Acquired Other Nationality. CAPMAS.
Capra, F. and C. Spretnak (1986). *Green Politics: The Global Promise*. Bear Factory & Company.
Caridi, P. (2015). 'Consensus Building in Al-Sisi's Egypt'. *Istituto Affari Internazionali*. Available at: https://www.iai.it/en/pubblicazioni/consensus-building-al-sisis-egypt. Accessed February 2021. Accessed May 2024.
Carlile, A. (2007). 'The Definition of Terrorism: A Report by Lord Carlile of Berriew Q.C'. Available at: https://www.gov.uk/government/publications/the-definition-of-terrorism-a-report-by-lord-carlile-of-berriew. Accessed December 2020.
Carothers, T. (2002). 'The End of the Transition Paradigm'. *Journal of Democracy*, 13 (1): 5–21.
Carothers, T. (2015). 'The Complexities of Global Protests', Carnegie Endowment for International Peace. October. Available at the Complexities of Global Protests – Carnegie Endowment for International Peace. Accessed December 2023.
Catusse, M. (2006) 'Ordonner, classer, penser la société: Les pays arabes au prisme de l'économie politique'. In E. Picard (ed.), *La Politique dans le monde arabe* (Paris: Armand Colin): 215–238.

Cavatorta, F. and H. Kraetzschmar (2010). 'The Convergence of Governance: Upgrading Authoritarianism in the Arab World and Upgrading of Democracy Elsewhere?' *Middle East Critique*, 19 (3): 217–232.

Cavatorta, F. and V. Resta (2019). 'Money and Morals: Salafi Economy in the Arab World'. Carnegie Middle East Center. Available at: https://carnegie-mec.org/2019/03/06/money-and-morals-salafi-economics-in-arab-world-pub-78509. Accessed September 2020.

CBE (Central Bank of Egypt) (2011). 'Annual Report 2010/2011'. Available at: https://www.cbe.org.eg/-/media/project/cbe/listing/research/annual-report/annual-report2010-2011.pdf. Accessed December 2020.

CBE (Central Bank of Egypt) (2015–2016). Annual Reports. Available at: https://www.cbe.org.eg/-/media/project/cbe/listing/research/annual-report/annual-report2014-2015.pdf. Accessed May 2024.

CBE (Central Bank of Egypt) (2017). 'Annual Report 2016/2017.' Available at: https://www.cbe.org.eg/-/media/project/cbe/listing/research/annual-report/annual-report-2016-2017.pdf. Accessed February 2021.

CBE (Central Bank of Egypt) (2018). 'Annual Report 2017/2018'. Available at: https://www.cbe.org.eg/-/media/project/cbe/listing/research/annual-report/annual-report-2017-2018.pdf. Accessed March 2021.

CBE (Central Bank of Egypt) (2019). 'Annual Report 2018/2019'. Available at: https://www.cbe.org.eg/-/media/project/cbe/listing/research/annual-report/annual-report-2018–2019.pdf. Accessed March 2021.

CBE (Central Bank of Egypt) (2022). 'Inflation Rates Historical Data'. Central Bank of Egypt. Available at: https://www.cbe.org.eg/en/economic-research/statistics/inflation-rates/historical-data. Accessed May 2023.

CBE (Central Bank of Egypt) (2023). 'Egypt Remittances'. Central Bank of Egypt. Available at: https://tradingeconomics.com/egypt/remittances. Accessed May 2024.

Chaichian, M.A. (1988). 'The Effects of World Capitalist Economy on Urbanization in Egypt, 1800–1970'. *International Journal of Middle Eastern Studies*, 20 (1): 23–43.

Chatham House (2011). 'Egypt's Economy in the Transition Period'. MENA Programme: Egypt Dialogue Workshop Report. Available at: Microsoft Word – 0911egypt_summary.docx (chathamhouse.org). Accessed March 2023.

Chehabi, E. and J.J. Linz (1998). *Sultanistic Regimes*. Baltimore, MD: Johns Hopkins University Press.

Chekir, H. and I. Diwan (2012). 'Crony Capistalism in Egypt'. Center for International Development at Harvard University. Available at: http://www.hks.harvard.edu/sites/default/files/centers/cid/files/publications/faculty-working-papers/250_Diwan_EGX+paper.pdf. Accessed May 2024.

Cleopatra Group (n.d.). 'Mohamed M. Abou El Enein'. Available at: http://www.abouelenein.com/wp-content/themes/exprimo_framework/img/landing-mediterraneo/Mohamed-M-Abou-El-Enein-en-Biography.pdf. Accessed May 2020.

Colgan, J. and J. Weeks (2015). 'Revolution, Personalist Dictatorships, and International Conflict'. *International Organization*, 69 (1): 163–194.

Collier, R.B. (2001). Populism. *International Encyclopedia of the Social and Behavioral Sciences*. Elsevier.

Cook, S.A. (2007). *Ruling But Not Governing: The Military and Political Development in Egypt, Algeria, and Turkey*. Baltimore: Johns Hopkins University Press.
CPI (Corruption Perception Index) (2013). Egypt. Available at: https://www.transparency.org/en/cpi/2013/index/egy. Accessed May 2024.
CPI (Corruption Perception Index) (2016). 'Transparency International Statement on Egypt's Corruption Perceptions Index Ranking for 2015'. Available at: https://www.transparency.org/en/press/transparency-international-statement-on-egypts-corruption-perceptions-index. Accessed February 2021.
CPI (Consumer Price Index) (2022). 'Egypt's Consumer Price Index'. Available at: https://tradingeconomics.com/egypt/consumer-price-index-cpi. Accessed May2024.
Crabbs, J. (1975). 'Politics, History, and Culture in Nasser's Egypt'. *International Journal of Middle East Studies*, 6 (4): 386–420.
Croke, K. *et al.* (2016). 'Deliberate Disengagement: How Education Can Decrease Political Participation in Electoral Authoritarian Regimes'. *Am. Polit. Sci. Rev.*, 110 (3): 579–600.
Croissant, A. and T. Eshcenauer (2018). 'Military and Politics in the Mediterranean'. In *Routledge Handbook of Mediterranean Politics*. London: Routledge: 157–170.
Dacin, T., C. Oliver and J.P. Roy (2007). The Legitimacy of Strategic Alliances: An Institutional Perspective. *Strategic Management Journal*, 28 (2): 169–187.
Dahl, R.A. (1971). *Polyarchy: Participation and Opposition*. New Haven, Connecticut: Yale University Press.
Daragahi, B. (2013). 'Recording Reveals al-Sisi's Political Ambitions in Egypt'. *Financial Times*. Available at: https://www.ft.com/content/e5c8f42e-359b-11e3-952b-00144feab7de. Accessed February 2021.
Daily News Egypt (2018). 'Al-Azhar, Dar al-Ifta Rejects al-Sisi Decision to Achieve Gender Equality in Inheritance'. *Daily News Egypt*. Available at: https://dailynewsegypt.com/2018/08/15/al-azhar-dar-al-ifta-reject-sibsi-decision-to-achieve-gender-equality-in-inheritance/. Accessed March 2020.
Darwish, P. (2015). 'Egypt's "War on Atheism"'. *Al-Ahram*, January. Available at: https://english.ahram.org.eg/NewsPrint/120204.aspx. Accessed January 2020.
Dau, M. (2012). How Saudi Petrodollars Fuel Rise of Salafism, France 24. Available at: How Saudi Petrodollars Fuel Rise of Salafism (france24.com). Accessed February 2021.
Davenport, C. (2007). 'State Repression and Tyrannical Peace'. *Journal of Peace Research*, (44): 485–504.
David, S. (1991). 'Explaining Third World Alignment'. *World Politics*, 43 (2): 233–256.
DCAF (Geneva Centre for Security Sector Governance) (2016). Available at: https://www.dcaf.ch/.
Della Porta, D. (2016). *Where Did the Revolution Go?* Cambridge: Cambridge University Press.
de la Torre, C. (2019). *The Routledge International Handbook of Global Populism*. New York: Routledge.
de Mesquita, B. and A. Smith (2011). *The Dictator's Handbook: Why Bad Behavior is Almost Always Good Politics*. New York: Public Affairs.

de Mesquita, B. et al. (1999). 'Policy Failure and Political Survival: The Contribution of Political Institutions'. *Journal of Conflict Resolution*, 43 (2): 147–61.

de Mesquita, B. et al. (2003). *The Logic of Political Survival*. New York: New York University Press.

Dekmejian, H. (1972). *Egypt under Nasir: A Study in Political Dynamics*. London: University of London Press.

Deknatel, F. (2019). 'Egypt's Sisi is Repeating Mubarak's Economic Mistakes, to the IMF's Applause'. *World Politics Review*. Available at: https://www.worldpoliticsreview.com/articles/27872/egypt-s-sisi-is-repeating-mubarak-s-economic-mistakes-to-the-imf-s-applause. Accessed April 2020.

Denis, S. (1994). *Private Voluntary Organizations in Egypt: Islamic Development, Private Initiative, and State Control*. Gainesville, FL: University of Florida Press.

Diamond, L. (2002). 'Thinking about Hybrid Regimes', *Journal of Democracy*, 13 (2): 21–35.

Diamond, L. and M.F. Plattern (eds) (2006). *Electoral Systems and Democracy*. Baltimore, MD: Johns Hopkins University Press.

Dillman, B. (2000). *State and Private Sector in Algeria: The Politics of Rent-Seeking and Failed Development*. Boulder, CO: Westview.

Dimitrov, M.K. (2009). 'Popular Autocrats'. *Journal of Democracy*, 20 (1): 78–81.

Diong, N.J.N. (2015). 'Sawt Al-Arab or Sawt Al-Nasser? The Case of Mass Media under Gamal Abdel Nasser and the Convoluted Rise of Pan-Arabism'. *Journal of Georgetown University/Qatar Middle Eastern Studies Student Association* 5. Accessed at: https://www.qscience.com/docserver/fulltext/messa/2015/1/messa.2015.5.pdf?expires=1612989863&id=id&accname=guest&checksum=AE59A295A8073D9D0F39F6E18661DF63. Accessed February 2021.

Diwan, I. and I. Vartanova (2020). 'Does Education Indoctrinate?' *International Journal of Educational Development*, 78.

Dodge, T. (2012). 'After the Arab Spring: Power Shift in the Middle East? Conclusions: The Middle East after the Arab Spring'. IDEAS Special Reports. London School of Economics and Political Science. Available at: http://eprints.lse.ac.uk/43469/1/After%20the%20Arab%20Spring_conclusion%28lsero%29.pdf. Accessed May 2024.

Dogan, M. (1992). 'Conceptions of Legitimacy'. In M. Hawkesworth and M. Kogan (eds), *Encyclopedia of Government and Politics*. London: Routledge: 116–126.

Dogan, M. (2009). 'Political Legitimacy: New Criteria and Anachronistic Theories'. *International Social Science Journal*, 60 (196): 195–210.

Dombos, T. et al. (2009). 'Critical Frame Analysis: A Comparative Methodology for the QUING Project'. Presented at the ECPR First European Conference on Politics and Gender, 21–23 January, Queens University Belfast.

Dorman, W.J. (2007). 'The Politics of Neglect: The Egyptian State in Cairo'. Unpublished PhD thesis, SOAS University of London.

Dorman, W.J. (2009). *Of Demolition and Donors: The Problematic of State Intervention in Informal Cairo*. Cairo: American University of Cairo Press.

Dorman, W.J. and E. Stein (2013). 'Informality Versus the State Islamists, Informal Cairo and Political Integration by Other Means'. *Turkish Journal of International Relations*, 12 (4): 5–19.

Downs, A. (1957). 'An Economic Theory of Political Action in a Democracy'. *Journal of Political Economy*, 65 (2): 135–150.
Drevon, J. (2014). 'Democracy and Islamist Violence: Lessons from Post-Mubarak Egypt'. *Domes*, 23: 1–14.
Drevon, J. (2015a). 'Assessing Islamist Armed Groups' De-Radicalization in Egypt'. *Peace Review*, 27 (3): 296–303.
Drevon, J. (2015b). 'The Emergence of Ex-Jihadi Political Parties in Post-Mubarak Egypt'. *Middle East Journal*, 69 (4): 511–526.
Dukalskis, A. and J. Gerschewski (2017). *The Authoritarian Public Space: Legitimation and Autocratic Power in North Korea, Burma, and China*. London: Routledge.
Dunne, M. (2019). 'Egypt's Trends in Politics, Economics, and Human Rights'. Carnegie Endowment for International Peace. Testimony US: Subcommittee on the Middle East, North Africa, and International Terrorism. Available at: https://carnegieendowment.org/2020/09/09/egypt-trends-in-politics-economics-and-human-rights-pub-82677. Accessed May 2020.
Dunne, M. and C. Bardos (2019). *Authoritarian Math*. Carnegie Middle East Center. Available at: https://carnegie-mec.org/diwan/78980. Accessed February 2021.
Dunne, M. and A. Miller (2019). 'Nine Reasons Why Declaring the Muslim Brotherhood a Terrorist Organization Would Be a Mistake'. Available at: https://carnegieendowment.org/2019/05/03/nine-reasons-why-declaring-muslim-brotherhood-terrorist-organization-would-be-mistake-pub-79059. Accessed January 2020.
Dupire, C. (2018). 'Competition Calls on Arab Youth to Share Positive Images of Change in Community'. *The Jordan Times*, November. Available at: https://www.jordantimes.com/news/local/competition-calls-arab-youth-share-positive-images-change-community. Accessed May 2022.
Durac, V. (2018). 'Opposition Party Political Dynamics in Egypt from the 2011 Revolution to Sisi'. In D. Conduit and S. Akbarzadeh (eds), *New Opposition in the Middle East*. Singapore: Palgrave Macmillan: 71–96.
Dusza, K. (1989). 'Max Weber's Conception of the State'. *International Journal of Politics, Culture, and Society*, 3 (1): 71–105.
Easton, D. (1965). *A Systems Analysis of Political Life*. New York: John Wiley.
Easton, D. (1975). 'A Reassessment of the Concept of Political Support'. *British Journal of Political Science*, 5: 435–457.
The Economist (2017). 'Egypt's Clerics are Resisting the President's Call to Renew Islam'. *The Economist*. Available at: https://www.economist.com/middle-east-and-africa/2017/02/18/reforming-islam-in-egypt. Accessed March 2020.
The Economist (2019). 'Egypt is Reforming its Economy, But Poverty is Rising'. *The Economist*. Available at: https://www.economist.com/middle-east-and-africa/2019/08/08/egypt-is-reforming-its-economy-but-poverty-is-rising. Accessed 14 December 2020.
Edel, M. and M. Josua (2017). 'How Authoritarian Rule Seeks to Legitimize Repression: Edelman, M. (1971). *Politics as Symbolic Action: Mass Arousal and Quiescence*. Elsevier.
Edelman, M. (1971). *Politics As Symbolic Action: Mass Arousal and Quiescence*. Chicago: University of Wisconsin.

Egypt Independent (2017). 'Rift Escalates, Becomes Public Between Sisi, Al-Azhar'. Available at: https://egyptindependent.com/rift-escalates-becomes-public-between-sisi-al-azhar/. Accessed April 2024.

Eickelman, D. and J. Piscatori (1996). *Muslim Politics*. Princeton, NJ: Princeton University Press.

Eisenstadt, S.N. (1968). *Max Weber: On Charisma and Institution Building*. Chicago: University of Chicago Press.

El-Amrani, I. (2005). 'The Mubarak Speech'. The Arabist. Available at: The Mubarak Speech – The Arabist. Accessed February 2021.

El-Ashwal, N. (2013). 'Egyptian Salafism: Between Religious Movement and Realpolitik'. Stiftung Wissenschaft und Politik. Available at: https://www.swpberlin.org/fileadmin/contents/products/comments/2013C27_ngw.pdf. Accessed March 2020.

El-Beblawy, H. (2014). 'New Suez Canal: Investment in the Future of Egypt'. *Studies and Research* (Arab magazine), n. 9,641, year 37.

El-Bernoussi, Z. (2021). *Dignity in the Egyptian Revolution*. Cambridge: Cambridge University Press.

El-Dabh, B. (2014). 'Sisi's Unconventional Campaign'. The Tahrir Institute for Middle East Policy. Available at: https://timep.org/presidential-elections-monitoring/sisis-unconventional-campaign/. Accessed July 2020.

El-Dine, C.C. (2014). 'Fragile Alliances in Egypt's Post-Revolutionary Order'. Stiftung Wissenschaft und Politik. Available at: https://www.swp-berlin.org/fileadmin/contents/products/comments/2014C46_chams_el_dine.pdf. Accessed January 2021.

el Issawi, F. (2014). 'Egyptian Media Under Transition: In the Name of the Regime… in the Name of the People?' London School of Economics and Political Science. Available at: Egyptian-Media-Under-Transition (essex.ac.uk). Accessed August 2020.

El-Naggar, L. (2022). 'Algeria's Hirak Movement: A Second National Liberation?' The Swedish Institute of International Affairs, February Paper 1. Link available at: https://www.ui.se/globalassets/ui.se-eng/publications/ui-publications/2022/ui-paper-no.-1-2022.pdf. Accessed May 2024.

El-Nawawy, M. and El-Masry, M.H. (2016). 'The Signs of a Strongman: A Semiotic and Discourse Analysis of Abdelfattah Al-Sisi's Egyptian Presidential Campaign'. *International Journal of Communication*, 10: 2275–2296.

El-Shafei, O. (1995). 'Workers, Trade Unions and the State in Egypt, 1984–1989'. *Cairo Papers in Social Science*, 18 (2).

El-Sherif, A. (2014). 'Egypt's Post-Mubarak Predicament'. Carnegie Middle East Center. Available at: http://carnegieendowment.org/files/post_mubarak_predicament.pdf. Accessed May 2024.

Entman, R.M. (1993). 'Framing: Toward Clarification of a Fractured Paradigm'. *Journal of Communication*, 43 (4): 51–58.

Entman, R.M., J. Matthes and L. Pellicano (2009). 'Nature, Sources and Effects of News Framing'. In K. Wahl-Jorgensen and T. Hanitzsch (eds), *The Handbook of Journalism Studies*. New York: Routledge: 175–190.

EODS (European Union Observation Mission to Egypt) (2014). *Final Report Presidential Elections 26/27 May 2024*. Available at: https://www.eods.eu/library/eueom-egypt2014-final-report_en.pdf. Accessed April 2024.
Epstein, N.L. et al. (2003). 'Distributive Justice and Attitudes toward the Welfare State'. *Social Justice Research* 16 (1): 1–27.
Escribà-Folch, A. and J. Wright, (2010). 'Dealing with Tyranny: International Sanctions and the Survival of Authoritarian Rulers'. *International Studies Quarterly*, 54 (2): 335–359.
Escribà-Folch, A. and J. Wright (2015). *Foreign Pressure and the Politics of Autocratic Survival*. Oxford: Oxford University Press.
Esterman, I. (2014). 'Despite Austerity, Spending in New Budget is Close to Last Year's'. Mada Masr. Available at: http://www.madamasr.com/sections/economy/despite-austerity-spending-new-budget-close-last-years.
European Commission (2014). 'ENP Country Progress Report 2013: Egypt'. Available at: https://ec.europa.eu/commission/presscorner/detail/en/MEMO_14_223. Accessed September 2020.
European Parliament (2012). 'The Dawn of Parliamentary Democracy in Egypt'. Directorate General for External Policies of the Union Policy Department. Available at: https://www.europarl.europa.eu/RegData/etudes/note/join/2012/457147/EXPO-AFET_NT(2012)457147_EN.pdf. Accessed May 2024.
European Parliament (2013). Salafis/Wahhabite Financial Support to Educational, Social and Religious Institutions. Directorate General for External Relations. Policy Department. Available at: https://www.europarl.europa.eu/RegData/etudes/etudes/join/2013/457136/EXPO-AFET_ET(2013)457136_EN.pdf. Accessed April 2024.
European Union Election Observation Mission (2014). 'Arab Republic of Egypt: Final Report: Presidential Election, 26/27 May 2014'. Available at: http://eeas.europa.eu/archives/eueom/missions/2014/egypt/pdf/eueom-egypt2014-final-report_en.pdf. Accessed November 2018.
European Union External Action Service (2016). 'Upgrading Informal Areas in Greater Cairo Region'. Available at: https://eeas.europa.eu/headquarters/headquarters-homepage/8741/upgrading-informal-areas-greater-cairo-region_en. Accessed February 2018.
Fahmy, K. (1999). 'The Police and the People in Nineteenth-Century Egypt'. *Die Welt Des Islams*, 39 (3): 340–377.
Fahmy, N. (2002). *The Politics of Egypt: State-Society Relationship*. London: Routledge.
Fahmy, K. (2012). 'The Army and the People are Not One Hand', *Egypt Independent*, January. Available at: https://egyptindependent.com/army-and-people-are-not-one-hand/. Accessed May 2022.
Fallows, J. (1997). *Breaking the News*. New York: Vintage.
FAO (Food and Agricultural Organisation of the United Nations) (2024). Egypt. Link available at FAOSTAT. Accessed May 2024
Farah, N.R. (2009). *Egypt's Political Economy: Power Relations in Development*. Cairo: American University in Cairo Press.

Fedi, L., M., Amer and A. Rashad (2019). 'Growth and Precariousness in Egypt'. *International Labour Organisation.* Available at: https://www.ilo.org/sites/default/files/wcmsp5/groups/public/@ed_emp/documents/publication/wcms_735169.pdf. Accessed February 2021.

Feuille, J. (2011). 'Reforming Egypt's Constitution: Hope for Egyptian Democracy?' *Texas International Law Journal*, 47 (1): 257–258.

Field, N. and A. Hamam (2009). *Salafi Satellite TV in Egypt*. Oxford: The Middle East Centre, St. Antony's College, University of Oxford.

Fjelde, H. (2010). 'Generals, Dictators, and Kings: Authoritarian Regimes and Civil Conflict, 1973–2004'. *Conflict Management and Peace Science*, 27 (3): 195–218.

Fouad, K. (2018). 'Militarisation of Political Parties'. Egyptian Institute for Studies. Available at: https://en.eipss-eg.org/wp-content/uploads/2018/07/Militarization-of-Political-Parties-in-Egypt.pdf. Accessed February 2021.

Foucault, M. (1988). *Michel Foucault: Politics, Philosophy, Culture. Interviews and Other Things, 1977–1984.* London: Routledge.

Fragile State Index (2016). 'Overall Trend in Egypt'. Available at: https://fragilestatesindex.org/country-data/. Accessed January 2020.

Frantz, E. and B. Geddes (2016). 'The Legacy of Dictatorship for Democratic Parties in Latin America'. *Journal of Politics in Latin America*, 8 (1): 3–32.

Frantz, E., A. Kendall-Taylor, Jia Li and J. Wright. (2021). 'Personalist Ruling Parties in Democracies'. *Democratization*, 1–21: 10.

Freedom House (2012). 'Egypt'. Available at: https://www.freedomhouse.org/sites/default/files/Egypt%202012.pdf. Accessed May 2019.

Freedom House (2013). 'Egypt: Freedom on the Net 2013'. Available at: https://www.freedomhouse.org/sites/default/files/resources/FOTN%202013_Egypt.pdf. Accessed March 2019.

Freedom House (2014). 'Egypt: Freedom on the Net'. Available at: https://freedomhouse.org/sites/default/files/resources/Egypt.pdf. Accessed November 2019.

Freedom House (2017). 'Egypt: Freedom in the World Country Report'. Available at: https://freedomhouse.org/country/egypt/freedom-world/2017. Accessed April 2024.

Freedom House (2018). 'Freedom in the World: Egypt'. Available at: https://freedomhouse.org/report/freedom-world/2017/egypt. Accessed February 2021.

Freedom House (2022). 'Egypt. Country Profile'. Available at: https://freedomhouse.org/country/egypt/freedom-world/2022. Accessed May 2024.

Freeman, J. and M.T. Hannan (1983). 'Niche Width and the Dynamics of Organizational Populations'. *American Journal of Sociology*, 88 (1): 116–145.

Freer, C. (2019). 'Challenges to Sunni Islamism in Bahrain since 2011'. Carnegie Middle East Center. Available at: Challenges to Sunni Islamism in Bahrain Since 2011 – Carnegie Middle East Center – Carnegie Endowment for International Peace (carnegie-mec.org). Accessed January 2021.

French, J. and B. Raven (1959). 'The Bases of Social Power'. In D. Cartwright (ed.), *Studies in Social Power*. Ann Arbor, MI: Institute for Social Research: 150–167.

Frerichs, S. (2016). 'Egypt's Neoliberal Reforms and the Moral Economy of Bread', Sadat, Mubarak, Morsi'. *Review of Radical Political Economics*, 48 (4): 610–632.

Fukuyama, F. (2013). 'What is Governance?' *Governance*, 26 (3): 347–368.

Gad, M. (2014). 'Austerity Without Protection: Egypt's 2014 Budget'. Middle East Institute. Available at: http://www.mei.edu/content/at/austerity-without-protection-egypts-2014-budget. Accessed February 2021.

Galal, A. (2003). 'Social Expenditure and the Poor'. ERF Working Paper 89. Cairo: Egyptian Centre for Economic Studies.

Galal, A. (2011). *Egypt in the Era of Hosni Mubarak*. Cairo: The American University in Cairo Press.

Galal, S. (2022) 'Quarterly Unemployment Rate in Egypt, 2019–2021, By Gender'. Statista. Available at: Egypt: quarterly unemployment rate by gender 2019-2021 | Statista. Accessed May 2024.

Gallagher, M. and J.K. Hanson (2013). 'Authoritarian Survival, Resilience, and the Selectorate Theory'. In Martin Dimitrov (ed.), *Why Communism Didn't Collapse: Understanding Regime Resilience in China, Vietnam, Laos, North Korea and Cuba*. Cambridge: Cambridge University Press.

Gamal, M. (2019a). 'Sisi's Policy of Constant Change of Military Leaders'. Egyptian Institute for Studies. Available at: https://en.eipss-eg.org/sisis-policy-of-constant-change-of-military-leaders/. Accessed June 2020.

Gamal, W. (2019b). 'Lost Capital: The Egyptian Muslim Brotherhood's Neoliberal Transformation'. Carnegie Endowment for International Peace. Available at: https://carnegieendowment.org/files/2-1-19_Gamal_Muslim_Brotherhood.pdf. Accessed May 2020.

Gandhi, J. and A. Przeworski (2006). 'Authoritarian institutions and the survival of autocrats'. *Comparative Political Studies*, 40 (11): 1279–1301.

Gandhi, J. and E. Lust-Okar (2009). 'Elections under Authoritarianism'. *Annual Review of Political Science*, 12: 403–422.

GCDCAF (2016). 'The Military, the Media and Public Perceptions in Egypt: Communication and Civil-Military Relations'. Egypt Civil-Military Relations Conference Paper Series Paper 3. Available at: https://www.dcaf.ch/sites/default/files/publications/documents/Egypt_Civil_Paper3_ENG.pdf. Accessed April 2024.

Geddes, B. (1999a). 'What Do We Know About Democratization After Twenty Years?' *Annual Review of Political Science*, 2: 115–144.

Geddes, B. (1999b). 'Authoritarian Breakdown: Empirical Test of a Game Theoretic Argument'. Paper presented at the annual meeting of the American Political Science Association, Atlanta.

Geddes, B. (2003). *Paradigms and Sand Castles: Theory Building and Research Design in Comparative Politics*. Ann Arbor, MI: University of Michigan Press.

Geddes, B. (2008). 'Party Creation as an Autocratic Survival Strategy'. Unpublished Working Paper. University of California, Los Angeles.

Geddes, B., J. Wright and E. Franz (2014). 'New Data Set: Autocratic Breakdown and Regime Transitions'. *Perspective on Politics*, 12 (1): 313–331.

Geddes, B., J. Wright and E. Frantz (2017). 'A Measure of Personalism in Dictatorships'. Pennsylvania State University. Available at: http://sites.psu.edu/dictators/files/2017/10/PersMeasure-1ph2gwp.pdf. Accessed February 2021.

Gellner, E. (1983) *Nations and Nationalism*. Ithaca, NY: Cornell University Press.

General Authority for Investments and Free Zone (2023). Government of Egypt. Available at: https://www.gafi.gov.eg/English/Pages/default.aspx. Accessed May 2023.

Gerschewski, J. (2013). 'The Three Pillars of Stability: Legitimation, Repression and Cooptation in Autocratic Regimes'. *Democratization*, 20 (1): 13–38.

Gerschewski, J. (2018) 'Legitimacy in Autocracies: Oxymoron or Essential Feature?' *Perspectives on Politics*, 16 (3): 652–665.

Gerschewski, J., W. Merkel, A. Schmotz, H.C. Stefes and D. Tanneberg (2013). 'Warum überleben Diktaturen? *Politische Vierteljahresschrift* (47): 106–131.

Ghitens-Mazer, J. (2005). *Cultural and political nationalism in Ireland: Myths and memories of the Easter Rising*. Unpublished PhD Thesis, London School of Economics and Political Science. Available at: https://etheses.lse.ac.uk/1838/. Accessed December 2019

Ghitens-Mazer, J. (2006). *Myths and Memories of the Easter Rising: Cultural and Political Nationalism in Ireland*. Dublin; Portland, OR: Irish Academic Press.

Gilbert, L. and P. Mohseni (2011). 'Beyond Authoritarianism: The Conceptualization of Hybrid Regimes'. *Studies in Comparative International Development*, 46 (3): 270–297.

Gilley, B. (2006). 'The Meaning and Measure of State Legitimacy: Results from 72 Countries'. *European Journal of Political Science*, 45: 499–525.

Gilley, B. (2012). 'State Legitimacy: An Updated Dataset for 52 Countries'. *European Journal of Political Research*, 51 (5): 693–699.

Ginsburg, T. and T. Moustafa (2008). *Rule by Law: The Politics of Courts in Authoritarian Regimes*. Cambridge: Cambridge University Press.

Glade, D. (2005). 'Dissonant Politics in Mubarak's Egypt'. *Res Publica*, 10 (1), 23–38.

Global Economy Index (2016). 'Egypt Political Stability 2016'. Available at: https://www.theglobaleconomy.com/Egypt/wb_political_stability/. Accessed September 2018.

Gramsci, A. (1971). *Selections from the Prison Notebooks*, ed. and trans. Quintin Hoare and Geoffrey Nowell-Smith. London: Lawrence & Wishart.

Goldberg, E. (2011). 'Mubarakism without Mubarak'. *Foreign Affairs*. Available at: https://www.foreignaffairs.com/articles/egypt/2011-02-11/mubarakism-without-mubarak. Accessed December 2020.

Gormus, E. (2017). 'Economic Liberalisation Policies and (Non-Islamic) Market Coalition in Egypt'. *Journal of North African Studies*, 22 (1): 60–77.

Gotowicki, S. (1999). 'The Military in Egyptian Society'. In Phebe Marr (ed.), *Egypt at the Crossroads: Domestic Stability and Regional Role*: Washington DC: National Defense University Press.

Grafstein, R. (1981). 'The Failure of Weber's Conception of Legitimacy: Its Causes and Implications'. *Journal of Politics*, 43 (2): 456–472.

Grimm, J.J. (2022). *Contested Legitmacy in Egypt*. Amsterdam: Amsterdam University Press.

Grönlund, K. and M. Setälä (2004). 'Low Electoral Turnout: An Indication of a Legitimacy Deficit?' Paper presented at ECPR Joint Session, Uppsala, 13–18 April.

Guardian (2015a). 'Eni discovers largest known gas field in Mediterranean'. *Guardian*. Available at: https://www.theguardian.com/business/2015/aug/30/eni-discovers-largest-known-mediterranean-gas-field. Accessed February 2021.

Guardian (2015b). 'How Media Has Become a Mouthpiece for the Military State'. *Guardian*. Available at: https://www.theguardian.com/world/2015/jun/25/egyptian-media-journalism-sisi-mubarak. Accessed December 2020.

Gutner, T. (1999). 'The political economy of food subsidy reform in Egypt,' FCND discussion papers 77, International Food Policy Research Institute (IFPRI).

Haber, S. (2006). 'Authoritarian Government'. In Barry Weingast and Donland Wittman (eds), *The Oxford Handbook of Political Economy*. New York: Oxford University Press: 693–707.

Hadenius, A. and J. Teorell (2007). 'Authoritarian Regimes: Stability, Change and Pathways to Democracy, 1972–2003'. Kellog Institute. Available at https://kellogg.nd.edu/documents/1639. Accessed May 2024.

Hafez, M.M. and Q. Wiktorowicz (2004). 'Violence as Contention in the Egyptian Islamic Movement'. In Q. Wiktorowicz (ed.), *Islamic Activism*. Bloomington, IN: Indiana University Press: 62–88.

Hallahan, K. (2008). 'Strategic Framing'. In W. Donsbach (ed.), *The International Encyclopedia of Communication*. Oxford: Wiley-Blackwell.

Hamid, S. et al (2017). 'Islamism after the Arab Spring: Between the Islamic State and the Nation-State'. *The Brookings Project on U.S. Relations with the Islamic World U.S.-Islamic World Forum Papers 2015*. Available at: https://www.brookings.edu/wp-content/uploads/2017/01/islamism-after-the-arab-spring_english_web_final.pdf Accessed April 2024.

Hamid, Y. (2018). 'Why President Morsi Rejected IMF Conditions'. *Middle East Observer*. Available at: https://www.middleeastobserver.org/2018/08/06/column-why-president-morsi-rejected-imf-conditions/. Accessed March 2020.

Hamza, M. and M. Beillard (2013). 'Grain and Feed Annual Forex Availability Impacts Grain Imports'. USDA Foreign Agricultural Service.

Hamzawy, A. (2005). 'Opposition in Egypt: Performance in the Presidential Elections and Prospects for the Parliamentary Elections'. Carnegie Endowment for International Peace. Available at: http://carnegieendowment.org/files/PO22.hamzawy.FINAL.pdf. Accessed May 2024.

Hamzawy, Amr (2014). 'On Religion, Politics and Democratic Legitimacy in Egypt, January 2011–June 2013'. *Philosophy and Social Criticism*, 40 (4–5): 401–406.

Hanieh, A. (2013). *Lineages of Revolt: Issues of Contemporary Capitalism in the Middle East*. Chicago: Haymarket Books.

Hannan, M.T. (1989). 'Competitive and Institutional Processes in Organizational Ecology'. In J. Berger, M. Zelditch and B. Andersen (eds), *Sociological Theories in Progress: New Formulations*. Newbury: Sage.

Haulslohner, A. (2014). 'Egypt's Abdel Fatah Al-Sissi Declares Intent To Run For Presidency'. *Washington Post*. Available at: https://www.washingtonpost.com/gdpr-consent/?next_url=https%3a%2f%2fwww.washingtonpost.com%2fworld%2fno-longer-a-general-abdel-fatah-al-sissi-is-poised-to-become-egypts-next-pres ident%2f2014%2f03%2f26%2f7c6440b9-1bed-468f-b315-735a32f7d9e8_story.html. Accessed December 2020.

Harders, C. (2009). 'Politik von unten — Perspektiven auf den autoritären Staat in ägypten' In M. Beck, C. Harders, A. Jünemann, and S. Stetter (eds.) *Der Nahe Osten im Umbruch. Zwischen Transformation und Autoritarismus* (Wiesbaden: VS Verlag für Sozialwissenschaften), pp. 299–323

Hechter, M. (2009). 'Legitimacy in the Modern World'. *American Behavioural Scientist*, 53 (3): 279–288.

Hadenius, A. and J. Teorell (2007). 'Authoritarian Regimes: Stability, Change and Pathways to Democracy, 1972–2003'. Kellog Institute. Available at: https://aei.pitt.edu/73636/1/eusrping_template_-pb_eg_pdf. Accessed May 2024.

Heilbroner, R. (1972). 'Growth and Survival'. *Foreign Affairs*, 51 (1): 139–153.

Heilbroner, R. (1973). 'Economic Problems of a Postindustrial Society'. *Dissent*, 20 (2): 163–176.

Henrich, J. and Gil-White, F.J. (2001). 'The Evolution of Prestige: Freely Conferred Deference as a Mechanism for Enhancing the Benefits of Cultural Transmission'. *Evolution and Human Behavior*, 22 (3): 165–196.

Helfont, S. (2014). 'Saddam and the Islamists: The Ba'thist Regime's Instrumentalization of Religion in Foreign Affairs'. *The Middle East Journal*, 68 (3): 352–366.

The Heritage Foundation (2006–2022). 'Egypt: Economic Freedom Country Profile'. Available at: https://www.heritage.org/index/pages/country-pages/egypt. Accessed May 2024.

Hertog, J. and D. Mcleod (2001). 'A Multiperspectival Approach to Framing Analysis: A Field Guide'. In S. Reese, O. Gandy and A. Grant (eds), *Framing Public Life*. Mahwah, NJ: Erlbaum: 139–161.

Heshmati, A. and R. Davis (2007). 'The Determinants of Foreign Direct Investment Flows to the Federal Region of Kurdistan'. *IZA Discussion Papers 3218*. Bonn: Institute for the Study of Labor (IZA).

Heydemann, S. (2007). 'Upgrading Authoritarianism in the Arab World'. Brookings Institution. Available at: https://www.brookings.edu/wp-content/uploads/2016/06/10arabworld.pdf. Accessed January 2020.

Heydemann, S. and R. Leenders (2014). 'Authoritarian Learning and Counter-revolution'. In Marc Lynch (ed.), *The Arab Uprisings Explained*. New York: Columbia University Press.

Hinnebusch, R. (1993). 'The Politics of Economic Reforms in Egypt'. *Third World Quarterly*, 14 (1): 159–170.

Hinnebusch, R. (2006). 'Authoritarian Persistence, Democratization Theory and the Middle East: An Overview and Critique'. *Democratization*, 13 (3): 373–395.

Hoekema, A.J., N.F. Manen, G. Heijden, B.D. Vroom and I. Vlies (1998). *Integraal bestuur: De behoorlijkheid, effectiviteit en legitimiteit van onderhandelend bestuur.* Amsterdam, Amsterdam University Press

Holbig, H. and B. Gilley (2010). 'Reclaiming Legitimacy in China'. *Politics and Policy*, 38 (3): 395–422.

Hollis, R. (2012). 'No Friend of democratization: Europe's Role in the Genesis of the "Arab Spring"'. *International Affairs*, 88 (1): 81–94.

Hollis, R. (2016). 'Europe in the Middle East'. In L. Fawcett (ed.), *International Relations of the Middle East*. Oxford: Oxford University Press: 380–399.

Howeidy, A. (2015). 'Matariyya, Egypt's New Theatre of Dissent'. *Middle East Research and Information Project* (MERIP), April. Available at: https://merip.org/2015/06/matariyya-egypts-new-theater-of-dissent/. Accessed September 2020.

Hudson, M.C. (2014). 'Arab Politics after the Uprisings'. In *Routledge Handbook of the Arab Spring*. London: Routledge: 28–38.

Human Rights Watch (2012). 'Egypt: Military Power Grab Creates Conditions for Abuse. Decrees Embed Armed Forces' Role in Law Enforcement'. Available at: https://www.hrw.org/news/2012/06/21/egypt-military-power-grab-creates-conditions-abuse. Accessed Aprill 2024.

Human Rights Watch (2014). 'Egypt: Painting "Terrorism" with a Very Broad Brush'. Available at: https://www.hrw.org/news/2014/05/05/egypt-painting-terrorism-very-broad-brush. Accessed March 2019.

Human Rights Watch (2016). 'Egypt: 7,400 Civilians Tried In Military Courts'. Available at: https://www.hrw.org/news/2016/04/13/egypt-7400-civilians-tried-military-courts. Accessed April 2024.

Human Rights Watch (2019). 'World Report 2019'. Available at: https://www.hrw.org/world-report/2019/country-chapters/egypt. Accessed May 2024.

Human Rights Watch (2020). 'IMF: Demand Transparency for Egypt Military's Firms'. Available at: https://www.hrw.org/news/2020/11/30/imf-demand-transparency-egypt-militarys-firms. Accessed December 2020.

Huntington, S.P. (1991). *The Third Wave: Democratisation in the Late Twentieth Century*. Norman, OK: University of Oklahoma Press.

Hurd, I. (1999). 'Legitimacy and Authority in International Politics'. *International Organization*, 53 (2): 379–408.

Hussein, E. and C. De Martino (2019). 'Egypt's Military Post-2011: Playing Politics without Internal Cracks'. *Contemporary Arab Affairs*, 12: 55–74.

Ibrahim, S.E. and H. Lofgren (1995). 'Successful Adjustment and Declining Governance. The Case of Egypt'. *Public Sector Development Department Paper n.8 World Bank*. Available at: https://documents1.worldbank.org/curated/fr/236971492969652301/pdf/multi0page.pdf. Accessed February 2021.

IFPRI (International Food Policy Research Institute) (2013). 'Food Security and Nutritional Status in Egypt Worsening Amidst Economic Challenges'. Available at: https://www.ifpri.org/news-release/food-security-and-nutritional-status-egypt-worsening-amidst-economic-challenges. Accessed May 2024.

Imad, Abdul Ghani (2019). 'Post-Islamism: Ideological Delusions and Sociological Realities'. *Contemporary Arab Affairs*, 3 September, 12 (3): 3–20.

IMF (International Monetary Fund) (2007). 'Arab Republic of Egypt – 2007 Article IV Consultation, Preliminary Conclusions of the IMF Mission'. Available at: https://www.imforg/en/News/Articles/2015/09/28/04/52/mcs091207. Accessed June 2024.

IMF (International Monetary Fund) (2015–2019). 'Inflation Consumer Price Egypt'. Available at: https://data.worldbank.org/indicator/FP.CPI.TOTL.ZG?end=2022&locations=EG&start=2010. Accessed March 2023.

IMF (International Monetary Fund) (2016). 'IMF Executive Board Approves US$12 billion Extended Arrangement Under the Extended Fund Facility for Egypt'. Available at: https://www.imf.org/en/News/Articles/2016/11/11/PR16501-Egypt-Executive-Board-Approves-12-billion-Extended-Arrangement. Accessed February 2021.

IMF (International Monetary Fund) (2018). 'Egypt Moving Forward: Key Challenges and Opportunities'. IMF Country Focus. Available at: https://www.imf.org/en/News/Articles/2018/07/16/na071618-egypt-moving-forward-key-challenges-and-opportunities. Accessed April 2020.

IMF (International Monetary Fund) (2019). 'Fourth Review Under the Extended Arrangement Under the Extended Fund Facility. April 2019'. Available at: https://www.imfconnect.org/content/dam/Compact%20with%20Africa/Countries/egypt/1EGYEA2019001.pdf. Accessed March 2021.

International Monetary Fund (2020). 'Inflation rate, average consumer prices'. Available at:https://www.imf.org/external/datamapper/PCPIPCH@WEO/OEMDC/ADVEC/WEOWORLD/EGY. Accessed March 2021.

ILO (International Labour Organization). (2014). 'Labour Force Statistics database (LFS). ILOSTAT. Available at: https://data.worldbank.org/indicator/SL.UEM.TOTL.NE.ZS?locations=EG. Accessed February 2024.

ILO (International Labour Organization (2014–2022). 'Data on Country Profiles'. Available at: https://ilostat.ilo.org/data/country-profiles/. Accessed March 2021.

ILO (International Labour Organization). 2017. 'Qanun Raqam 213 li-Sana 2017 [Law No. 213 of 213]'. Available at: www.ilo.org/dyn/natlex/docs/ELECTRONIC/107361/132117/F1934495720/213.pdf. Accessed August 2020.

IRIS (Institute de Relations Internationales et Strategiques) (2017). 'The Impact of Military Consolidation on Long-Term Resilience'. Available at: https://www.iris-france.org/wp-content/uploads/2017/05/Obs-ProspHuma-EGYPT-2020-May-2017.pdf. Accessed March 2021.

Isaac, S.K. (2015). 'Gulf Assistance Funds Post-2011: Allocation, Motivation and Influence'. European Institute of the Mediterranean IEMed. Available at: https://www.iemed.org/publication/gulf-assistance-funds-post-2011-allocation-motivation-and-influence/. Accessed May 2024.

Ismail, S. (1998). 'Confronting the Other: Identity, Culture, Politics and Conservative Islamism in Egypt'. *International Journal of Middle East Studies*, 30 (2): 199–225.

Ismail, S. (2006a). *Political Life in Cairo's New Quarters: Encountering the Everyday State* (NED-New edition). Minneapolis, MN: University of Minnesota Press.

Ismail, S. (2006b). *Rethinking Islamist Politics: Culture, the State and Islamism*. London: I.B.Tauris.

Ismail, S. (2012). 'The Egyptian Revolution against the Police'. *Social Research*, 79 (2): 435–462.

Janowitz, M. (1977). *Military Institutions and Coercion in the Developing Nations: The Military in the Political Development of New Nations*. Chicago: University of Chicago Press.

Johnson, C. (1964). *Revolution and the Social System*. Stanford, CA: Stanford University Press.
Joya, A. (2020). *The Roots of Revolt: A Political Economy of Egypt from Nasser to Mubarak*. Cambridge: Cambridge University Press.
Kailitz, S. (2013). 'Classifying Political Regimes Revisited: Legitimation and Durability'. *Democratization*, 20 (1): 39–60.
Kailitz, S. (2015). 'Regime Legitimation, Elite Cohesion and the Durability of Autocratic Regime Types'. *International Political Science Review*, 38 (3): 332–348.
Kailitz, S., and Stockemer, D. (2017). 'Regime legitimation, elite cohesion and the durability of autocratic regime types'. *International Political Science Review*, 38(3), 332–348.
Kandil, H. (2012). *Soldiers, Spies and Statesmen: Egypt's Road to Revolt*. London: Verso.
Kandil, H. (2016). *The Power Triangle: Military, Security and Politics in Regime Change*. Oxford: Oxford University Press.
Kaufman, S.J. (2001). *Modern Hatreds: The Symbolic Politics of Ethnic War*. Ithaca, NY: Cornell University Press.
Kelly, I. (2016). *Regime Elites and Transition from Authoritarian Rule: A Comparative Analysis of the Tunisia and Egyptian Uprisings*. Unpublished PhD Thesis, Dublin City University.
Ketchley, N. (2014).*Contentious Politics and the 25th January Egyptian Revolution*. Unpublished PhD thesis, LSE.
Khaldun, I. (1958). *The Muqadimmah: An Introduction of History*, trans. Franz Rosenthal. London: Routledge.
Khalid, M. (2020). 'Egypt's Emboldened Military Courts'. *Sada*. Available at: https://carnegieendowment.org/sada/2020/06/egypts-emboldened-military-courts?lang=en. Accessed May 2024.
Khalifa, M.A. (2015). 'Evolution of Informal Settlements Upgrading Strategies in Egypt: From Negligence to Participatory Development'. *Ain Shams Engineer Journal*, 6 (4): 1151–1159.
Khalil, J. (2017). 'Egypt's Real Estate Boom has Turned from Economic Safe Haven to Rubble'. Pulitzer Center. Available at: https://pulitzercenter.org/reporting/egypts-real-estate-boom-turned-economic-safe-haven-rubble. Accessed February 2021.
King, S.J. (2009). *The New Authoritarianism in the Middle East and North Africa*. Bloomington, IN: Indiana University Press.
Kingsley, P. (2014). 'Egypt's Atheists Number 866 Precisely'. *Guardian*. Available at: https://www.theguardian.com/world/2014/dec/12/egypt-highest-number-atheists-arab-world-866. Accessed March 2020.
Kingsley, P. (2015). 'Egypt's War on Atheism'. Ahram Online. Available at: http://english.ahram.org.eg/NewsContent/1/151/120204/Egypt/Features/Egypts-war-on-atheism.aspx. Accessed April 2020.
Kirkpatrick, D. (2013). 'Ousted General in Egypt is Back, as Islamists' foe', New York Times, 30 October. Available at: https://www.nytimes.com/2013/10/30/world/middleeast/ousted-general-in-egypt-is-back-as-islamists-foe.html?pagewanted=all. Accessed May 2020.

Kneuer, M. (2013). 'Die Suche nach Legitimität: Außenpolitik als Legitimationsstrategie auto- kratischer Regime'. *Politische Vierteljahresschrift*, special issue (47): 205–236.

Koella, J.C. (2003). 'The Impact of Interest Groups and New Media Framing on Public Opinion: The Rise and Fall of the Clinton Health Care Plan'. Paper presented at the Annual Meeting of the Midwest Association for Public Opinion Research, October.

Korany, B. (1998). 'Restricted Democratization from Above: Egypt'. In B. Korany, R. Brynen and P. Noble (eds), *Political Liberalization and Democratization in the Arab World*. Boulder: Lynne Rienner Publishers.

Korany, B., M. El-Sayyad and B. Serag (2016). 'A Ticking Bomb. Egypt's Youth Unemployment'. *SAHWA Policy Paper, 06, 2016*. AUC Forum, The American University in Cairo.

Koubaa S.M. (2012). 'Democratic transition in Tunisia: A Rewarding Path'. *Security and Human Rights*, 23 (3): 223–226.

Kurer, T. et al. (2019). 'Economic Grievances and Political Protest'. *European Journal of Political Research*, 58 (3): 866–892.

Laclau, E. (1977). *Politics and Ideology in Marxist Theory*. London: NLB.

Lacroix, S. (2012). *Sheikhs and Politicians: Inside the New Egyptian Salafism*. Doha: Brookings Doha Center Publications.

Lacroix, S. (2013). 'Symbolic System, Power and Politics: Understanding the Egyptian Muslim Brotherhood as an Islamic Socio-Political actor'. Available at: KSP_Paper_Award_Spring_2013_Neron-Bancel_Arthur.pdf (sciencespo.fr). Accessed January 2021.

Lacroix, S. (2016). 'The Salafi's Pragmatism: The Politics of Hizb al-Nour'. Carnegie Endowment for International Peace. Available at: https://carnegieendowment.org/files/Brief-Lacroix_al-Nour_Party.pdf. Accessed February 2021.

Landau, M.J., D. Sullivan and J. Greenberg (2009). 'Evidence that Self-Referent Motives and Metaphoric Framing Interact to Influence Political and Social Attitudes'. *Psychological Studies*, 20: 1421–1427.

Lawrence R.G. (2000) 'Game-Framing the Issues: Tracking the Strategy Frame in Public Policy News'. *Political Communication*, 17 (2): 93–114.

Leber, A., C. Carothers and M. Reichert (2023). 'When Can Dictators Go It Alone? Personalization and Oversight'. *Authoritarian Regimes. Politics & Society*, 51 (1): 66–107.

Leoussi, A.S. and S. Grosby (eds) (2007). *Nationalism and Ethnosymbolism: History, Culture and Ethnicity in the Formation of Nations*. Edinburgh: Edinburgh University Press.

Levi, M. and A. Sacks (2009). 'Legitimating Beliefs: Sources and Indicators'. *Regulation & Governance*, 3: 311–333.

Levitsky, S. and L. Way (2002). 'The Rise of Competitive Authoritarianism'. *Journal of Democracy*, 13 (2): 51–65.

Levitsky, S. and L. Way (2010). *Competitive Authoritarianism Hybrid Regimes after the Cold War*. Cambridge: Cambridge University Press.

Linz, J.J. (1975). *Totalitarian and Authoritarian Regimes*. Boulder, CO: Lynne Rienner Publishers.

Linz, J.J. (1988). 'Legitimacy of Democracy and the Socioeconomic System'. In M. Dogan (ed.), *Comparing Pluralist Democracies: Strains on Legitimacy*. Boulder, CO: Westview Press.

Linz, J.J. and Stephan, A.C. (2013). *Problems of Democratic Transition and Consolidation: Southern Europe, South America and Post-Communist Europe*. Baltimore, MD: Johns Hopkins University Press.

Lipset, S.M. (1959). 'Some Social Requisites of Demcracy: Economic Development and Political Legitimacy'. *The American Political Science Review*, 53 (1): 69–105.

Lipset, S.M. (1960). *Political Man*. New York: Doubleday.

Lipset, S.M. (1984). 'Social Conflict, Legitimacy, and Democracy'. In William Connolly (ed.), *Legitimacy and the state*. New York: New York University Press: 88–103.

Lipset, S.M. (1994). 'The Social Requisites of Democracy Revisited: 1993 Presidential Address'. *American Sociological Review*, 59 (1): 1–22.

Lipset, S.M. and S. Rokkan (1967). *Party Systems and Voter Alignments: Cross-National Perspectives*. New York: The Free Press.

Lipton, D. (2018). 'Statement by IMF First Deputy Managing Director David Lipton on Meeting with Egypt's President'. *International Monetary Fund*, 18 (164). Available at: https://www.imf.org/en/News/Articles/2018/05/08/pr18164-statement-by-imf-fdmd-david-lipton-on-meeting-with-egypt-president. Accessed February 2021.

Listhaug, O. (1998). 'Confidence in Political Institutions: Norway 1982–1996'. Paper presented to the research seminar of the Centre for Nordic Policy Studies, University of Aberdeen. Available at: https://journals.sagepub.com/doi/10.1177/000169938402700202. Accessed September 2020.

Loewe, M., T. Zintl and A. Houdret (2020). 'The Social Contract as a Tool of Analysis: Introduction to the Special Issue on Framing the Evolution of New Social Contracts in the Middle East and North African countries'. *World Development* 145: 1–16.

Lorenzon, F. (2016) 'The Political Economy of Food Subsidies in Egypt: Reforms and Strengthening of Social Protection', *The Public Sphere: Journal of Public Policy*, 4 (1): 105–133.

Lucca-Silveira, M. (2016). 'The Subject of Social Justice: A Defence of the Basic Structure of Society'. *Brazilian Political Science Review*, 12 (2): 1–26.

Lunenburg, F.C. (2012). 'Power and Leadership: An Influence Process'. *International Journal of Management, Business and Administration*, 15 (1): 1–9.

Lust-Okar, E. (2005). *Structuring Conflict in the Arab World: Incumbents, Opponents and Institutions*. Cambridge: Cambridge University Press.

Lust-Okar, E. (2006). 'Elections under Authoritarianism: Preliminary Lessons from Jordan'. *Democratization*, 13 (3): 455–470.

Lust-Okar, E. (2009). 'Competitive Clientelism in the Middle East'. *Journal of Democracy*, 28 (3): 122–135.

Lynch, M. (2013). *Origins and Development of Authoritarian and Single Party States*. London: Hodder Education.

Makara, M. (2013). 'Coup-Proofing, Military Defection, and the Arab Spring'. *Democracy and Security*, 9 (4): 334–359.

Magaloni, B. (2006). *Voting for Autocracy: Hegemonic Party Survival and its Demise in Mexico*. Cambridge: Cambridge University Press.

Magaloni, B. (2008). 'Credible Power-Sharing and the Longevity of Authoritarian Rule'. *Comparative Political Studies*, 20 (10): 1–27.

Maged, M. (2019). 'Hosni Mubarak Talks on 6th October War Memories in his Latest Appearance'. *Egypt Independent*. Available at: https://egyptindependent.com/video-hosni-mubarak-talks-about-6th-of-october-war-memories-in-his-latest-appearance/. Accessed November 2019.

Malashenko, A. (2013). 'Russia and the Arab Spring'. Carnegie Moscow Centre. Available at: https://carnegiemoscow.org/2013/10/01/russia-and-arab-spring-pub-53137. Carnegie Endowment for International Peace. Accessed August 2020.

Malthus, T. (1798). *An Essay on the Principle of Population*. Printed for J. Johnson, in St. Paul's Church-Yard.

Mandour, M. (2017). 'Sisi's Expanding Authority'. Carnegie Endowment for International Peace, October. Available at: Sisi's Expanding Authority – Carnegie Endowment for International Peace.

Mandour, M. (2019). 'Generalissimo Sisi', Sada Carnegie Endowmrnt for International Peace February. Available at: https://carnegieendowment.org/sada/78363. Accessed April 2024.

Mandour, M. (2024). *Egypt under Sisi: A Nation on the Edge*. London: Bloomsbury.

Mansfield, E., H. Milner and P. Rosendorff (2000). 'Free to Trade: Democracies, Autocracies, and International Trade', *American Political Science Review*, 94 (2): 305–321.

Mansour, S. (2009). 'Enough is Not Enough: Achievements and Shortcomings of Kefaya, the Egyptian Movement for Change'. In Maria J. Stephan (ed.), *Civilian Jihad: Nonviolent Struggle, Democratization, and Governance in the Middle East*. New York: Palgrave Macmillan: 205–218.

Mansour, S. (2015). 'Stifling the Public Sphere: Media and Civil Society in Egypt'. *National Endowment for Democracy*. Available at: https://www.ned.org/wp-content/uploads/2015/10/Stifling-the-Public-Sphere-Media-Civil-Society-Egypt-Forum-NED.pdf. Accessed February 2020.

Mansour, D. (2016). 'The Socioeconomics of Exclusion: Re-Questioning Citizenship in Relation to Social Justice in Post-Arab Spring Egypt'. *Policy Brief on Socio-Economic Rights in Egypt*. Available at: euspring_template_-pb_eg_final.pdf (pitt.edu). Accessed May 2020.

Marks, M. and J. Abdelhalim (2018). 'Introduction: Identity, Jeopardy and Moral Dilemmas in Conducting Research in "Risky" Environments'. *Contemporary Social Science*, 13 (3–4): 305–322.

Marshall, M.G. and K. Jaggers (2013). 'Polity IV Project: Political Regime'. *Characteristics and Transitions, 1800–2010*. Available at: https://www.systemicpeace.org/polity/polity4.html.

Marshall, S. (2015). 'The Egyptian Armed Forces and the Remaking of an Economic Empire'. Carnegie Middle East Center. Available at: https://carnegie-mec.org/2015/04/15/egyptian-armed-forces-and-remaking-of-economic-empire-pub-59726. Accessed February 2021.

Marshall, S. and J. Stacher (2012). 'Egypt's Generals and Transitional Capital'. *Middle East Research and Information Project* 262. Available at: https://merip.org/2012/03/egypts-generals-and-transnational-capital/. Accessed August 2020.

Marx, K. and F. Engels (1959). *Basic Writings on Politics and Philosophy*. Garden City, NY: Doubleday & Company.
Massoud, M.F. (2013). *Law's Fragile State: Colonial, Authoritarian, and Humanitarian Legacies in Sudan*. Cambridge: Cambridge University Press.
Matthes, J. (2012). 'Framing Politics: An Integrative Approach'. *American Behavioural Scientist*, 56 (3): 247–259.
Mattheson, C. (1987). 'Weber and the Classifications of Forms of Legitimacy'. *The British Journal of Sociology*, 38 (2): 199–215.
Mazepus, H. et al. (2016). 'A Comparative Study of Legitimation Strategies in Hybrid Regimes'. *Policy Studies*, 37 (4): 350–369.
McClelland, D.C. (1970). 'The Two Faces of Power'. *Journal of International Affairs*, 24: 29–47.
McClelland, D.C. (1975). *Power: The Inner Experience*. Nowy Jork: Wiley.
McCullough, A. (2015). *The Legitimacy of States and Armed Non-State Actors: Topic Guide*. Birmingham, UK: GSDRC, University of Birmingham.
McLoughlin, C. (2014). 'When Does Service Delivery Improve the Legitimacy of a Fragile or Conflict-Affected State?' *Governance*, 28 (1): 341–356.
McLoughlin, C. (2015). 'When Does Service Delivery Improve the Legitimacy of a Fragile or Conflict-Affected State?' *Governance*, 28 (1): 341–356.
Mead, N. and J. Maner (2010). 'The Essential Tension between Leadership and Power: When Leaders Sacrifice Group Goals for Self-Interest'. *Journal of Personality and Social Psychology*, 99 (3): 482–497.
Meddeb, H. (2019). 'Ennahda's Uneasy Exit From Political Islam'. Carnegie Middle East Center. Available at: https://carnegie-mec.org/2019/09/05/ennahda-s-uneasy-exitfrom-political-islam-pub-79789?fbclid=IwAR19mRZeOMgi9 2nC6sxDuUJHm_0xHmvsmy_2XRCTe_3an0ZZjMHp6OFhIs. Accessed December 2020.
Meijer, R. (2012). 'The Muslim Brotherhood and the Political: An Exercise in Ambiguity'. In Edwin Bakker and Roel Meijer (eds), *The Muslim Brotherhood in Europe*. New York: Hurst/Columbia University Press: 291–316.
Meijer, R., J.M. Sater and Z.R. Babar (2020). *Routledge Handbook of Citizenship in the Middle East and North Africa*. London, Routledge.
Meital, Y. (2006). 'The Struggle over Political Order in Egypt: The 2005 Elections'. *Middle East Journal*, 60 (2): 257–279.
Mellor, N. (2018). *Voice of the Muslim Brotherhood: Da'wa, Discourse and Political Communication*. London: Routledge.
Merkel, W. and J. Gerschewski (2011). 'Autocracies at Critical Junctures: A Model for the Study of Dictatorial Regimes'. *Schlossplatz*, 3 (11): 14–17.
Middle East Eye (2016). 'Ennahda leader Ghannouchi: "We are Muslim Democrats, not Islamists"'. *Middle East Eye*. Available at: https://www.middleeasteye.net/news/ennahda-leader-ghannouchi-we-are-muslim-democrats-not-islamists. Accessed February 2020.
Middle East Eye (2018). 'Rabaa: The Massacre that Ended the Arab Spring', *Middle East Eye*. Available at: https://www.middleeasteye.net/news/rabaa-massacre-ended-arab-spring. Accessed May 2023.

Middle East Institute (2013). 'SCAF and the Muslim Brotherhood. Middle East Institute'. Available at: https://www.mei.edu/publications/scaf-and-muslim-brotherhood. Accessed March 2021.

Middle East Monitor (2019). 'Egypt's Sisi Prohibits Travel of Senior Officials, Al-Azhar Grand Imam'. Middle East Monitor. Available at: https://www.middleeastmonitor.com/20190116-egypts-sisi-prohibits-travel-of-senior-officials-al-azhar-grand-imam/. Accessed February 2020.

Miller, M.M. (1997). 'Frame Mapping and Analysis of News Coverage of Contentious Issues'. *Social Science Computer Review*, 15 (4). 367–378.

Ministry of Defence (2020–2021). 'Egyptian Armed Forces' website'. Available at: https://www.mod.gov.eg/ModWebSite/Default.aspx. Accessed January 2020.

Ministry of Finance (2015–2017). Monthly/ Yearly reports. Available at: https://mof.gov.eg/en/archive/monthlyFinancialReport/general/Monthly%20Finance%20Report. Accessed May 2024.

Ministry of Planning and Economic Development (2019–2020). 'Executive Summary Financial Bulletin'. Available at: https://mped.gov.eg/AdminPanel/sharedfiles/d_2020-19.pdf. Accessed March 2023.

Ministry of Petroleum (up to 2020) 'Egypt's Fuel Subsidies Reform Development'. Available at: egyptoil-gas.com/reports/egypts-fuel-subsidy-reform-development/. Accessed May 2023.

Minsky, M. (1977). 'Thinking: Reasings in Cognitive Science, Frame theory'. In P.N. Johnson-Laird and P.C. Wason (eds), *Thinking Reasings in Cognitive Science*. Cambridge: Cambridge University Press: 355–376.

Mitchell, T. (2002). *Rule of Experts: Egypt, Techno-Politics, Modernity*. Berkeley, California: University of California Press.

Mittiga R. (2022). 'Political Legitimacy, Authoritarianism, and Climate Change'. *American Political Science Review*, 116 (3): 998–1011.

Moughira, M.A. (2015). *Les Armées Arabes et le Pouvoir d'Etat, Militaires du Peuple ou du Régime?* [Arab Armies and State Power, Militaries of the People or of the Regime?] Paris: Karthala.

Mohammed, A. (2015). 'Cairo's Metropolitan Landscape Segregation'. *Failed Architecture*. Available at: https://www.failedarchitecture.com/cairos-metropolitan-landscape-segregation-extreme/. Accessed February 2021.

Mohammed, N. et al. (2023) 'Informal Employment in Egypt, Morocco and Tunisia: What Can we Learn to Boost Inclusive Growth?' World Bank.

Momani, B. (2003). *IMF-Egyptian Debt Negotiations*. Cairo: American University in Cairo Press.

Monier, E.I. and A. Ranko (2013). 'The Fall of the Muslim Brotherhood: Implications for Egypt', *Middle East Policy*, 20 (4): 111–123.

Moody's (2013). 'Egypt Credit Rating'. Available at: https://tradingeconomics.com/egypt/rating. Accessed May 2024.

Moody's (2018). 'Egypt Credit Rating'. Available at: https://tradingeconomics.com/egypt/rating. Accessed March 2023.

Moody's (2024). 'Moody's Changes Outlook on Egypt to Positive, Affirms Caa1 Ratings'. Available at: https://ratings.moodys.com/ratings-news/416475. Accessed May 2024.

Moore, M. (2008). 'Between Coercion and Contract: Competing Narratives around Taxation and Governance'. In D. Bautigam, o-H Fjieldstad and M. Moore (eds), *Taxation and State Building in Developing Countries*. Cambridge: Cambridge University Press.

Morlino, L. (2009). 'Are There Hybrid Regimes? Or Are They Just an Optical Illusion?' *European Political Science Review*, 1 (2): 273–296.

Morsy, A. (2013). 'The Grand Sheikh and the President'. Middle East Institute. Available at: https://www.mei.edu/publications/grand-sheikh-and-president. Accessed February 2020.

Moustafa, T. (2000). 'Conflict and Cooperation between the State and Religious Institutions in Contemporary Egypt'. *International Journal of Middle East Studies*, 32 (1): 3–22.

MSIT (Ministry of Supply and Internal Trade) (2014). Available at: http://www.msit.gov.eg. Accessed May 2024.

Muasher, M. (2013). 'Freedom and Bread Go Together'. *Finance and Development International Monetary Fund*, Available at: https://www.imf.org/external/pubs/ft/fandd/2013/03/pdf/muasher.pdf. Accessed December 2020.

Mueller, H. (2015). 'Insulation or Patronage: Political Institutions and Bureaucratic Efficiency'. *The B.E. Journal of Economic Analysis & Policy*, 15 (3): 961–996.

Munson, Z. (2001). 'Islamic Mobilization: Social Movement Theory and the Egyptian Muslim Brotherhood'. *The Sociological Quarterly*, 42 (4): 487–510.

Nagarajan, K.V. (2013). 'Egypt's Political Economy and the Downfall of the Mubarak Regime'. *International Journal of Humanities and Social Science*, 3 (10): 21–39.

Nasralla, S. (2014). 'Tempers Fray, Prices Rise as Egypt Cuts Fuel Subsidies'. *Reuters*. Available at: https://www.reuters.com/article/us-egypt-subsidies/tempers-fray-prices-rise-as-egypt-cuts-fuel-subsidies-idUSKBN0FB0N920140706. Accessed March 2020.

Nasser, G.A. (1955). *Egypt's Liberation: The Philosophy of the Revolution*. Washington DC: Public Affairs Press.

Nelson, R.M. and J.M. Sharp (2013). 'Egypt and the IMF: Overview and Issue for Congress'. Congressional Research Service. Available at: https://fas.org/sgp/crs/mideast/R43053.pdf. Accessed May 2024.

Newman, S. (2004). 'The Place of Power in Political Discourse'. *International Political Science Review*, 25 (2): 139–157.

Noakes, J.A. and H. Johnston (2005). *Frames of Protests: Social Movements and the Framing Perspective*. Washington, DC: Rowman & Littlefield Publishers.

Noll, J. (2017). 'Ägyptens Militär zementiert seine ökonomische Macht: Die wirtschaftliche Expansion der Streitkräfte verhindert Strukturreformen im Land'. Stiftung Wissenschaft und Politik. Available at: https://www.swp-berlin.org/fileadmin/contents/products/aktuell/2015A47_rll_noj.pdf. Accessed February 2021.

Noll, J. (2019). 'Fighting Corruption or Protecting the Regime? Egypt's Administrative Control Authority'. POMED. Available at: https://pomed.org/report-corruption-egypts-administrative-control-authority/. Accessed February 2021.

Nordlinger, E. (1977). *Soldiers in Politics: Military Coups and Governments*. Englewood Cliffs, NJ: Prentice-Hall.

Obaid, N. (2017). 'Muslim Brotherhood: A Failure in Political Evolution'. Harvard Kennedy School, Belfer Center for Science and International Affairs.

O'Leary, B. (1997). 'On the Nature of Nationalism: A Critical Appraisal of Ernest Gellner's Writings on Nationalism'. *British Journal of Political Science* (27): 191-222.

Olidort, J. (2015). 'Egypt's Elections (Part 2): Salafis Use Education to Campaign'. The Washington Institute for Near and East Politics. Available at: https://www.washingtoninstitute.org/policy-analysis/egypts-elections-part-2-salafis-use-education-campaign. Accessed January 2021.

Omelicheva, M.Y. (2016). 'Islam and Power Legitimation: Instrumentalisation of Religion in Central Asian States'. *Contemporary Politics*, 22 (2): 144–163.

Ophuls, W. (1977). *Ecology and the Politics of Scarcity: Prologue to a Political Theory of the Steady State*. San Francisco: W.H. Freeman.

Ouaissa, R. (2020). 'Algeria: Has the Hirak Failed Politically?' Rosa Luxemburg Stiftung. Available at: https://rosaluxna.org/publications/algeria-has-the-hirak-failed-politically/. Accessed May 2024.

Pan, Z. and G. Kosicki (1993). 'Framing Analysis: An Approach to News Discourse'. *Political Communication*, 10: 55–75.

Parreira, C. (2020). *The Art of Not Governing: Local Politics in Postwar Lebanon*. PhD Diss., Department of Political Science, Stanford University, Palo Alto, CA.

Parsons, T. (1963). 'On the Concept of Influence'. *Public Opinion Quarterly*, 27 (1): 37–62.

Patriotta, G.G. and F. Schultz (2011). 'Maintaining Legitimacy: Controversies, Orders of Worth and Public Justifications'. *Journal of Management Studies*, 48: 1804–1836.

Patterson, T.E. (1993). *Out of Order*. New York: Vintage.

Perthes, V. (2008). 'Is the Arab World Immune to Democracy?' *Survival*, 50 (6): 151–160.

Pevehouse, J.C. (2005). *Democracy from Above: Regional Organizations and Democratization*. Cambridge: Cambridge University Press.

Platteau, J.P. (2011). 'Political Instrumentalization of Islam and the Risk of Obscurantist Deadlock'. *World Development*, 39 (2): 243–260.

Polimeno, M.G. (2022). 'COP27 in Egypt: The Archipelago of Political Lies'. *The Loop, European Consortium for Political Research*. Available at: https://theloop.ecpr.eu/cop27-in-egypt-an-archipelago-of-political-and-environmental-lies/. Accessed May 2022.

Polity IV (2010). 'Political regime characteristics and transitions, 1800–2010'. Link available at: http://www.systemicpeace.org/polity/polity4.html. Accessed February 2020.

Polity Project V (2017). 'Global Report 2017 Conflict, Governance, and State Fragility'. *Center for Systemic Peace*. Available at: https://www.systemicpeace.org/vlibrary/GlobalReport2017.pdf. Accessed May 2024.

POMPES (2013). 'Egypt's Political Reset'. *Project on the Middle East*. Available at: https://pomeps.org/wp-content/uploads/2013/07/POMEPS_BriefBooklet20_Egypt_web.pdf. Accessed December 2019

Postel, C. (2007). *The Populist Vision*. Oxford: Oxford University Press.

Posusney, M.P. and M.P. Angrist (2005). *Authoritarianism in the Middle East: Regimes and Resistance*. Boulder, CO: Lynne Rienner Publishers.

Powell J. (2012) 'Determinants of Attempting and Outcome of Coups D'état'. *Journal of Conflict Resolution*, 56 (6): 1017–1040.

Pratt, N. and D. Rezk (2019). 'Securitizing the Muslim Brotherhood: State Violence and Authoritarianism in Egypt after the Arab Spring'. *Security Dialogue*, 50 (3): 239–256.

Priewasser, R. (2014). 'The Missing Revolution: El-Sisi's Presidency in the Light of the Army's Historical Role in Egypt'. *Journal of African Studies*, 13: 55–78.

Przeworski, A. (1986). 'Some Problems in the Study of the Transition to Democracy'. In G. O'Donnell et al. (eds), *Transitions from Authoritarian Rule: Prospects for Democracy*. Baltimore, MD: Johns Hopkins University Press.

Przeworski, A. and F. Limongi (1993). 'Political Regimes and Economic Growth'. *The Journal of Economic Perspectives*, 7 (3): 51–69.

Pridham, G. (1995). 'Democratic Transition and the International Environment'. In G. Pridham (ed.), *Transitions to Democracy: Comparative Perspectives from Southern Europe, Latin America and Eastern Europe*. Aldershot: Dartmouth.

Quinlivan, J. (1999). 'Coup-Proofing: Its Practice and Consequences in the Middle East'. *International Security*, 24 (2): 131–165.

Racimora, W. (2013). 'Salafist/Wahhabite Financial Support to Educational, Social and Religious Institutions'. Directorate-General for External Policies of the European Union. Available at: https://www.europarl.europa.eu/RegData/etudes/etudes/join/2013/457136/EXPO-AFET_ET(2013)457136_EN.pdf. Accessed January 2021.

Radnitz, S. (2012). 'Oil in the Family: Managing Presidential Succession in Azerbaijan'. *Democratization*, 19 (1): 60–77.

Rahbek, B. (2005). *Democratisation in the Middle East: Dilemmas and Perspectives*. Aarhus: Aarhus University Press.

Ramey, G. and V.A. Ramey (1995). 'Cross-Country Evidence on the Link Between Volatility and Growth'. *The American Economic Review*, 85 (5): 1138–1151.

Ranko, A. (2015). 'The State and the Brotherhood under Nasser and Sadat (1954–1981)'.p.). In A. Ranko (ed.), *The Muslim Brotherhood and its Quest for Hegemony in Egypt*. New York: Springer: 43–71.

Rasha, A. (2012). 'Mapping Digital Media: Egypt'. Open Society Foundation. Available at: https://www.opensocietyfoundations.org/uploads/9c6d2b03-8fb7-43e3-94a9-4ba2e00ff595/mapping-digital-media-egypt-20130823.pdf. Accessed May 2020.

Raz, J. (1985). 'Authority and Justification'. *Philosophy and Public Affairs*, 14 (1): 3–29.

Reiter, D. (2020). 'Avoiding the Coup-Proofing Dilemma: Consolidating Political Control While Maximizing Military Power'. *Foreign Policy Analysis*, 16 (3): 312–331

Reiter, D. and A.C. Stam (2003). 'Identifying the Culprit: Democracy, Dictatorship, and Dispute Initiation'. *American Political Science Review*, 97 (2): 333–337.

Richards, A. (1992). 'Higher Education in Egypt'. *Working Paper, World Bank*. Available at: documents1.worldbank.org/curated/ar/163341468770080097/pdf/multi-page.pdf. Accessed March 2023.

Ridge, H.M. (2022). 'Dismantling New Democracies: The Case of Tunisia. *Democratization*, 29 (8): 1539–1556.

Riker, W.H. (1962). *The Theory of Political Coalitions*. New Haven, CT: Yale University Press.

Ritchie, A. (2019). *Inclusive Populism: Creating Citizens in the Global Age*. Notre Dame, IN: University of Notre Dame Press.

Roll, S. (2016). 'Managing Change: How Egypt's Military Leadership Shaped the Transformation'. *Mediterranean Politics*, 21 (1): 23–43.

Roll, S. and L. Miehe (2019). 'Egypt Engulfed by Militarism'. *IEMed Mediterranean Handbook 2019*. Link available at: https://www.iemed.org/wp-content/uploads/2021/01/Egypt-Engulfed-by-Militarism.pdf. Accessed May 2024.

Runciman, D. (2003). 'Review of Legitimating Identities: The Self-Presentation of Rulers and Subjects', ed. R. Barker. *Contemporary Political Theory*, 2 (1): 113–115.

Russett, B. (2011). *Hegemony and Democracy*. New York: Routledge.

Rutherford, B. (2013). *Egypt after Mubarak: Liberalism, Islam, and Democracy in the Arab World*. Princeton, NJ: Princeton University Press.

Rutherford, B. (2018). 'Egypt's New Authoritarianism under Sisi'. *Middle East Institute*, 72 (2): 185–208.

Ryan, C.R. (2001). 'Political Strategies and Regime Survival in Egypt'. *Journal of Third World Studies*, 18 (2): 26–46.

Sabry, M. and D. Levy (2015). 'Egyptian Private Higher Education at a Crossroads'. *International Higher Education*, Fall 65: 13–15.

Sabry, S. (2005). 'The Social Aid and Assistance Programme of the Government of Egypt – A Critical Review'. *Environment and Urbanization*, 17 (2): 27–41.

Saif, I. (2013). 'The Private Sector in Post-Revolutionary Egypt'. Carnegie Middle East Center. Available at: https://carnegieendowment.org/files/egypt_private_sector1.pdf. Accessed December 2020.

Saikal, A. (2011). 'Authoritarianism, Revolution and Democracy: Egypt and Beyond'. *Australian Journal of International Affairs*, 65 (5): 530–544.

Saliba, I. (2014). 'Legitimacy Through Reforms: The Impact of Authoritarian Learing on Reforms and Legitimacy on Contested Regimes'. *Paper prepared for ECPR joint session in Salamanca*.

Sartori, G. (2001). 'The Party Effects of Electoral Systems'. In Larry Diamond and Richard Gunther (eds), *Political Parties and Democracy*. Baltimore, MD: Johns Hopkins University Press.

Saward, M. (1992). *Cooptive Politics and State Legitimacy*. Aldershot: Dartmouth Publishing.

Sayigh, Y. (2012). 'Above the State: The Officers' Republic in Egypt'. Carnegie Middle East Center. Available at: https://carnegie-mec.org/2012/08/01/above-state-officers-republic-in-egypt-pub-48972. Accessed January 2021.

References 263

Sayigh, Y. (2019). 'Owners of the Republic: An Anatomy of Egypt's Military Economy'. Carnegie Middle East Center. Available at: https://carnegie-mec.org/2019/11/18/owners-of-republic-anatomy-of-egypt-s-military-economy-pub-80325. Accessed January 2021.

Sayigh, Y. (2020). 'The Implications of Egypt's Military Economy'. Carnegie Middle East Center. Available at: https://carnegie-mec.org/2020/10/26/implications-of-egypt-s-military-economy-pub-83032. Accessed February 2021.

Schafer, I. (2015). 'The Tunisian Transition: Torn Between Democratic Consolidation and Neo-Conservatism in an Insecure Regional Context'. IEMED Papers, 25. Available at: https://www.idos-research.de/uploads/media/Tunisian_Transition_EuroMeSCo_Paper_25_Isabel_Schaefer.pdf. Accessed July 2020.

Scharpf, Fritz W. (1970). *Demokratietheorie Zwischen Utopie und Anpassung*. Konstanz: Universitätsverlag.

Schedler, A. (2002). 'Elections Without Democracy: The Menu of Manipulation'. *Journal of Democracy*, 13 (2): 36–50.

Schedler, A. (ed.) (2006). *Electoral Authoritarianism: The Dynamics of Unfree Competition*. Boulder, CO: Lynne Rienner.

Scheufele, D.A. (1999). 'Framing as a Theory of Media Effects'. *Journal of Communication*, 49: 103–122.

Schlumberger, O. (2000). 'The Arab Middle East and the Question of Democratization: Some Critical Remarks'. *Democratization*, 7 (4): 104–132

Schlumberger, O. (2010). 'Opening Old Bottles in Search of New Wine: On Non-democratic Legitimacy in the Middle East'. *Middle East Critique*, 19 (3): 233–250.

Schlumberger, O. and T. Matzke (2012). 'Path Toward Democracy? The Role of Economic Development'. *Swiss Political Science Review*, 18 (1): 105–109.

Schmitter, P.C. (2010). 'Micro-Foundations for the Science(s) of Politics: The 2009 Johan Skytte Prize Lecture'. *Scandinavian Political Studies*, 33 (3): 316–330.

Schweitzer, A. (1974). 'Theory and Political Charisma'. *Comparative Studies in Society and History*, 16 (2): 150–181.

Schweitzer, A. (1984). *The Age of Charisma*. Chicago: Nelson-Hall.

Sdralevich, C. et al. (2014). 'Subsidy Reforms in the Middle East and North Africa. Recent Progress and Challenges Ahead'. International Monetary Fund. Available at: _1403mcd.pdf. Accessed February 2021.

Seligson, M.A. (2002). 'The Impact of Corruption on Regime Legitimacy: A Comparative Study of Four Latin American Countries'. *Journal of Politics*, 64 (2): 408–433.

Shadmehr, M. (2014). 'Mobilization, Repression, and Revolution: Grievances and Opportunities in Contentious Politics'. *Journal of Politics*, 76 (3): 621–635.

Shahin, A.F. (2017). *The Quest for Legitimacy: The Egyptian State from Nasser to Sisi*. Unpublished PhD thesis, St Andrews University.

Shahira, A. (2021). 'Egypt's President Slices Bread Subsidies'. Al-Monitor, August. Available at: https://www.al-monitor.com/originals/2021/08/egypts-president-slices-bread-subsidies. Accessed September 2022.

Sharp, J.M. (2011). 'Egypt: The January 25 Revolution and Implications for U.S. Foreign Policy'. Congressional Research Service. Available at: https://www.refworld.org/reference/countryrep/uscrs/2011/en/78112. Accessed December 2020.

Shenker, J. (2008). 'Protests in the Smog'. *Guardian*. Available at: https://www.theguardian.com/commentisfree/2008/apr/07/protestsinthesmog. Accessed February 2021.

Shenker, J. (2016). *The Egyptians: A Radical History of Egypt's Unfinished Revolution*. New York: New Press.

Sherry, V. (1992). *Behind Closed Doors: Torture and Detention in Egypt*. A Middle East Watch Report. Human Rights Watch.

Sika, N. (2012). 'Youth Political Engagement in Egypt: From Abstention to Uprising'. *British Journal of Middle Eastern Studies*, 39 (2): 181–199.

Sika, N. (2019). 'Repression, Cooptation, and Movement Fragmentation in Authoritarian Regimes: Evidence from the Youth Movement in Egypt'. *Political Studies*, 67 (3), 676–692.

Sims, D. (2003). 'The Case of Cairo, Egypt'. UNHabitat Global Report on Human Settlements: Slums and Poverty in the City. University College London. Available at: https://www.ucl.ac.uk/dpu-projects/Global_Report/pdfs/Cairo.pdf. Accessed December 2020.

Sims, D. (2012). *Understanding Cairo: The Logic of a City Out of Control*. Cairo: American University in Cairo Press.

Singerman, D. (1996). *Avenues of Participation: Family, Politics, and Networks in Urban Quarters of Cairo*. Princeton, NJ: Princeton University Press.

Singerman, D. (2009). *Cairo Contested*. Cairo: American University in Cairo Press.

Slater, D. and S. Fenner (2011). 'State Power and Staying in Power: Infrastructural Mechanisms and Authoritarian Durability'. *Journal of International Affairs*, 65 (1): 15–29.

Smith, A. (1986). *The Ethnic Origins of Nations*. Malden, Blackwell Publishing.

Smith, A.D. (1991). *The Ethnic Origins of Nations*. Oxford: Wiley-Blackwell.

Smith, A.D. (1998). *Nationalism and Modernism: A Critical Survey of Recent Theories of Nations and Nationalism*. London: Routledge.

Smith, A.D. (2009). *Ethno-Symbolism and Nationalism: A Cultural Approach*. London: Routledge.

Smith, B. (2015). Resource Wealth as Rent Leverage: Rethinking the Oil-Stability Nexus. *Conflict Management and Peace Science*, 34 (6): 597–617.

Snow, D.A. and R.D. Benford (1988). 'Ideology, Frame Resonance and Participant Mobilization'. In B. Klandermans, H. Kriesi and S. Tarrow (eds), *International Social Movement Research 1*. London: JAI Press: 197–217.

Snow, D.A. et al. (2014). 'The Emergence, Development and Future of the Framing Perspective'. *Mobilization: An International Quarterly*, 19 (1): 23–45.

Snyder, R. and J. Mahoney (1999). 'The Missing Variable: Institutions and the Study of Regime Change'. *Comparative Politics*, 32 (1): 103–122.

Sokhey, S.W. and A.K. Yildirim (2012). 'Economic Liberalization and Political Moderation: The Case of Anti-System Parties'. *Party Politics*, 19 (2): 230–255.

Soliman, M. (2020). 'Egypt's Informal Economy: An Ongoing Cause of Unrest'. *Journal of International Affairs*, Columbia University. Available at: https://

jia.sipa.columbia.edu/egypts-informal-economy-ongoing-cause-unrest. Accessed September 2020.
Spencer, M.E. (1973). 'What is Charisma?' *The British Journal of Sociology*, 24 (3): 341–354.
Springborg, R. (2007). 'The Middle East's Democracy Gap: Causes and Consequences'. *The Brown Journal of World Affairs*, 13 (2): 233–245
Springborg, R. (2015). 'President Sisi's Delegative Authoritarianism'. Instituto Affari Internazionale. Available at: https://www.iai.it/sites/default/files/iaiwp1526.pdf. Accessed May 2024.
Springborg, R. (2017). 'The rewards of failure: Persisting military rule in Egypt'. *British Journal of Middle Eastern Studies*, 44 (4): 478–496.
Springborg, R. (2020). 'Sisi's Egypt Moves from Military Economy to Family Firm'. ISPI. Available at: https://www.ispionline.it/en/pubblicazione/sisis-egypt-moves-military-economy-family-firm-28504. Accessed March 2021.
Springborg, R. (2022). 'Egypt is Backing Private Schools, While Public Education is Starved of Funds'. *Middle East Eye*, May. Available at: https://www.middleeasteye.net/opinion/egypt-public-education-neglected-backing-private-schools. Accessed February 2022.
Stacher, J. (2004). 'Parties Over: The Demise of Egypt's Opposition Parties'. *British Journal of Middle Eastern Studies*, 31: 215–233.
Stacher, J. (2011). 'Egypt without Mubarak'. *Middle East Research and Information Project*. Available at: http://www.merip.org/mero/mero040711.
Stacher, J. (2020). *Watermelon Democracy: Egypt's Turbulent Transition*. Syracuse, New York: Syracuse University Press.
Standard & Poor's (2016). 'Research Update: Arab Republic of Egypt Outlook Revised to Negative; "B-/B" Ratings Affirmed'. Standard and Poor's. Available at: https://disclosure.spglobal.com/ratings/en/regulatory/article/-/view/sourceId/20020680. Accessed May 2024.
State Information Service (2015). 'Speech by H.E. President Abdel Fattah El Sisi at the Inauguration Ceremony of the New Suez Canal'. Available at: https://beta.sis.gov.eg/en/presidency/speeches-and-interviews/speech-by-he-president-abdel-fattah-el-sisi-at-the-inauguration-ceremony-of-the-new-suez-canal/ Accessed January 2021.
State Information Service (2020a). 'Al-Azhar's Int'l Conference on Renewal of Islamic Thought'. Available at: https://www.sis.gov.eg/Story/143554/Al-Azhar%E2%80%99s-Int%E2%80%99l-Conference-on-Renewal-of-Islamic-Thought?lang=en-us. Accessed March 2020.
State Information Service (2020b). 'New Administrative Capital'. Available at: https://www.sis.gov.eg/section/352/5238?lang=en-us. Accessed May 2020.
State Information Service (2023). 'CAPMAS: Monthly Inflation Rate Up by 2% in July'. Available at: https://sis.gov.eg/Story/185139/CAPMAS-Monthly-inflation-rate-up-by-2%25-in-July?lang=en-us. Accessed May 2024.
State Information Service (2024). 'Egypt, UAE Sign Historic Deal to Develop Ras El Hekma Area on Northern Coast. Egypt'. Available at: https://www.sis.gov.eg/Story/191740/Egypt%2C-UAE-Sign-Historic-Deal-to-Develop-Ras-El-Hekma-Area-on-Northern-Coast?lang=en-us. Accessed May 2024.

Stein, E. (2012). 'After the Arab Spring: Power shift in the Middle East?' In Nicholas Kitchen (ed.), *Revolutionary Egypt: Promises and Perils*. London School of Economics and Political Science.
Stepputtat, F. and J. Larsen (2015). 'Global Political Ethnography: A Methodological Approach to Studying Global Politicly Regimes'. Danish Institute for International Studies. Available at: https://www.diis.dk/files/media/publications/publikationer_2015/wp2015-01.pdf.
Stinchcombe, Arthur L. 1968. *Constructing Social Theories*. New York: Harcourt, Brace and World.
Storm, L (2022). 'Political Dynamics in the Arab World and the Future of Ideologies. *IEMed, Mediterranean Handbook*.
Strömbäck, J. and D.V. Dimitrova (2006). 'Political and Media Systems Matter: A Comparison of Election News Coverage in Sweden and the United States'. *The Harvard International Journal of Press/Politics*, 11 (4): 131–147.
Strömbäck, J. and O.G. Luengo (2008). 'Polarized Pluralist and Democratic Corporatist Models: A Comparison of Election News Coverage in Spain and Sweden'. *The International Communication Gazette*, 70 (6): 547–562.
Strömbäck, J. and A. Shehata (2007). 'Structural Biases in British and Swedish Election News Coverage'. *Journalism Studies*, 8 (5): 798–812.
Supreme Electoral Committee (2012). 'Candidates for the Presidency of the Arab Republic of Egypt 2012'. Available at: https://web.archive.org/web/20120505151311/https://www.elections.eg/index.php/candidacy/applicants. Accessed October 2019.
Suez Canal Authority (2021). 'Egypt Maritime Transport: Suez Canal Revenues'. Available at: https://www.ceicdata.com/en/egypt/maritime-transport-revenues/maritime-transport-suez-canal-revenues. Accessed March 2021.
Suez Canal Authority (2022). 'New Suez Canal'. Government of Egypt. Available at: https://www.suezcanal.gov.eg/English/About/SuezCanal/Pages/NewSuezCanal.aspx. Accessed February 2021.
Svolik, M.W. (2008). 'Power-Sharing and Leadership Dynamics in Authoritarian Regimes'. SSRN. Available at: https://papers.ssrn.com/sol3/papers.cfm?abstract_id=860744.
Svolik, M.W. (2012).*The Politics of Authoritarian Rule*. Cambridge: Cambridge University Press.
Szelenyi, I. (2016). 'Weber's Theory of Domination and Post-Communist Capitalisms'. *Theoretical Sociology*, 45 (1): 1–24.
Tadros, M. (2007). 'State welfare in Egypt Since Adjustment: Hegemonic Control with a Minimalist Role'. *Review of African Political Economy*, 33 (108): 237–254.
Tallberg, J., M. Lundgren, T. Sommerer and T. Squatrito (2020). 'Why International Organizations Commit to Liberal Norms'. *International Studies Quarterly*, 64 (3): 626–640.
Tamer, H. (2017). 'Awaiting the Promise of the Suez Canal Zone', *Business Monthly*, American Chamber of Commerce in Egypt. Available at: http://bit.ly/2krePzR. Accessed February 2021.
Tammam, H. (2011). Islamists and the Egyptian Revolution. *Egypt Independent*, February. Available at: https://www.egyptindependent.com/islamists-and-egyptian-revolution/. Accessed May 2024.

Tavana, D.L. (2013). 'Party Proliferation and Electoral Transition in Post-Mubarak Egypt'. In G. Joffe (ed.), *North Africa's Arab Spring*. Abingdon: Routledge: 51–68.

Teti, A. (2004). 'A Role in Search of a Hero: Construction and Evolution of Egyptian Foreign Policy, 1952–67'. *Journal of Mediterranean Studies*, 14 (1/2): 77–105.

Teti, A. and P. Abbott (2016). Arab Transformations Framework Project Paper. Working Paper 4, 21 July.

Teti, A. and P. Abbott (2018). 'Sink-Holes of Insecurity: The Structural Causes of Weaknesses in Six Arab Countries'. Arab Transformations Project *Policy Brief* 11. Available at: https://www.researchgate.net/publication/320170921_Sinkholes_of_Insecurity_The_Structural_Causes_of_Weaknesses_in_Six_Arab_Countries_Arab_Transformations_Policy_Brief_11. Accessed September 2020.

Teti, A. (2012). 'The EU's First Response to the "Arab Spring": A Critical Discourse Analysis of the Partnership for Democracy and Shared Prosperity'. *Mediterranean Politics* 17 (3): 266–284.

Teti, A. et al. (2018). *The Arab Uprisings in Egypt, Jordan and Tunisia*. London: Palgrave Macmillan.

Totten, M.J., D. Schenker and A. Abdul-Hussain (2012). 'Arab Spring or Islamic Winter?' *World Affairs*, 174 (5): 23–42.

Transparency International Index (2020). 'Our Work in Egypt'. Available at: https://www.transparency.org/en/countries/egypt. Accessed July 2020.

Transparency International (2022). 'Corruption Perception Index'. Available at: https://www.transparency.org/en/cpi/2022/index/egy. Accessed March 2023.

Transparency International (2023). 'Egypt Corruption Perceptions'. Corruption Perception Index. Available at: https://www.transparency.org/en/cpi/2023/index/egy. Accessed April 2024.

Tuchman, G. (1978). *Making News*. New York: Free Press.

Tucker, R.C. (1977). 'Personality and Political Leadership'. *Political Science Quarterly*, 92 (3): 383–393.

Tullock, G. (1987). *Autocracy*. New York: Springer.

UNDP (United Nations Development Programme) (n.d.). 'Egypt 2030: A New Decade Towards Sustainable Development'. Available at: https://www.undp.org/sites/g/files/zskgke326/files/migration/arabstates/English_Full-Report_Sep-12-287-298.pdf. Accessed March 2021.

Utych, S.M. and C. D. Kam (2014). 'Viability, Information Seeking, and Vote Choice'. *Journal of Politics*, 76 (1): 152–166.

Van den Bosch, J. (2015). 'Personalism: A Type or characteristic of authoritarian regimes?' *Czech Political Science Review (Politologicka revue)*, 21 (1): 11–30.

Van den Bosch, J. (2016). *Personalism: A Type of Characteristic of Authoritarian Regimes?* Mckiewicz University.

Van Dijk, T. (2001). 'Multidisciplinary CDA'. In R. Wodak and M. Meyer (eds), *Methods of Critical Discourse Analysis*. London: Sage.

Varieties of Democracy Project (2023). 'Educational Equality'. Available at: https://v-dem.net/data_analysis/VariableGraph/. Accessed April 2021

Vayda, A, and B. Walters (1999). 'Against Political Ecology'. *Human Ecology*, 27 (1):167–179.

Verme, P. (2016). *The quest for subsidies reforms in the Middle East and North Africa Region: A microsimulation approach to policy making.* Springer: World Bank Group.

Viney, S. (2011). 'Liberal Groups Merge to Form New Political Party'. *Al-Masry Al-Youm*. Available at: http://www.almasryalyoum.com/en/node/379828. Accessed July 2020.

Volpi, F. (2012). 'Explaining (and Re-Explaining) Political Change in the Middle East during the Arab Spring: Trajectories of Democratization and of Authoritarianism in the Maghreb'. *Democratization*, 20 (6): 969–990.

Volpi, F. and Stein, E. (2015). 'Islamism and the State after the Arab Uprisings: Between People Power and State Power'. *Democratization*, 22: 276–293.

Voltolini, B. et al. (2017). 'The EU and Islamist Parties in Tunisia and Egypt after the Arab Uprisings: A Story of Selective Engagement'. *Mediterranean Politics*, 23 (1): 83–102.

von Haldenwang, C. (2011). *Mapping legitimation: How do states manage situations of stress and change?* Bonn: German Development Institute/Deutsches Institut für Entwicklungspolitik (DIE).

von Haldenwang, C. (2016). 'Measuring Legitimacy – New Trends, Old Shortcomings?' German Development Institute. Available at: https://www.die-gdi.de/uploads/media/DP_18.2016.pdf. Accessed May 2020.

von Soest, C. and J. Graugovel (2017). 'Identity, procedures and performance: How authoritarian regimes legitimize their rule'. *Contemporary Politics*, 23 (3): 287–305.

Wahman, M., A. Hadenius and J. Teorell (2013). 'Autocratic Regime Types Revisited: Updated Data in Comparative Perspective'. *Contemporary Politics*, 19 (1): 19–34.

Wallerstein, I. (1997). 'Eurocentrism and its Avatars: The Dilemmas of Social Science'. *Sociological Bulletin*, 46 (1): 21–39.

Walt, S.M. (1985). 'Alliance Formation and the Balance of World Power'. *International Security*, 9 (4): 3–43.

Waltz, K. (1979). *Theory of International Politics*. New York: Random House.

Waterbury, J. (1983). *The Egypt of Nasser and Sadat: The Political Economy of Two Regimes*. Princeton, NJ: Princeton University Press.

Waterbury, J. (1989). 'The Political Management of Economic Adjustment and Reform'. In J.M. Nelson et al. (eds), *Fragile Coalitions: The Politics of Economic Adjustments*. Washington DC: Overseas Development Council.

Way, C. and J. Weeks (2014). 'Making it Personal: Regime Type and Nuclear Proliferation'. *American Journal of Political Science*, 58 (3): 705–719.

Weatherford, M.S. (1992). 'Measuring Political Legitimacy'. *The American Political Science Review*, 86 (1): 149–166.

Weber, M. (1947). *The Theory of Economic and Social Organization*. Oxford: Oxford University Press.

Weber, M. (1963). *The Sociology of Religion*. Boston: Beacon Press.

Weber, M. (1968). *Economy and Society: An Outline of Interpretative Sociology* (Vol. 1). New York: Bedminster Press.

Weber, M. [1922] 1978. *Economy and Society*. Berkeley, CA: University of California Press.

Weeks, J. (2012). 'Strongmen and Straw Men: Authoritarian Regimes and the Initiation of International Conflict'. *American Political Science Review*, 106 (2): 326–347.

Weinbaum, M.G. (1985). 'Egypt's "Infitah" and the Politics of US Economic Assistance. *Middle Eastern Studies*, 21 (2): 206–222.

Weyland, K. (2001). 'Clarifying a Contested Concept: Populism in the Study of Latin American Politics'. *Comparative Politics*, 34: 1–22.

Whetstone, J.T. (2002) 'Personalism and Moral Leadership: The Servant Leader with a Transforming Vision'. *Business Ethics: A European Review*, 11: 385–392.

Wickham, C.R. (2002). *Mobilizing Islam: Religion, Activism and Political Change in Egypt*. New York: Columbia University Press.

Wickham, C.R. (2012). *The Muslim Brotherhood: Evolution of an Islamist Group*. Princeton, NJ: Princeton University Press.

Winter, D.G. (1973). *The Power Motive*. New York: Macmillan.

Wood, M.L. (2018). 'Schemas and Frames'. *Sociological Theory*, 36 (3): 244–261.

World Bank (2009). '2009 Economic Development and Prospects: navigating through the global recession'. Available at: https://documents1.worldbank.org/curated/en/615711468278680679/pdf/522260WP0MENA1101Official0Use0Only1.pdf. Accessed December 2020.

World Bank (2011–2020). 'Unemployment Total % of Total Labour Force'. Available at: https://data.worldbank.org/indicator/SL.UEM.TOTL.NE.ZS?locations=EG-ZQ. Accessed May 2024.

World Bank (2014a). 'Corrosive Subsidies'. *MENA Economic Monitor*. Available at: https://documents1.worldbank.org/curated/en/922481468275944547/pdf/912100WP0Box380RSION0OCTOBER0402014.pdf. Accessed February 2021.

World Bank (2014b). 'Egypt: Too Many Regulations Breed Corruption'. Available at: https://www.worldbank.org/en/news/feature/2014/12/09/egypt-bureaucracy-regulations-and-lack-of-accountability-inspire-corruption. Accessed February 2021.

World Bank (2017). 'Egypt Literacy Rate 1986–2017'. Macrotrends. Available from: https://www.macrotrends.net/countries/EGY/egypt/literacy-rate. Accessed April 2020.

World Bank (2020). 'Inflation, Consumer Prices (annual %) – Egypt, Arab Rep., Middle East & North Africa'. Available at: https://data.worldbank.org/indicator/FP.CPI.TOTL.ZG?end=2019&locations=EG-ZQ&start=2005. Accessed February 2021.

World Economics (2022). 'Egypt Shadow Economy Size'. Available at: https://www.worldeconomics.com/country-reviews/egypt/. Accessed March 2021.

World Economic Forum (2007). 'The Global Competiveness Report'. Available at: https://www3.weforum.org/docs/WEF_GlobalCompetitivenessReport_2006-07.pdf. Accessed May 2024.

Worldwide Governance Indicators (2018). 'Egypt Good Governance Indicators'. World Bank. Available at: https://databank.worldbank.org/Egypt-Good-Governance-Indicators/id/a6c7b5a1. Accessed March 2021.

World Health Organisation (2021). Available at: https://data.worldbank.org/indicator/SH.XPD.CHEX.GD.ZS?locations=EG. Accessed February 2021.

Wright, J. (2016). 'Measuring Autocratic Regime Stability'. *Research and Politics*, 3 (1): 1–7.

Yazbeck, D.G. (2018). 'Limiting Change Through Change: The Key to Algerian's Regime Longevity'. Carnegie Endowment for International Peace. Available at: https://carnegieendowment.org/files/CMEC_70_Yazbeck_Algeria_Final.pdf. Accessed March 2020.

Yefet, B. and L. Lavie (2021). 'Legitimation in Post-Revolutionary Egypt: Al-Sisi and the Renewal of Authoritarianism'. *Digest of Middle East Studies*, 30: 170–185.

Yehoshua, Y. (2020). 'Dispute at Al-Azhar's "International Conference on the Renewal of Islamic Thought" Reflects Institution's Long-Standing Rejection of Religious Reforms in Egypt', MEMRI. Available at: https://www.memri.org/reports/dispute-al-azhars-international-conference-renewal-islamic-thought-reflects-institutions. Accessed March 2020.

Yezza, H. (2013). 'What Algeria 1992 Can, and Cannot, Teach us about Egypt 2013'. *Open Democracy*. Available at: https://www.opendemocracy.net/en/what-algeria-1992-can-and-cannot-teach-us-about-egypt-2013/. Accessed July 2020.

Youssef, N. (2015). 'How Egyptian Media has Become a Mouthpiece for the Military State'. Available at: https://www.theguardian.com/world/2015/jun/25/egyptian-media-journalism-sisi-mubarak. Accessed December 2020.

Zeghal, M. (1999). 'Religion and Politics in Egypt: The Ulema of al-Azhar, Radical Islam and the State (1952–94)'. *International Journal of Middle Eastern Studies*, 31 (3): 371–399.

Zhu, Yuchao. (2011). '"Performance Legitimacy" and China's Political Adaptation Strategy'. *Journal of Chinese Political Science*, 16: 123–140.

Zhukov, Y.M. (2015). 'Egypt's Gift from God: What the Discovery of Offshore Gas Means for Cairo'. Available at: https://www.foreignaffairs.com/articles/cyprus/2015-09-23/egypts-gift-god. Accessed January 2021.

Zimmerer, K. and T. Bassett (2003). *Political Ecology: An Integrative Approach to Geography and Environment-Development Studies*. The Guilford Press.

Zollner, B. (2018). 'Does Participation Lead to Moderation? Understanding Changes in Egyptian Islamist Parties Post-Arab Spring'. In H. Kraetzschmar and P. Rivetti (eds), *Islamists and the Politics of the Arab Uprisings: Governance, Pluralisation and Contention*. Edinburgh: Edinburgh University Press.

Zollner, B. (2019a). 'The Metamorphosis of Social Movements into Political Parties: The Egyptian Muslim Brotherhood and the Tunisian al-Nahda as Cases for a Reflection on Party Institutionalisation Theory'. *British Journal of Middle Eastern Studies*, 46. Available at: https://www.tandfonline.com/doi/full/10.1080/13530194.2019.1609413. Accessed May 2024.

Zollner, B. (2019b). 'Surviving Repression: How Egypt's Muslim Brotherhood has Survived Repression'. Carnegie Middle East Center. Available at: https://carnegie-mec.org/2019/03/11/surviving-repression-how-egypt-s-muslim-brotherhood-has-carried-on-pub-78552.

Zuhur, S. (2007). 'Egypt: Security, Political and Islamist Challenges'. Strategic Studies Institute. Available at: https://publications.armywarcollege.edu/pubs/1884.pdf. Accessed February 2021.

Index

Abu-Lughod 20, 25, 27–28–29, 35
   de-Westernising and decolonising 4, 20, 60, 193
agenda 2030 20, 175, 181, 209, 216, 221
   green transitions 20–22, 197
al-Azhar 21, 46, 48–50, 64, 111, 134, 136–138, 140–142, 145, 147–156, 158–165, 173, 175, 195, 218–219
Algeria 14, 64, 65, 135, 215, 220
   Algeria military model 14, 124
   Islamic Salvation Front in 140
Al-Sisi, Abdel Fattah 3–6, 9, 11–14, 18, 21–25, 27, 33, 39, 41–42, 44–46, 48–49, 55–56, 58, 60, 62–65, 67–71, 73–77, 80, 90, 92, 94, 97–113, 115–132, 134, 136, 140, 144–165, 169–195, 199–201, 203, 212, 215–222
amendments 19, 49, 60, 78, 84, 87, 92, 98, 100–102, 121, 187
Anti-Muslim Brotherhood 69–70, 125, 148, 159
anti-terrorism 79, 87, 88, 91–92, 94–95, 102, 110, 125, 147, 210
Arab Organisation for Industrialisation AOI 14, 68, 103, 122, 186, 188, 209, 219
armed forces 7, 9, 11–12, 14, 20–21, 34, 37, 46, 49–51, 68–72, 77, 80–81, 83, 85, 88–89, 91–93, 95, 97, 102–104, 109–110, 117, 121, 125–127, 132, 168, 185, 194, 206, 209–210, 213, 215, 217–218, 220–222
   Supreme Council of Armed Forces 7, 158

authoritarianism 1, 20, 26, 27
   changing dynamic of 25
   Egyptian authoritarianism 3
   electoral 52
   fluid authoritarianism 2, 3, 8, 24, 66, 77, 128, 130
   historical legacy of 27
   military 25
   personalist and electoral 67
   political variation in 11
   populist 57
   reinvention of and taxonomy of 65
   sub-categories of 56
   theocratic 77
   theories of 130–131
   transformation of and scalation in 101
   upgraded 13
Ayubi, Nazeem 4, 10, 25, 41

Bauman, Zygmunt, and Baumanian thought 2, 217
Baumanian-Gramscian inspired background 2
Baumanian-Gramscian reinterpretation 1
Bauman with Gramsci 217
Beetham, David 26, 31–32, 40, 150
belief system 10, 40
   construction of 223
   dissemination and reproduction of 136
   theory of 183
   understanding of 150
black economy 182, 185, 191, 193, 211
bread 19, 122, 192–195
   democracy and intifada of 192
   democratisation of 192

moral economy of 211
riots 19, 194
subsidised 192
budget 97, 103, 123, 152, 168–169,
    184, 192, 206
  food subsidies budget and monetary
    budget 192
  military budget 123
  state budget 192

Cairo 16, 23, 78, 167
  the desert of 127
  Golden Parade in 114
  hardship of life in 175, 177
  Hezbet el-Haggana in 148
  political groups based in 142
  relocation of 206
  riots in 192
  social divisions in 70
  Summit, opening of 198
capitalism 13, 15, 24, 207, 221
  neoliberal 13
  post-1990s crony 50
charisma 2, 4–5, 19, 21–22, 30–31,
    38–39, 41, 46, 50, 107, 109,
    118, 120, 128, 130–131, 133,
    139, 150, 157, 159, 163, 218
  charismatisation 82
  personalisation of 12, 120
civil society 16, 19, 21, 47, 54, 57, 69,
    71, 74, 79, 89, 91, 94, 97,
    101–102, 104, 108, 121, 131,
    148, 161, 175, 188, 195, 205,
    214, 223
clientelism 33, 216
  corruption 216
  pyramidal 199, 219
consensus 2, 4, 8, 18, 25, 31, 36, 44,
    46, 50, 59, 75, 78, 82, 86,
    98–99, 102, 107, 109, 121, 125,
    147, 152–153, 182–183, 191,
    193, 195, 207, 213–214,
    217–218
  degradation of consensus 90
  diplomatic consensus 178, 215
  erosion in consensus 62
  external 161
  indirect consensus 85
  internal consensus 159, 190
  international consensus 159–161
  intra-NDP consensus 130
  legitimacy and consensus 64
  popular consensus 84, 86
  social 18, 166
  societal consensus 71, 84, 97, 131,
    147–148, 154, 201
  Washington consensus 13, 16, 23,
    166
corruption 3, 8, 18, 23, 26, 38, 45, 48,
    69–70, 74, 90–91, 102–103, 126,
    136, 141, 154, 169–170, 180,
    182, 185, 192, 195, 198–202,
    209, 211–213, 219, 221, 223
  architecture of 219
  economic 141, 167, 179
  institutionalised 154
  National Anti-Corruption Strategy
    and state corruption 199
coup (2013) 7, 12–14, 18, 20–21, 22,
    27–28, 50, 55–56, 63, 75, 77,
    79–80, 82, 84, 87, 121–122,
    125–126, 128, 134–135, 146,
    148, 183, 215
cronyism 13, 15, 167, 171, 178, 198
  pyramidal 130, 198, 201
currency 181, 225
  devaluation of 210
  floating of 195, 211
  foreign 170–171, 183, 194, 196,
    201–202, 205, 209, 214
  hard 194

David, Stephen R. 25, 28–30, 35–38,
    216
debt 169, 181, 208
  Egyptian 170
  external 202, 205
  foreign 170
  government 211
  internal 169, 219
  national 202
  public 170, 203
  structural 169
decrees 41, 80, 91–92, 97–98, 111,
    116, 128
  presidential 46, 60, 80, 88, 91–92,
    102, 127–128, 192, 206
defective 5, 100–102, 226
  autocracy 85
  defective democracies 52

Index

democracy 1, 52–53, 54, 56, 65, 67, 70–71, 88, 89, 92, 105, 108, 109, 111, 140, 192, 226
   liberal 54
   parliamentary 98
   participatory 207
   Partnership for Democracy and Shared Prosperity (PfDSP) 67
   perceptions of 51
   process of 80
   roadmap for 81
   Varieties of Democracy Project 47
democratisation 4–5, 13, 31, 40, 53–57, 64
   a façade form of 52
   process of 15, 63, 75, 82, 106, 139, 175, 180, 195, 213, 247, 223
   resistance to 49
   third wave of 52
desert 127, 181, 207, 222
   greening of 7, 23, 206
destabilisation 62, 66, 193, 214
dispositive 40
   political dispositive 3
dissent 19, 23, 62, 83, 92, 102, 107, 148, 155, 161, 173, 176, 183, 221
   bottom-up 10, 222
   diffused 69
   political 44, 79, 94
   popular 101, 217
   structured 19
   social 63, 107, 191, 195–196, 209
   societal 66, 196, 213
   virtual domestic 98, 195

economic liberalisation 15, 16
economic recovery 8, 82, 106–107, 180, 190, 203–204
ecosystem 22, 167, 197, 217, 226
education 16, 22, 32, 105, 108. 127, 173–177, 205, 211, 219
Egypt 1–20, 22–28, 32–40, 43–51, 53–56, 58, 60–72, 74, 76–77, 79–81, 83–92, 94, 96–101, 103–109, 111–126, 128–130, 133–157, 165, 167, 167–177, 179–180, 182, 184–198, 200, 202–225

elections 4, 23, 33, 42, 52–54, 57, 106, 128, 139, 141–142, 165, 172, 192
   democratic 54
   multi-candidate 83–84
   multi-party 13, 53, 66–67, 128, 198
   non-competitive 220
   parliamentary 55, 74, 144–145, 154
   presidential 6, 68–69, 73–74, 82–83, 87, 99, 101, 124–125, 143
   semi competitive 31
elite 4, 5, 19, 30, 37, 53–54, 65, 74, 79, 86, 114, 147, 167, 207, 209, 212, 214, 226
   business elite 119, 12
   civilian business elite 68
   intellectual elite 115
   landowning elite 124
   military elite 13, 37, 109, 130, 201
   Mubarak-era elite 126
   Muslim Brotherhood elite 143
environment 4, 7, 23, 27, 194
   environmentalism 39, 104, 188, 196, 207–208
   environmental ethics and politics 79
   Minister of the 146
   neo-Malthusian 186
   United Nations Environment Programme 187
establishment 11, 17, 39, 75, 119, 125, 132, 134, 136–138, 140, 142, 144, 146, 148–151, 178, 153–156, 158–159, 162–163, 166, 175, 178, 181, 188–191, 219, 222

fiscal reforms 172, 175, 181, 183
   politics of fiscal reforms 177
floating 172, 185, 195, 200, 211
fluidity 10, 41, 46, 81, 103, 121, 217
   regime fluidity 131
foundations 5, 8, 25–26, 56, 69, 72, 90, 93–94, 131, 150, 185, 208, 225
   economic foundations 6, 207
   Egyptian republic's foundations 218
   normative/legal/juridical foundations 20 –21, 49, 106, 176, 217

state foundations 19, 137, 163, 216, 222, 224
Foreign Direct Investments 6, 23, 169–170, 184–185, 189, 202, 205, 219
foreign policy 7, 22, 103, 117, 135, 150, 156, 160, 162, 171, 216
fragile 4, 6, 11, 17, 57, 147, 220, 222, 226
   Fragile State Index (FSI) 111
fragmentations 60, 148, 216
   internal 21, 153
   intra-ideological 132
   intra-NDP 34
   intra-party 144
frames 41–42, 44, 80–81, 101, 111, 159, 170, 185
   diagnostic 104
   meta-frames 63, 89, 104
   strategic and tactical 60, 205
   strategic 73
   tactical 159
framing analysis 40–41, 45, 48, 83, 87, 129, 178, 180
Freedom and Justice Party 5, 9, 29, 35, 44, 56, 66, 68–73, 75, 80–81, 84–85, 91, 100, 101, 107–108, 113, 120, 126, 130, 134, 137, 139, 142, 145, 148, 151, 153, 163, 167, 169–171, 179, 189, 192–193, 195

Gerschewski, Johannes 38, 45–46, 48, 50–52, 54–59, 62, 70, 185, 189, 242, 247
Global South 5, 15, 224–225
governance 41, 53, 56, 61, 69, 80, 111, 121, 200, 222
Gramsci, Antonio, and Gramscian thought 1, 2, 20
green energy 172, 185
Gross Domestic Product 6, 33, 127, 169–172, 176, 182–184, 188–190, 192, 202, 205, 209–211, 214
   military expenditure of 123
   national 193
   real 167
growth rate 167, 190–191, 205, 209

hero 61, 69, 72, 74, 104, 106, 115, 122, 218
   hero-complex 104, 115
   national 84, 116
   military 84
   political 39, 10
Hizb al-Nour 49, 51, 87, 134, 140–146, 148 –149, 161, 163–164, 218
human rights 33, 48, 54, 62, 65, 88, 94, 101, 104, 111, 208
   human rights abuses 180
   international human rights law 22

identity 3, 38, 45, 114–115, 117, 135–136, 141, 159, 164, 215, 218, 224
   authoritarian1
   civilisational 119
   cultural 164, 168, 224
   ethnic 72, 114
   fluid 226
   Islamic-rooted 163
   militarised nationalistic 73, 77
   nationalistic 25, 118
   Pharaonic 114, 132
   political 142, 152
   populist 120
   regime 3
   societal 149
   structural 24
   threats to 119, 216
incumbent 56, 104, 113–114, 116, 129–130, 156, 162, 164, 209–211, 215, 218, 221–222
   incumbent armed forces relations 168
   pro–incumbent support 163
inflation 33, 127, 193–195, 202–203, 211–212
informal economy 169–170
infrastructural 4, 5, 7, 11, 14, 43, 63, 72, 107, 121, 131, 172, 180, 189, 194, 197, 213, 219, 221, 225
inputs 26, 28, 39–40, 196, 209
interregnum 1, 2, 20, 222
   Baumanian reinterpretation of 20
   liquid 24, 75, 214

Index

international system 4, 7, 10, 44, 220, 225
intra-systemic 3, 10–11, 225
International Monetary Fund 15, 22, 45, 49, 65, 120, 128, 154–155, 167, 169–172, 181, 182, 184, 188–191, 194–196, 202–206, 208–209, 210–211, 214
   IMF's Structural Adjustment Programme 15, 128, 169
Islam 44, 47, 66, 107, 118, 120, 134–139, 141, 147–153, 154–160, 162–164, 210, 218
Islamism 20, 64, 137, 145–146, 148
   Egyptian 139
Islamists 16, 79, 103, 135, 137–138, 148, 153, 213
   Egyptian 147

Julten, Abdelhalim 20, 25, 27, 29, 35

Khaldunian 2, 20

leadership 11–12, 14, 17, 28, 36, 48, 58, 63, 82–84, 88, 90, 92, 97, 99, 100, 103, 107, 114, 129, 131, 134, 135, 139, 146, 150, 154, 161, 174, 177, 180, 183, 185, 203, 204, 207, 215, 223
   al-Sisi's 98
   civilian 6, 106
   dynamics of 46
   militarised 199
   political 2, 14, 147, 159, 186, 200, 202, 209, 217, 221
   political leadership 2, 12, 14, 147, 159, 161, 172, 186, 200, 209, 217, 221
   servant 58
   transformational 46
Lebanon 40, 45, 48–49, 186
legitimacy 2, 3, 5–6, 8–9, 12, 15, 17, 20, 23–40, 43, 46, 49–51, 53, 55, 62–66, 72–76, 78, 82–83, 86–87, 90, 98–104, 118, 121, 125, 128, 132–133, 134, 137, 147, 149, 152, 156, 162–163, 173, 177–179, 183, 185, 188, 191, 197–198, 201, 203, 209, 211, 213, 217, 221, 226

internal political 2, 4–5, 7–9, 11, 13–14, 17, 19–20, 22, 24–27, 30–32, 34–36, 38, 40, 42, 44–45, 50, 54, 62, 67, 79, 82, 119, 137–138, 196, 213, 216, 217, 223–225
legitimation claim 2, 10, 21, 28, 41, 77, 100, 121
loans 172, 182–183, 206, 208
   IMF loans 65
   international 182, 219
   unsustainability of 170
   World Bank and IMF 120

macroeconomic indicators 6, 48, 171, 202, 204–205, 209–210, 219
manipulation 26, 29, 31, 58, 74–75, 84, 121, 128, 177
Marks, Monique 20, 25, 27, 29, 35
Mediterranean 3–5, 7, 9, 22–23, 27, 45, 54, 67, 113, 122–123, 160, 177, 180, 193–194, 204, 208, 215, 220, 222–223, 225
   Euro–Mediterranean partnership 53
mega-projects 127, 196, 201–202, 206–207, 212
micro-structural 11, 13, 63, 121, 224
Middle East 2, 3, 8, 13, 15, 20, 25–26, 28, 31, 56, 64, 66–68, 76, 113, 118–120, 123, 135, 138, 170, 176, 198, 213–214, 224
militarism 3, 48–49, 58, 61, 130, 215, 217, 225
   electoral 129
   upgraded 112
modified framework 26, 28, 37, 40, 217
Morsi, Mohammed 20, 49, 56, 59, 72, 75, 83, 113, 123, 125–127, 139, 142, 145–146, 153, 157, 167, 170–171, 189, 207
Mubarak, Gamal 119, 127
Mubarak, Hosni 6, 12–14, 16, 20, 23, 38, 50, 56, 62, 65, 71, 73, 75–77, 81, 87, 92, 98, 102, 109, 122, 128, 132, 137, 140, 142–143, 158, 176, 191, 199, 201, 207, 209, 214, 219–220

multi-party 3, 60, 62, 66, 74
  multi-party elections 13, 53, 66–67, 198
  multi-party system 33, 37, 53
Muslim Brotherhood 5, 9, 16, 21, 23, 28, 35, 48–51, 55, 62–63, 66, 68–70, 73, 75, 80, 84, 88, 91–92, 113, 125–126, 132, 134, 138–141, 143–145, 147–150, 154, 156, 159–160, 162–165, 171, 173, 175, 192, 210, 215, 218–221
myth-symbols 10
  myth-symbol complex 72, 112, 113, 122
  myth-symbolism 74

Nasser, Gamal Abdel 5, 12, 22, 27, 50, 73, 103, 107–108, 109, 112–113, 115–122, 124, 126, 130–132, 135–136, 138, 140, 152, 158, 163, 189, 191–193, 196, 200
  Nasserisation 12, 64, 112, 116, 118, 130, 218
  Nasserites 6
National Democratic Party 7, 11, 13–14, 16, 18, 23, 27, 34, 49, 51, 65–67, 69–73, 75, 77, 81, 88, 91, 93, 101–102, 107, 112, 123, 128, 130–132, 138, 143, 152, 167, 169, 171, 179, 185, 189, 192, 196, 198–199, 202, 206–207, 212, 215
nationalism 39, 113–115, 118
  Arab 117, 119, 122, 132
  Egyptian 190
  façade of 203
  military 119
  variation of 118, 120
nature 1–8, 13–14, 17, 22, 28, 52–53, 83, 93, 95, 99–100, 107, 109, 111, 126, 128, 150, 168, 187–188, 191, 196–197, 207–208, 210, 217, 220
neoliberalism 119, 169, 173, 197, 210
  capitalist 19
  Western imposed 185
non-exclusivist 14, 37, 214, 220, 226

omnibalancing 37, 38, 51, 162, 216
  internal rebalance of power 7, 213
  intra-alignments 29, 39
  intra-realignments 37
opposition 3, 6–7, 14, 16, 36–37, 51, 53, 62–63, 67, 79–80, 87, 98, 102, 116, 119, 121, 124, 128, 131, 137, 150, 159, 179, 191, 210, 221
  Islamist opposition 26, 66, 92, 153
  political opposition 13, 94, 124
outputs 26, 33, 38–40, 196–197
  legitimacy by 183
  legitimation by 209

parliamentary assembly 7, 55–56, 61, 79, 101, 116, 121, 139, 141, 149
  bureaucratisation of 131, 220
  depoliticization of 28, 101
patronage 15, 26, 51, 67, 132, 150, 198
penal code 19, 49, 60, 78, 84, 87, 92–93, 97–98, 100–102, 110, 121, 130, 150, 176, 187, 207, 217, 221
  amendments to 19, 49, 60, 78, 84, 87, 92, 98, 100–102, 121, 187, 207, 217
performance 24, 32–33, 37–41, 48, 51, 56, 83, 98–99, 132, 139, 178, 180, 189–190, 200, 203–205, 219, 223
  economic 22, 32–33, 39, 44, 46, 50, 120, 167, 173, 179, 185, 202, 204–205, 208–209, 216
  government 8, 18, 109, 111, 171, 172, 173, 201
  market 16
  political 9
  regime's 33
personalism 13, 27, 57–61, 116, 128, 210, 220
  non-exclusivist personalism 3, 14, 37, 210
political authority 7, 11, 13, 26, 28, 35, 50, 63, 87, 90, 92, 98, 102, 106–107, 111, 116, 126, 131, 135–136, 138, 146, 150–151, 157, 162–164, 175, 185, 190

political ecology 22, 197, 208, 216, 225–226
political participation 80, 105, 140, 142, 176
political parties 49, 54–55, 80, 94, 116, 118, 140, 144, 146, 202, 207, 221
political power 3–4, 11, 17, 19–20, 28, 38, 40, 69, 73, 134–136, 138, 152, 186, 208, 213, 216, 219
populism 2, 11, 21, 118–120, 130
  eco-populism 219
  post-populism 119, 121
  religious 159
  socialist populism 118
  technocratic populism 118
poverty rate 172, 184, 193, 196, 209–210
private sector 23, 74, 147, 167, 169, 176, 179, 188, 196
protests 9, 13, 15, 17, 19, 31, 34, 77, 92–95, 102, 104, 125, 129, 138, 142, 146, 164–165, 167, 169, 184, 193–194, 196, 221, 223
  2011 protests 3, 18–19, 70, 76, 91, 119, 138, 142, 199, 213
  shockwaves protests 2, 8, 38
  social 24, 28, 53, 66

repression 15, 19, 59, 67, 85–86, 97, 100, 113, 122, 161, 169, 212
  authoritarian 106
  political 55, 79, 91, 177, 186
  politics of 18, 127
resistance 11, 29, 35, 40, 44, 47, 69, 98, 102, 149, 154, 172, 213
  Muslim Brotherhood's resistance 75, 79
restrictions 17, 80, 87, 92–93, 97, 102, 148, 195
revenues 65, 169, 171, 183, 189–191, 193, 196, 202–205, 208
rule of law 2, 4, 21, 39, 41, 45–46, 54, 69–70, 72–73, 75, 79–81, 83, 85, 87–88, 90, 92

Sadat, Anwar 5, 11, 38, 50, 54, 64, 73, 94, 105, 108, 112–113, 122, 129, 136–138, 193

Salafism 20, 48–49, 134, 137, 139–143, 147–148, 156, 162
  Egyptian 142, 146
  political 20, 139, 144–145, 147
  pro-regime Salafism 35, 49, 134, 139–140, 144
salvation narrative 84, 106–107
selectorate 37, 59, 107, 124, 129, 225
  absence of 131, 220
  real 65
Sharia 107, 135–136, 138, 141, 144, 148, 157
shockwaves 2, 4–5, 8, 20, 22, 31, 35, 38, 64, 129, 213, 216, 224, 226
social justice 6, 46–47, 82, 90, 103, 107–108, 169, 174, 178–179, 180, 199, 205–206, 212, 214, 223
specific support 25, 29, 34–35, 37–38, 216
stability 5–7, 9, 12–13, 18, 27, 30, 33, 36, 53, 56, 59, 62, 66, 70, 74, 88–90, 94, 102, 106–108, 111, 125, 131, 145, 169, 170, 174, 177, 180, 185–186, 195, 200, 203, 206, 208–209, 214, 221–223
  political 18, 39, 59, 130, 180, 192
state structures 7, 12, 14, 25, 36–37, 40, 66, 87, 90, 100, 107, 124, 127–128, 130, 156, 162–163, 210
  authoritarian 28
  sub-transformed 14, 38
  transformation of 130
state violence 3, 21, 62, 76–79, 98, 101
Structural Adjustment Programme 15, 120, 128, 169
struggle 2, 3–5, 7, 17, 22, 41–42, 49, 65, 68, 70, 75, 79, 87, 90, 97, 99–100, 102–103, 106, 130, 138, 144, 146, 158, 159, 160, 162, 188, 194, 197, 208, 211, 215, 219
  al-Sisi's struggle 70, 87, 110, 159, 163
  legitimation struggle 7, 90, 122, 135, 187, 210

subsidies 120, 154–155, 169, 171–172, 177–178, 182–183, 185, 192, 206, 209, 211
   cuts to 181, 184, 189, 191, 194, 195
   reforms to 197
Suez Canal 81, 127, 179, 189–190, 203, 214
   Suez Canal Authority 189
   Suez Canal Zone 172, 183, 189, 200, 203, 206, 209
sustainable development 6, 22, 173, 198, 212, 214

Tahrir Square 69, 72, 77–78, 104
taxonomy 36, 52, 57, 60, 65, 103, 121, 157, 224
top-down 2, 6, 9, 28, 40–42, 44–46, 73, 107, 130, 134, 151, 174, 186, 208, 215, 218, 222
torture 76, 104, 121, 128
tradition 4, 19, 22, 26, 31, 34, 39, 43, 50, 64, 99, 104, 118–119, 122, 142, 154–156, 158–159, 161, 217, 224, 226
transition 2, 3, 5, 9, 24, 30, 38, 41, 44, 52, 54–56, 59, 68, 70, 73–75, 79, 81, 86, 101–102, 112, 114, 138, 141, 144, 171, 177, 214, 217, 220, 224–225;
   Egyptian 69
   green 4, 20–22, 172, 214
   political 3, 9, 72–74, 122, 223
Tunisia 68, 121, 135–136, 138, 144–145, 164–165, 186, 223–224

unemployment 5, 16, 33, 72, 74, 126, 154, 168–169, 176, 184, 188, 193, 196, 210, 219

United Nations 104, 185, 187, 194, 209
upgrade 1, 37, 64, 170, 204, 219, 225
   authoritarian 13
   militarism 112

vacuum 5, 49, 64, 139, 142, 187–188, 213, 215
   al-Sisi's 178
   internal 101, 128
   social 152
violence 15, 69–70, 74–79, 94, 98, 124–125, 140, 169, 173, 186–187
   political 75, 124
   routinisation of state violence 3
   state violence 21, 62, 76–77, 101

Wahhabi 50, 138, 164, 219
   Wahhabism 163
Wallerstein 20, 25, 27
Washington Consensus 13, 16, 23, 167
Weber, Max, and Weberian thought 8–9, 22, 25, 28, 30–31, 35, 38–40, 50, 79, 82, 86, 100, 129, 199, 216–217
Western actors 22, 59, 110, 207, 222, 226
wheat 182, 192–194
   crisis 194, 207
   subsidised 193
winning coalition 37, 59, 65, 107, 129, 131, 225
World Bank 98, 45, 47–49, 72, 120, 170, 172, 181, 184, 200, 204, 209